CONSTITUTIONAL EVOLUTION IN CENTRAL AND EASTERN EUROPE

Studies in Modern Law and Policy

Series Editor: Ralf Rogowski,
Professor of Law, University of Warwick

Also in the series

Central and Eastern Europe After Transition
Towards a New Socio-legal Semantics
Edited by Alberto Febbrajo and Wojciech Sadurski
ISBN: 978-1-4094-0390-6

Democracy, Law and Governance
Jacques Lenoble and Marc Maesschalck
ISBN: 978-1-4094-0395-1

Judicial Accountabilities in New Europe
From Rule of Law to Quality of Justice
Daniela Piana
ISBN: 978-0-7546-7758-1

The European Social Model and Transitional Labour Markets
Law and Policy
Edited by Ralf Rogowski
ISBN: 978-0-7546-4958-8

The Changing Law of the Employment Relationship
Comparative Analyses in the European Context
Nicola Countouris
ISBN: 978-0-7546-4800-0

Property in Work
The Employment Relationship in the Anglo-American Firm
Wanjiru Njoya
ISBN: 978-0-7546-4587-0

Contract and Control in the Entertainment Industry
Dancing on the Edge of Heaven
Steve Greenfield and Guy Osborn
ISBN: 978-1-85521-561-0

Constitutional Evolution in Central and Eastern Europe

Expansion and Integration in the EU

Edited by
KYRIAKI TOPIDI and ALEXANDER H.E. MORAWA
School of Law, University of Lucerne, Switzerland

Routledge
Taylor & Francis Group
LONDON AND NEW YORK

First published 2011 by Ashgate Publishing

2 Park Square, Milton Park, Abingdon, Oxon OX14 4RN
711 Third Avenue, New York, NY 10017, USA

Routledge is an imprint of the Taylor & Francis Group, an informa business

First issued in paperback 2016

British Library Cataloguing in Publication Data
Constitutional evolution in Central and Eastern Europe :
expansion and integration in the EU. -- (Studies in modern
law and policy)
1. Constitutional law--Europe, Eastern. 2. International
and municipal law--Europe, Eastern. 3. European Union--
Europe, Eastern.
I. Series II. Topidi, Kyriaki. III. Morawa, Alexander H. E.
342.2'4-dc22

Library of Congress Cataloging-in-Publication Data
Constitutional evolution in Central and Eastern Europe : expansion and integration in the EU / by Kyriaki Topidi and Alexander H.E. Morawa.
p. cm. -- (Studies in modern law and policy)
Includes index.
ISBN 978-1-4094-0327-2 (hardback)
1. Constitutional law--Europe, Eastern. 2. International and municipal law--Europe, Eastern. 3. European Union--Europe, Eastern. I. Topidi, Kyriaki. II. Morawa, Alexander H. E.
KJC4436.C66 2010
342.24--dc22

2010021939

ISBN 978-1-4094-0327-2 (hbk)
ISBN 978-1-138-25445-9 (pbk)

Contents

List of Contributors

Tomas Dubrovsky Mgr. et Mgr. he is a PhD Candidate at the European Law Department, Charles University Law Faculty.

Prof. Dr Tanel Kerikmae He is Jean Monnet Professor of European Union Law at the Tallinn Law School of the Tallinn University of Technology.

Dr Piotr Mikuli He is a constitutional lawyer, an Adjunct Professor in the Chair of Comparative Constitutional Law of the Jagiellonian University in Cracow.

Prof. Dr Alexander H.E. Morawa He holds the Chair in Comparative and Anglo-American Law at School of Law at the University of Lucerne. He is also Delegate for Internationalization (Global) of the Law School and directs the Transnational Legal Studies Program.

Prof. Dr Katrin Nyman-Metcalf She is Professor and acting Director of the Chair of Law and Technology at the School of Law of the Tallinn University of Technology. She is also a freelance independent media and telecommunications law consultant.

Dr Daniel Smilov He is a comparative constitutional lawyer and political scientist. He is Programme Director at the Centre for Liberal Strategies, Sofia, Recurrent Visiting Professor of Comparative Constitutional Law at the Central European University, Budapest, and Assistant Professor of Political Theory at the Political Science Department, University of Sofia.

Dr Bernadette Somody She is an Assistant Lecturer of Constitutional Law at Eötvös Loránd University since 2005. She is specialized in human rights protection, especially children's rights and ombudsman-institutions.

Prof. Dr Simina-Elena Tanasescu She is Professor and Vice-Dean of the Faculty of Law of the University of Bucharest. She is Romania's representative with the EU's Fundamental Rights' Agency (FRA) and the Director of the Centre for Constitutional Law and Political Institutions (Bucharest, Romania).

Dr Kyriaki Topidi She is lecturer and senior researcher at the Chair of Comparative and Anglo-American Law of the School of Law of the University of Lucerne.

Prof. Dr Jiri Zemanek He is Jean Monnet Professor of European Law at the Faculty of Law of the Charles University Prague.

Foreword

The process of democratic transition in Central and Eastern Europe has already attracted many scholars and has found descriptions and assessment, in numerous publications, by lawyers, economists, sociologists and almost everybody else in the academic world. While the initial period of research was, sometimes, rather adventurous and often lacked any solid basis of intellectual theories (the rapid pace of transformation processes caught politicians as well as scholars by surprise), soon a new generation of experts replaced the old group of "Sovietologists". This new generation was better prepared intellectually and less enclosed within the "classic" picture of the communist world. Today, it is possible to note that the initial period of transformation, understood as a departure from the previous regime, has found a competent and detailed presentation in academic writings.

At the same time, however, the transition continues, as – by definition – it is a process involving constant change or/and evolution. It has twofold consequences. On the one hand, it assumes a good deal of dynamism: the stage of transition that has already been successfully reached may no longer be suitable for the situation today and, certainly, will not be sufficient for the needs of tomorrow. The pace of changes in Central and Eastern Europe is still quite rapid and the changes lead to the need for constant updating of academic literature. It should also be observed that transition, while constant in its dynamism, neither remains uniform for all "new democracies" nor develops identically everywhere. Quite the contrary, with the passage of time, differences between the more and the less "successful" countries seem to widen.

On the other hand, the process of transition is not only multidimensional, but also multidirectional: the changing realities of the countries of Central and Eastern Europe necessarily influence changes in the "old democracies" that must cope with the new face of what once constituted the communist world. Absorption, at least of those who managed not to waste their chances, became one of the favourite policies of the West – the new composition of NATO and EU enlargement constitutes the formal expression of this approach.

The dynamic and multidirectional nature of the Central and Eastern European transformation represents an important challenge for the academic community as well – research successfully completed 10 years ago may have become hopelessly obsolete today and, in any case, it requires constant updating. That is also why new projects and publications have a good chance to establish new facts and trends, as well as to elaborate on new theoretical concepts.

This book, *Constitutional Evolution in Central and Eastern Europe: Expansion and Integration in the EU*, represents an interesting example of a new generation of writings on the European transition. Its aim is to reflect on legal and institutional aspects of the current stage of the transformation process, namely on the transition of the "winners" during the initial period of EU membership. In particular, the authors of the 10 chapters address the question: "Has the body of constitutional cultures of traditions of a union of 27 member states been affected by the 2004 and 2007 enlargement and if so, in what ways?"

The attempt to answer these questions was taken by a group of 10 scholars from different countries, almost exclusively from Central and Eastern Europe. The volume is organized into three separate sections: Foundations and Methods of Constitutional Dialogue in Central and Eastern Europe (Estonia – Kerikmae; Romania – Tanasescu; and a general chapter on EU constitutionalization after enlargement – Topidi); The Role of Courts in the New Legal Order (the Czech Republic and Slovakia – Dubrovsky and Zemanek; Poland – Mikuli; and a general chapter on the reactions of the European courts – Morawa); The Rule of Law and Policy-Making in Central and Eastern Europe after Enlargement (Hungary – Somody; Bulgaria – Smilov; and a more general chapter on public media in the region – Nyman-Metcalf).

Thus, there is no geographical parallelism in the structure of each of the three sections, nor is there any parallelism within the structure of each of the three sections. But this was exactly the original intent of both authors and editors. We are offered an interesting collection of chapters that depict actual pictures of several important institutions of the new members of the European Union, as well as some institutional and political responses of the European Union to developments in Central and Eastern Europe. In brief, both the informational value and the conceptual attractiveness of those chapters clearly make them worth careful study by all those who are ready to undertake serious research on the changing picture of our continent.

Lech Garlicki
Judge at the ECtHR

Acknowledgements

This book is the final outcome of a research project undertaken at the School of Law of the University of Lucerne, in Switzerland. It was realized between 2009–2010, with the generous financial support of the Gebert Ruef Foundation. We are indebted to the commitment of a number of people. We are particularly grateful to Patrick Nasciuti as well as to all of the contributors to this volume for their dedication to our project and their precious insights and collaboration.

We would also like to take this opportunity to thank Alison Kirk and the team at Ashgate for their assistance, guidance and patience throughout the publication process.

'He who has a why to live can bear with almost any how'
[F. Nietzsche]

To EMK and GK, K.T.

To Nam, Hannah and Sarah, A.M.

Chapter 1

Prologue: Constitutional Transition in Central and Eastern Europe

Kyriaki Topidi and Alexander H.E. Morawa

It would have been difficult – if not impossible – to predict in 1989 that the European Union would embrace the process of transition of Central and Eastern European states to the extent of assisting the states concerned to move from repression and communism to democracy in a relatively short period. The laborious and highly complex adjustment to the *acquis communautaire* accompanied by fundamental reforms in the direction of more open and democratic governance allowed states in that region to satisfy their desire for redress of the historical balance in the European continent and the creation of new opportunities.[1] The transformation of post-communist societies contributed to the otherwise difficult realignment of ideas for two parts of the same continent that had followed substantially different directions for a good part of the twentieth century. Enlargement was about making the "parallelism of the unparallel" a possibility, even a reality.[2] As a result of the process, the enlarged EU, according to Bet-El, resembles today a modern couple that has learned to live together, but refuses absolute final commitment.[3] Ambiguity is present with regards to the future direction of European integration and we are still investigating whether "there will be enough affection to keep the family together".[4]

Perceptions, narratives and expectations on and from the European Union have not always been shared between "old" and "new" Member States. Martin Krygier in his *Parables of Hope and Disappointment* pertinently noted that questions posed in Central and Eastern Europe about the benefits of EU membership have

1 Bet-El, I. (2009), Post-Cold War Enlargement and the Coming of Age of the European Union, in *Twenty Yeats After: Post-Communist Countries and European Integration*, Heinrich Böll Stiftung, 12. Available at http://www.boell.cz/downloads/Twenty_years_after_UK_web.pdf, accessed 5 July 2010.

2 Kühnhard, L. (2009), The Fall of the Berlin Wall and European Integration. Available at http://www.kas.de/upload/Publikationen/Panorama/2009/1/kuehnhardt.pdf, at 14, accessed 5 July 2010.

3 Bet-El (n 1), at 15–16.

4 Ibid.

not stopped changing ever since the collapse of communism in 1989.[5] While in the first years after the collapse there was question of free elections, politicians being voted out of office, important court decisions being finally followed with no objections by the executive and other equivalent developments, such achievements soon lost their novel character. Following signs of transition to more democratic practices and particularly with the admission of a large number of states in the region to the European Union, new questions emerged. This book was born out of the need to discuss these *new* questions. There is little disagreement among the authors of this volume that as soon as these questions begin to receive some answers a new set of questions will automatically surface to replace the previous ones. In that sense, the goal of the book is to advance discussion on the current issues pertaining to constitutionalization in Central and Eastern Europe and not to provide definite, permanent answers. In a construction that evolves in the way that the European Union does, such as an assumption would be too perilous.

To return to Krygier once more, the end of communism delivered high hopes for a successful "return to Europe", but at the same time it also brought disappointment with regards to the price that the peoples of Central and Eastern Europe have had to pay in order to leave behind any and all of the attachments to their communist past.[6] Following a decade (which in some cases stretched longer than that) of intense economic and political reforms, applicant countries of the region joined the Union in two waves in 2004 and 2007. Their legal systems were required to respond and adapt to a complex and highly novel body of rules. Earlier experiences of statehood and of constitutional practice have inevitably been challenged, but overall it would be difficult and perhaps unfair to claim that these newly independent states have not passed the "beginner course in constitutional democracy".[7]

Following Ralf Dahrendorf's conceptualization of constitutional democracy as comprised of a constitution laying down the values and principles of the polity, of a market economy and finally of an active civil society,[8] the contributions in this book focus on the first element, but occasionally intersect with the other two in their analyses. While Dahrendorf suggested that the stage of constitution-making would last six months, the underlying assumption in all of the chapters to this volume is that we have not finished dealing with the effects of this first stage despite the fact that the constitutions of certain states have been in existence for

5 Krygier, M. (2002), Parables of Hope and Disappointment, *East European Constitutional Review*, 11(3). Available at http://www1.law.nyu.edu/eecr/vol11num3/special/krygier_print.html, at 2, accessed 5 July 2010.

6 Ibid., at 4.

7 Maruste, R. (2007), The Role of the Constitutional Court in Democratic Society, *Juridica International*, XIII, 8–13, at 8.

8 Dahrendorf, R. (1990), *Reflections on the Revolution in Europe*, Times Books, New York, at 86 et seq.

two decades. These effects in the aftermath of constitution-making have been made even more prominent by the complexities of the EU legal order.

Judge Maruste is right to point out that constitutional law, along with its implementation and supervision, in the form of judicial review, remain the most political and legal activities of all both during and after transition.[9] It is precisely these intensely political and legal activities, particularly their methods and limits that one finds challenging to observe within the perspective of the European legal order, as it was experienced in the "new" Member States.

The sensitive balance of power in a constitutional democracy requires the distribution of tasks to three sovereign centres of power: the parliament, the executive and the courts. In the case of transition in Central and Eastern Europe, the last centre of power has emerged prominently and has voiced relevant questions of a constitutional and occasionally of a political nature, at the domestic, regional and supra-national levels.[10] The task for legal systems and their actors in Central and Eastern Europe was not simple, it was complex. On the one hand, institutions and actors had to consolidate democracy and, on the other hand, they had to align themselves to the requirements of EU/EC law. The latter aspect has proved more complex, especially with an eye to the development of a common European legal area and the new needs that arise from it. If we are to argue thus that the main constitutional parameters in Europe are being harmonized, then the immediate question that is asked is whether the current domestic constitutional arrangements are adequate to address these parameters and, if not, how should they be redesigned. In other words, would a mere adaptation in the form of, perhaps, a differing interpretation be sufficient to respond to these needs or is a new constitutional arrangement required to satisfy the new constitutional demands? There are of course a number of nuances between the two options, but the question remains intact. The various options that courts tend to favour in the region of the world concerned range from ignorance of the domestic constitutional text, to favourable interpretation of the constitution to meet the new juridical requirements (in essence adaptation), to adoption of a new constitutional text that fits precisely the needs and requirements of the present circumstances.

In retrospect, and perhaps surprisingly for some, constitutional experimentation in Central and Eastern Europe was not as intense as one could have foreseen in the early 1990s. Sadurski has put forward two factors that explain, but not justify, the lack of constitutional boldness:[11] first, the force of *emulation* and, second, the relevance of post-communist transition. For the first factor, the explanation that is

9 Maruste (n 7), at 9.

10 See Part II of this volume.

11 Sadurski, W. (2009), Twenty Years After the Transition: Constitutional Review in Central and Eastern Europe, *Sydney Law School Legal Studies Research Paper* No.09/69, Available at http://ssrn.com/abstract=1437843, at 2–3, accessed 5 July 2010. He discusses these factors, however, in the context of modes of constitutional review selected by individual states after the collapse of communist rule.

offered advances the requirements of EU membership, in the form of conditionality, that have dictated the vast number of constitutional and constitutionalizing reforms in Central and Eastern Europe. The point immediately becomes weaker once the author observes, a bit further through his analysis, that EU conditionality did not contain any precise benchmarks on preferred models for the exercise of constitutional democracy. What counts, however, is that despite this noticeable gap in the transition process, Central and Eastern European states seemed to perceive a certain type of constitutional arrangement as the "most favoured" in Western Europe. The perception of European norms as a factor of legitimization of the process is not, after all, a unique phenomenon in the history of international and comparative law. It is therefore not surprising that a degree of convergence, with a strong preference for the Kelsenian features of constitutionalism, has been observed, with only a handful of exceptions.

Sadurski's second determining factor that led to uniformity in the constitutional feature of the newly independent states stems from the very essence and purpose of democratic transition. The underlying tension between continuity and rupture with the past triggered distrust towards politics and politicians, and left ample scope for constitutional courts, in particular, to emerge as key players in the transition process. What mattered most at the time was to create constitutional texts that reflected the "safe" aspects of Western-style democracy. The "return to normalcy" proved stronger in that sense than experimentation in constitutional design. The strongly perceived need for control of power and efficient checks and balances elevated these courts to a moral position beyond reach for other institutions, and with the task of interpreting the new constitutions in accordance with the recently declared democratic values. As contributions in this book will also support in various ways and domestic contexts, the activism of these courts has been and continues to be considered determinant in the consolidation of democracy. More than 20 years after the beginning of transition, this sort of activism has moved beyond consolidation of democracy and has also undertaken the crucial task of consolidating European integration too. This gradual shift or expansion in the courts' targets has meant that what has been of interest in the past few years for these bodies increasingly revolves around their understanding of the limits of the constitutional relationship between their state and the EU as a whole. Constitutional dialogue in Central and Eastern Europe is about methods and principles as interpreted by national supreme courts and the implications of the new relationship(s) that arose from EU membership in policymaking. Trapped between the desire to secure continuity with pre-existing law and the need to proceed with transformation that was called for by appurtenance to the EU, legal systems in Central and Eastern Europe were led to reflect on their own position within the European legal landscape.

In essence, this book attempts to offer Central and Eastern European perspectives on the way legal systems and institutions are taking stock and problematizing their future within the European legal order. There are of course few, or often no, straightforward solutions as to the most efficient way to ensure harmony between the domestic and the supranational. But is that not the case with most transnational legal phenomena? Previous scholarship has focused on the question of the fit of constitutional cultures of new member states with the common constitutional traditions of older Member States.[12] We add to this question the following one: has the body of constitutional cultures of traditions of a Union of 27 Member States been affected by the 2004 and 2007 enlargement and, if so, in what ways? Methodologically, the contributions in the book do not adopt a uniform approach. In addition to their diverse geographical focus, they tend also to take quite different approaches to the epiphenomenon of enlargement in Central and Eastern European legal systems. What seems important, however, to any student of European integration is not uniformity, but the study of diversity and the impact that it has had in the shaping of a common European constitutional future.

In line with our earlier observation that the current questions – determined by equally current and thus fluctuating political and societal realities – will be replaced by other ones sooner or later, the contributors to the present volume were asked to link the historical, contemporary and future dimensions of constitutionalization by means of both Europeanization and intra-state consolidation. With this agenda, the authors embarked on an adventurous journey exploring the processes of adjustment of the legal orders of Central and Eastern Europe to the European "ideal" and the actors instrumental in that venture. Like every process that involves learning, the initial one-way street that positioned the West as the teachers and the East as the eager students changed over time – one might say rather rapidly – and acquired a new dimension. In today's constitutionalization reality, the former students have become influential young graduates with minds of their own, knowledge that matches that of their teachers and agendas that make them players of influence on the European stage.

The volume is organized in three sections, with most of the authors in each one combining a topical focus with a corresponding look at a particular country. This can be explained by the special local expertise of the authors, but also by the need to examine the particularities of the new EU Member States in the East. Too many times the accession states have been placed in a box and labelled superficially and incorrectly as synonymous. The historical contexts of each country differ profoundly, however, and so do the details of their legal systems and state structures, with the constitutions being the prominent feature.

The first cluster of contributions centres around the foundations and methods of constitutional dialogue in Central and Eastern Europe. Tanel Kerikmae advances the concept of "deliberative supranationalism" as a suitable tool for new Members States to become not just efficient, but influential, EU actors that can help shape the emerging European constitution, as well as the

12 See in that respect the very important work by Sadurski, W. (2008), *Rights Before Courts: A Study of Constitutional Courts in Postcommunist States of Central and Eastern Europe*, Dordrecht: Springer.

changing national constitutions – the Estonian constitution in particular. Simina Tanasescu explores international constitutionalism in the broader sense with a particular focus on the Romanian judiciary's response to European "duties". Her contribution points towards the prevalent question of transnational constitutional borrowing, supremacy and/or primacy of supranational law, and the struggles of domestic actors to consolidate such external influences with the supposedly firm ground of national law they are used to. Kyriaki Topidi focuses on the role that fundamental rights have played in demonstrating the possibilities and need for constitutional dialogue in a European Union of 27 Member States. She argues more specifically that, following enlargement, fundamental rights are necessary to foster essential constitutional communication between the various "languages" that courts speak within and beyond Central and Eastern Europe.

The second cluster of chapters pertinently emphasizes the relevance of courts in establishing – and sometimes challenging – the new legal order of pan-European constitutionalism. Tomas Dumbrovsky sets the stage by discussing the Czech and Solvak courts' response to demands of adopting European law. He introduces us to what he calls a "dense and complicated net of channels and modes of [judicial] cooperation" which is, however, compromised by a mentality that places national unilateralism above the common goals of an ever-closer union. This, the question of whether inter-judicial dialogue is sufficient for European constitutionalization, reappears in the other contributions in this section. Piotr Mikuli in his contribution calls for both a more refined and better defined role of national as European judges, but also for an explicit formulation of the status of national constitutions in primary EU law. Jiri Zemanek then explores the Czech Constitutional Court's Lisbon Treaty cases in light of a pluralistic judicial dialogue and calls for a respect-based approach to the primacy of EU law. Alexander H.E. Morawa's contribution concludes this section, and he proposes both to reconsider the Kelsenian triangle as a suitable basis for building a multi-layered substantive European constitution and to empower the European citizenry to become strong actors of future European constitutionalization by making the best use of litigation strategies aimed at advancing a beneficial give-and-take between the European Court of Justice (ECJ) and national constitutional courts.

The third cluster of chapters addresses the rule of law and policymaking in Central and Eastern Europe after enlargement. Fundamental rights take centre stage in this section, as Bernadette Somody's contribution on the Hungarian courts' indicates. Using data retention as an example, she points out that European standards can be a double-edged sword and can indeed not only boost, but also dominate in better national standards to the detriment of individual rights protection. Katrin Nyman-Metcalf subsequently explores the role of the media in constitutional transition and suggests ways in which legislation can contribute to a firm foundation for liberal press freedoms in an evolving Europe. Last but not least, Daniel Smilov takes a critical look at the effect of populism on national–European relations and the failure of the judiciary to offer a corrective to that influence.

The editors hope that the thought-provoking, and sometimes simply provoking, contributions to this volume will contribute to a better understanding of the current questions of post-enlargement constitutionalization in Europe. Beyond that, the issue of transnational constitutional dialogue through its foremost proponents, courts of a constitutional stature, is of unwavering importance in global context. First and foremost, however, this volume aims to open the door for new questions which will undoubtedly invite new dialogues, new proposed solutions and new controversies. After all, constitutions thrive amidst – civilized – controversy.

PART I
Foundations and Methods of Constitutional Dialogue in CEE

Chapter 2
Estonia as an EU Member State: Lack of Pro-active Constitutional Dialogue

Tanel Kerikmäe

Introduction[1]

Membership of the European Union is an impulse for several reforms for Member States in the context of the rethinking of their constitutionalism and legal reasoning. "Many of the vital problems that society is trying to deal with are *multidimensional*, *complex* and to some extent, *transnational* – in their origin, their causes and the problem solving stage. All these three qualities represent substantial challenges to our present political and legal decision-making systems."[2]

European Union membership brings us to multilevel governance that complicates the decision-making process. Estonia, as a Member State of the European Union, certainly has choices. There is a contra-argument for those who are praising political realism and ultra-superiority of EU rules over any national initiative. According to Sverdrup, "implementation also involves a balancing act between, on the one hand, securing homogeneous implementation and, on the other hand, allowing for some domestic discretion".[3] This discretion should be based not so much on the margin of appreciation and exceptions enabled by supranational EU law, but rather on the principles derived from the domestic constitution as a living instrument that reflects the values of society. The dialogue between the two constitutional levels is inevitable for securing the rule of law. According to Martinico: "As the distinction between interpretations and politics diminishes, the

1 Theoretical framework of the following contribution is reflected by the author in his doctoral dissertation, Estonia in the European Legal System: Protection of the Rule of Law through Constitutional Dialogue, Dissertations on Social Sciences, Tallinn University, Tallinn 2009.

2 Inger-Johanne Sand, Polycontextuality as an Alternative to Constitutionalism, in Christian Joerges, Inger-Johanne Sand and Gunther Teubner (eds) *Transnational Governance and Constitutionalism*, Oxford and Portland Oregon, Hart Publishing, 2004, 62–63.

3 Ulf Sverdrup, Implementation, in Paolo Graziano and Maarten P. Vink (eds) *New Research Agendas*, New York, Palgrave Macmillan, 2008, 199–200.

need for pluralism in interpretation increases."[4] Even within the EU legal system we need not abandon the rule of law.

European (legal) identity cannot be seen as a final goal, but as an ongoing process. The European Union is not just a post-national union, but it is a problem-solving and value-based construct. Implementation of European values that are common to the EU should be a primary task for any Member State, including Estonia. The general recognition of a need for legitimacy as a component of the rule of law for the European project does not need another apologism and "a shared collective identity (a European one) would seem to be a good means to the end envisaged."[5]

Deliberative Supranationalism

The relationship between EU law and national law is one of the most debated issues of European constitutional law.[6] Member States hold three basic views[7] on the primacy of EC/EU law:

1. primacy of EC law because of its very nature, i.e., faithful to European Court of Justice case-law (Belgian *Cour de Cassation* in Le Ski 1971);[8]
2. primacy of EC law based on national law (French *Cour de Cassation* in Vabre 1975);[9] and
3. primacy of EC law based on national law, and only within certain limits (German *Solange* I 1974 and II 1987).[10]

Primacy of EU law over Member States' constitutions has always been controversial as the national constitutions are the sources that allow EU law to enter the domestic legal systems. Verhoeven proposes constitutional homogeneity to be a precondition for loyalty to European Union. The author agrees that multiple

---

4 Giuseppe Martinico, A Matter of Coherence in the Multilevel Legal System: Are the "Lions" Still "Under the Throne"? Jean Monnet Working paper, 2008, 16/08, 37.

5 Enikö Horváth, *Mandating Identity. Citizenship, Kinship and Plural Nationality in the European Union*, The Netherlands, Kluwer Law International, 2007, 72.

6 Franz C. Mayer, Supremacy – Lost? Comment on Roman Kwiecień, in Philipp Dann and Michal Rynkowski (eds) *The Unity of the European Constitution*, Berlin, Heidelberg, New York, Springer, 2006, 87.

7 Christa Tobler and Jaques Beglinger, *Essential EC Law in Charts*, Budapest, Hvg-orac, 2007, 88.

8 Cour de Cassation, Arrêt du 27 mai 1971, *Etat belge v Fromagerie franco-suisse Le Ski*, JT, 1971, 471.See also 23 CMLRev (1986) 253–286.

9 Cour de Cassation, *Cafés Jaques Vabres*, Judgment of 24 May 1975, 2 CMLRev (1976).

10 BVerfGE 37, 271 2 BvL 52/71 Solange I-Beschluß and BVerfGE 73, 339 2 BvR 197/83 Solange II-decision.

masters (EU law and national constitution) are *per se* a source of conflict, but also states that "that conflict cannot be properly resolved *ex ante*, say, making the European law automatically "trump" national constitutions".[11] This kind of homogeneity cannot be (legally) framed, but must be seen as a process where the values emerge and develop through the communications between the two levels. To assume that supranationalism is a dogma and the competence of the EU cannot be influenced by the Member States is misleading, taking account the principle of Maastricht Treaty, which in Article 6(1) stipulates:

> The Union is founded on the principles of liberty, democracy, respect for human rights and fundamental freedoms, and the rule of law, principles which are common to the Member States.

A rather radical view is that EU law supremacy can be conceived as a conflict rule, entailing, in the first place, the "obligation to disapply".[12] The very idea, though, is not to deny the supremacy of EU law in general, but to urge the national legislator to interpret, think and consult. Even if the hierarchical relationship between national and supranational legal systems can be assumed, the automatic hierarchical relationship of the legal norms in the implementation process cannot be presumed. As Prechal suggests: "Despite some scholarly efforts, this conclusion cannot be drawn from the case law of the European Court of Justice which, moreover, leaves the necessary space to the national legal systems to accommodate Community law provisions."[13]

Under the rule of law we cannot presume the absolute autonomy of European law even if the EU legal system is often declared to be *sui generis*. Barents warns, "that in such an approach, Community law is in danger of being conceived in a visionary way, strongly influenced by ideology and idealism".[14] However, contemporary theories of legal argumentation are more advanced in comparison with purely formalistic approaches which prevailed decades ago.

---

11 Amaryllis Verhoeven, 319.

12 Sacha Prechal, Direct Effect, Indirect Effect, Supremacy and the Evolving Constitution of the European Union, in Catherine Barnard (ed.) *The Fundamentals of EU Law Revisited. Assessing the Impact of the Constitutional Debate*, Oxford, Oxford University Press, 2007, 55; see also analysis of what constitutes the breach of European law: Bert Van Roosebeke, *State Liability for Breaches of European Law. An Economic Analysis*, Wiesbaden, Deutscher Universitäts-Verlag, 2007, especially Part II, section 3, subsection 3.4, Why do Member States breach? Theory and Empirics.

13 Sacha Prechal, Direct Effect, Indirect Effect, Supremacy and the Evolving Constitution of the European Union, in Catherine Barnard (ed.) *The Fundamentals of EU Law Revisited. Assessing the Impact of the Constitutional Debate*, Oxford, Oxford University Press, 2007, 55–56.

14 René Barents, *The Autonomy of Community Law*, The Hague, London, New York, Kluwer Law International, 2004, 16.

In order to protect the rule of law, the judgement should be based on deliberation. The modern theories concerning the EU legal system and primacy of the supranational law lead to an interpretation that takes account of arguments from both national and EU levels. Zürn concludes that the so-called "deliberative supranationalism" (deriving from the ideas of Habermas, Weiler, Haltern, Mayer and Koh) must guarantee:

a. that in the deliberations surrounding the enactment of a particular regulation the grounds brought forward for and against it are *acceptable* to all the parties involved;
b. that it requires "arguing" about relevant problems;
c. that the general public is given the chance to articulate its opinions on matters.[15]

In general, deliberative supranationalism seems to be a modified version of Habermas's theory of "deliberative democracy" by which democracy is seen, in essence, as a process of institutionalized public deliberation on matters of common concern.[16] It follows, as stated by Verhoeven, "that real constitutions are never static or complete but are constantly open to *critique* and review. What the constitution is, must rather be sought in the living and evolving *aquis* of constitutional rules and principles of a particular community."[17] Therefore, the Estonian constitution cannot be seen just as a channel to the EU legal system, but as a forum for state authorities by which the mediation of reciprocal Europeanization process to (legal) society is made possible.

Walker's proposal to build a metaconstitutional frame with the cosmopolitan nature, "which lacks tradition, well-defined and well-respected rules of amendment, and lives in the shadow of a pluralist conception of authority which shares and challenges their jurisdiction ...",[18] is a utopian and vague concept. Deliberativist ideas are more close to what Tully calls common constitutionalism, by which "a constitution should be seen as a form of activity, an intercultural dialogue in

15 Michael Zürn, Law and Compliance at Different Levels, in Michael Zürn and Christian Joerges (eds) *Law and Governance in Postnational Europe. Compliance Beyond the Nation-State*, Cambridge, Cambridge University Press, 2005, 37.

16 See analysis of Habermas and Alexy by Amaryllis Verhoeven, *The European Union in Search of a Democratic and Constitutional Theory*, The Hague, London, New York, Kluwer Law International, 2002, 39–50.

17 Ibid., 53.

18 Neil Walker, Flexibility within a Metaconstitutional Frame: Reflections on the Future of Legal Authority in Europe, in Gráinne de Búrca and Joanne Scott, (eds) *Constitutional Change in the EU. From Uniformity to Flexibility*, Oxford, Portland Oregon, Hart Publishing, 2001, 29.

which culturally diverse sovereign citizens of contemporary societies negotiate agreements on their forms of association over time…”.[19]

Estonia could secure the prevalence of the rule of law also in order to avoid possible political influences from other Member States. By establishing the constitutional dialogue between national and EU constitutional levels, Estonia can minimize any foreign political impact. This aspect of deliberativism, described by Raadschelders, sees the European Union's supranational character as a universal authority. He adds that “when the universal authority crumbles …, horizontal integration becomes the need to establish an absolute independence from neighbors”.[20] On one hand, there is a contradiction – the EU is a combination of values (and norms reflecting them) that derive from systems of different cultures. However, the most influential Member States are not changing their state functions and legal reasoning as dramatically as Members States that joined later, under the conditions that were elaborated before their accession. On the other hand, there is no contradiction between the idea of reciprocity and deliberative supranationalism, as the EU authority should be autonomous or not independent from any Member State. However, we should reject the naïve question of “bottom-up or bottom down?” and be inspired by the concept of “societal constitutionalism” (which is an alternative to the normative, state-linked constitutionalism). The EU legal system (including the legal systems of Member States) must be based unconditionally on the rule of law, not economic and political influences of different interest groups.

Joerges, concluding and promoting Teubner's concept, gives a definition of societal constitutionalism: “Societal constitutionalism is autonomous, self-creating and self-legitimating: globalization is not just about economy, but is driven by many more social sub-systems which create a new global pluralism which exerts (self-)control through a ‘decentralized multiplicity of spontaneous communication processes’”.[21] This is a combination of, what Allot describes as “the ideal constitution” which self-constitutes in the form of ideas, and “the real constitution” which self-constitutes through the everyday willing and acting of society members.[22]

---

19 See analysis of Tully's ideas in: Jo Shaw, Relating Constitutionalism and Flexibility in the European Union, in Gráinne de Búrca and Joanne Scott (eds) *Constitutional Change in the EU. From Uniformity to Flexibility*, Oxford, Portland Oregon, Hart Publishing, 2001, 347–351.

20 Jos C.N. Raadschelders, *Handbook of Administrative History*, New Brunswick and London, Transaction Publishers, 2000, 217.

21 Christian Joerges, Constitutionalism and Transnational Governance: Exploring a Magic Triangle, in Christian Joerges, Inger-Johanne Sand and Gunther Teubner (eds) *Transnational Governance and Constitutionalism*, Oxford and Portland Oregon, Hart Publishing, 2004, 373.

22 Philip Allott, The Concept of International Law, in Michael Byers (ed.) *The Role of Law in International Politics. Essays in International Relations and International Law*, Oxford, Oxford University Press, 2001, 69.

Even if the EU law can less and less be considered to be foreign law for Estonia (and other Member States), the dangers and obstacles in the use of legislation not adopted by the national legislator can be enumerated, as proposed by Markesinis and Fedtke,[23] as follow:

- the lack of precise information;
- the lack of up-to-date information;
- the issue of detailed consideration versus generalities (related to the overlapping legal acts and norm hierarchy);
- the impact of the socio-economic and political environment;
- the lack of legal certainty;
- the question of whether domestic courts have enough time (as well as willingness and knowledge) to deal with other legal systems;
- the lack of "depth" of analysis of foreign legal ideas.

The constitutional dialogue could be instrumentalized by using Kordela's[24] system of EU general principles, by which the need for deliberativism can be tested. Before applying European Union legal norms, the legal practitioners (lawyers and judges, mostly) should test them using the following system of principles:

a. substantial premise (EU legal norm must be justified by fundamental human rights, and the principle of legitimate expectations should be taken into account);
b. formal premise (the EU legal norm cannot contradict the principles clearly formulated at the supranational level, such as proportionality, legal certainty, non-retroactivity, equality, subsidiarity);
c. procedural premise (the EU legal norm must be adopted according to the competences given to the EU institutions).

Only after successfully examining the legal norm through the abovementioned test, the argument of praxeological necessity, i.e., supremacy and direct effect, can be assumed. The examining process should take account of the legal reasoning from both the national and supranational levels.

EU law is not only about written norms, it is, in large part, about the jurisprudence of European Court of Justice (ECJ) that reflects the implementation issues. Besides that, there exists a kind of European argumentative dualism, as

23 Basil Markesinis and Jörg Fedtke, *Judicial Recourse to Foreign Law. A New Source of Inspiration?* London, University College London Press, 139–173.

24 Marzena Kordela, Principles of Law as a Theoretical Category – Remarks on the Background of the General Principles of Community Law, in Adam Bodnar, Michal Kowalski, Karen Raible and Frank Schoropf (eds) *The Emerging Constitutional Law of the European Union. German and Polish Perspectives*, Berlin, Heidelberg, New York, Springer, 2003, 581–582.

the opinions of Advocates General (suggestions to the judiciary of ECJ) have at least the same relevance or weight as ECJ jurisprudence, operating in the field of "the discourse of the personal and subjective construction of purposive judicial solutions".[25] It is also important to bear in mind that the Estonian judiciary is not used to shifting from normative interpretation to teleological interpretation, which, as suggested by several authors, is the preferred method much of the European Court[26] and represents best the principle of "legal effectiveness" or *effet utile*, used by ECJ as a main doctrinal method. Our state representatives should obtain knowledge not only of technical implementation procedures of EU law, but also be familiar with the legal reasoning that concerns the dynamic development of EU law. Legal pluralism must always be in the mind of those who apply or prepare the implementation of EU norms.[27]

The problems in positioning the EU law into the domestic legal system are even more evident in the cases where the EU rule or precedent is not commonly understood or is interpreted in difference ways. According to Williams: "Identifying a central principle is an essential step in the process of judgment. But it is not enough. A mere rhetorical observation … is patently insufficient. We need to look further for guidance. What concerns us is how the principle is or is not fulfilled. In other words, the principle is not the last word in values. We must also consider the means by which it is brought into effect. Only then can effective evaluation be made as to the extent to which the principle has been and is realized."[28]

Clarity of conception, capacity for evolution and enforcement, transparency,[29] certainty, foreseeability, analysis of cost–benefit balance, cultural dimension and preconditions are the keywords that must establish EU-related (legal) policy in Member States. We should be aware of the categorization of competences and be able to effectively use different techniques and levels of competence (European or domestic) in making strategies that work for Estonian welfare, such as infra-

25 Mitchel de S.O.-L'E. Lasser, *Judicial Deliberations. A Comparative Analysis of Judicial Transparency and Legitimacy*, Oxford, Oxford University Press, 2004, 141.

26 Trevor C. Hartley, *European Union Law in a Global Context*, Cambridge, Cambridge University Press, 2004, 118. G. Burca, The European Court of Justice and the International Legal Order after *Kadi* Jean Monnet Working Paper 01/09, New York, New York School of Law. Available at www.JeanMonnetProgram.org, accessed 3 September 2009.

27 See: Albertine Veldman, Legal System, Theory and Legal Methods of Research into the Enforcement and Effectiveness of Community Law, in J.A.E. Vervaele (ed.) *Compliance and Enforcement of European Community Law*, The Hague, London, Boston, Kluwer Law International, 1999, 125–141.

28 Andrew Williams, Respecting Fundamental Rights, in Catherine Barnard (ed.) *The Fundamentals of EU Law Revisited: Assessing the Impact of the Constitutional Debate*, Oxford, Oxford University Press, 2007, 82.

29 Andrew Williams is using the concept particularly in the context of protecting human rights; however, it can be and must be used in broader terms (see Williams, ibid., 87–107).

nationalism,[30] intergovernmental negotiations and the seeking of consensus among lawyers of other Member States before presenting a legal argument against the possible violation of rule of law by the EU institutions.

Every transition (e.g., formation and development of the European Union) is a result of interaction of ideas. Amongst social scientists there are different approaches supporting the idea:

1. Political scientists propose a qualitative step from executive multilateralism to a form of socially consented multilateralism in the age of globalization.
2. Lawyers, by contrast, tend to develop a constitutional perspective of law production where the deliberation becomes the normative leitmotif that inspires the organization of transnational problem solving and assessment.[31]

It seems quite expected that in a multilevel system there must be a certain coordination between the national and the supranational order. There are several meanings of "constitutional dialogue", the term that reflects reciprocal and interactive relations between national and supranational legal societies. Authors are using expressions such as "constitutional tolerance" and "cosmopolitan communitarism", the former inspired by Weiler and the latter by Bellamy.[32] Other authors use the term "interpretative pluralism". Stihl argues that legal professionals believe less and less that law is science rather than politics. He proposes that interpretative pluralism (or pluralist interpretation) can be used as "the absence of a single binding or authoritative interpretation".[33] The interpretative pluralism is revealed to be a method of comparative law. Stihl concludes his thoughts with the observation that "whether final interpretation is united in a single court or

30 Such as infranationalism: opportunities in lobbying at forums related to comitology, as stated by Joseph Weiler: "comitology is responsible directly for fundamental societal decisions on the allocation of risk and its costs and indirectly for significant decisions on the allocation of resources and redistribution", see Joseph Weiler, *The Constitution of Europe. "Do the New Clothes have an Emperor?" and Other Essays on European Integration*, Cambridge. Cambridge University Press, 2000, 277–278.

31 Michael Zürn, Law and Compliance at Different Levels, in Michael Zürn and Christian Joerges (eds) *Law and Governance in Postnational Europe. Compliance Beyond the Nation State*, Cambridge, Cambridge University Press, 2005, 37.

32 Giuseppe Martinico, A Matter of Coherence in the Multilevel Legal System: Are the "Lions" Still "Under the Throne"? Jean Monnet Working paper 2008, 16/08. See also, J.H.H. Weiler, European Democracy and the Principle of Constitutional Tolerance: The Soul of Europe, in F. Cerutti and E. Rudolph (eds) *A Soul of Europe*, Leuven, Peeters 2001, 33–54; R. Bellamy and R. Warleigh, Cementing the Union: The Role of European Citizenship, in F. Cerutti and E. Rudolph (eds) *A Soul of Europe*, Leuven, Peeters, 2001, 55–72.

33 Richard Stith, Securing the Rule of Law through Interpretive Pluralism: An Argument from Comparative Law. Jean Monnet working paper, 2008 01/07.

divided among many institutions, the rest of us are left subject not to the law itself but to the interpretations of the law handed down by fallible human beings, interpretations that may over time distance themselves greatly from the original legal sources".[34] According to Martinico, there must be judicial dialogue that represents a privileged perspective for studying the relations between interacting legal orders.[35]

The modern approach in multilevel relations is to secure the equilibrium between national and supranational interests through constitutional dialogue. Supreme courts (Irish, Greek, Danish and Finnish) have been innovatively active to keep up the dialogue that constitutional courts of some Member States (Italian, French, Spanish) have avoided. The Estonian judicial system should, following this logic, belong to the first category of Member States as the highest judicial body is the Supreme Court.

The present author's position on the cruciality of constitutional dialogue has, at a general level, been recently (4 May 2009) reflected by the debate at the Commission of European Affairs, and the Estonian parliament (*Riigikogu*). Attention was drawn to the need of Estonia to become a more proactive Member State and to the need to test the decisions related to the implementation of EU law through the Estonian constitution and guarantee the high-level training of the public officials whose professional activities are related to the EU issues. More consistent formation of constitutional doctrine (i.e., interpretative pluralism) is indirectly supported by the Commission as one of its suggestions includes the demand for deliberate alternative solutions when implementing EU law. This is a clear sign that Estonia needs to be acquainted with modern theories of deliberative supranationalism in order to become better positioned among Member States on the basis of solid legal arguments derived from constitutional dialogue between the national and European Union levels.

There are certain techniques for dialogue to take place. One of the most important ones is the technique which distinguishes between supremacy and primacy. According to the *Tribunal Constitucional*: "supremacy is sustained in the higher hierarchical character of a regulation and, therefore, is a source of validity of the lower regulations, leading to the consequent invalidity of the latter if they contravene the provisions set forth imperatively in the former. Primacy, however, is not necessarily sustained on hierarchy, but rather on the distinction between the scopes of application of different regulations, principally valid, of which, however, one or more of them have the capacity for displacing others by virtue of their

34 Stihl, ibid., 28.

35 Giuseppe Martinico, A Matter of Coherence in the Multilevel Legal System: Are the "Lions" Still "Under the Throne"? Jean Monnet Working paper, 2008, 16/08. See also J.H.H. Weiler, European Democracy and the Principle of Constitutional Tolerance: The Soul of Europe, in F. Cerutti and E. Rudolph (eds), "A Soul of Europe, Leuven, Peeters 2001, 33–54; R. Bellamy and R. Warleigh, Cementing the Union: The Role of European Citizenship, in F. Cerutti and E. Rudolph (eds) *A Soul of Europe*, Leuven, Peeters 2001.

preferential or prevalent application due to various reasons."[36] Another technique consists of the distinction between disapplication and non-application: a Member State cannot disapply the national law that contradicts the EU norm, but must not apply the national rule contrasting with directly applicable EU law.

In general, "the process of ascertaining conformity of national rules implementing EU norms to the constitution is not carried out through a strict application of the unassailable rule of EU law primacy over the whole domestic law, nor by assuming unconditioned supremacy of the constitution over any other source of law, but rather with the objective of identifying the best solution to fulfil the ideals underlying legal practice in the European Union and its Member States".[37] According to Pollicino, "today more than ever, the courts (especially, in relation to the national legal orders, the constitutional courts) are the institutions which, in their respective legal orders, occupy a privileged position to forge closer ties between different but interacting legal regimes".[38]

When analyzing the EU Member State relations from the perspective of legal communication, the Lisbon Treaty cannot be ignored. The rejection of the constitutional treaty was a shock for its self-assured conceivers and supporters. Nevertheless, as Barnard points out, at least some of the opposition used the referenda (where they took place) "as an opportunity to give a bloody nose to the incumbent national governments".[39] In the context of this chapter, the author agrees with Weiler who remarked that "[w]hat Europe needs … is not a constitution but an *ethos* and *telos* to justify, if they can, the constitutional order it has already embraced".[40] There are many academic contributions[41] about the Constitution of Europe, Constitutional Treaty for Europe, Reform Treaty or Lisbon Treaty that demonstrate the inevitable link between EU and Member States constitutional law.

36 *Declaración del Pleno del Tribunal Constitucional* 1/2004, de 13 de diciembre de 2004. Requerimiento 6603–2004.

37 M. Kumm, The Jurisprudence of Constitutional Conflict: Constitutional Supremacy in Europe Before and After the Constitutional Treaty, *European Law Journal*, 11, 2005, 262–286.

38 Oreste Pollicino, New Emerging Judicial Dynamics of the Relationship Between National and the European Courts after the Enlargement of Europe, Jean Monnet Working paper 2008 14/08.

39 Catherine Barnard, Introduction: The Constitutional Treaty, the Constitutional Debate and the Constitutional Process, in Catherine Barnard (ed.) *The Fundamentals of EU Law Revisited: Assessing the Impact of the Constitutional Debate*, Oxford, Oxford University Press, 2007.

40 Joseph Weiler, European Neo-constitutionalism: In Search of the Foundations for the the European Constitutional Order, *Pol. S.* 44, 1996, 517–533.

41 One of the best collections of articles is by Bruno de Witte (ed.) *Ten Reflections on the Constitutional Treaty for Europe*, Robert Schuman Centre for Advanced Studies, European University Institute, 2003, available at http://www.cadmus.eui.eu/dspace/bitstream/1814/2538/1/DeWitte_ConsTreaty.pdf, accessed 28 August 2010.

According to Sand, "the more classical theories of law and politics have presupposed that politics can presume to handle any theme and any policy orientation, and that all such themes and policies are communicable or translatable into a common political language of social *interests*".[42] The solution lies in "continuous learning processes, deliberation, comparisons, exchange of experiences". Interdependence and reciprocity are the keywords that Member States should follow to solve the *problématique* of transnational legal society.

The issue of how to interpret constitutional law is common to many legal societies. Trying to find an answer to the question of whether a specialized methodology is needed for European constitutional law, Dann declares that "the systematic and pan- European comparison of constitutional methodologies and its reflection onto issues facing Europe, as a whole, are still desiderata".[43] Even if Dann is not sure that the existing constitutional jurisprudence of Member States is able to compose the methodology of European Constitution, "the cognitive interests of academia (in contrast to those of courts)"[44] may have relevant influence on the process.

As it is noticed by Kowalski, "… respect for various European identities, cultures, traditions should not be destroyed or hindered by European integration".[45] The interdependence of the EU and its Member States is demonstrated by the work of several researchers.[46] Estonia should recognize the unavoidable effect of reciprocity in relations with the European Union and follow the reasoning that derives from multi-level constitutional culture.

Estonian Legal Policy *vis-à-vis* EU Constitutionalism

The main issue in the domestic context is the concordance of Estonia's constitutional legal policy with the EU legal dynamism. The self-positioning in the context of European Union membership requires from Member States an adaptive capacity and the establishment of proactive, coherent and consistent orientation in a dynamic, multi-level legal system. The principle of the rule of law must remain

42 Inger-Johanne Sand, Polycontextuality as an Alternative to Constitutionalism, in Christian Joerges, Inger-Johanne Sand and Gunther Teubner (eds) *Transnational Governance and Constitutionalism*, Oxford and Portland Oregon, Hart Publishing, 2004.

43 Philipp Dann, Thoughts on a Methodology of European Constitutional Law, in Philipp Dann and Michal Rynkowski (eds) *The Unity of the European Constitution*, Berlin, Heidelberg, New York, Springer, 2006, 47.

44 Ibid., 46.

45 Michal Kowalski, Comment on Daniel Thym: United in Diversity or Diversified in the Union, in Philipp Dann and Michal Rynkowski (eds) *The Unity of the European Constitution*, Berlin, Heidelberg, New York, Springer, 2006, 382.

46 See, for example, Jochen Herbst, Observations on the Right to Withdraw from the European Union, in Philipp Dann and Michal Rynkowski (eds) *The Unity of the European Constitution*, Berlin, Heidelberg, New York, Springer, 2006, 388.

the basis for the legal society and state activities. The constitution should be a tool that achieves equiprobable harmony of the national and supranational interests.

The current practice in Estonia consists of positioning supranational law through the Estonian constitutional order. Placing supranational law through the domestic constitutional legal order is inadequate because it fails to protect the principle of the rule of law in the dynamic environment of the European Union.

The following questions are of particular relevance:

1. Can the role of the Estonian constitution in the context of EU membership be identified?
2. Is Estonia ready to use the constitution as a central tool of mediation between national and supranational legal systems?
3. Are the used methods to position the Estonian constitution in an EU context sufficient to secure the rule of law?
4. Is the principle of legal certainty in Estonia guaranteed concerning the validity of the constitution after the accession to the European Union?
5. Is there sufficient constitutional dialogue to take account of the dynamic nature of the European Union?
6. Is Estonian contemporary legal education in conformity with the need for European legal thinking and reasoning?

To analyse the positions taken by Estonia, the author has constructed the conceptual framework summarized in Table 2.1 and further developed the approaches discussed in the theoretical part of this chapter. The key idea is to generalize the diametric differentiation between rigid and dynamic approaches of constitutional doctrines in the context of EU membership. The indicators are elaborated as a result of the analysis and generalization of theoretical approaches. There is a generalized analysis of the research of relevant authors in the field and the author's own empirical research. This analysis enables the author to present the main features of contemporary constitutional doctrine in the context of EU membership, and to evaluate and compare the rigid (traditional) and dynamic (deliberative) in a manner to create theoretical methodology for further research.

The five indicators included are used to measure and identify the positions of Estonia which are discussed in the empirical part of this chapter.

Table 2.1 Diametric measurement of constitutional doctrine

	INDICATORS (and authors whose contributions have been the basis in ascertaining the indicators)	**A. RIGID APPROACH (traditional supranationalism)**	**B. DYNAMIC APPROACH (deliberative supranationalism)**
1	Relationship and communication between national and supranational (EU) law Pollicino 2008 McCormick 2007 Kordela 2003 Martinico 2008 Kowalski 2006 Zürn 2005 Walker 2001 Shaw 2001 Warleigh 2001	Passive positioning. Communication is unilateral (*ex parte*). Supremacy and primacy are synonyms. Supranational character of EU law is sufficient basis for validating legal norms in domestic legal system. Interaction of national and supranational legal systems is not supported. Member state is acting under the principle of constitutional loyalty assuming that supranational interests take account the national interests	Pro-active positioning. "Primacy" (distinction between the scopes of application) is distinguished from "supremacy" as a general principle. Legitimacy of EU norm is analyzed by a test composed of the constitutional principles and substantial, formal and procedural premises (see Kordela´s test in section 3.2). Member state attempts to generate a interactive dialogue (based on equilibrium and balanced interests) between *domain reservé* of national and supranational levels (reciprocity)
2	Implementation and *techniques* of interpretation of EU law Bateup 2008 Williams 2007 Stihl 2007 Lasser 2004 Lenaerts 2003 Bodnar, Kowalski, Raible, Schoropf 2003	Implementation is automatic, based on technical-grammatical interpretation and rhetorical observations. Subsidiary sources (court decisions, opinions of Advocate Generals and *academia*) are often rejected. Only European Court of Justice (ECJ) can interpret EU legal norms and analyze the compliance of domestic law with supranational law	Implementation is based on deliberative observations, teleological interpretation and the doctrine of *effet utile*. Subsidiary sources are having great relevance. Interpretative pluralism prevails, skills of legal reasoning of the public officials are relevant determinators of the member state's capacity

Table 2.1 Continued

3	Collision between national and supranational law Aragáo 2008 Grossi 1999 Hay, Lister 2006 Sorensen 2006 Kumm 2005	Conflict is eliminated *ex ante* by disapplication of domestic legal norm. Exceptions and deviations (margin of appreciation) from EU rule must be prescribed by the EU legal norm	Conflict is possible or even assumed. Domestic legal norm is not applied until the just argument is adopted through interpretative *techniques*. Margin of appreciation is deriving from common European constitutional values reflected by the member state's constitution
4	Status and relevance of the Constitution Sverdrup 2008 Martinico 2008 Mayer 2006 Prechal 2007 van Roosebeke 2007 Zürn 2005 Raadschelders 2000 Joerges 2004	Constitution is seen as a text to acknowledge of the supreme position of the EU law in general. EU law determines the validity and content of the constitution of the member state. The scope of legal bindingness of the constitution as independent legal text remains unframed. The continuous dynamics of EU legal environment is not taken into account due to the principle of absolute autonomy of EU law. Amendments in interpretation of EU law can be initiated only from supranational level	Constitution is seen as a living instrument that safeguards the position of member state in the EU. The content and bindingness of the constitution is not formally dependent from EU law. The constitution can be interpreted through "common constitutionalism" and "constitutional dialogue". Changing legal environment is taken into account by analyzing EU developments, using constitutional dialogue and interpretative pluralism
5	Approach to the Rule of Law Mann 2003 Gearey 2005 Vincent 1996 Verhoeven 2002 Pierson 2007 Markensis, Fedke 2006 Weiler 1996; 2000; 2004	Rule of law is determined by the EU exclusively. For state authorities, it becomes an apologist construct in justifying interference of political and economic influences that prevail over the legal framework. The dependence from other member states is significant. Rule of law is endangered because of recognition of only one interpreter of EU law (ECJ)	Rule of law remains to be the most important criteria, which can be analyzed independently from socio-economic and political environment. The impact of other member states in domestic decision-making and implementation of EU law is minimized as much as possible

Estonia's Positions: Empirical and Theoretical Analysis

Estonian Constitution in Light of EU Membership

In previous work,[47] the present author provided an analysis of the main theoretical discussions that were held in Estonia before its accession. As (the delegation of) sovereignty has been the central topic, that chapter was an analytical overview of the proposed amendments. The author supported the idea that a constitution should be deemed to be a type of contract and discussed the problems of *pouvoir constituant* related to the (re)delegation of sovereignty. The chapter concluded with the assumption that the answer to the question, "What is the constitutional future of the Union?", was also the answer to many questions of how to reach a compromise in our legal society. The future of the EU (and its own developing constitutionalism) was also taken into account: the article included suggestions and analysis of the most sensitive areas of Estonian public interest. Separate research presented was related to the EU Charter of Fundamental Rights,[48] demonstrating the change of EU (legal) values following a shift from market values to the prioritization of human rights and freedoms.

Elsewhere,[49] the suggestion to rethink the role of the Estonian parliament was also made. As the main representative at the EU level (making supranational binding decisions for Estonia) is the Estonian government, the balance in decision-making is gradually shifting towards the executive branch of state power, which appears to be a deviation from the rule of law.[50] The author adopted a critical approach to the technique used by the Estonian state in positioning EU law *vis-à-vis* the Estonian constitution. In general, the research area can be comprehensibly divided into three periods: before, during and following EU accession.

Preparing for accession — The European Union gives free choice to a candidate state as to if, when and how to amend or modernize its constitutional law. The criticism of the European Commission in the so-called "success reports" never concerned questions related to the constitution. Of course, the compliance of prospective Member States' constitutions with certain criteria set up in Copenhagen

47 T. Kerikmäe, Estonian Constitutional Problems in Accession to the EU, in A.E. Kellermann, J.W. de Zwaan and J. Czuczai (eds) *EU Enlargement. The Constitutional Impact at EU and National Level*, The Hague, T.M.C Asser Press, 2001.

48 T. Kerikmäe and Kari Käsper, *European Charter of Fundamental Rights*, Lexis Nexis Expert Commentaries, Matthew Bender & Co, 2007/2008 (online resource).

49 Tanel Kerikmäe, Euroopa *Zeitgeist* ja Eesti valikud Põhiseaduslikkuse mõtestamisel [European *Zeitgeis*t and Estonian Choices in interpretation of Constitutionalism], Tartu, 2009.

50 In the article, the author provided an overview of his expert opinions related to the position of Estonian constitution before, during and after the accession.

criteria[51] is taken into account during the process of accession. At the same time, neither the European Commission nor other institutions have made any pertinent remarks claiming that the Constitution of the Republic of Estonia does not meet the criteria. Calls for pre-accession constitutional reforms in candidate states have been finalized with a conclusion that it is not possible to form a sample constitution, listing provisions that should be copied into the prospective Member States' constitutions.

The constitution has been an important factor in building up the rule of law in Estonia. According to Vahtre:

> [the] ... Estonian decision – to start with [building] the constitution was justified. Despite a few disagreements, the constitution built a solid legal base for the state, making it easier to do the following restructuring work. Laws and the importance of their mutual suitability for a whole society in the process of a systematic restructuring cannot be underestimated.[52]

Moreover, the question of constitutional compliance became important in the context of the desired European Union membership.

During the pre-accession period, the legal expert commission[53] came to conclusion that "[the] current constitution does not allow Estonia to access the European Union". At the same time, the commission did take into consideration the constitution "as a living legal document".

This author suggested that the goals of the Estonian state could be achieved efficiently through membership of the European Union without contradicting the Estonian constitution. Accession to the European Union had to be viewed as a process under international law based on the people's right to self-determination. It was suggested that the state's authority was an intermediary between the individual and the EU and that the constitution was a regulator for relations between the national and supranational level. At that time, the state's main function was to explain to the electorate how the EU could be useful to Estonia.

In his opinion to the Legal Chancellor in 2002, this author also suggested that, first, people should decide on the accession to the European Union and only after that could the need for amendment of the constitution arise. Insofar as Estonian

51 The use of criteria is considered politicized. For an indicative example of the negotiations with Turkey, see Lutz Sommer, Accession of Turkey to the European Union – A Question of Advantage? IABR & TLC Conference Proceedings San Juan, Puerto Rico, 2008, available at: www.cluteinstituteonlinejournals.com/-Programs/Puerto_Rico_2008/Article%20159%20Sommer.pdf, accessed 28 August 2010.

52 Lauri Vahtre, *Eesti rahva lugu* [Story of Estonian People], Tallinn, ILO, 2005, 264 (extract translated by the author of the current chapter).

53 The Estonian government established a constitutional commission of legal experts by the order dated 4 May 1996. See also Paul Varul, Põhiseaduse juriidiline ekspertiis: eesmärgid, töökorraldus ja töötulemused, RITO 18, Tallinn 2008.

objectives were in conformity with the principles prescribed in the constitution, then they should be realized in a new historical situation by interpreting constitutional provisions according to the European Union's primary law (viewed as an international treaty). In case the principles contained in the constitution were no longer protected by the EU, then, according to the international law, it was possible to step away from such a contractual relation. Therefore, the constitution would not provide an obstacle for Estonia to become a Member State. A constitution cannot *per se* restrict the people's exercise of self-determination. On the other hand, it cannot be preclude that performing such a right can further establish a need for the constitutional amendment (Indicator 2).

This author believes that the interpretation (and, if required, the amendment) of the constitution depends upon the people as the "high bearer of state's supreme power". The constitution should be treated as a process the objectives of which depend on the people's will. The aforementioned expert commission concluded that sovereignty has two dimensions – an internal one and an external one. However, taking account of the status of international law in the Estonian legal order, it should be noted that this kind of division cannot be taken as absolute. An example is the binding character of the judicial decisions of the European Court of Human Rights. The European Convention on Human Rights and Fundamental Freedoms, ratified as an international treaty, is an integral part of national law, and the European Court of Human Rights is the one and only institution that can interpret the treaty. Therefore, due to the fact that the Estonian judiciary is obliged to take account of the standards of international judgements, the relation between external obligations and internal legal order is apparent.

The main theoretical question asked at the time of pre-accession on the conditions and reasons for which the constitution should be amended was left without solution. Today, it is clear that the answers can vary depending on whether they concern general (conceptual) or more specific points. The general questions deal with the delegation of jurisdiction to international organizations (e.g., to the European Community or European Union). A specific question, which has provided great discussion, is the transfer of legislative drafting and decision-making from the parliament to the government representing Estonia at the supranational level. Affordable solutions can be found, for instance, in the effective performance of European Union Affairs Committee in the Estonian parliament. The role of the Estonian people's representation – the Parliament – is also changing in the context of EU membership and the state faces the problem of how to secure the control over executive power[54] at the European level. If at first the question was not deemed relevant, later *Riigikogu* amended its statute in March 2004. That amendment gave ways to the parliament to exercise control over activities of the government

54 Tanel Kerikmäe, The Role of the Estonian Parliament after Accession to the European Union, Riigikogu's edition IV [Estonian parliamentary journal], Tallinn 2001. For experiences of other states see, e.g, Elspeth Deards and Sylvia Hargreave, *EU Law*, Oxford, Oxford University Press 2007, 37–44.

on the European level. It also ensured the involvement of legislative power in EU's decision-making process and solved questions on the internal coordination mechanism[55] (Indicators 3 and 4).

The Treaty of Accession concluded with the European Union is by its nature an international agreement. The dispute in the context of EU membership has been the scope of interpretation of Article 123 of the Estonian constitution. Although the provision sets forth an *ex ante* control mechanism in order to measure the compliance between an international agreement and the constitution, it does not set forth an *a posteriori* control. In case of a ratified agreement, the constitution should be, then, interpreted in the light of an international agreement. According to Article 46 of the Vienna Convention on the Law of Treaties, a state may not invoke its non-compliance with an international obligation on the basis of internal law.

This author also differentiates the aspect of delegation of sovereignty "from final transaction" and assumes that the process can be turned back. The part that has been delegated can be taken back and redelegated. This means that the delegated powers cannot either decrease or increase without respective authorization. One of the Euro-sceptic views – according to which the departure from the European Union is impossible – relies on the Vienna Convention on the Law of Treaties.[56] Article 54 provides: "The termination of a treaty or the withdrawal of a party may take place: (a) in conformity with the provisions of the treaty; or (b) at any time by consent of all the parties after consultation with the other contracting States." The treaty of establishment and the treaties amending and improving it do not talk about the termination of the treaty. It would still become politically complicated for a Member State to get the consent of the contracting parties. A second option is contained in the Convention's Article 56 that sets out the general rule: "(1). A treaty which contains no provision regarding its termination and which does not provide for denunciation or withdrawal is not subject to denunciation or withdrawal unless: (a) it is established that the parties intended to admit the possibility of denunciation or withdrawal; or (b) a right of denunciation or withdrawal may be implied by the nature of the treaty."

The final solution lies in the Convention's Article 60(2), according to which: "material breach of a multilateral treaty by one of the parties entitles: the other parties by unanimous agreement to suspend the operation of the treaty in whole or in part or to terminate it either." According to Article 60(3)(b), a material breach of a treaty consists of the violation of those provisions, which have significant meaning. According to this provision, the right to denounce the treaty would guarantee that the institutions of EU would not misuse what has been delegated by Estonia. The emphasis should be put on the interpretation of the constitution: it should be assumed that constitutional law protects Estonian sovereignty. Potential

55 Clarification regarding the nature of amendments by European Union Affairs Committee 25.01.2008, available at: http://www.riigikogu.ee/index.php?id=48788&parent_id=48709, accessed 28 August 2010.

56 Convention on the Law of Treaties RTII, 11.05.1993, 13/14, 16.

conflicts or a collision between the two legal orders should be possible to solve in the light of the constitution. In case of hesitation on how to interpret internal law, including constitutional provisions, judges should preferably use interpretation that is in compliance with the EU primary law – international treaties to which Estonia party.

The limits of interpretation of the constitution are determined by the will of the carrier of the supreme power – the people. The intention of the people can be clarified by referendum. Accordingly, this author did not support the idea to amend the constitution before the accession for the purpose of puttin the Treaty of Accession to a vote (as the constitution prohibits holding a referendum on international treaties). Instead, this author concluded his vision as follows: amendment of the constitution is necessary only when it cannot be interpreted according to the provisions it contains (Indicator 2). Mandate, or in other words limits on interpretation, can be given by referendum. Accordingly, in his expert opinion to the Legal Chancellor, this author suggested having a referendum with the following question: "Would you delegate the powers to state authorities in order to take steps, which would lead Estonia to European Union membership?"

Accessing the European Union – At the referendum[57] on 14 September 2003, the Estonian people, according to Article 162 of the Constitution, adopted a law[58] to amend the constitution of the Republic of Estonia as follows:

1. Estonia may belong to the European Union in accordance with the fundamental principles of the Constitution of the Republic of Estonia.

2. As of Estonia's accession to the European Union, the Constitution of the Republic of Estonia applies, taking account of the rights and obligations arising from the Accession Treaty.

3. This Act may be amended only by a referendum.

4. This Act enters into force three months after the date of proclamation.

---

57 Referendum was followed by court action: an Estonian citizen, K. Kulbok, submitted a claim in which he challenged the action of the government's electoral committee regarding the validity question on a ballot paper. The Supreme Court found that a question put to a vote and wording entered on a ballot paper was not decided by the government's electoral committee, but by a decision of *Riigikogu* on 18 December 2002, and the deadline for challenging the text had expired. Also, according to the law, individuals are not entitled to challenge the accordance of the foreign treaty (accession treaty) and the constitution directly from the Supreme Court. See: Decision No 12 of the Constitutional Review Chamber of the Supreme Court 29.09.2003, RT III 2003, 28, 287.

58 Amendment Act to the Constitution (*Eesti Vabariigi Põhiseaduse täiendamise seadus*). RT I 2003, 64, 429.

Clearly, it was the case of a compromise solution where the text of the constitution would not be amended directly. Was it possible to guarantee the supremacy of constitution by avoiding the amendment procedure of the constitution? In this case it would be arguable as to how to interpret the constitution by an Act which is hierarchically positioned as subordinate law.

In his expert opinion given in 2003 to the Chancellor of Justice, this author posed a question regarding the change for Estonia, as a monist state, in becoming a dualist state,[59] which would also change the prevailing approaches to the constitution. In other words, the question was whether the Act entered into force was constitutional legislation or just incorporation of the Act of the Treaty of Accession. Though the theory of dualism/monism does not have much relevance for Member State law when implementing[60] EU supranational law, favouring dualism can contravene the constitution (Articles 3 and 123) and endanger former judicial practice[61] by giving different subjects the legal grounds to demand further additional incorporation of international law.[62] The Treaty of Accession referred to in the text of the draft legislation was in itself a kind of (international) incorporation act, the form of which did not depend on Estonia. It could have been qualified as an internal implementation Act by which the constitution was to be interpreted.[63] During the assessment of draft legislation, this author conducted comparative analyses considering different Member States' specific laws as practical solutions in accession to the European Union. The aim of bringing out similar features was used to study the experiences deriving from different "techniques" (Indicator 4).

Relying on these experiences (the previously mentioned comparative analyses), this author found that the amendment of the constitution would not be legally correct and would bring political and legal complications. The proposed draft legislation was a political compromise between those who considered its amendment necessary and those who considered it unnecessary. This meant that

59 In monistic countries, internal and international law form a single legal order internally, but for dualistic countries, in order to adopt international treaties they adopt a special act, which limits the implementation of the treaty within the state's legal order.

60 The argument does not only apply with regard to supranational law. As the Community's legal system itself is dual and regulates the status of international agreements in the Community's legal order, then Member States are subject to their own method of delegating foreign jurisdiction judicially as it comes from the loyalty principle of The Rome Treaty.

61 Important examples contained in the practices of Supreme Court, e.g., decision of 30 December II-4/A-5/94.

62 A few deviations from the principle of monism have done so (see, e.g, notice of Ministry of Defence (No 2) 10.07.1998, RT Annex 1998 238/239), but they have been mistakes rather than by virtue of applications.

63 Opinion to the Chancellor of Justice about the draft legislation of Ministry of Justice, Põhiseaduse rakendamine Euroopa Liidu liikmeks oleku tingimustes (21.03.2002).

the text of the constitution shall not be amended, but an act supplementing the constitution would be adopted instead.[64]

Later controversies related to the following phrase in Article 1: "in accordance with the fundamental principles of the Constitution of the Republic of Estonia". This is the so-called "defence clause", which was added to the draft legislation text. As the constitution itself is not listing *expressis verbis* fundamental principles, it can be presumed that the principles referred to are contained in the preamble of the constitution and in chapter 1 of the general provisions (Indicators 1 and 2).

This author believes that after the debates about the accession to the European Union and conditions regarding membership, the Estonian legal society reached a certain maturity. However, the Amendment Act to the constitution does not comply with the Estonian constitution as the mechanisms to guarantee the rule of law are not clearly formulated. Furthermore, taking into account the dynamic nature of the EU, the text of the law needs constant analysis (Indicator 4).

Denial of Constitutional Dialogue

In order to understand whether the concept of deliberative supranationalism is employed in Estonia, we have to analyse the implementation of the Amendment Act to the Estonian constitution. On 25 January 2006, the *Riigikogu* passed a resolution to request the opinion of the Supreme Court on the interpretation of Article 111 of the constitution in conjunction with the constitution of the Republic of Estonia Amendment Act and EU law. In its opinion (11 May 2006, 3-4-1-3-06), the Supreme Court (the constitutional review chamber) of Estonia demonstrated its apathy concerning innovative approaches in the implementation of EU law. As the Supreme Court opinion is not conducive to a more advanced understanding of the position of EU law, it is important to take account not only of the opinion of the Court, but also of statements made by participants in the proceedings.

According to the facts included in the opinions, the Chancellor of Justice (Ombudsman) considered that the situation wherein the grammatical provision of the Constitution and the actual substance thereof have grown apart is a regrettable one. According to him, the best solution for ensuring the applicability of the Constitution "would be a Constitution wherein the amendments arising from the Accession Treaty and following from the transposition of European Union law were introduced." On the opposite side, the Minister of Justice was convinced that "only a grammatical (formal) conflict is possible". However, the minister mentioned that the national provision which is not compatible with the European Union law shall nevertheless remain in force (Indicator 2).

64 See different opinions from the state's Chancellery information sheet, "Eesti ja Euroopa Liit": Põhiseadus ja rahvahääletus, available at: http://www.riigikantselei.ee/failid/v_haaletus_2003, accessed 28 August 2010.

The opinion of the Supreme Court attempted to clarify the position of the Amendment Act adopted by a referendum on 14 September 2003. The Court stated that:

> the text of the Constitution must always be read with its amendments and only that part of the constitutional text shall be applied which is not in conflict with the amendments. Thus, the Constitution of the Republic of Estonia must be read together with the Constitution of the Republic of Estonia Amendment Act, applying only the part of the Constitution that is not amended.

This is a clearly formalist approach (Indicator 4) that is further explained by the Court:

> To find out, which part of the Constitution is applicable, it has to be interpreted in conjunction with EU law, which became binding for Estonia through the Accession Treaty. [At that,] only that part of the Constitution is applicable, which is in conformity with EU law or which regulates the relationships that are not regulated by the EU law. The effect of those provisions of the Constitution that are not compatible with the European Union law, and thus inapplicable, is suspended. This means that within the spheres which are within the exclusive competence of the European Union or where there is a shared competence with the European Union, the European Union law shall prevail in the case of a conflict between Estonian legislation, including the Constitution, with European Union law.

In general, the Supreme Court denied any possibility of taking into account the dynamics of the relationship between two legal systems, and endorsed the dogmatic view that unconditionally subordinated the Estonian Constitution to EU law (Indicator 1).

There were two dissenting opinions supplementing the opinion of the Supreme Court (both related to Indicators 1 and 3). First, the dissenting opinion of Justice Kõve argues that the legal effect of the opinion is doubtful because of the constitutional review mechanism established by the constitution itself. According to Kõve, "consequently, in the present case, it would have been necessary at least to consider the issue of constitutionality of the amendments to the Constitutional Review Court Procedure Act". Also criticism towards the improper use of the "defence clause" is presented in the dissenting opinion. According to the Justice, "for the time being, the relationship between Article 1 and 2 of the Amendment Act, as well as, for example, the meaning of Chapter I of the Constitution in its entirety, after accession to the European Union, remain unclear". In general, this dissenting opinion found that "the Chamber 'overestimated' the principle of supremacy of the European Union law over the Estonian legal order when it found that as a result of the Amendment Act the Constitution in its entirety has been changed and that that the Constitution continues to have an effect only to the extent that it regulates the issues not regulated by the European Union law or to the extent that it is in conformity with the European Union law". Justice Kõve agreed with the justification or the primacy of the Treaty over the constitution.

In the second dissenting opinion, Justice Kergandberg agreed with the previously mentioned dissenting opinion concerning the non-use of the "defence clause", stating that "it is regrettable that the opinion of the Supreme Court contains no explanation as to why it has not considered it necessary to include the provisions of Article 1 of Amendment Act into the analysis of constitutionality". He also found that "such an analysis, one related also to the fundamental principles of the Constitution of the Republic of Estonia, would have been imperative ...".

Laffranque, one of the judges who contributed to the aforementioned majority opinion, justified the opinion adopted as follows: "the Estonian Supreme Court finally clarified the meaning of the Amendment Act of the Constitution, rightly stating that the Estonian Constitution must be read together with the Amendment Act of the Constitution, applying only those parts of the Constitution that were not amended by the Amendment Act."[65] This remark concluded a view supporting traditional supranationalism as explained by Table 2.1 on formalist and innovative approaches (see Indicator 5).

The author of the present chapter finds that the task of the Supreme Court should not have been that of questioning EU legal supremacy, but analysing the conformity of the Estonian constitution with the EU legal system, and setting the methods for testing the dynamic nature of the EU law. The Supreme Court did not refer to the difference of EC law and EU law (from the perspective of the three-pillar system) that carries some importance from the point of view of the binding nature of norms and decisions. Overall, the Supreme Court's decision can be seen as disappointing. The position of the Amendment Act remained vague and meaningless. The expectations that the Supreme Court would finally provide a doctrine that positions the relationship between the national and supranational law through the constitution were not fulfilled. As said by Cox:

> Values, interests and capacity to act matter, but so too do vision and political will. Reflecting actual and perceived national and regional issues and interests, many EU states and regions clearly struggle to assimilate new global realities. Too often, our leaders – and I refer here not just to political leaders – preach radical reform but [also] practice conservative corporatism. They crave for transformation but resist change. They preach cure but refuse the necessary medicine."[66]

---

65 Julia Laffranque, Ratification of the European Constitution in Estonia: A New Constitution for Estonia? in Anneli Albi and Jacques Ziller (eds) *The European Constitution and National Constitutions. Ratification and Beyond*, The Netherlands, Kluwer Law International, 2007, 88.

66 Pat Cox, Europe's Challenges in a Globalised World. Visions of leading policy makers and academics, speech at opening session of the Global Jean Monnet Conference,

General Conclusions and Suggestions

The above discussion aimed to analyse the problems in securing the principle of the rule of law in the context of European Union membership. The author presumes that the rule of law cannot be abandoned in any circumstance and suggests taking into account modern theories reflected in the phenomenon called "deliberative supranationalism".

As a conclusion, the author finds that a clear doctrine of constitutionalism in the context of Estonia's EU membership is missing and this absence endangers the rule of law. Therefore, Estonia is not prepared to use the constitution as a central tool for mediation between domestic and supranational legal systems. It is not sustainable to use technical–minimalist methods to position the Estonian constitution in the EU context. As it is not clear which parts of the constitution are valid after accession to the EU, the Estonian state is not guaranteeing the principle of legal certainty for its citizens.

The author also has claimed that there is no sufficient constitutional dialogue to analyse the developments in the European Union (e.g., Lisbon Treaty, EU Charter of Fundamental Rights) and legal education, supported by state, is not taking account of the need for European legal thinking.

Estonia, through the Amendment Act to the Constitution and the opinion of the Supreme Court, is not supporting innovative methods of deliberative supranationalism. but remains formalist when applying EU law. In general, the contributions emphasize that rule of law is not adequately protected in Estonia in the context of being an EU Member State.

The role of the Estonian constitution in the context of EU membership is vague as it is not interpreted in a way to become a central tool of mediation between national and supranational legal systems. The principle of legal certainty in Estonia is not guaranteed taking into account the interpretation of the Supreme Court of the validity of the constitution after the accession to the European Union. There is a lack of constitutional dialogue and the dynamic nature of the European Union has not been taken into account. Estonian contemporary legal education needs to be in accordance with the needs of a Member State from the point of view of generating European legal thinking and reasoning. In conclusion, the used methods to position Estonian constitution in EU context are not sufficient to secure the rule of law.

The author suggests that primacy of EU law cannot be taken as dogma and supra-national does not mean supra-rational. The European Union and its legal system are dynamic and must, therefore, operate as a testing area for our constitutional values (fundamental principles). According to reciprocity as a principle in a multi-governance system such as the European Union, the interpretation of these values must be combined with European constitutional principles. The rule of law can

---

ECSA World Conference, Brussels, 23–24 November 2006, Brussels, Education and Culture DG, Office for Official Publications of the European Communities, 2007.

be guaranteed only if the formalistic approach prevailing today is replaced by interpretative pluralism.

Estonia should take account of the approach of deliberative supranationalism to secure the rule of law. The automatic transposition of EU legal norms leads to stagnation in legal reasoning and bars Estonia from becoming an efficient Member State, as purely political influences may have priority over the rule of law. The interpretation of the position of EU law should take account of arguments both from the national and the EU level. The normative–technical understanding, purely rhetorical observations and the lack of depth of analysis of the EU legal system create the asymmetric positioning of Estonia as a Member State. It should be replaced with constitutional dialogue between the national and supranational levels. Estonian state authorities should not act in an apologist manner, but instead secure their positions in the EU through legal reasoning that derives from constitutional dialogue. There must be a constructive relationship with the EU on the basis of certainty and stability provided by the rule of law and constitutionalism. In the implementation of EU law, Estonia should take into account the general principles, innovative methods of interpretation (*effet utile*) and reciprocal character of the EU multilevel system.

Estonian and EU constitutional law must become sources of inspiration for further constitutional dialogue. Estonia cannot underestimate its possible contribution to the process of building up a common EU legal space. Estonia should take steps to create the basis for a European legal education that provides awareness of theories, sources and techniques in the implementation of EU normative acts.

References

Allott, P., The Concept of International Law, in Michael Byers (ed.) *The Role of Law in International Politics. Essays in International Relations and International Law*, Oxford, Oxford University Press, 2001.

Alter, K.J., *Establishing the Supremacy of European Law. The Making of an International Rule of Law in Europe*, Oxford, Oxford University Press, 2001.

Aragáo, A., European Governance in the Treaty of Lisbon and the European Paradox, Temas de Integracáo, 1 semestre de 2008 n 25. After Fifty Years: The Coming Challenges/Governance and Sustainable Challenges, Coimbra, Almedina, 2008.

Arnull, A., The Rule of Law in the European Union, in Anthony Arnull and Daniel Wincott (eds) *Accountability and Legitimacy in the European Union*, Oxford, Oxford University Press, 2002.

Barents, R., *The Autonomy of Community Law*, The Hague, London, New York, Kluwer Law International, 2004.

Barnard, C., Introduction: The Constitutional Treaty, the Constitutional Debate and the Constitutional Process, in Catherine Barnard (ed.) *The Fundamentals of EU Law Revisited: Assessing the Impact of the Constitutional Debate*, Oxford, Oxford University Press, 2007.

Bateup, C., The Dialogic Promise: Assessing the Normative Potential of Theories of Constitutional Dialogue, *Brooklyn Law Review*, 71, NYU Law School, 2006.

Bellamy, R. and Castiglione, D., Building the Union: The Nature of Sovereignty in the Political Architecture of Europe, in Neil MacCormick (ed.) *Constructing Legal Systems: "European Union" in Legal Theory*, Dordrecht, Boston, London, Kluwer Academic Publishers, 1997.

Bellamy, R. and Warleigh, R., Cementing the Union: The Role of European Citizenship, in F. Cerutti and E. Rudolph (eds) *A Soul of Europe*, Leuven: Peters, 2001, 55–72.

Bodnar, A., Kowalski, M., Raible, K. and Schoropf, F. (eds) *The Emerging Constitutional Law of the European Union. German and Polish Perspectives*, Berlin, Heidelberg, New York, Springer, 2003.

Bulmer, S., Theorizing Europeanization, in Paolo Graziano and Maarten P. Vink (eds) *New Research Agendas*, New York, Palgrave Macmillan, 2008.

Burca, G., The European Court of Justice and the International Legal Order after *Kadi* Jean Monnet Working Paper 01/09, New York, New York School of Law. Available at www.JeanMonnetProgram.org, accessed 3 September 2009.

Chernilo, D., *A Social Theory of the Nation-State. The Political Forms of Modernity beyond Methodological Nationalism*, London and New York, Routledge, 2007.

Clark, I., *Legitimacy in International Society*, Oxford, Oxford University Press, 2005, 175.

Commission Communication, A Citizens Agenda: Delivering Results for Europe, COM (2006) 211 final (10.05.2006).

Cox, P., Europe's Challenges in a Globalised World. Visions of leading policy makers and academics, speech at opening session of Global Jean Monnet Conference, ECSA World conference, Brussels, 23–24 November 2006, Brussels, Education and Culture DG, Office for Official Publications of the European Communities, 2007.

Crasier, D., Higher Educational Trends and Developments. A European Success Story? EIAE Forum, Spring 2007.

Dann, P., Thoughts on a Methodology of European Constitutional Law, in Philipp Dann and Michal Rynkowski (eds) *The Unity of the European Constitution*, Berlin, Heidelberg, New York, Springer, 2006.

Deards, E. and Hargreave, S., *EU Law*, Oxford, Oxford University Press 2007, 37–44.

Eijsbouts, W.T., Introduction, in Tom Thomas, A.J.A. Vandamme and Jan-Herman Reestman (eds) *Ambiguity in the Rule of Law. The Interface between National and International Legal Systems*, Groningen, Europa Law Publishing, 2001.

Gearey, A. *Globalization and Law. Trade, Rights, War*, Oxford, Rowman & Littlefield Publishers Inc, 2005.

Grossi, P., Historical Models and Present Plans in the Formation of a Future European Law, in A. Gambaro and A.M. Rabello (eds) *Towards a New European Ius Commune*, Jerusalem, The Harry and Michael Sacher Institute for Legislative Research and Comparative Law, The Hebrew University of Jerusalem, 1999.

Hackney, J.R. Jr, *Under Cover of Science*, Durham and London, Duke University Press, 2007.

Hartley, T.C., *European Union Law in a Global Context*, Cambridge, Cambridge University Press, 2004.

Hattenhauer, H., *Europäische Rechtsgeschichte*, Heidelberg, C.F. Müller Verlag, 2004.

Hay, C. and Lister, M., Theories of the State, in Colin Hay, Michael Lister and David March (eds) *The State. Theories and Issues*, New York, Palgrave Macmillan, 2006.

Helvetius, C.A., *De l'esprit* (Disc. III, ch. 14) Paris, 1758.

Herbst, J. Observations on the Right to Withdraw from the European Union, in Philipp Dann and Michal Rynkowski (eds) *The Unity of the European Constitution*, Berlin, Heidelberg, New York, Springer, 2006, p. 388, referring to George Orwell, *The Collected Essays, Journalism and Letters of George Orwell*, volume 4, In the Front of your Nose, 1945–1950, 1968, 152, 153.

Horváth, E., *Mandating Identity. Citizenship, Kinship and Plural Nationality in the European Union*, The Netherlands, Kluwer Law International, 2007, 72.

Joerges, C., Constitutionalism and Transnational Governance: Exploring a Magic Triangle, in Christian Joerges, Inger-Johanne Sand and Gunther Teubner (eds) *Transnational Governance and Constitutionalism*, Oxford and Portland, Oregon, Hart Publishing, 2004.

Johnston, A., "Euro-visions?" Some Thoughts on Prospects and Mechanisms for Future Constitutional Change in the European Union, in Catherine Barnard (ed.) *The Fundamentals of EU Law Revisited: Assessing the Impact of the Constitutional Debate*, Oxford, Oxford University Press, 2007.

Kerikmäe, T., Estonian Constitutional Problems in Accession to the EU, in A.E. Kellermann, J.W. de Zwaan and J.Czuczai (eds) *EU Enlargement. The Constitutional Impact at EU and National Level*, The Hague, T.M.C Asser Press, 2001.

Kerikmäe, T., Eesti parlamendi roll pärast liitumist Euroopa Liiduga, [The role of Estonian Parliament after the Accession with EU] Riigikogu Toimetised [*Parliament Journal*] IV, 2001.

Kerikmäe, T., Achilleus Heel of Estonian Ownership Reform: The Case of Baltic Germans, *European Journal of Law Reform*, vol. 6(172), 2006, cited in European Integration Current Contents.

Kerikmäe, T., The Labyrinth of Priorities for Legal Education: Estonia [Prioriteetide labürint õigushariduses Eesti kontekstis], in Silvia Kaugia (ed.) *Vaateid Õiguspoliitikale* [Views on Legal Policy], Tallinn Avatar, 2008.

Kerikmäe, T., Euroopa Zeitgeist ja Eesti valikud Põhiseaduslikkuse mõtestamisel [European Zeitgeist and Estonian Choices in Interpretation of Constitutionalism], *Tartu Ulikooki Kirjastus* [Tartu University Law Review], 2009.

Kerikmäe, T. and Käsper, K., European Charter of Fundamental Rights, Lexis Nexis Expert Commentaries, Matthew Bender & Co, 2007/2008; summary available at http://law.lexisnexis.com/international-foreignlaw/blogs/internationalandforeignlawcommentary/archive/2008/05/22/The-European-Charter-of-Fundamental-Rights, accessed 28 August 2010.

Kordela, M., Principles of Law as a Theoretical Category – Remarks on the Background of the General Principles of Community Law, in Adam Bodnar, Michal Kowalski, Karen Raible and Frank Schoropf (eds) *The Emerging Constitutional Law of the European Union. German and Polish Perspectives*, Berlin, Heidelberg, New York, Springer, 2003.

Kowalski, M., Comment on Daniel Thym: United in Diversity or Diversified in the Union, in Philipp Dann and Michal Rynkowski (eds) *The Unity of the European Constitution*, Berlin, Heidelberg, New York, Springer, 2006.

Kratochwil, F.V., How Do Norms Matter? in Michael Byers (ed.) *The Role of Law in International Politics. Essays in International Relations and International Law*, Oxford, Oxford University Press, 2001.

Kronman, A.T. and Weber, M., *Jurists: Profiles in Legal Theory*, London, Edward Arnold Publishers, 1983.

Kumm, M., The Jurisprudence of Constitutional Conflict: Constitutional Supremacy in Europe Before and After the Constitutional Treaty, *European Law Journal* 11, 2005, 262–286.

Laffranque, J., Ratification of the European Constitution in Estonia: A New Constitution for Estonia? in Anneli Albi and Jacques Ziller (eds) *The European Constitution and National Constitutions. Ratification and Beyond*, The Netherlands, Kluwer Law International, 2007.

Lasser, M. de S.O.-L'E *Judicial Deliberations. A Comparative Analysis of Judicial Transparency and Legitimacy*, Oxford, Oxford University Press, 2004.

Lenaerts, K., Interlocking Legal Orders in the EU and Comparative Law, *International and Comparative Law Quarterly* 905, 2003.

Mann, M. The Autonomous Power of the State: Its Origins, Mechanisms and Results, in Neil Brenner, Bob Jessop, Martin Jones, and Gordon MacLeod (eds) *State/Space. A Reader*. Oxford, Blackwell Publishing, 2003.

McCormick, J.P., *Weber, Habermas, and Transformators of the European State. Constitutional, Social, and Supranational Democracy*, Cambridge, Cambridge University Press, 2007.

Markesinis, B. and Fedtke, J., *Judicial Recourse to Foreign Law. A New Source of Inspiration?* London, University College London Press, 2006.

Martinico, G., A Matter of Coherence in the Multilevel Legal System: Are the "Lions" Still "Under the Throne"? Jean Monnet Working paper 16/08, New York University School of Law, 2008.

Mayer, F.C. Supremacy – Lost? Comment on Roman Kwiecień, in Philip Dann and Michal Rynkowski (eds) *The Unity of the European Constitution*, Berlin, Heidelberg, New York, Springer, 2006, 87.

Pierson, C. *The Modern State* (2nd edn), London, New York, Routledge, 2007.

Pollicino, O., New Emerging Judicial Dynamics of the Relationship Between National and the European Courts after the Enlargement of Europe, Jean Monnet Working paper, 14/08. New York University School of Law. Available at www.centers.law.nyu.edu/jeanmonnet/papers/08/081401.html, accessed 28 August 2010.

Prechal, S., Direct Effect, Indirect Effect, Supremacy and the Evolving Constitution of the European Union, in Catherine Barnard (ed.) *The Fundamentals of EU Law Revisited. Assessing the Impact of the Constitutional Debate*, Oxford, Oxford University Press, 2007.

Raadschelders, J.C.N., *Handbook of Administrative History*, New Brunswick and London, Transaction Publishers, 2000.

van Roosebeke, B., *State Liability for Breaches of European Law. An Economic Analysis*, Wiesbaden, Deutscher Universitäts-Verlag, 2007.

Sand, I.-J., Polycontextuality as an Alternative to Constitutionalism, in Christian Joerges, Inger-Johanne Sand and Gunther Teubner (eds) *Transnational Governance and Constitutionalism*, Oxford and Portland Oregon, Hart Publishing, 2004.

Shapiro, M., Implementation, Discretion and Rules, in J.A.E. Vervaele (ed.) *Compliance and Enforcement of European Community Law*, The Hague, London, Boston, Kluwer Law International, 1999.

Shaw, J., Relating Constitutionalism and Flexibility in the European Union, in Gráinne de Búrca and Joanne Scott (eds) *Constitutional Change in the EU. From Uniformity to Flexibility*, Oxford, Portland Oregon, Hart Publishing, 2001.

Sorensen, G., The Transformation of the State, in Colin Hay, Michael Lister and David March (eds) *The State. Theories and Issues*, New York, Palgrave Macmillan, 2006.

Stern, B., How to Regulate Globalization, in Michael Byers (ed.) *The Role of Law in International Politics. Essays in International Relations and International Law*, Oxford, Oxford University Press, 2001.

Stith, R., Securing the Rule of Law through Interpretive Pluralism: An Argument from Comparative Law. Jean Monnet working paper, 01/07. Available at www.centers.law.nyu.edu/jeanmonnet/papers/07/070101.html, accessed 28 August 2010.

Sverdrup, U., Implementation, in Paolo Graziano and Maarten P. Vink (eds) *New Research Agendas*, New York, Palgrave Macmillan, 2008.

Thym, D., "United in Diversity" – The Integration of Enhanced Cooperation into the European Constitutional Order, in Philipp Dann and Michal Rynkowski (eds) *The Unity of the European Constitution*, Berlin, Heidelberg, New York, Springer, 2006.

Tobler, C. and Beglinger, J. *Essential EC Law in Charts*, Budapest, Hvg-orac, 2007.

Vahtre, L., Eesti rahva lugu [Story of the Estonian People], Tallinn, ILO, 2005, 264 (extract translated by the author of the current chapter).

Varul, P., Põhiseaduse juriidiline ekspertiis: eesmärgid, töökorraldus ja töötulemused [The Constitution, a Legal Expert: Objectives, Organization and Performance], RITO 18, Tallinn, 2008.

Veldman, A., Legal System, Theory and Legal Methods of Research into the Enforcement and Effectiveness of Community Law, in J.A.E. Vervaele (ed.) *Compliance and Enforcement of European Community Law*, The Hague, London, Boston, Kluwer Law International, 1999.

Verhoeven, A., *The European Union in Search of a Democratic and Constitutional Theory*, The Hague, London, New York, Kluwer Law International, 2002, 39–50.

Vincent, A., Law and Politics, in Philip A. Thomas (ed.) *Legal Frontiers*, Aldershot, Dartmouth Press, 1996, 115.

Waldron, J. *The Dignity of Legislation*, Cambridge, Cambridge University Press, 1999.

Walker, N. Flexibility within a Metaconstitutional Frame: Reflections on the Future of Legal Authority in Europe, in Gráinne de Búrca and Joanne Scott (eds) *Constitutional Change in the EU. From Uniformity to Flexibility*, Oxford, Portland Oregon, Hart Publishing, 2001.

Walter, C., Constitutionalising (Inter)national Governance: Possibilities for and Limits to the Development of an International Constitutional Law, 170 *German Yearbook of International Law*, 2001.

Weiler, J.H.H., European Neo-constitutionalism: In Search of the Foundations of the European Constitutional Order, *Pol. Studies* 44,1996, 517–533.

Weiler, J.H.H., *The Constitution of Europe. Do the New Clothes have an Emperor? and Other Essays on European Integration*, Cambridge, Cambridge University Press, 2000.

Weiler, J.H.H., European Democracy and the Principle of Constitutional Tolerance: The Soul of Europe, in F. Cerutti and E. Rudolph (eds) *A Soul of Europe*, Leuven, Peeters, 2001, 33–54.

Weiler, J.H.H., On the Power of the World: Europe's Constitutional Iconography, in Deidre Curtin, Alfred E. Kellermann and Steven Blockmans (eds) *The EU Constitution: the Best Way Forward?* The Hague, T.M.C. Asser Press, 2004.

Williams, A., Respecting Fundamental Rights, in Catherine Barnard (ed.) *The Fundamentals of EU Law Revisited: Assessing the Impact of the Constitutional Debate*, Oxford, Oxford University Press, 2007.

de Witte, B. (ed.), Ten Reflections on the Constitutional Treaty for Europe, 2003. Available at www.cadmus.eui.eu/dspace/bitstream/1814/2538/1/DeWitte_ConsTreaty.pdf, accessed 28 August 2010.

Zürn, M., Law and Compliance at Different Levels, in Michael Zürn and Christian Joerges (eds) *Law and Governance in Postnational Europe. Compliance Beyond the Nation State*, Cambridge, Cambridge University Press, 2005, 37.

Chapter 3
The Constitutionalization of EU Law in Romanian Jurisprudence

Simina Tănăsescu

The terms "constitution" and "constitutionalization" are used with increasing frequency, exceeding the classic boundaries of the state, which was the structure in which these terms were conceived. The ideas of constitution and constitutionalization have grown to include not only state-level conceptions, but also European- and international-level conceptions. While, several years ago, the association of the terms European Union and constitution would have represented a linguistic revolution, or at least an unusual transplant, today such conceptions verge on commonplace. The Romanian jurisprudence seems to be divided on the legal consequences of EU constitution and constitutionalization process, but the source of the divide lies rather in the approach taken with regard to the relationship between national and EU law than in the conceptual meaning of the words.

Terminological References

The terms used in the legal doctrine, "constitution", "constitutionalism" and "constitutionalization", are totally different, although interdependent.

The philosophical evolution of the idea of constitutionalism and the advent of written constitutions both developed the idea of the constitution as a means of modernization and allowed for its global spread and philosophical–legal prominence. Yet, at the same time, individual constitutions represented the concretization of ideas and principles offered by constitutionalism as influenced by "the constitutional moment"[1] and the historical, economical, political and national particularities of the individual state.

The constitutionalisation of law is a reality that emerged long before formal legal doctrine and legal theory named it as such, particularly in national (domestic)

1 B. Ackermann, The Rise of World Constitutionalism, *Virginia Law Review* 83, 1997, 775, and also in the Constitutional Politics/Constitutional Law, *Yale Law Review* 99, 1999, 453.

law. Different studies conducted on the French,[2] German,[3] Spanish[4] or Romanian[5] legal systems show that constitutionalization is a complex legal phenomenon which influences the entire legal system, maintaining its unity through established relationships between the norms enshrined in the fundamental law and the norms holding a status inferior to the constitution. Neither the existence of the constitutional foundations of a legal system nor the supremacy of the constitution can be identified as the constitutionalization of law. Yet, both are indispensable prerequisites for the constitutionalization process. Irrespective of the normative system considered, the constitutionalization of law begins with the adoption and effective implementation of a constitution and the establishment of a jurisdictional guarantee for the supremacy of such a constitution. In this context, the legal literature reminds us that "it is certain that without constitutional justice this process would have never existed".[6]

Many authors with backgrounds in EU law are of the opinion that it is now possible to transplant the terminology of constitutional law, once exclusive to states and their constitutional law, to the supranational entity of the European Union.[7] This approach is reinforced by the language of the European Union's founding treaties concerning the creation of "an ever closer Union" and by the constructive jurisprudence, almost inventive in some parts, of the European Court of Justice. The Court of Justice has affirmed not only the structure and coherence of EU law, but also the legal order's autonomy from both national legislations of Member States and public international law. The Court has even designated the founding treaties of the EU as the "constitutional charter"[8] of the newly proclaimed legal order.

2 L. Favoreu, *L'influence de la jurisprudence du Conseil Constitutionnel sur les diverses branches du droit, Mélanges Léo Hamon*, Paris, Economica, 1982, 235 et seq.; L. Favoreu, L'apport du Conseil Constitutionnel au droit public, *Pouvoirs* 13, 1980, 17; L. Favoreu, La constitutionnalisation du droit, *Mélanges en hommage à Roland Drago*, Paris, Aix, Marseille, PUAM Economica, 1999, 25 et seq.

3 M. Fromont, Les droits fondamentaux dans l'ordre juridique de la R.F.A., in *Mélanges Eisenmann*, Paris, Cujas, 1977, 9 *et seq.*; J.C. Béguin, *Le contrôle de la constitutionnalité des lois en R.F.A.*, Paris, PUAM Economica, 1982.

4 P. Bon, La constitutionnalisation du droit espagnol, *Revue Française de Droit Constitutionnel* 5, 1991.

5 I. Muraru and S. Tănăsescu, La constitutionnalisation du droit roumain, in J.-C. Colliard and Y. Jegouzo (eds) *Le nouveau constitutionnalisme – Mélanges en l'honneur de Gérard Conac*, Paris, Editura Economica, 2001, 234 et seq.

6 L. Favoreu, La constitutionnalisation du droit, op. cit., 28.

7 The structural principles of community law are analysed by K. Lenaerts and P. van Nuffel, *EU Constitutional Law*, London, Sweet and Maxwell, 2004. Jurgen Habermas explained why Europe needs a Constitution (Why Europe needs a Constitution, *New Left Review* 11, 2001, 5).

8 *The Green Party "Greens" v European Parliament* (ECJ 1986, C294/83).

Nevertheless, it is important to remember that the European constitution as an instrument emerged in close connection with the state.[9] Therefore, using the concept in relation to para- or extra-state entities is still hard to accept, at least for scholars of domestic law. The constitution became the fundamental law of the state at the moment the state power truly became democratic. The passage from traditional constitutionalism, illustrated by British parliamentarism,[10] to a new perspective on the legitimacy of the state, as marked by the Philadelphia Convention, explains the indestructible connection created between the constitution and the state. From that moment on, modern constitutionalism has so strongly intertwined the concepts of constitution and state that it is difficult to conceive of them separately, even today. The constitution became the fundamental law of the state: it not only establishes the rules of the political game, but also sets up the "competence of competences". This allocation of competencies grants the constitution (and, therefore, its authors) the power to regulate the production of norms in a state and, thus, to become itself the foundation of the state legal order.

Today, at the international level, there are numerous types of multinational and international organizations comprised of states, animated by common objectives, constituted in a more or less structured way and regulated by consensually adopted legal norms. Yet, despite the similarities of these systems to formal state apparatuses, it is not clear that such *vinculum juris* are sufficient to constitute real constitutions, within the proper meaning of the term. The member states of some such associations have reached a high level of integration, as is the case with the European Union. Many organizations have democratically created not only a simple set of common principles, but also common institutions with normative, executive and judicial powers to which member states willingly submit, thus limiting their own sovereignty. Despite all that, there is no guarantee that the documents that lie at the foundation of such constructions comply with the criteria and, more significantly, with the specific functions of genuine constitutions because the basis of comparison is, and will remain, the state.

Despite all this, the term "constitution" is increasingly being used in a context that goes far beyond its state origins. If, up until the end of the twentieth century, the term "constitution" was rarely used in connection with supranational or international entities,[11] then the twenty-first century has been marked by a serious

9 A. Pizzorusso, L'emergence d'un droit constitutionnel européen – rapport italien, *General Reports of the XVIIth Congress of Comparative Law* – Utrecht, 16–22 July 2006, K. Boele-Woelki and S Erp (eds), Bruxelles/Utrecht, Bruylant/Eleven Publishing, 2007.

10 G. Ionescu, *Opoziția*, Humanitas, București, 1992, 15.

11 B. Fassbender, The United Nations Charter as Constitution of the International Community, *Columbia Journal of Transnational Law* 36, 1998, 529 et seq.

step towards such usage,[12] despite both confusion and controversy.[13] Beyond the context of orthodox legal doctrine, the progress of European integration has created an opportunity to associate these two irreconcilably contradictory terms[14] within the title of a European Union treaty. The Treaty establishing a Constitution for Europe, which is itself an oxymoron, reminds us of Carl Schmitt's theories concerning the constitutive treaty of a (con)federation, regarded as an act of the constitutive power (*pouvoir constituant*).[15]

In the given context (and regardless of the outcome of this particular treaty in any of its iterations), a legitimate question is raised: whether, at the moment, we can talk about a genuine Constitution of the European Union,[16] and, therefore, talk about a constitutionalization of European integration. In a more general context, in which the term "constitutionalization" is used even in connection with public

12 Among the specialists in public international law there seems to be an agreement concerning the concept of an international constitution; see, for example, J. Klabbers, Constitutionalism Lite, *International Organisations Law Review* 1, 2004, 31 *et seq.*; R. St. J. Macdonald and D. M. Johnston (eds), *Towards World Constitutionalism: Issues in the Legal Ordering of the World Community*, La Haye, Nijhoff, 2005. Equally, specialists in the field of community law have taken the case law of the ECJ a step forward and adapted the constitutional terminology to the European Union realities; see K. Lenaerts and P. van Nuffel, *Constitutional Law of the EU*, London, Sweet & Maxwell, 2004; J. Habermas, Why Europe needs a Constitution, *New Left Review* 11, 2001, 5 et seq.

13 The constitutional law and history of law specialists, in particular, raised some questions concerning the excessive use, and sometimes even misuse, of some classic concepts in an improper context; see L. Favoreu, Au carrefour des droits, in *Mélanges en l'honneur de Louis Dubouis*, Paris, Dalloz, 2002, 35 et seq.; D. Grimm, Ursprung und Wattel des Verfassung, in J. Isensee and P. Kirchof (eds) *Handbuch des Staatsrecht des Bundesrepublik Deutschland*, Heidelberg, C.F. Müller, 2003, 3 et seq. (unpublished translation mentioned with the permission of the translator); E.S. Tănăsescu, Sur la possible constitutionnalisation du droit communautaire, *AUB* 1, 2004, 1 et seq. Also, relevant for the idea of an original use of constitutional terminology, see V. Constantinesco, Des racines et des ailes, in *Au carrefour des droits – Mélanges en l'honneur de Louis Dubouis*, Paris, Dalloz, 2002, 315 et seq.

14 E.S. Tănăsescu, Between a Treaty with Constitutional Authority and The Authority of a Constitutional, in Iancu Bogdan (ed.) *The EU as the Paradigm of Future European Statehood,* Bucharest, IANCU, New Europe College, 2006, 61 et seq.

15 It is interesting to mention that, according to Carl Schmitt, the confederation does not have a constitutive power of its own, but is based on a convention that is the result of an initial constitutive power, whose members are the all the states that are party to this association. Nevertheless, a "genuine constitutional treaty of a (con)federation is a special act of the constitutive power" since the affiliation to a (con)federation forces the state to integrate in the political system framework. Carl Schmitt even used the concept of "constitutional treaty" without seeing in that a *contradictio in terminis*. See C. Schmitt, *Théorie de la Constitution*, Paris, Quadrige/PUF, 1993, 514–515.

16 The term European Union is used here as generic concept covering the European Economic Community, The European Community or the European Union.

international law,[17] another question occurs: is it possible for specific parts of this normative system (such as the EU law) to be more advanced on this path than others? Does the recent development of these fairly original quasi-legal processes at international level justify the borrowing *tale quale* or the simple transplant of the concepts and reasoning developed at state level for such processes?

To test this theory, in the context of the legal order of the European Union, one must verify the existence of two indispensable prerequisites for the constitutionalization process: first, the existence of a constitution (A) and, secondly, the existence of efficient jurisdictional guarantees to uphold constitutional supremacy in light of the other norms enshrined in existing European Union law (B).

The Constitution – Descriptive vs Prescriptive Approach

The term "constitution" is protean in nature. It can acquire different meanings over time and it can cover very distinct realities concurrently. The term and concept of a constitution can be analysed from two different perspectives: descriptive and prescriptive. Therefore, the contemporary use of the concept of constitution can easily adapt to include both state-level and supranational structures such as the European Union.

The Descriptive Approach of the Concept of Constitution

Viewed from a descriptive point of view, the concept of a European Union Constitution builds on the objective reality that the founding treaties of an international organization are the structural foundation of the given institutional ensemble. The existence of a European constitutional law,[18] having at its foundations a *corpus* of norms with fundamental values found in the EU's founding treaties and on which the entire normative process of such a subsystem can rely, is a concept neither new nor shocking.

Following this approach, scholars and students of EU legal doctrine began citing a genuine "constitutional system of the communities"[19] as early as the 1980s. Such a system was thought to be fundamentally original compared to the traditional organization of state-level power. In other words, the founding treaties of the European Union are legally binding documents that differ from the traditional concept of a constitution; however, they do fulfil at least one of the specific functions of a constitution, namely, they establish the grounds and regulate the issuance of norms for the subsequent normative subsystem.

One cannot help but notice the influence of theories developed between the two World Wars concerning the international legal order. The positivist school of law of

17 B. Fassbender, op. cit., 529 et seq.

18 L. Favoreu, Au carrefour des droits, op. cit., 35 et seq.

19 D. Symon, *Le système juridique communautaire*, Paris, PUF, 2001, 177 et seq.

that period upheld the existence, even at that time, of an international constitutional law, arguing that a constitution is nothing else other than the normative foundation of a legally created community. In this paradigm, the constitution of the international legal system encompasses the "collection of norms establishing the structure, the sub-divisions and the allocation of competences in a community".[20] In other words, the international constitution states how subsequent public international law norms are created, the nature of the legal effects of norms and norm violations, and the body or bodies responsible for interpreting norms and resolving conflicts between them. Similarly, a European Union constitution establishes the way acts of secondary legislation are adopted and applied and further establishes bodies to interpret legislation and resolve legislative conflicts.

This image corresponds to the temporal evolution of the European Union and to a purely descriptive approach to the classic concept of constitution. Nevertheless, it does not justify the claim of inherent originality, as is strongly advocated by authors in the EU law field for the subject they are studying. The functionality of a legal act is not sufficient to give it the status of a genuine constitution. Even though the founding treaties of the European Union function as a structural guide for EU law and for the organization and functioning of EU institutions, there are other international organizations that use the term with a similar meaning.[21] Indeed, one author drolly noted that, by this standard, even golf clubs have constitutions.[22]

Furthermore, a second function of classic constitutions is partially[23] met by what is usually defined by the term "European constitution". The European Union has made all necessary efforts to ensure to its citizens a certain protection of their fundamental rights within the European Community's legal order. This endeavour was sometimes more difficult than it appeared.[24] Therefore, before references to European citizenship were inserted into the EU treaties, the ECJ had already mentioned that the law of the European Community encompassed both subjective and individual rights that are part of an individual's legal patrimony and can be raised directly in front of the national authorities.[25] Later, the ECJ upheld the fundamental rights of European citizens as a general principle of the European

---

20 A. Verdross, *Die Verfassung des Völkerrechtsgemeinschaft*, Wien/Berlin, Springer Verlag, 1926, v.

21 The International Organization for Migration, The World Health Organization, The International Labour Organization and the UNESCO all called their founding treaties Constitutions.

22 J.H. Weiler, On the power of the word: Europe's constitutional iconography, I-CON, Vol 3(2–3), Special Issue May 2005, 173–190.

23 Or extremely originally, to be just to EU law authors.

24 See the already established jurisprudence: *Frontini*, in the Italian Constitutional Court, and *So lange*, in the German Constitutional Tribunal, quoted before, where the constitutional jurisdictions found that they remain the last-instance guardians of the fundamental rights of their citizens as long as there were/are no adequate and efficient protection mechanisms implemented in the community law.

25 C-26/62, decision *Vand Gend en Loos*, 5 February 1963.

legal order.[26] The codification (Article 6, para. 2 Treaty on European Union (TEU)) of the "constitutional traditions of Member States" was, to a large extent, made possible by this constant jurisprudence of the ECJ. When confronted with this difficult problem, the ECJ absolutely refused to acknowledge the possibility of using sources of law not part of the Community law, other than those from the normative orders of Member States, as a legal foundation for the fundamental rights of European citizens.[27] Finally, the supranational entity has endowed itself with a non-binding Charter of fundamental rights, following an assembly known as a Convention, which emerged from a *mélange* of internationalist methods and state institutions and decisional procedures. Even so, the protection of fundamental rights of European citizens is still primarily tasked to national jurisdictions, mainly constitutional courts, which provide only complementary jurisdiction to EU bodies where it merely concerns the relations between European citizens and European Union institutions.

In conclusion, the European Union founding treaties are nothing more than the legal grounds for an autonomous legal order, characterized by a certain originality, but which do not accommodate the characteristics of the concept of constitution as defined at state level. This assertion does not hinder an original, rather empirical, application, purely descriptive and functional, of the classic concept to new entities, such as the European Union, that do not yet fall under a strict legal classification. Certainly, such an approach represents a revolution for the accuracy of legal terminology, but then just think of how many revolutions started simply as a *coup d'etat*.

The Prescriptive Approach of the Concept of Constitution

From a prescriptive point of view, or even a normative one, using constitutional terminology in the supranational context signals the promotion, via legal acts, of a particular human behaviour in connection with selected values. This (implicit) selection of values is specific to a particular moment in the evolution of a human community and is protected by formally instituted legal norms, driven by rules that can fulfil the functions of a constitution.

Therefore, the rules commonly agreed to by the Member States of the European Union, are, in the first place, the expression of their agreement on a set of essential values for them, their citizens and the Union. Secondly, those rules are legally binding on the Member States and impose on them certain obligations that may differ from those that would have been possible (or desirable) in the absence of European integration process. The principles of good faith and *pacta sunt servanda* compel Member States to accept and comply with the treaties to which they are

---

26 C-11/70, decision *Internationale Handelsgesellschaft mbH*, 17 December 1970.

27 See the ECJ's Advisory Opinion n° 1/1994 concerning the adhesion of the European Union to the European Convention on Human Rights.

party and, furthermore, to submit to the international jurisdiction (ECJ) instituted by the same treaties which act as guardians of their provisions.

The ECJ's case law, particularly its early cases, was characterized by a significant creativity and cannot be fully understood without the constitutional dimension of the founding treaties. The fact that the Community law is internally coherent and autonomous is due to the rules imposed by the treaties, and their binding character on Member States.

On the other hand, Member States retain the competence to make decisions on integration matters, although the outcome of the integration process is out of their reach. The ECJ never could have identified the original and specific features of Community law unless there was an agreement among the Member States concerning the *telos* of such an endeavour. Nevertheless, this *telos* is only implicitly mentioned in the treaties. It justifies the constitutional value of the founding treaties, but it is never clearly expressed in them. As long as we consider that the EU founding treaties contribute to the process of defining a *telos* belonging to this supranational entity, such as the integration itself,[28] and different from the *telos* specific to Member States, we can say that we already have a European constitution. Surely, this constitution has its originality and is still developing, since its ultimate purpose has yet to be determined.

The significant activism of the ECJ and its determination to identify and underline the particularities of the Community law as distinct from both the domestic law of Member States and from public international law, has led some authors to argue that the European Union law is evolving into something resembling the public law of a federal state[29] or of a republic *in statu nascendi*.[30] Such a development, they argue, makes legitimate the use of constitutional law terminology when describing the existing realities of the European Union's political and legal development.

In any case, the term constitution is not only protean, but also an evolving concept. Originally, the constitution was a set of legal norms regulating the social relations necessary for the exercise of state power, with a self-referential normative effect, defined in relation to precise goals. Among these goals are the establishment of the human collectivity as a community, the integration of all the individual members of that community and the definition of the characteristics that allow for self-identification of the group and its members using the commonly accepted values (*telos*). The constitution is the "frame and the measure of law"[31]

28 Integration cannot be perceived other than as an instrument to reach the desired goal. For a critique of the expectations related to the integration through law, see D. Grimm, Integration by Constitution, *International Journal of Constitutional Law* 3(2–3), 2005, 193–208.

29 J. Habermas, op. cit., 5 et seq.

30 A. von Bogdandy, The Prospect of a European Republic: What European Citizens are Voting On, *Common Market Law Review* 42, 2005, 913.

31 C. Starck, *La Constitution – cadre et mesure du droit*, Paris, PUAM Economica, Collection Droit Public Positif, 1997, *passim*.

inside a state. It establishes the limits and the internal organization of the state's power and provides the rights and liberties of the state's citizens. According to contemporary democratic theory, power is exerted at state level through collectively adopted decisions of citizens and citizens have no choice in surrendering to this prerogative.

The complexity of the European Union realities is in danger of being undermined if a quick, unreasonable and simplistic analogy is made to the domestic law context in order to explain it. For example, the mere use of language specific to the democratic use of power at the state level does not require democratic effects at a supranational level.[32] The integration of citizens in the modern state was prior to their democratic emergence and, consequently, to their constitutions. Therefore, the integration of European citizens within the European Union should be the prerequisite, and not the effect, of a future European constitution.

As has already been shown, it is imperative to notice that, at present, European citizens have their legal status determined primarily at the state level, and only secondarily (or complementarily) at the European Union level. Citizens are direct participants in the decision-making process only in their states. At the European level, the decision-makers remain the Member States, particularly with regard to the fate of the European Union itself and/or its *telos*. This situation is substantially different from the one observed at the state level.

Therefore, from a prescriptive approach, the European Union is still engaged in the search for its own, ultimate purpose, one that has to be different from integration itself; the integration is one of the means to achieve the supranational entity, even though it can be considered as a common goal for the Member States. The value selection, operated in accordance with this ultimate and defining purpose, can be logically and sequentially made only after clearly affirming its acceptance by all those involved. The European Union has yet to express a clearer and more complete objective than that of "an ever closer Union between the peoples of Europe". Further, it has not made sufficient efforts to integrate European citizens and involve them in a project that will make them go beyond the tight bounders of states and step confidently in a supranational space, in a situation that is at least comparable to the status they have now at state level.

To sum up, from a descriptive perspective, the European constitution has existed since the beginnings of the European integration, but, from a prescriptive perspective, it is still in a process of self-definition and evolution.

---

32 *Mutatis mutandis*, the same argument was used by D. Grimm, op. cit., *passim*, when he asserted that social integration specific to the national constitutions is more of a prerequisite that is pre-existent and facilitates the adoption of a fundamental law, than a paralegal effect of it. Any legal text would face some difficulties in determining *ipso facto* this effect in practice, and even more so would an international treaty that does not directly engage the citizens.

Guaranteeing Supremacy of the Constitution – A Prerequisite of Constitutionalization

Even if the mere transposition of legal concepts from the state level to the international level is not possible, a historic perspective can be instructive through a different interpretative lens. In public international law doctrine some authors have noticed that legal sedimentation leading to informal, "organic" constitutions is not particular to the European constitution, but is a widely spread phenomenon among the so-called historical or traditional constitutions.[33] As a result, such constitutional texts that cannot be overlooked, given their historical importance, take the form of a set of normative acts, deposited in time, and formally overlapped, and not the form of a unique piece of legislation with fundamental character. The constitution of Great Britain gives the most notable example, but the constitution of Sweden with its four organic laws[34] and the French[35] and Spanish blocks of constitutionality[36] are also worth mentioning. Over time, such sedimentation of principles, and their subsequent prioritization over other types of rules and norms through the mutual consent of Member States, does not come as a surprise in the EU: the process is internationally known and appears rather common.[37]

It is important to clarify the particularities that make the European constitution truly original. If we accept that the result of any given legal sedimentation/evolution can have the specific functions of constitutions of the historic type,[38] we should also notice that its effects are closer to the ones of a modern constitution.

---

33 B. Fassbender, The meaning of International Constitutional Law, op. cit., p. 307 et seq.

34 The Swedish constitutional system is composed of four documents considered as fundamental laws of the state: the Constitution (*Regeringsformen*), the law of succession to the throne (*Successionsordningen*), the law concerning the liberty of the press (*Tryckfrihetsförordningen*), and the fundamental law concerning freedom of expression. (*Yttrandefrihetsgrundlagen*). To those we should add the Riksdag Rules (*Riksdagsordningen*), which are on a lower level to the four above-mentioned acts, but above the ordinary laws.

35 L. Favoreu, Le bloque de constitutionnalité, in O. Duhamel and Y. Mény (eds) *Dictionnaire constitutionnel,* Paris, PUF, 1992, 87 et seq.

36 M. Rodriguez-Pinero and J. Leguina Villa, "Rapport espagnol" à la VIII-ème Conférence des Cours Constitutionnelles européennes sur "L'hiérarchie des normes constitutionnelles et sa fonction dans la protection des droits fondamentaux", *AIJC* VI, 1990, 99 et seq. (particularly 113).

37 P. Eleftheriadis, The Standing of States in the European Union, in N. Tsagourias (ed.) *Transnational Constitutionalism: International and European Perspectives*, Cambridge, Cambridge University Press, 45–70.

38 For an attempt to classify the constitutions according to time, introducing a separation between historic constitutions and modern constitutions, see H. Dippel, Modern Constitutionalism, an Introduction to a History in Need of Writing, *The Legal History Review* 73(1–2), 2005, 153 et seq.

The constitution of Great Britain stands out because it is flexible and does not occupy a superior position in the domestic hierarchy of normative acts. This is not necessarily the case for the other "complex" fundamental laws, and is certainly not applicable to the case of the European constitution.

Repeatedly, the ECJ has mentioned not only the priority/primacy of the founding treaties over the community secondary legislation, but also their character as a "fundamental charter", endowed with supremacy within the European Union legal order. This hierarchic positioning of the sources of law of a constitutional nature compared to the rest of the normative system is a feature of modern constitutions. At a jurisprudential level, it was marked by the famous case of the US Supreme Court, *Marbury v. Madison* (5 U.S. (1 Cranch) 137 (1803)), and, in general, it is institutionally guaranteed through the constitutionality control in most modern constitutional systems.

If, on the one hand, the ECJ managed to beautifully provide arguments for the hierarchically superior position of the founding treaties of the European Union then, on the other hand, these treaties do not afford a genuine jurisdictional guarantee of this position. At the beginning, the ECJ's jurisdiction to check upon the legality of the secondary Community legislation was limited to legal acts adopted under the first pillar of the European Union, and was lately extended, with significant precautions, to some legal acts in the field of the third pillar.[39] The coming into force of the Treaties of Lisbon on 1 December 2009 has considerably changed the situation, as the pillars architecture of the EU has disappeared, while the jurisdiction of the ECJ has been considerably expanded. The decisions taken by the Court on the preliminary ruling requests are not directly compulsory for their addressees since the characteristic of this procedure is the cooperation that needs to be established between national courts and the ECJ. The ECJ is not a court of last instance, and even less a supreme court within the legal system of the European Union, which has the effect of depriving this jurisdiction of the possibility to guarantee the supremacy of the European constitution within the community law. Therefore the EU lacks the ability, in its current form, to guarantee the normative aspect of the supremacy of the constitution. This is one of the prerequisites of the

39 In the field covered by the third pillar of the European Union, the ECJ holds a classic type of jurisdiction, specific to public international law – a jurisdiction that is conditional to the formal recognition by Member States. From a material point of view, the ECJ can decide upon preliminary questions only in relation to decisions, framework decisions and conventions. In fact, this competence is dependent on an express declaration of accepting its jurisdiction, which is a declaration that has to be made by each state, in accordance with Art. 35 TEU. Furthermore, the effects of this declaration can be limited by Member States, who have the discretionary power to allow preliminary questions to be sent only by the courts of last instance, without making it an obligation. For a detailed analysis of the ECJ's specific jurisdiction in the area covered by the third pillar of the European Union, see S. Peers, *EU Justice and Home Affairs Law*, 2nd edn, London, Oxford University Press, 2007,17 et seq.

constitutionalization of (domestic) law which is strictly related to the emergence of modern constitutionalism.

Furthermore, the fact that the number of legal acts declared by the ECJ to hold supreme value in the normative system of the European Union is constantly increasing[40] does not help to change the existent situation. Constitutionalization does not mean any unregulated process of normative inflation or of abusing the control function in a rationally structured legal order. At national level, the above-mentioned processes are instead associated with the collateral damage of the rule of law.[41] Just as the constitutionalization of (domestic) law implies the existence of a constitution, the rule of law requests, and implies,[42] the existence of a fundamental law, but none of these two realities can be confounded with the constitution itself.

EU Constitutionalization seen by Romanian Scholars

In Romania, the debate over the European constitution or the potential constitutionalization of EU law has been hindered by the relatively long process of accession[43] and the necessary revision of the Romanian fundamental law in view of that accession.[44] Although this may come as a surprise, the so-called "constitutional treaty" did not raise much controversy in Romanian academia, and its implicit and premature ratification was made almost in silence by Parliament, without the control of the constitutional judge.[45] However, Romanian scholars seem to be interested in the original nature of the European Union and particularly by the inherent originality of the relations established between the Romanian legal order and EU law.

---

40 Although not incorporating it into the founding treaties, the Lisbon Treaty granted the Charter of Fundamental Rights the same legal value as any original treaty.

41 J.P. Henry, Vers la fin de l'Etat de droit ? *RDP*, 1977, 1207–1235.; J. Chevallier, L'Etat de droit, *RDP*, 1988, 313 et seq.

42 L. Favoreu, La constitutionnalisation du droit, op. cit., 28.

43 Which lasted between 1993, the date of the signature of the Association Agreement between Romania and the EU, and 2007, when the effective accession of Romania to EU was achieved.

44 The Romanian Constitution was adopted on 8 December 1991 and has been revised once, in October 2003, in order to facilitate Romania's accession to the EU.

45 E.S. Tănăsescu, Between a Treaty with Constitutional Authority and The Authority of a Constitutional, in I. Bogdan (ed.) *The EU as the Paradigm of Future European Statehood*, Bucureşti, IANCU, New Europe College, 2006, 61 et seq.

Thus, the European Union has been qualified as "a recent reality, which is difficultly classified among classical categories of law",[46] an "original entity, *sui generis*".[47] Since the treaties of Westphalia, at international level there are only states, as equal actors; they may agree to create new entities such as international organizations. The intermediary level of supranational organizations, such as the European Union, has not been necessarily foreseen. However, one must accept that nowadays the European Union is such a supranational entity, which may establish legal norms directly applicable to citizens (including at national level), but which may also play an important role at international level, concurrently with Member States that have created it and without affecting their own international capacity.[48] Through successive limitations of their sovereignty, Member States have given to the European Union more and more important decision-making power, thus losing exclusive competencies which used to belong to them.[49] This did not result in a change of the nature of Member States nor of that of the European Union, but, according to the number and importance of competences transferred, this may impact on the relations between Member States and the European Union. If these transfers remain limited and controlled by Member States, a mere accepted limitation of sovereignty can be noticed; if, on the contrary, these transfers become uncontrollable and irreversible a mere question of degree may become an issue and the EU could develop into a totally different entity than the supranational one we know nowadays. This plainly illustrates the uncertainty surrounding the future of the European Union, but also its ever-evolving nature. While declaring the EU the successor of EC and endowing it with legal personality, the Treaties of Lisbon have not helped to dissipate the doubts with regard to the legal nature and actual status of the supranational organization.

To simplify, one may group the opinions expressed by Romanian scholars in two categories: those claiming the existence of an European constitution, endowed with supremacy over national legal systems according to a simple monistic view, and those defending pluralist positions, where national legal orders remain autonomous, and recognize only the supremacy of the national constitutions, while Community law enjoys priority over national law, but remains within the realm of international public law.

---

46 O. Manolache, *Tratat de drept comunitar*, 5 edn, Bucureşti, C.H. Beck, 2006, 11 et seq.; G. Gornig and I.E. Rusu, *Dreptul Uniunii Europene*, Bucureşti, C.H. Beck, 2007, 25.

47 I. Deleanu, *Instituţii şi proceduri constituţionale*, Bucureşti, C.H. Beck, 2006, 269 et seq.

48 O. Manolache, op. cit.

49 G. Gornig and I.E. Rusu, op. cit., 235–236.

European Constitution and Supremacy

Romanian scholars in community law[50] or public international law[51] tend to accept without hesitation the doctrine of the supremacy of EU law, without questioning the constitutional nature (or lack of it) of the legal norms declared supreme. The hierarchy thus established between EU and national law is based upon the implicit assumption that a European constitution is already in place and that it belongs to its own jurisdiction to provide for rules in this area. According to this doctrine, the supremacy of EU law is based on its intrinsic originality and concerns all EU rules and regulations; also, this is the only possible interpretation of Article 148[52] of the Romanian Constitution as revised in 2003.

According to this approach, the supremacy of EU law on the entire national legal order stems directly from the Romanian Constitution. Since Article 148, paragraph 2, of the Romanian Constitution allows for "mandatory community regulations" to take precedence over the opposite provisions of national law, it means that the Romanian constituent power decided that any contradiction between EU law and Romanian law is not allowed within the framework of the fundamental law. The argument could be read in between the lines of a landmark decision of the Romanian Constitutional Court,[53] where the constitutional judges did not want to advance more in the "mined field" of the relations between EU and national law,

50 T. Ştefan, *Introducere în dreptul comunitar*, Bucureşti, C.H. Beck, 2005, *passim*; Ionuţ Gâlea, Augustina Dumitraşcu and Cristina Morariu, *Tratatul instituind o Constituţie pentru Europa*, Bucureşti, C.H. Beck, 2005, 27.

51 C.L. Popescu, Controlul constituţionalităţii tratatelor internaţionale, *Dreptul* 11, 2005, 9 et seq.; C.L. Popescu, Comentariu la decizia Curţii Constituţionale, *CJ* 308(6), 2006, 3.

52 Article 148 – Integration into the European Union – provides:

(1) Romania's accession to the constituent treaties of the European Union, with a view to transferring certain powers to community institutions, as well as to exercising in common with the other member states the abilities stipulated in such treaties, shall be carried out by means of a law adopted in the joint sitting of the Chamber of Deputies and the Senate, with a majority of two-thirds of the number of deputies and senators.

(2) As a result of the accession, the provisions of the constituent treaties of the European Union, as well as the other mandatory community regulations shall take precedence over the opposite provisions of the national laws, in compliance with the provisions of the accession act.

(3) The provisions of paragraphs (1) and (2) shall also apply accordingly for the accession to the acts revising the constituent treaties of the European Union.

(4) The Parliament, the President of Romania, the Government, and the judicial authority shall guarantee that the obligations resulting from the accession act and the provisions of paragraph (2) are implemented.

(5) The Government shall send to the two Chambers of the Parliament the draft mandatory acts before they are submitted to the European Union institutions for approval.

53 Decision of the Constitutional Court n°148/2003 concerning the law on the revision of the Constitution.

but they did want to underline the fact that the revised Constitution dealt with the issue. However, neither the constitutional judges nor the jurisprudence clarify one important aspect, namely the relationship which might exist between concepts such as precedence/priority and supremacy of EU law. If synonymy is taken for granted, as it appears in the approach here presented, at least it should be made clear.

One has to notice that the Romanian Constitution makes use of the word "supremacy" only in an auto-referential manner, while with regard to other legal norms it uses terms such as "precedence". Indeed, Article 11[54] of the Romanian Constitution deals with the relationship between national and international law and provides for the ratification of international treaties which might be found (by the Constitutional Court) contrary to the Constitution only pending the revision of the fundamental law, whereas Article 20 of the Constitution[55] enshrines the principle of *lex mitior* in the Romanian legislation. Supremacy is mentioned only with regard to the Constitution[56] and to the mission of the Constitutional Court.[57] A bit more hermeneutics could have helped clarify the issue.

Another line of argument lies in the intrinsically original nature of the EU law and the well-known case law of the ECJ with regard to the constitutional nature of the founding treaties of EU.[58] When holding such positions, Romanian authors, mainly publishing in the area of EU law, are quoting other (foreign) authors, who, in turn, base their opinions on series of decisions of the European Court in Luxembourg. Thus, this argument is exogenous to the Romanian doctrine and merely takes on board issues and solutions considered to be clarified long since by authoritative scholars elsewhere.

---

54 Article 11 – International law and national law – provides:

(1) The Romanian State pledges to fulfil as such and in good faith its obligations as deriving from the treaties it is a party to.

(2) Treaties ratified by Parliament, according to the law, are part of national law.

(3) If a treaty Romania is to become a party to comprises provisions contrary to the Constitution, its ratification shall only take place after the revision of the Constitution.

55 Article 20 of the Constitution – International treaties on human rights – provides:

(1) Constitutional provisions concerning the citizens' rights and liberties shall be interpreted and enforced in conformity with the Universal Declaration of Human Rights, with the covenants and other treaties Romania is a party to.

(2) Where any inconsistencies exist between the covenants and treaties on the fundamental human rights Romania is a party to, and the national laws, the international regulations shall take precedence, unless the Constitution or national laws comprise more favourable provisions.

56 Article 1 – The Romanian State – provides in paragraph 5: "In Romania, the observance of the Constitution, its supremacy and the laws shall be mandatory."

57 Article 142, paragraph 1, provides : "The Constitutional Court shall be the guarantor for the supremacy of the Constitution."

58 O. Manolache, op. cit., 11 et seq.; G. Gornig and I.E. Rusu, op. cit., 25 et seq.; I. Deleanu, op. cit., 269 et seq.

A singular voice offered "an affirmative nuanced"[59] answer to the question regarding the very existence of a European constitution, but it only referred to the constitutional treaty and did not address the general issue. It concluded that "since the European Union reminds of a federation without really being one", the founding treaties "may difficultly be qualified [as] anything but a fundamental law". Later, the same voice considered that "European constitutionalism equates constitutionalisation of the European integration process" and the very concepts of constitution, constitutionalism and constitutionalization need to be redefined as to include different meanings than those originally theirs.[60]

The coming into force of the Treaties of Lisbon has not much altered this line of thinking within the Romanian jurisprudence. What elsewhere has been considered "power politics with a vengeance"[61] passed merely unnoticed in Romania, where its insertion in the national legal order was with no hesitations and no problems. This seems difficult to understand given the context and debates surrounding the Lisbon Treaties in other EU Member States and the more so since the backdrop of the "constitutional treaty" did not seem to hamper the replication of almost all innovations there included in the new legal form of classical EU treaties. The debate on the constitutional nature of the founding treaties and the constitutionalization process should not be halted nor diminished by the fact that national courts have started to use the preliminary question as a new tool at their disposal, thus acknowledging EU's legal precedence.[62] On the contrary, this could have been an opportunity to continue and enhance a discussion which is far from at its end.

European Constitution and Primacy

On the other hand, Romanian scholars in constitutional law,[63] and even some in community law,[64] instead opt for the doctrine of the primacy of EU over national

---

59 G. Vrabie, Constitution, Etat, souveraineté – concepts qu'il faut repenser, *Revista de Drept Public* 3, 2004, 14 et seq.

60 G. Vrabie, Le constitutionnalisme européen – phénomène complexe et intégrateur, in G, Vrabie (ed.) *L'évolution des concepts de la doctrine classique de droit constitutionnel*, Iasi, Institutul European, 2007, 202.

61 P. Craig, The Treaty of Lisbon: Process, architecture, and substance, *European Law Review* 33, 2008, 139.

62 N.D. Ploesteanu, The first cause solved by the European Communities Court of Justice as a result for a prejudicial decision presented by a Romanian Court, *Revista de drept public* 3,2008, 112.

63 Ion Deleanu, op. cit., 274, 277–278, E.S. Tănăsescu, Comment on Article 148 of the Constitution, in I. Muraru and E.S. Tănăsescu (eds), *Constituția României comentata*, Bucureşti, C.H. Beck, 2008, 1425 et seq.

64 O. Manolache, op. cit., p.67 et seq.; Ion Filipescu and Augustin Fuerea, *Drept instituțional comunitar european*, Bucureşti, Actami, 1994, 48 et seq.; G. Gornig and I.E. Rusu, op. cit., 94–95.

law, which does not necessarily imply the existence of a European constitution. By embracing a pluralist doctrine based on a dualist relation between national and EU law, such authors consider that the primacy of the EU law is based not on its intrinsic nature, but on the express provisions of national constitutions.[65] However, the endogenous argument is framed in a different way. The interpretation of Article 148 of the Romanian Constitution shows to these authors that nothing comes above the national constitution[66] and, even if a European constitution may exist, it does not have the same meaning as the concept has had since its creation.[67] Thus, in this approach, according to Article 148 of the Romanian Constitution, the relationship between EU law and the national legal order is not necessarily hierarchical, but rather complex and depending on the normative content of the individual legal acts put under scrutiny. Only a comparison between the normative substance of each EU legal act and the national legal order allows the observer to draw a conclusion with regard to the position each one holds. The same applies to the relationship between constitution and treaties in the area of human rights, but while Article 20 of the Romanian Constitution provides for *lex mitior* in the latter case, in the former case Article 148 secures a constant precedence of the EU law over Romanian national law. The solution found by the Romanian constituent power may seem baroque at a first glance; however, it secures flexibility and it enables further evolutions both with regard to national and international legal order, while preserving the interests of the pluralist argument.

Mention has to be made here that this approach does not claim to provide a clear answer with regard to the constitutional nature of the founding treaties of EU, nor does it hold a strong position in relation to the constitutionalization process. In this view, the existence (or not) of an EU constitution and constitutionalization process is separate from the issue of the relationship between legal systems. The two concepts may evolve distinctively and enjoy autonomy. This partly explains why the coming into force of the Lisbon Treaties could not have a major impact on this line of thinking. While consideration has been given to the potential impact that the Lisbon Treaties might have on the integration process, including at the level of the EU citizen,[68] the pluralist approach enables a variety of positions to be

65 I. Muraru and E.S. Tănăsescu, *Drept constituţional*, vol. I, XII edn, Bucureşti, C.H. Beck, 2005, 12–14.

66 See also the decision of the Constitutional Court n°59/2007, E.S. Tănăsescu, Commentary, *Curierul Judiciar* 5,2007, 1 et seq.

67 E.S. Tănăsescu, Sur la Constitution européenne ou l'émergence d'un droit constitutionnel européen, in G. Vrabie (ed.) *L'évolution des concepts de la doctrine classique de droit constitutionnel*, Iasi, Institutul European, 2007, 185.

68 E.S. Tănăsescu, The potential benefit and impact on people in the EU of the Charter of Fundamental rights, a paper given at Fundamental rights in the EU in view of the accession of the Union to the European Convention on Human Rights and Fundamental Liberties, a seminar jointly organized by the Spanish Presidency of the European Union and the Fundamental Rights Agency of the EU, 2–3 February 2010, Madrid, Spain.

held on the issue at stake here, and without preventing factual observations on the conceptual differences between words used.

In an attempt to reconcile these two positions, another singular voice[69] noticed that, in fact, currently in use there are two completely different meanings of the concept of constitutionalization: one in domestic law and another one in European law. According to this author, "the concept of constitutional European law has developed along with the ideas concerning the constitutional treaty", and, given the important influence community law has on national legal systems, the two can be considered as elements of a new and multilayered constitutional system. This intermediary approach came at a moment in time when the so-called EU constitution was still under debate. That author was a constant observer of new legal phenomena;[70] unfortunately, he is no longer among us to share his views with regard to the Lisbon Treaties. The position he took had the advantage that it allows for a complex use of identical words and yet different concepts, according to the context in which they are placed, but it does not go without noticing that it owes much to the better-known doctrine of the "multilevel constitution" developed by Ingolf Pernice[71] towards the beginning of the twenty-first century that is earlier than the official beginning of the constitutionalization process of EU.

Conclusion

Constitutional sedimentation and codification are not new processes, at either national or at international level. In this context, from an internal perspective, constitutional sedimentation was the process that characterized the emergence of the first constitution in the world – in England – and is a process that should not be ignored, even though the frequency of its use is almost zero. At the international level, we witness an ever more concentrated sedimentation of some rules and principles that gain precedence over other types of norms. Such a process enjoys the consensual acceptance of a growing number of states involved in international relations. We can acknowledge the same phenomenon, but with an increased intensity, at the level of the European Union. This phenomenon could determine the materialization of a future constitution within the proper meaning of the term. It alone, totally isolated, however, cannot lead to the constitutionalization of the European law.

---

69 V. Duculescu, Le droit constitutionnel européen, un défi à l'adresse du droit constitutionnel classique ou un nouveau concept de droit ? in S.E. Tănăsescu and S. Deaconu (eds) *Despre constituţie şi constituţionalism, Liber amicorum*, Bucureşti, Ioan Muraru, Hamangiu, 2006, 289 et seq.

70 V. Duculescu, Impactul globalizarii si privatizarii asupra procesului de constitutionalizare a dreptului, *Revista de drept public* 1, 2008, 1.

71 I. Pernice, *Fondements du droit constitutionnel européen*, Paris, Editions Pédone, 2004, *passim*.

International constitutionalism can be considered a progressive movement, directed towards supporting international cooperation through consolidating the relations (in the field of material law) between states and the organizational structures (formally institutionalized) existent at international level. The corollary of this approach could be that, worldwide, there is an increasing unity of actors engaged at the international level. This integration trend is even more visible in the European Union, for the goal expressed by the Member States is to realize "an ever closer Union". The obviously established hierarchy of legal norms, both at the international level and in Community law, is just an element that provides more strength to this trend.

In this context, with due regard to the absence of the necessary and indispensable prerequisites for constitutionalization, we consider that we cannot, at this moment, discern such a process at European Union level, even though the existence of an ever closer cohesion and of an increased efficiency of its normative system cannot be denied. In other words, a revolution can also be a successful *coup d'etat*, and a patricide can legitimate a new monarchic line, but a mere transplant, even a legal one, does not guarantee the survival of the patient. The concept of constitutionalization is in danger of sharing the fate of the child disputed by two mothers, if it follows its multiple vocation and claim to cover, at the same time, two fundamentally different realities.

References

Romanian authors

Deleanu, I., *Instituţii ţi proceduri constituţionale*, Bucureşti, C.H. Beck, 2006.

Duculescu, V., Le droit constitutionnel européen, un défi à l'adresse du droit constitutionnel classique ou un nouveau concept de droit? in S.E. Tănăsescu and S. Deaconu (eds) *Despre constituţie ţi constituţionalism – Liber amicorum Ioan Muraru*, Bucureşti, Hamangiu, 2006.

Duculescu, V. Impactul globaliztrii ţi privatiztrii asupra procesului de constituţionalizare a dreptului, *Revista de drept public* 1, 2008.

Filipescu, I. and Fuerea, A., *Drept instituţional comunitar european*, Bucureşti, Actami, 1994.

Gâlea, I., Dumitraţcu, A. and Morariu, C., *Tratatul instituind o Constituţie pentru Europa*, Bucureşti, ALL Beck, 2005.

Gornig, G. and Rusu, I.E., *Dreptul Uniunii Europene*, Bucureşti, C.H. Beck, 2007.

Ionescu, I., *Opoziţia*, Bucureşti, Humanitas, 1992.

Manolache, O., *Tratat de drept comunitar*, Bucureşti, C.H. Beck, 2006.

Muraru, I. and Tănăsescu, S., La constitutionnalisation du droit roumain, in Jean-Claude Colliard and Yves Jegouzo (eds) *Le nouveau constitutionnalisme – Mélanges en l'honneur de Gérard Conac*, Paris, Editura Economica, 2001.

I. Muraru and E.S. Tănăsescu, *Drept constituţional*, vol. I, Bucureşti, C.H. Beck, 2005.

I. Muraru and E.S. Tănăsescu (eds) *Constituţia României comentata* Bucureşti, C.H. Beck, 2008.

Ploesteanu, N.D., The first cause solved by the European Communities Court of Justice as a result for a prejudicial decision presented by a Romanian Court, *Revista de drept public* 3, 2008.

Popescu, C.L., Controlul constituţionalitţţii tratatelor internaţionale, *Dreptul* 11, 2005.

Popescu, C.L., Comentariu la decizia Curtii Constitutionale nr.308/2006, *Curierul Judiciar* 6, 2006.

Stefan, T., *Introducere în dreptul comunitar*, Bucureşti, C.H. Beck, 2006.

Tănăsescu, E.S., Sur la possible constitutionnalisation du droit communautaire, Analele Universitatii din Bucuresti – seria Drept 1, 2004.

Tănăsescu, E.S., Between a Treaty with Constitutional Authority and The Authority of a Constitutional, in Bogdan Iancu (ed.) *The EU as the Paradigm of Future European Statehood*, Bucuresti, New Europe College, 2006.

Tănăsescu, E.S., Sur la Constitution européenne ou l'émergence d'un droit constitutionnel européen, in Genoveva Vrabie (ed.) *L'évolution des concepts de la doctrine classique de droit constitutionnel*, Iasi, Institutul European, 2007.

Tănăsescu, E.S., Comentariu la decizia Curtii Constitutionale n°59/2007, *Curierul Judiciar* 5, 2007.

Tănăsescu, E.S., The potential benefit and impact on people in the EU of the Charter of Fundamental rights, a paper given at Fundamental rights in the EU in view of the accession of the Union to the European Convention on Human Rights and Fundamental Liberties, a seminar jointly organized by the Spanish Presidency of the European Union and the Fundamental Rights Agency of the EU, 2–3 February 2010, Madrid, Spain (manuscript with author).

Vrabie, G., Constitution, Etat, souveraineté – concepts qu'il faut repenser, *Revista de Drept Public* 3, 2004.

Vrabie, G., Le constitutionnalisme européen – phénomène complexe et intégrateur, in Genoveva Vrabie (ed.) *L'évolution des concepts de la doctrine classique de droit constitutionnel*, Iasi, Institutul European, 2007.

Foreign authors

Ackermann, B., Constitutional Politics/Constitutional Law, *Yale Law Review* 99(3), 1989.

Ackermann, B., The Rise of World Constitutionalism, *Virginia Law Review* 83, 1997.

Béguin, J.C., *Le contrôle de la constitutionnalité des lois en R.F.A.*, Paris-Aix-Marseille, PUAM Economica, 1982.

von Bogdandy, A., The Prospect of a European Republic: What European Citizens are Voting On, *Common Market Law Review* 42, 2005.

Bon, P., La constitutionnalisation du droit espagnol, *Revue Française de Droit Constitutionnel* 5, 1991.

Chevallier, J., L'Etat de droit, *Revue du droit public et de la science politique en France et à l'étranger* 2, 1988.

Constantinesco, V., Des racines et des ailes, in *Au carrefour des droits – Mélanges en l'honneur de Louis Dubouis*, Paris, Dalloz, 2002.

Craig, P., The Treaty of Lisbon: Process, architecture, and substance, *European Law Review* 33, 2008.

Dippel, H., Modern Constitutionalism, an introduction to a history in need of writing, *The Legal History Review* 73, 2005.

Duhamel, O. and Mény, Y. (eds), *Dictionnaire constitutionnel*, Paris, PUF, 1992.

Fassbender, B., The United Nations Charter as Constitution of the international community, *Columbia Journal of Transnational Law* 36, 1998.

Favoreu, L., La constitutionnalisation du droit, in Jean-Bernard Auby et al. (eds), *L'unité du droit – Mélanges en hommage à Roland Drago*, Paris-Aix-Marseille, PUAM Economica, 1999.

Favoreu, L., L'apport du Conseil Constitutionnel au droit public, *Pouvoirs* 13, 1980.

Favoreu, L., L'influence de la jurisprudence du Conseil Constitutionnel sur les diverses branches du droit, in G. Conac, H. Maisl and J. Vandiaux (eds) *Itinéraires – Mélanges en hommage à Léo Hamon*, Paris, Economica, 1982.

Fromont, M., Les droits fondamentaux dans l'ordre juridique de la R.F.A., in *Recueil d'études en hommage à Mélanges Eisenmann*, Paris, Cujas, 1975.

Grimm, D., Integration by Constitution, *International Journal of Constitutional Law* 3, 2005.

Habermas, J., Why Europe needs a Constitution, *New Left Review* 11, 2001.

Henry, J.P., Vers la fin de l'Etat de droit ?, *Revue du droit public et de la science politique en France et à l'étranger* 5, 1977.

Klabbers, J., Constitutionalism Lite, *International Organisations Law Review* 1, 2004.

Lenaerts, K. and van Nuffel, P., *EU Constitutional Law*, London, Sweet & Maxwell, 2004.

Macdonald, R. St.J. and Johnston, D.M. (eds), *Towards World Constitutionalism: Issues in the Legal Ordering of the World Community*, La Haye, Nijhoff, 2005.

Peers, S., *EU Justice and Home Affairs Law*, London, Oxford University Press, 2007.

Pernice, I., *Fondements du droit constitutionnel européen*, Paris, Editions Pédone, 2004.

Pizzorusso, A., *L'émergence d'un droit constitutionnel européen – rapport italien*, Utrecht, Congrès international de l'Académie de droit comparé, 2006.

Rodriguez-Pinero, M. and Leguina Villa, J., "Rapport espagnol" à la VIII-ème Conférence des Cours Constitutionnelles européennes sur "L'hiérarchie des normes constitutionnelles et sa fonction dans la protection des droits fondamentaux", *Annuaire International de Justice Constitutionnelle* VI, 1990.

Schmitt, C., *Théorie de la Constitution*, Paris, Quadrige/PUF, 1993.

Starck, C., *La Constitution – cadre et mesure du droit*, Paris-Aix-Marseille, PUAM Economica, 1997, 28.

Symon, D., *Le système juridique communautaire*, Paris, PUF, 2001.

Tsagourias, N. (ed.), *Transnational Constitutionalism – International and European Perspectives*, Cambridge–New York, Cambridge University Press, 2007.

Weiler, J.H., On the power of the word: Europe's constitutional iconography, *International Journal of Constitutional Law* 3, 2005.

Chapter 4
Fundamental Rights in the EU's Post-enlargement Landscape: An Exercise in Constitutional Translation?

Kyriaki Topidi

Introduction

One of the many possible definitions of European integration that draws on organizational theory suggests that the term refers to the "process of combining or adding parts or elements into a systematic whole".[1] With the experience of the recent enlargements, the European Union (EU) is at present a strongly plural legal system, but at the same time is striving to become an equally pronounced and distinct normative context. In other words, it is still engaged in the process of singling out the parts that constitute its systemic whole. Fundamental rights fit in the wider picture of the Union normative landscape and are customarily viewed either through the prism of European identity or citizenship[2] or even as a self-standing paradigm. From either perspective, human and fundamental rights stand for a bridge between the differences and particular legal or political systems as well as identities within a polity such as the EU due to their universal appeal.

European integration closely interlinked with Europeanization is often depicted as co-linear or parallel to constitutionalization. Constitutionalization initially referred to the law-making activity of the ECJ, and particularly to the judicial creation of the principles of direct effect and the supremacy of EC law. Today, lawyers use the term to describe the gradual transformation of the EU into a political system that rests on certain constitutional legal bases.[3] Constitutionalization is

1 Andersen, S.S. and Sitter, N. (2006), Differentiated Integration: What is it and How Much Can the EU Accommodate?, *Journal of European Integration*, 28(4), 313–30, at 319.

2 See indicatively on European citizenship, Wiener, A. Comment: Fact or Artefact? Analysing Core Constitutional Norms in Beyond-the-state Contexts, *Journal of European Public Policy*, 13(8), 1308–13; Føllesdal A., Union Citizenship: Unpacking the Beast of Burden, *Law and Philosophy*, 20(3), 313–43.

3 Peters, A. (2006), The Constitutionalisation of the European Union – Without the Constitutional Treaty, in S. Puntscher Riekmann and W. Wessels (eds) *The Making of a*

also often depicted as co-linear or parallel to Europeanization.[4] Their respective contents have been heavily influenced by the decision of the EU to enlarge on a great scale to Central and Eastern Europe (CEE). The former concept is of course more concerned with the complexities that stem from the plurality of legal orders in the European legal space (a typical example of which is the clash between constitutional supremacy versus EC law primacy). The latter concept studies the effects of membership on states, belonging or aspiring to belong to the union, with an eye for the characteristics of their gradual "transformation" and adaptation.

Within these quite broad semantic parameters, this contribution aims to approach fundamental rights in what has not been considered – before the EU enlargement to include CEE – their natural environment: the EU. The analysis proposed below will argue that in the post-enlargement era, and possibly with an eye for further enlargements to come, the dynamics of constitutionalization are gradually affecting fundamental rights protection in the Union, placing them in an increasingly prominent position within the system.

Systemically and methodologically, the discussion in this chapter is grounded in constitutional law considerations, yet it assumes that constitutions at the state level have now ceased to be considered what Peters calls "total constitutions".[5] They do not regulate the entirety of areas in the same way, and hence there is a practical, real need to study the constitutionalizing trends at European level.

In order to give a sense of the type of constitutional dialogue on fundamental rights undertaken after enlargement, this analysis will borrow Walker's paradigm on *constitutional translation*.[6] Constitutional translation, according to Walker, is based on at least three premises: contextual appropriateness, generality of explanatory scope and depth of normative foundations.[7] If we transpose this theoretical scheme to the discussion of fundamental rights after CEE countries have joined the Union, one can argue that the *depth of normative foundations* hints at the ongoing constitutionalizing process (together with its implications) of fundamental rights with special focus placed on the now legally binding Charter.

European Constitution: Dynamics and Limits of the Convention Experience, Wiesbaden, VS Verlag, 35–67, at 36.

4 Czuczai J. (2001), Practical Implementation by the Acceding Candidate Countries of the Constitutional *Acquis* of the EU: Problems and Challenges, in Kellerman, A. et al. (eds) *EU Enlargement: The Constitutional Impact at EU and National Level*, The Hague, T.M.C. Asser Press, 411–422, at 411–12.

5 Peters (2006), at 46. She argues further that the neat distinction between *pouvoir constituant* and *pouvoir constitué* has also become rather obsolete at EU level since both powers now are undertaken in turns by the actors involved in EU constitutionalization (op. cit., at 51–2).

6 As discussed in Walker, N. (2003), Postnational Constitutionalism and the Problem of Translation, in J. Weiler and M. Wind (eds) *European Constitutionalism Beyond the State*, Cambridge, Cambridge University Press, 27–54, in particular 45.

7 He adds, however, the need for the quest of fundamental and generalized sets of normative concerns to complete the three other ingredients. Ibid., at 45.

Contextual appropriateness corresponds quite conveniently to the domestic reactions that are being provoked by EU law on fundamental rights. These reactions are informed by the constitutional traditions of new and old Member States. They are also conditioned by considerations on the perennial question of the quantitative and qualitative resonance of fundamental rights defended at EU level in the domestic contexts. Finally, *generality of explanatory scope* is explored through the identification of the domestic and supranational legal systems with a certain number of fundamental rights norms that represent the Union internally and externally, particularly in the context of a continuing enlargement to include south-western Europe or Turkey. These three elements, or more appropriately directions, guide the process of discovery and reconciliation of the core values of the Union with the type of multilevel constitutionalism that the Union represents. Accordingly, the structure that the chapter follows tackles each of these three components of constitutionalization of fundamental rights following the 2004 and 2007 enlargements. The chapter finally concludes that the translation of fundamental rights into meaningful domestic and European practice, so timely at present, presupposes a different approach in the balance of methods and institutions.

Constitutionalization through *Text*: The Role of the Charter

The debate on the need for a "constitution" for the EU carries many implications. What are relevant for this discussion are the ways in which a constitutional text may reflect the characteristics of a given legal order. More specifically, a constitutional text at EU level carries internal and external dimensions that respectively concern the identification of the most salient constitutional norms within the system and the distinctiveness of the overall legal order from other systems.[8] The admission of 12 new Member States rendered structural, including constitutional, reform and update relevant, if not imperative.[9] While it is not possible to identify a single transformative constitutional moment in the case of the EU, the recent ratification of the Lisbon Treaty represents a convenient point at which to attempt a consideration of the constitutionalizing trends that have prevailed in the EU in the area of fundamental rights.

European rights are usually the subject of interpretation within individual legal systems, but as Aziz correctly notes, "[i]t is often said that much may be lost in translation. It may also be the case, however, that much can be gained, given the

8 Walker, N. (2005), Constitutionalism and New Governance in the European Union: Rethinking the Boundaries, *EUI Working Papers* No.2005/15; available at http://cadmus.iue.it/dspace/index.jsp at 5, accessed 20 July 2010.

9 Grimm, D. (2005), Integration by Constitution, 3 *International Journal of Constitutional Law*,193–208, at 196.

rich tapestry of constitutional traditions in the EU …".[10] At the same time, rights remain at the heart of a constitutionalizing process due to their salience for the characterization of the type of governance sought and practised from both the perspective of the institutions as well as from that of citizens as holders of rights. The inclusion of the Charter in the failed Constitution for Europe, as well as in the (now ratified) Lisbon Treaty, signifies the setting of a clear standard for the orientation of the Union's policies, without nevertheless necessarily signalling a restructuring of the European legal order.[11] In other words, the rights, contained in the Charter and that have now found their place in the Lisbon Treaty, summarize the values, rights and principles of the Union while placing the citizen at the centre of the European polity as a beneficiary of a number of these rights. By virtue of the Charter and the level of visibility that it has created for fundamental rights, the Community judges, advocate generals, plaintiffs and their lawyers have less and less hesitation to refer to the Charter.

In a sense and as others have already said elsewhere, the Charter can now operate as a point of reference in the composite constitutional system of the EU, solidifying the ECJ's jurisprudence in this area.[12] It fulfils that role in two directions and dimensions: it legitimizes the human rights policy of the Union that has now become an important identity and policy element, and at the same time it provides ample space for further constitutional dialogue and interpretation of such rights.[13]As a result, fundamental rights will acquire the following functions: first, they will contribute towards the more efficient delimitation of the Union's competences regarding the rights of the individual, reflecting at the same time more coherently the principles of subsidiarity and proportionality; second, they will provide guidance on the implementation of other provisions of EU law, to citizens, institutions and practitioners in the light of the *effet utile* of the disputed provision in each context; finally, they will gradually clarify the legal status of individuals as citizens.[14]

Increasingly, these rights are influenced by both national and supranational agents, "disturbing" in that way the pre-conceived hierarchical model of sources of law.[15] As an expression of a polity's values of social organization, there has

10 Aziz, M. (2004), *The Impact of European Rights on National Legal Cultures*, Oxford, Hart Publishing, at 2.

11 Pernice, I. and Kanitz, R. (2004), Fundamental Rights and Multilevel Constitutionalism in Europe, Walter Hallenstein Institut Paper 7/04, at 4, in particular footnote 7.

12 Ibid., at 6.

13 Cartabia refers to these dimensions respectively as legitimizing and hermeneutical effects. See Cartabia, M. (2009), Europe and Rights: Taking Dialogue Seriously, *European Constitutional Law Review*,5, 5–31, at 15.

14 Ibid., at 7–8.

15 For an illustration of the complications that this process might create, see Bernadette Somody's article in this volume on the effects of EC law on human rights standards in Hungary.

been, so far, little in the way of organizing the multiplicities and divergences that stem from the different layers of protection. In that sense, fundamental rights, from the right to equality, non-discrimination and diversity to more procedural issues such as the applicability of constitutional rights horizontally or their limits within the internal market, are worth reflecting upon, especially in a context where sovereignty and its anchoring elements of people, state and territory are being transformed and challenged.[16] Perhaps the multiplication of instruments and sets of rules that aim at the protection of fundamental rights in Europe will push in the direction of more accommodating jurisdictions,[17] without excluding the risk of fragmentation of standards. National courts will remain competent to scrutinize the compatibility of national implementing law with EU law. The ECJ (and the Court of First Instance (CFI) will, on the other hand, be competent to strike down EU measures that violate fundamental rights. Both levels of jurisdiction will inspire each other in the quest for concrete standards for these rights.

Grimm argues that there is a close link between a constitution's integrative power and a polity's fundamental rights: both confer elements of identity, in different ways of course. The Charter embodies probably the closest that the Union has come to both a text on fundamental rights of constitutional nature and to a distinct polity governed by certain principles and norms which will "feed" each other in their attempt to provide concrete meaning to the applicable standards for fundamental rights protection.

Constitutionalization through *Context:* Domestic Repercussions of EU Law on the Protection of Fundamental Rights

Europeanization in the new Member States has had distinctive characteristics. The "romantic" European project was quickly institutionalized to the extent of demanding "a wholesale transfer of Western institutional structures to Eastern Europe'.[18] Because the process of post-communist transformation in Central and Eastern Europe coincided with the quest for EU membership, the Union encountered less resistance *vis-à-vis* the institutional paradigms that were required for Union accession.[19] The technocratic approach to the large volume of legislation to be adopted signified at least two things: first, due to the fast pace of adoption of legislation there was very little control or awareness of the content of the

16 For a similar point see Aziz (2004), at 5.

17 Jiri Zemanek's conclusions on the increasing maturity of the Czech Constitutional Court seem to suggest a similar point. See Zemanek in this volume.

18 Jacoby, W. (1999), Priest and Penitent: The European Union as a Force in the Domestic Politics of Eastern Europe, 8 *East European Constitutional Review*, 62–7, at 66.

19 Grabbe, H. (2001), How does Europeanization affect CEE Governance? Conditionality, Diffusion and Diversity, *Journal of European Public Policy*, 8(6), 1013–31, at 1014.

legislation that was being passed; and, second, the goal of accession, in particular the speed of adoption and the lack of parliamentary debates, gave more control to the executive to master the process leading to an increasing centralization of decision-making.[20] Prior to accession, the countries in question were exposed to an adjustment process that relied on softer, policy-oriented instruments, such as conditionality, persuasion or normative pressure. The nature of this process has been, however, clearly more intrusive and intense than what new members have experienced post-2004 and -2007 respectively.[21] Adoption of EU norms prior to accession had a distinct administrative flavour with the implication and risk that it would (and it did) erode public support for European integration.

At the same time, the post-communist internal legal methodology of adaptation remained to a large extent attached to the Kelsenian concept of a legal system, following the classical hierarchy of legal sources.[22] The new Member States' legal systems therefore had difficulties in adjusting to a more pluralist understanding of the EU legal space, without insinuating here that Western Europe had never in the past experienced similar issues or that it has indeed completely solved them. Moreover, in CEE the nature of the judicial activity was organized in such a way that the ordinary judges were asked to simply apply the law while judicial matters concerning international and, of course, European law were concentrated in the hands of the constitutional courts.[23]

The Role of Central and Eastern European Courts in European Integration after Enlargement

Following the acquisition of EU membership, constitutional courts in CEE embarked on a quest to set the application of *controlimiti*, for fear of the ECJ trespassing, by maintaining in a balanced way their already declared intention to adopt a constitutional discourse that sought judicial interpretations that were consonant, to the extent possible, with EU law. This was especially given that constitutional courts emerged as powerful institutional players throughout transition, often dictating the rules of the political game.[24] Their stance was particularly characterized by what Sadurski pertinently calls the "sovereignty

20 On this point see Sedelmeier, U. (2006), Europeanisation in new Member and Candidate States, *Living Review in European Governance*, 1, at 3; available at http://www.livingreviews.org/lreg-2006-3, at 17, accessed 20 July 2010, and Grabbe (2001) at 1017.

21 Sedelmeier (2006), at 5.

22 Kühn, Z. (2005), Making a European Transnational Constitution: Some Central European Perspectives, in I. Pernice and R. Zemanek (eds) *A Constitution for Europe: The IGC, the Ratification Process and Beyond*, Baden-Baden, Nomos, 127–39, at 132–3.

23 Kühn (2005), at 133.

24 For a demonstration on this point, see the contribution of Daniel Smilov in this volume.

conundrum" and the fear that EU membership rendered the recently reacquired membership obsolete again.[25]

The following examples precisely address the various dimensions of the sovereignty conundrum", yet with the accent placed on the restraint that domestic jurisdictions demonstrated towards the supremacy of EU law. The Hungarian Constitutional Court, in one of the first post-enlargement cases, used the method of isolating the challenged act in that instance from EU law and declared the case a purely domestic one.[26] In that way it avoided a direct confrontation between the domestic legal act and an EU regulation, which had been subsequently transposed in its entirety by the Hungarian act. With the aim being to artificially eliminate the possibility for a clash with the Hungarian Constitution, the Constitutional Court adopted this approach in order not to appear uncooperative towards the application of EC law.

The Polish Constitutional Tribunal, in its controversial *European Arrest Warrant* case (EAW),[27] approached the issue of conflict between EC and domestic law in a more direct fashion. It accepted that although the Polish Constitution prohibited extradition in absolute terms, domestic provisions implementing the EAW decision would apply, even if declared unconstitutional. The rule contained in the Constitution was thus left aside and the obligation to implement European law prevailed. A month later, the same court made more explicit its stance towards the conditions for the application of EU law on the occasion of the case on Poland's membership of the Union, while at the same time issuing a word of caution.[28] The Polish court indicated that, particularly for fundamental rights protection, "... the norms of the Constitution within the field of individual rights and freedoms indicate a minimum and unsurpassable threshold which may not be lowered or questioned as a result of the introduction of Community provisions".[29]

Lawmakers at EU level should not fall outside delegated competences, the principle of subsidiarity should be observed by the ECJ and the Luxembourg court should embrace a duty to be sympathetically disposed towards the national legal system in order for there to be respect for Community norms.[30] This mutual respect was therefore presented as a form of dialogue that requires consideration of the other side's legal context from both interlocutors.

---

25 Sadurski, W. (2008), 'Solange, Chapter 3': Constitutional Courts in Central Europe – Democracy – European Union, *European Law Journal*, 14(1), 1–35, at 3–4.

26 Hungarian Constitutional Court, Decision 17/2004 (V.25) AB.

27 Polish Constitutional Tribunal, *European Arrest Warrant*, 27 April 2005, No.1/05.

28 Polish Constitutional Tribunal, *Poland's Membership in the European Union (Accession Treaty Case),* 11 May 2005, K18/04. Part 8 of the judgement stipulated that Polish constitutional provisions "do not authorize the delegation of competences to such an extent that it would signify the inability of the Republic of Poland to continue functioning as a sovereign and democratic state".

29 Part 14 of decision K18/04.

30 Ibid., at paragraph 16 of the judgement.

Similarly, the Czech Constitutional Court in its own *European Arrest Warrant* case,[31] was faced with a similar question: the law implementing the EAW decision was found not to be contrary to the domestic Charter of Rights contained in the Czech Constitution, but only because the Court tried to eliminate every possibility for a potential clash between the EU norm and the Constitution. To quote a very representative part of the judgement: '… if the Constitution … can be interpreted in several manners, only certain of which lead to the attainment of an obligation which the Czech Republic undertook in connection with its membership to the EU, then an interpretation must be selected which supports carrying out that obligation, and not an interpretation which precludes it.'[32]

Likewise and even more unambiguously, in the Baltics, in the context of a case brought before the Estonian Supreme Court,[33] the court opted for an openly pro-European approach on the question of supremacy by declaring its incapacity to set aside domestic law that implements Community law.

Overall, it emerges clearly that CEE constitutional courts have been prepared to accommodate and accept EC law supremacy, yet with an eye for the recognition of their own constitutional legal traditions. If this condition is not respected, the balance of constitutional interests runs the risk of being seriously jeopardized. In that sense and while uncertainty on the precise limits of delegation of national sovereignty to the EU persists, a different process seems to be taking place at the same time: that of gradual abandonment of the search for the "ultimate [constitutional] authority" between national and supranational legal orders in Europe.[34] Methodologically, the new approach, which clearly distinguishes itself from the one "older" Member States adopted in Solange-type decisions, is enhanced by efforts at EU level to endow the Union with the Charter, a fundamental rights catalogue, that has so far been one of the most crucial arguments for the intervention of domestic constitutional courts in the constant questioning of who stands as the "ultimate authority" in the Union's legal space.

The Conditions of the Fundamental Rights Dialogue between Domestic Courts and the ECJ

Walker argues that "[t]he EU's most venerable and still its most intense constitutional claim is in the juridical sphere".[35] While this is accurate with reference to the role of the ECJ, the description of course does not take into

31 Czech Constitutional Court, Judgment Pl. US 66/04.

32 Ibid., as quoted in Piqani, D. (2008), Constitutional Courts in Central and Eastern Europe and their Attitude towards European Integration, *EJLS*, 1(2), 1–22, at 16–7.

33 General Assembly of the Estonian Supreme Court, Case No. 3-4-1-1-05, 19 April 2005.

34 Sadurski (2008), at 30.

35 Walker, N. (2008), Taking Constitutionalism beyond the State, *Political Studies*, 56, 519–43, at 534.

account the judicial interplay between the Luxembourg court and the courts within Member States. The quality of the dialogue in this context appears to suffer from a different "translation" of fundamental rights in their wider systemic functionality. Cartabia notes that this significant divergence is most visible in the approach that the EU and national constitutions adopt towards fundamental rights: she explains that while the Union endorses an individualistic conception of fundamental rights, in the national context, constitutional texts insist on a personalistic/dignitarian understanding of these rights.[36] The implication that this distinction carries is that the Court, due to its individual-centred perception of fundamental rights, does not hesitate, at the cost of neglecting the national particularities of its Member States, to focus on vulnerable groups such as women and migrant workers or on sensitive issues such same-sex marriage, abortion, bioethics and so on. Member State jurisdictions, on the other hand, prefer to consider the individual within the intermediate social body that he/she belongs. To the extent, however, that this exercise would lead to a uniformization of the content of fundamental rights, it probably creates unity *without* diversity and threatens directly the foundations of the Union's constitutional balance. This dynamic, however, does not seem to be seriously affected by the entry into the Union of the Central and Eastern European Member States.

Yet to insist on the national trajectory, the role assumed by national courts when interpreting EU law differs significantly from one Member State to another. A number of both old as well as new Member States have not yet fully accepted the principle of primacy of EC law that flows from the autonomy of the European legal order. Most Central and Eastern European constitutions expressly establish the principle that the constitution is the highest legal source.[37] They claim that it is up to the national constitution and to the national courts to adjudicate on the circumstances of this primacy.[38] This is largely because, when interpreting European law, national courts tend to engage themselves in the exercise of delineation of the margins of decision-making that the national authorities should enjoy each time.[39] In that sense, Andersen and Sitter, paraphrasing Lenin, rightly note that so far European integration has generated a regime that is *European in form but national in content*.[40] Within this context, constitutional courts appear as the interlocutors

---

36 Cartabia (2009) at 18, in particular her footnote 40.

37 See indicatively Article 8 of the Polish Constitution, Article 77(1) of the Hungarian Constitution, Article 1(5) of the Romanian Constitution. For more on this point, see Anneli Albi (2005), *EU Enlargement and the Constitutions of CEE*, Cambridge, Cambridge University Press, at 171.

38 For an overview of the variety of reactions in that respect in CEE, see the contributions of Mikuli, Dubrovsky and Zemanek in this volume.

39 Slepcevic, R. (2009), The Judicial Enforcement of EU Law through National Courts: Possibilities and Limits, *Journal of European Public Policy*, 16(3), 378–94, at 382.

40 Ibid., at 318.

par excellence of the ECJ in their capacity as *viva vox constitutionis*[41] as well as conveyors of the constitutional tradition of each legal system through their participation in the dialogue with the Court in Luxembourg.

Ideally, both the national courts and the ECJ should contribute to the development of a new legal order as the outcome of the so-called *interpretive* competition that requires coordination between different levels, comparisons and even mediation.[42] Supremacy, direct effect and preliminary rulings have been instrumental in creating for the ordinary judges in both older and newer Member States the scope for them to participate in the application of EC law. Recent ECJ case law however took a bold and perilous step further and attempted to introduce a *de facto* hierarchy in order to build further coherence and unity,[43] bearing in mind that the discretion as to whether to refer a preliminary question to the ECJ remains in the hands of the national judge.[44] With *Kuehne and Heinz*, the Court seemed to be attacking the domestically cherished principle of *res judicata* by accepting that under certain circumstances a final administrative decision that was wrongly applying EU law could be reopened so as to provide to the applicant an effective judicial remedy to protect an EU fundamental right. Subsequent case law, re-established the status quo by recognizing the finality of judgements of national courts.[45]

By the same token, the ECJ withheld its aspirations for a "final solution" for the sovereignty conundrum. A different but parallel strategy was used when, by widening the scope of Community fundamental rights, the ECJ, on the occasion of cases regarding the rights of transsexuals, crossed the limits of EU competences.[46]

41 Term borrowed by Cartabia (2009), 23.

42 Martinico, G. (2009), European Constitution and European Evolution: Why does the ECJ matter?, *STALS Research Paper* N.4/2009; available at http://stals.sssup.it, at 8, accessed 20 July 2010.

43 Referred to here are cases C-224/01 *Köbler*, ECR I-10239 [2003]; C-129/00 *Commission v. Italy*, ECR I-837 and C-453/00 *Kühne and Heitz* ECR I-837. Some authors, such as J. Komarek (2005), wrote about the "end of the sincere cooperative relationship", in Federal Elements in the Community Judicial System-building coherency in the Community Legal Order, *Common Market Law Review*, 42(1), 9–34, at 21.

44 In the same direction, the ECJ in *Köbler* acknowledged that: "The principle that it is for the legal system of each Member State to determine which court or tribunal has jurisdiction to hear disputes involving individual rights derived from Community law, subject to the reservation that effective judicial protection be ensured, is applicable to actions for damages brought by individuals against a Member State on the basis of an alleged breach of Community law by a supreme court."

45 See indicatively, Joined Cases C-392/04 and C-422/04 *i-21 Germany and Arcor v. Germany* [2006], ECR I-8559; Case C-234/04 *Kapferer v. Schlank & Schick* [2006], ECR I-2585 and Case C-2/06 *Willy Kempter KG* [2008], ECR I-411.

46 Cases C-117/01 *K.B.,* 7 January 20004 and C-423/04 *Richards*, 26 April 2006 are being referred to here. As Cartabia (2009) well explains at 10–1, the area of application of fundamental rights before these cases covered acts of EU institutions as well as acts of

In the cases at issue, the Court found that British legislation on the registration of personal data had a discriminatory effect on one of the conditions of one's right, as a survivor, to his partner's pension. The ECJ thus penetrated the space of the national legal order in an attempt to safeguard the individual's right to non-discrimination. Both the vertical as well as the horizontal attempts to firmly privilege fundamental rights despite the systemic constraints of the EU legal edifice demonstrate the limits of the construction and of course reflect a certain underlying fear of Kelsenian legal anarchy.

Due to the unsettled legal contours of EU law with regards to the modalities of constitutional dialogue and the wider issue of competences, particularly from the ECJ's position, the relationship between national and European courts is currently at a crossroads. So far, techniques of constitutional dialogue between constitutional courts and the ECJ have involved *consistent interpretation* introduced by *Marleasing*,[47] as well allowing for consideration of national constitutional structures, especially when there is an exception to the application of rules resulting from the *acquis*.[48] A third suggestion, Kumm's *mutual deliberative engagement*,[49] disposes, however, of one non-negligible advantage for fundamental rights protection when compared to other techniques: by allowing national courts to consult their counterparts in other Member States and cite each other's decisions, this prompts a reasonable and appropriate consideration as well as an accommodation of the concerns of other national courts. At the same time, by doing so, this enables the ECJ to continue developing its fundamental rights jurisprudence in the spirit of national constitutional traditions. If the development of a self-conscious and coherent European constitutional tradition in the area of fundamental rights protection is indeed desired, courts at both levels could play the role of mediators leading towards greater sensitivity to points of legislative jurisdiction with equal, if not more, emphasis provided for fundamental rights analysis. Such a methodological development would undoubtedly constitute the most valuable legacy of enlargement to CEE.

Member States when implementing EC law and in cases where the state act constituted an exception to one of the fundamental freedoms of the internal market.

47 C-106/89 Marleasing/Comercial Internacional de Alimentación, 1990, ECR I-4135.

48 See for example case C-244/06 Dynamic Medien ECR I-505 [2008], which held inter alia that: "In that connection, it is not indispensable that restrictive measure laid down by the authorities of a Member State to protect the rights of the child, referred to in paragraphs 39 to 42 of this judgment, correspond to a conception shared by all Member States as regards the level of protection and the detailed rules relating to it (see, by analogy, Omega, paragraph 37). As that conception may vary form one Member State to another on the basis of, inter alia, moral or cultural views, Member States must be recognized as having a definite margin of discretion."

49 Kumm, M. (2005a), The Jurisprudence of Constitutional Conflict: Constitutional Supremacy in Europe before and after the Constitutional Treaty, *European Law Journal*, 11(3), 262–307 at 301–2.

The Principle of Favourable Interpretation of EC Law in Central and Eastern Europe

A third and quite salient component in the contextualized analysis of fundamental rights protection in the CEE domestic context concerns the quite unique principle of favourable interpretation of EC law. The duty of domestic judges to construe their own law as closely as possible to EU law constitutes one of the most loaded, in terms of implications, principles in CEE judicial practice. From such a duty follows the obligation for the judge to set aside any domestic legislation found to be incompatible with European law. The Polish Constitutional Tribunal was referring to this duty when it declared, in 1998, prior to full membership, that the court holds "the obligation to interpret the existing legislation in such a way as to ensure the greatest possible degree of such compatibility."[50] Similarly, prior to EU accession, the Czech Constitutional Court declared that the interpretation of European law by European authorities is valuable for the interpretation of Czech rules,[51] adding later that even general principles formed by common European values assist the Court in adjudicating claims, including in the area of fundamental rights.[52] At the same time, the Czech Court highlighted the limits of the principle of favourable interpretation by remarking that: "The Constitutional Court also considers it necessary to emphasise that the holding it now adopts in no way signifies that the Constitutional Court would abdicate its powers of constitutional review of national legal enactments which are complementary to Community law, as has been done by several courts of EC Member States."[53] The delegation of powers to the Union was thus conditioned by their exercise in a compatible way to the preservation of state sovereignty. In other words, the limits of the duty to Euro-friendly interpretation were related to democratic principles.

The 2004 case before the Hungarian Constitutional Court, on measures concerning agricultural surplus stock,[54] by setting aside the European dimension of the issue and by treating the points involved in the case on the basis of the strict application of national Hungarian law and not implementation of EC law, generated an additional dimension to the discussion of the principle of favourable interpretation of EC law in Member States. EC law can be approached from the perspective of domestic law, in this case Hungarian national law, instigating almost the opposite of a Euro-friendly interpretation, one that reflects and insists more on

50 Decision K. 15/97 *Orzecznictwo Trybunalu Konstytucyjnego* Nr.19/1997, available in English 5 E. EUR. CASE REP.OF CONST.L. 271, at 284 (1998), as quoted in Kühn, Z. (2005b) The Application of European Law in the New Member States: Several (Early) Predictions, *German Law Journal*, 6(3), 565–82, at 566.

51 *Re Skoda Auto,* Collection of decisions of the Constitutional Court, col. 8, 149.

52 *Milk Quota Case*, n.410/2001 Sb [Official Gazette].

53 Part VI of Decisions Pl US 50/04.

54 Cf. footnote 26 of this chapter.

the constitutional flavour of Member States,[55] in denial of the possibility that a conflict between the two legal orders may exist.

Although therefore not all CEE courts embraced the penetration of EU law into their domestic legal systems with the same degree of openness,[56] it remains the position that following accession, judges of national courts in CEE have to act in their capacity as European judges by enforcing European secondary law, but also by reverting to the principle of favourable disposition to EU law and the wider integration process whenever required.[57] Enlargement in this sense is not entirely disconnected from the empowerment of the judiciary, particularly taking into account the tradition of judicial restraint in CEE. In fact, it may well challenge in a substantial manner the centralized structure of the national judiciaries while relieving the judge from the constraining effects of judicial precedent.[58]

Constitutionalization through *Values:* Continuing Enlargement and the Transfer of Fundamental Rights Norms

The recent and future enlargements of the Union have added the consideration of a supplementary layer on the issue of the centrality and gravity of fundamental rights in the Union's legal and political system. They have directly challenged and empirically tested how cosmopolitan the EU has become.[59] The example of Turkey is illustrative of the challenge as the prospective Turkish membership of the Union has ignited the conflict "between the old national and a new Cosmopolitan

55 Sadurski (2008) (at 16–8) read this decision in the light of the Hungarian Constitutional Court's earlier decision of 25 June 1998 that found unconstitutional a rule of Hungarian law implementing the Europe Agreement on the basis that the *acquis* had no direct effect in Hungary prior to accession.

56 Kühn (2005a) mentions the example of the Slovak Supreme Court in its decision of 25 August 1999, where the Court declared the contents of an EU directive as non-binding and irrelevant on the basis of Slovakia's then non-membership of the EU (cf. *Zbierka stanovísk Najvyššieho súdu a rozhodutí súdow Slovenskej republiky*, Slovak Case Reporter Decision No.76, Vol.4/2000, at 55).

57 See decision K 15/04 of the Polish Constitutional Tribunal, at para. 10, where the Court declared that: "Whilst interpreting legislation in force, account should be taken of the constitutional principle of favorable predisposition towards the process of European integration and the cooperation between States", available at http://www.trybunal.gov.pl/eng/summaries/documents/K_15_04_pp_GB.pdf, accessed 20 July 2010.

58 In the same direction see Kühn (2005b) at 581–2.

59 Adelman, S. (forthcoming 2010), Cosmopolitanism Sovereignty, in Baillet, C. and Aas, K. (eds) Cosmopolitanism and its Discontents [working title], London and Milton, Routledge, in particular his point about Europe being "an idea, ideal and ideology as much as a physical space".

Europe",[60] that requires both the EU and Turkey to rethink their identity and the ideas that lie at their respective foundations. What Beck calls the "language of human rights" embodies well the legitimate and legitimizing discourse that cosmopolitanism is based on, with the risk however that it carries by creating at the same time a right to intervention in the affairs of states anywhere in the world.[61]

According to Olli Rehn, what differentiates the EU from other supranational organizations is that "values make the borders of Europe".[62] One of the most important reasons for CEE countries to join the Union following the collapse of Communist rule was their quest and desire to consolidate their democracy and to establish a net of protection for fundamental rights.[63] The process of Europeanization of Central and Eastern European Member States suggests that, given the particular socio-economic characteristics of post-communist countries, the EU attempted an ambitious transfer of norms and rules prior to accession. This transfer was generated by the willingness to align legal systems of the applicants to the distinct legal order that the EU claims to be. There is a great wealth of academic literature that criticizes accession conditionality, particularly for its top-down approach and the significant power asymmetry that it provoked.[64]

Despite the variety of methods and policy tools employed, the operational contours of this transfer of values from the normative perspective, while obviously and tightly connected to enlargement, remain unclear in their operation, content and efficiency. They are also quite difficult to observe and measure in their full epistemological dimensions. Nevertheless and for the narrow purposes of this discussion, Ceva and Calder introduce a useful distinction between two categories of values: those that can be legally secured (e.g., the rule of law) and those that

60 Beck, U. (2006), *Cosmopolitan Vision*, Cambridge Polity Press, at 164, as quoted in Baban, F. and Keyman, F. (2008), Turkey & Postnational Europe: Challenges for the Cosmopolitan Political Community, *European Journal of Social Theory*, 11(1), 107–24, at 108.

61 Beck, U. (2005), at 64.

62 Rehn, O. (2006), Europe's Next Frontiers, Baden-Baden, Nomos, as quoted in Williams, A.W. (2009), Taking Values Seriously: Towards a Philosophy of EU Law, *Oxford Journal of Legal Studies*, 9(3), 549–77, at 553.

63 Sadurski (2008), at 4.

64 See indicatively, Börzel T.A. and Sedelmeier, U. (2005), The EU Dimension in European Politics, in Heywood, P. et al. (eds) *Developments in European Politics*, Houndmills, Basingstoke/New York, Macmillan, 54–70; Goetz, K.H. (2005), The New Member States and the EU: Responding to Europe, in Bulmer, S. et al. (eds) *The Member States of the European Union*, Oxford, Oxford University Press; Hughes, J. and Sasse, G. (2003), Monitoring the Monitors: EU Enlargement Conditionality and Minority Protection, *Journal on Ethnopolitics and Minority Issues in Europe* Issue 1, 1–37; available at http://www.ecmi.de/jemie, accessed 20 July 2010; Schimmelfennig, F. and Sedelmeier, U. (2005), *The Europeanization of Central and Eastern Europe*, Ithaca, New York, Cornell University Press.

cannot be secured through legislation (e.g., solidarity).[65] Quite predictably, EU founding treaties did not provide any definition of either category. The Lisbon Treaty, however, signed on 13 December 2007, provides in Article 2 TEU that "[t]he Union is founded on the values of respect for human dignity, liberty, democracy, equality, the rule of law, and respect for human rights, including the rights of persons belonging to minorities".[66] The recognition of such values expresses and reflects the political nature of the Union. Furthermore, these values constitute guidance for further enlargements as well as for the establishment and maintenance of relations with third-party countries. In that sense, they characterize both the European historical heritage and, at the same time, a universal standard that third-party countries should aspire to. They also serve the purpose of accentuating the dichotomy between the EU and countries outside its borders in terms of value-based assumptions.[67]

The declared EU common values, by laying down a foundation of the identity of the EU, establish at the same time a path for the future evolution of the Union, not only as a political and economic entity, but as a legal one too.[68] The implementation of these values has so far suffered from a great degree of abstraction. The values are shared to the extent that they are inserted in constitutions and legal acts both domestically and at the European level, yet remain abstract and subject to different judicial or other legal interpretations in terms of how they should be implemented in concrete circumstances.[69] Does that signify that EU common values have little or no contractual value within the EU or among the EU's neighbouring countries and partners? The answer is probably positive, but only insofar as these values receive no concrete meaning through legal and political interpretation. To quote Leino and Petrov, "common values receive their meaning in the processes through which they are implemente". The terms of the 2004 and 2007 enlargement conditionality have in this sense operated as guidance with respect to certain aspects of the legal nature and dimensions of at least some of these values. The same terms have also been instrumental in highlighting the gaps in the process. In retrospect, it would

---

65 Ceva, E. and Calder, G. (2009), Values, Diversity and the Justification of EU Institutions, *Political Studies*, 57, 828–45, at 829.

66 Article 2 TEU was amended by the Lisbon Treaty to substitute the contents of Article 6(1) EU. Article 2 TEU continues: "… These values are common to the Member States in a society in which pluralism, non-discrimination, tolerance, justice, solidarity and equality between women and men prevail."

67 Turkey is a very good example of this dichotomy.

68 Leino, P. and Petrov, R. (2009), Between "Common Values" and Competing Universals – The Promotion of the EU's Common Values through the European Neighbourhood Policy, *European Law Journal*, 15(5), 654–71, at 656.

69 Significantly in this direction, despite measures in the opposite direction, both the UK and Poland have added Protocol No. 30 on the application of the Charter (OJ 2007 C306/156) limiting its applicability to their national authorities, and this is despite Article 52(5) of the Charter that stipulates that principles are not to have direct effect unless they have been implemented by legislative and executive acts.

be monolithic to claim that the values connected to fundamental rights protection remain exclusively legal: in fact, they have become a political instrument of mobilization for EU institutions as well, and in particular one for the Commission, to influence reforms in partner or prospective Member States.

But the example of the Turkish candidacy denounces the limits of the well-advertised discourse on values: what it means to be "European" and be also perceived as such is a stand-alone debate at present. Unity in diversity, in practice often denotes an acceptance of diversity only to the extent that it does not disrupt unity.[70]

A number of authors, including Habermas, have put forward the *cosmopolitan* image of the EU in order to suggest that the Union based on a set of abstract universalistic principles, such as human and fundamental rights, can evolve, with the help of constitutionalization, into a "post-national constellation" in a position to export the rule of law, democracy and human rights worldwide.[71] In that respect, the EU Charter of Fundamental Rights, now legally biding since the ratification of the Treaty of Lisbon in December 2009, stands as an illustration of this dynamic. Thus the case of fundamental rights reveals that, in particular, following the collapse of Communism and the beginning of accession negotiations with CEE has been gradually elevated to a *grundnorm* through two simultaneous processes: first, by the control and willingness of the ECJ,[72] although rights' definitions are lacking,[73] and, second, through the amendment of the treaties and the increasing awareness of the common values between Member States as a salient element of constitutional identity with repercussions both internal and external to the EU.

The process of recognition has not been, however, uninterrupted, with the example of the *Kadi* case suggesting a momentary retreat from the initial intention. The case concerning the compatibility of the Council's imposition of a regulation (Council Regulation No 881/2002), applying restrictive measures to the detriment of the applicant's fundamental rights under EU law in implementation of UN Security Council resolution on international terrorism, was decided by the CFI. The Court found that the measures did not constitute a breach of European law, although it did attempt to present human rights as *ius cogens*.[74] Being unable in the first instance to protect its declared values prompted the ECJ to declare that

70 Williams (2009), at 554 referring to the cultural values of the EU.

71 Habermas, J. (2001), *The Post-national Constellation*, Cambridge, Polity Press; Habermas, J. (2003), Towards a Cosmopolitan Europe, *Journal of Democracy*, 14(4), 86–100.

72 See for example the cases C-112/00 *Schmidberger v. Austria* [2003] ECR I-5659 or C-36/02 *Omega v. Bonn* [2004] ECR I-9609 that are examples of how the ECJ moved beyond a general preference for the market over rights. Case T-315/01 *Yassin Abdullah Kadi v. Council of the European Union and Commission of the European Communities*. O.J. 2005, C281.

73 Williams (2009), at 570–1.

74 For more on this point see Williams (2009), at 573.

the restrictions imposed in *Kadi* were in breach of his fundamental right to a fair hearing.[75] Beside the obvious implication that the ECJ was claiming the autonomy of the EU's legal system, its decision was also a clear statement on the level of protection of values, in line with Article 297 TEC.[76]

Conclusions: Inconsistency as the Heart of Pluralism

One of Kelsen's arguments has been that ranking rules and other legal principles is conducive to the elimination of inconsistencies.[77] In the case of the European Union, this has been the approach that both scholars and practitioners were trying to apply for a number of years before the 12 new Member States joined the Union. After 2004, it seems legitimate to question this approach, especially if one sides with those that argue in favour of constitutional pluralism. Thinking about law (and politics) beyond the EU may in fact also require a rethinking of the basic assumptions underlying national practices. The practice of national constitutional or international legal practice may not suffice in that respect.[78]

Most of the CEE national courts, with few notable exceptions, have avoided addressing the issue of supremacy in a confrontational manner. Instead, they have limited themselves to issue (discrete) warnings about the limits of sovereignty. To address the point of conflict of rules, the current state of scholarship discusses three options: the change of EU law, the amendment of national constitutional law or the toleration of the occasional discrepancy between national and EU law.[79] In light of the enlargement, CEE experience and the reaction of domestic jurisdictions to the particularities of the EU legal order, it may be said with relative safety that the best way to solve conflicts is for the national judge and the ECJ to adopt the solution that seems each time to realize best the ideals and goals that characterize (and distinguish) legal practice in the European legal space.[80] In an

75 Cases C-402/05P and C-415/05P *Yassin Abduallh Kadi and Al Barakaat International Foundation v. Council* [2008] where the ECJ held at para.303 that "... the obligations imposed by an international agreement cannot have the effect of prejudicing the constitutional principles of the EC Treaty, which include the principle that all Community acts must respect fundamental rights ...".

76 Article 297 TEC stipulates that Member States are allowed to take measures interfering with the common market, but cannot authorize any derogation from the principles of liberty, democracy and respect for human rights and fundamental freedoms enshrined in Article 6(1) EU (now Article 2 TEU) as a foundation of the Union.

77 As quoted in Barber, N.W. (2006), Legal Pluralism and the European Union, *European Law Journal*, 12(3), 306–29, at 309.

78 Kumm (2005), at 268.

79 See for example the very detailed analysis in Kumm (2005), in particular 270.

80 Ibid., at 286. As Kumm cautiously points out however at 288, decision-making in the EU and the identification of principles does not happen independently of national interests.

EU with the kind of diversity that stems from 27 different members, the goal of safeguarding fundamental rights within a group of nation-states largely justifies and compensates for the complexities in constitutional translation.

One can, of course, claim that "legal systems are artificial normative structures, and, as such are not constrained to comply with all the dictates of logic",[81] but it is not clear how this would help, for example, the national judge to decide whether to accept the supremacy claims of the ECJ or the rival similar claims of the national court. The fragmentation of the domestic legal orders is clearly not the aim of European integration either. Under a pluralist model, however, both the national and supranational positions can coexist to the extent that they exercise mutual respect and restraint. In that sense inconsistency may be viewed as constructive.[82]

Holmes said quite some time ago that "the life of the law has not been logic, it has been experience".[83] Constitutions of Member States, as well as EU treaties, carry a number of principles. In particular, the ones that concern fundamental rights tend to have broad normative contexts and ambitions, and rightly so.[84] Regardless of the intentions surrounding their initial conceptualization, they are condemned to openness to development and reinterpretation if they are to survive in an environment of constitutional pluralism. Adaptability in the course of their implementation, exactly as Holmes described it, is thus the most important prerequisite that they should dispose in order to meet the requirements that national constitutionalism imposes on them. It is probably a necessary quality in making sure that the ECJ's interpretative normative guidance remains relevant and that the system is its wholeness responds to the demands of a post-national and post-sovereign European Union.

References

Adelman, S. (forthcoming 2010), Cosmopolitanism Sovereignty, in Baillet, C. and Aas, K. (eds) *Cosmopolitanism and its Discontents* [working title], London and Milton, Routledge.

Albi, A. (2005), *EU Enlargement and the Constitutions of CEE*, Cambridge, Cambridge University Press.

Andersen, S.S. and Sitter, N. (2006), Differentiated Integration: What is it and How Much Can the EU Accommodate?, *Journal of European Integration*, 28(4), 313–30.

81 Barber (2006), at 311.

82 For a similar argument see ibid., at 328.

83 Wendell Holmes, O. (1880), Review of CC Langdell "Summary of the Law of Contracts", 14 *American Law Review*, at 234, as quoted in Aziz (2004), at 13.

84 Poiares Maduro, M. (2007), Interpreting European Law: Judicial Adjudication in a Context of Constitutional Pluralism, *EJLS*, 1(2), 1–21, at 12.

Aziz, M. (2004), *The Impact of European Rights on National Legal Cultures*, Oxford, Hart Publishing.

Baban, F. and Keyman, F. (2008), Turkey & Postnational Europe: Challenges for the Cosmopolitan Political Community, *European Journal of Social Theory*, 11(1), 107–24.

Barber, N.W. (2006), Legal Pluralism and the European Union, *European Law Journal*, 12(3), 306–29.

Beck, U. (2005), *Power in the Global Age: A New Global Political Economy*, Cambridge, Polity Press.

Beck, U. (2006), *Cosmopolitan Vision*, Cambridge, Polity Press, at 164, as quoted in Baban, F. and Keyman, F. Turkey & Postnational Europe: Challenges for the Cosmopolitan Political Community, *European Journal of Social Theory*, 11(1),107–24.

Börzel, T.A. and Sedelmeier, U. (2005) The EU Dimension in European Politics, in Heywood, P. et al. (eds) *Developments in European Politics*, Houndmills, Basingstoke/New York, Macmillan, 54–70.

Cartabia, M. (2009), Europe and Rights: Taking Dialogue Seriously, *European Constitutional Law Review*, 5, 5–31.

Ceva, E. and Calder, G. (2009) Values, Diversity and the Justification of EU Institutions, *Political Studies*, 57, 828–45.

Czuczai, J. (2001), Practical Implementation by the Acceding Candidate Countries of the Constitutional *Acquis* of the EU: Problems and Challenges, in Kellerman, A. et al. (eds) *EU Enlargement: The Constitutional Impact at EU and National Level*, The Hague, T.M.C. Asser Press, 411–22.

Føllesdal, A. (2001), Union Citizenship: Unpacking the Beast of Burden, *Law and Philosophy*, 20(3), 313–43.

Goetz, K.H. (2005), The New Member States and the EU: Responding to Europe, in Bulmer, S. et al. (eds) *The Member States of the European Union*, Oxford, Oxford University Press.

Grabbe, H. (2001), How does Europeanization affect CEE governance? Conditionality, diffusion and diversity, *Journal of European Public Policy*, 8(6), 1013–31.

Grimm, D. (2005), Integration by Constitution, 3 *International Journal of Constitutional Law*,193–208.

Habermas, J. (2001), *The Post-national Constellation*, Cambridge, Polity Press.

Habermas, J. (2003) Towards a Cosmopolitan Europe, *Journal of Democracy*, 14(4), 86–100.

Holmes, O.W. (1880), Review of CC Langdell "Summary of the Law of Contracts", 14 *American Law Review*.

Hughes, J. and Sasse, G. (2003), Monitoring the Monitors: EU Enlargement Conditionality and Minority Protection, *Journal on Ethnopolitics and Minority Issues in Europe*, Issue 1, 1–37; available at http://www.ecmi.de/jemie, accessed 20 July 2010.

Jacoby, W. (1999), Priest and Penitent: The European Union as a Force in the Domestic Politics of Eastern Europe, 8 *East European Constitutional Review*, 62–7.

Komarek, J. (2005), Federal Elements in the Community Judicial System-building Coherency in the Community Legal Order, *Common Market Law Review*, 42(1), 9–34.

Kühn, Z. (2005a), Making a European Transnational Constitution: Some Central European Perspectives, in Pernice, I. and Zemanek, R., *A Constitution for Europe: The IGC, the Ratification Process and Beyond*, Baden-Baden, Nomos, 127–39.

Kühn, Z. (2005b), The Application of European Law in the New Member States: Several (Early) Predictions, *German Law Journal*, 6(3), 565–82.

Kumm, M. (2005), The Jurisprudence of Constitutional Conflict: Constitutional Supremacy in Europe before and after the Constitutional Treaty, *European Law Journal*, 11(3), 262–307.

Leino, P. and Petrov, R. (2009), Between "Common Values" and Competing Universals – The Promotion of the EU's Common Values through the European Neighbourhood Policy, *European Law Journal*, 15(5), 654–71.

Maduro, M.P. (2007), Interpreting European Law: Judicial Adjudication in a Context of Constitutional Pluralism, *EJLS*, 1(2), 1–21.

Martinico, G. (2009), European Constitution and European Evolution: Why does the ECJ matter?, *STALS Research Paper* N.4/2009; available at http://stals.sssup.it/judicial-dialogue/ accessed 20 July 2010.

Pernice, I. and Kanitz, R. (2004), Fundamental Rights and Multilevel Constitutionalism in Europe, Walter Hallenstein Institut Paper 7/04.

Peters, A. (2006), The Constitutionalisation of the European Union – Without the Constitutional Treaty, in S. Puntscher Riekmann and W. Wessels, *The Making of a European Constitution: Dynamics and Limits of the Convention Experience*, Wiesbaden, VS Verlag, 35–67.

Piqani, D. (2008), Constitutional Courts in Central and Eastern Europe and their Attitude towards European Integration, *EJLS*, 1(2), 1–22.

Rehn, O. (2006), *Europe's Next Frontiers*, Baden-Baden, Nomos.

Sadurski, W. (2008), "Solange, Chapter 3": Constitutional Courts in Central Europe – Democracy – European Union, *European Law Journal*, 14(1), 1–35.

Schimmelfennig, F. and Sedelmeier, U. (2005), *The Europeanization of Central and Eastern Europe*, Ithaca, New York, Cornell University Press.

Sedelmeier, U. (2006), Europeanisation in new Member and Candidate States, *Living Review in European Governance*, 1, at 3: available at http://www.livingreviews.org/lreg-2006-3, accessed 20 July 2010.

Slepcevic, R. (2009), The Judicial Enforcement of EU Law through National Courts: Possibilities and Limits, *Journal of European Public Policy*, 16(3), 378–94.

Walker, N. (2003), Postnational Constitutionalism and the Problem of Translation, in J. Weiler and M. Wind (eds) *European Constitutionalism Beyond the State*, Cambridge, Cambridge University Press, 27–54.
Walker, N. (2005), Constitutionalism and New Governance in the European Union: Rethinking the Boundaries, *EUI Working Papers* No.2005/15; available at http://cadmus.iue.it/dspace/index.jsp, accessed 20 July 2010.
Walker, N. (2008), Taking Constitutionalism Beyond the State, *Political Studies*, 56, 519–43, at 534.
Wiener, A. (2006), Comment: Fact or Artefact? Analysing Core Constitutional Norms in Beyond-the-state Contexts, *Journal of European Public Policy*, 13(8), 1308–13.
Williams, A.W. (2009), Taking Values Seriously: Towards a Philosophy of EU Law, *Oxford Journal of Legal Studies*, 29(3), 549–77, at 553.

PART II
The Role of Courts in the New Legal Order

Chapter 5
Constitutional Pluralism and Judicial Cooperation in the EU after the Eastern Enlargements: A Case Study of the Czech and Slovak Courts[1]

Tomáš Dumbrovský

Introduction

Pluralism, the purpose of law, and cooperation blow like a gentle breeze through the new European constitutional space. They chase away the stuffy atmosphere of the Kelsenian world of absolute unity, formalist interpretation and hierarchy out of their rooms. Does the opening of doors to the new Member States stifle the fresh breeze?

The European Union and its Member States operate in a constitutional space where multiple actors claim final constitutional authority. The functioning of the system is ensured through the cooperation of these actors. Cooperation has been enshrined in the Treaty establishing the European Community through the institute of preliminary reference. The European Court of Justice (ECJ) has envisaged this cooperation as a dialogue between a national court and the ECJ itself. Constitutional pluralism has taken the dialogue-like idea into its framework and extended its use into an area of "cooperation" that goes beyond (and indeed against) the preliminary reference system. In this chapter, the impact of the Eastern enlargement of the European Union on the common European constitutional space and the challenge it has posed to the theory of constitutional pluralism are analysed. After a brief

1 This chapter forms part of the project GAUK 2570/2007 and the project GAČR 09/1747. The author would like to thank Luboš Tichý, Eric Stein, Daniel Halberstam, Armin von Bogdandy, Alexander Morawa, Kyriaki Topidi, Bilyana Petkova, Jan Komárek, Anelli Albi, Christoph Hönnige, Sylvain Brouard and Běla Plechanovová for their valuable comments at various stages of the research, and especially the participants at the Roundtable on Constitutionalization in Central and Eastern Europe held in Lucerne on 17–18 July 2009. The author is delighted to express his gratitude to the University of Lucerne, the Law Faculty of Charles University in Prague, the University of Michigan Law School and the Max-Planck Institute for Comparative Public Law and International Law for providing him with generous research support. All errors are the author's.

overview of the theory and its recent criticisms, two areas of judicial cooperation – formal and material – are conceptualized. Both areas are governed by different modes of cooperation – dialogue and bargaining[2] respectively (Hopmann 1995: 24–47). This chapter claims that as a consequence of the Eastern enlargement, material cooperation has broadened and dialogue has been increasingly overridden by bargaining. More and more, bargaining has trumped dialogue and diminished cooperation, thus endangering the very essence of constitutional pluralism.

As a case study, the development of these two types of cooperation in the European doctrines of the Czech and the Slovak Constitutional Courts is examined. Finally, an explanation is offered for the inability of the new Member States' judiciaries to grasp the idea of constitutional pluralism and dialogue. Such inability stems mainly from their different constitutional development during communist rule, which has directly impacted on the way legal transformation took place in the transition period.

Notions of Pluralism, Dialogue and Bargaining

Constitutional Pluralism

Constitutional pluralism is "the idea of competing claims of constitutional authority within a single system of governance" (Halberstam 2009a: 327–328). It "recognises that in the post-Westphalian world there exists a range of different constitutional sites and processes configured in a heterarchical rather than a hierarchical pattern" (Walker 2002: 317). The functioning of such a system, which following competing claims of authority lacks a single hierarchy of norms, is ensured through a cooperation of multiple constitutional interpreters in a dialogue between the ECJ and the national constitutional courts (Mayer 2003: 39).

The origins of the idea of constitutional pluralism may be traced back to the constructivist debate on the nature of the European Union (Community) during the 1990s. The constructivists broadly built on the premises of the plurality of actors (state and non-state) and/or the existence of different levels of governance (Stone Sweet and Brunell 1998; Marks, Hooghe and Blank 1996). These premises found their way into the constitutional law scholarship in the form of "constitutional" multi-level governance (Pernice 2002, 2006, 2009) and constitutional pluralism. Both are variants of a constitutional theory for a system, which lacks a single hierarchically built legal order and single supreme (final) constitutional interpreter. Legal pluralism, yet another intellectual source for constitutional pluralism, arose from rethinking the concept of sovereignty (MacCormick 1999: 113–136; Walker 2003: 6 et seq.), which has became untenable *vis-à-vis* challenges to

2 In main negotiation theories, bargaining is usually opposed to dialogue-like problem-solving strategies. While the former presupposes zero-sum outcomes, the latter offer positive-sum results.

the exclusive authority of the state both within (constitutionally) and externally (internationally) in the second half of the twentieth century. An important incentive for the establishment of the constitutional pluralist movement was the Maastricht decision of the German Constitutional Court, which offered an empirical base for this theory (Baquero Cruz 2008: 412).

According to constitutional pluralism, there is more than one competing constitution in the European constitutional space, without the constitutions of the Member States or the EU being able to claim the status of supreme law of the land.[3] It follows from constitutional pluralism that there is not a single institution entrusted to have the final say on what the law is; that is, to decide which one of the constitutions is supreme or, in other words, to decide what is the relationship between a Member State constitution and European law. If there were one, the pluralism of constitutions would be but formal. Nevertheless, an institution entrusted to interpret the constitution is designated by each constitution. Although there may be more institutions or entities competing for the authoritative interpretation of a constitution,[4] it is the judiciary[5] that is foremost entrusted with this task. Therefore the enquiry in this chapter will be limited to the highest courts.

Critique of Constitutional Pluralism

The possible benefits of pluralism are obvious – it stirs better solutions as a result of competition and fosters dynamics through conflict. First, pluralism offers a plethora of ideas (within constitutional law for instance, it gives ideas on the extent of human rights protection, on the level and means of protection, or on the division of competences horizontally and vertically within a state). Second, this competition of ideas inevitably creates conflict and conflict is what makes the system dynamics.

However, within the sphere of law, pluralism becomes a problematic concept. It is indeed beneficial to have more ideas on what the law shall be. It is much less

---

3 It is presupposed here that there is a constitution (either in a formal or in a material sense) in every of the 27 Member States and that there is a constitution (in material sense) of the European Union (Community). It is not the purpose of this article to deal with this matter. However, the author is persuaded that the overwhelming majority of the European legal scholarship (including the ECJ itself) agrees on the constitutional substance of the Treaties.

4 Daniel Halberstam calls this "institutional pluralism" (2009b) or "interpretive pluralism" (2009a), which he perceives as a structural feature of the American constitutional system. In his interpretation, "institutional pluralism" gives the system the necessary dynamics, comparable to the dynamism of the European system based on the "competition' of constitutions (constitutional pluralism).

5 To be sure, some institutions which we consider today as judicial were originally, or are still, doctrinally parts of either the executive branch (e.g., *Conseil d'État* in France) or the legislature (e.g., Appellate Committee of the House of Lords in the UK, up until October 2009).

desirable to have two or more competing norms without being able to doctrinally decide which one is applicable. Baquero Cruz (2008: 414) contrasts discursive pluralism with radical pluralism (pluralism in law application). While plurality in legal discourse and interpretation, as well as in law-making is beneficial, pluralism in the sphere of judicial activity and law application may endanger the rule of law, legal certainty and the effective protection of individual rights due to "the lack of clear relationships among judicial institutions" (Baquero Cruz 2008: 415).

Another line of criticisms goes into the specific consequences of constitutional pluralism for the European constitutional space. The European Court of Justice has never softened its views on the Treaties as an autonomous source of validity for European law and on the absolute supremacy of any given European norm when in conflict with any norm of a Member State's legal order. Constitutional pluralists thus do not offer anything to the ECJ. Their theory serves only the needs of those national courts that object to absolute supremacy of EU law. That is because constitutional pluralism is based on a thesis that breaches European law, although the breach is, so far, indirect and rather hypothetical. Despite a danger of becoming a self-fulfilling prophecy, constitutional pluralism well captures reality. The theory conceptualizes reality in a way that limits conflict and ensures the functionality of the system. However, in doing so it inevitably signifies compromise with the unified application of EU law and backs up the wrongdoing of some national supreme judiciaries (Baquero Cruz 2008: 412–415).

Conditions for Effective Pluralism

Within the scholarship on the relationship between EU law and national (constitutional) law we may identify two major claims. The first one was described above and is about the nature of the European constitutional space and the structural benefits of the plurality of constitutions. The second focuses on the development of doctrines of Member States' constitutional courts *vis-à-vis* the European Court of Justice's case law. For scholars dealing with the second topic, the central question becomes how constitutional courts and the ECJ can coexist given the contradiction in their doctrinal approaches. These scholars find explanation in the constitutional dialogue initiated between different constitutional interpreters. The two strands of the scholarship are overlapping and the distinction between the consequences of their claims is often blurred. This is so because both build foremost on the ECJ's and the Member States' constitutional courts' case law without actually differentiating enough between the system features and its consequences, i.e., between the state of things (plurality of constitutions) and the means to make the system work (dialogue). This confusion is to a certain extent understandable because the relationship of plurality and dialogue goes both ways: constitutional pluralism is a consequence of the courts' decisions understood as both actions and reactions (as neither of the courts accepts the other court's doctrine fully, which means that there is no agreed hierarchy of norms in the European constitutional space). This in turn creates necessity for dialogue in order to understand each other's arguments and limits of discretion and to adapt the courts' doctrines accordingly.

Once we have differentiated between the two – the substance of the system (constitutional pluralism) and the means to get it running (cooperation – e.g., dialogue) – we shall be able to research deeper into the interactions among the courts in the European Union's constitutional space, enriching the predominant "dialogue idea", as it will be called in this chapter, with more refined insights.

Two Types of Cooperation

Pluralism is an ever-growing phenomenon in our time, and the legal sphere is not immune to it. However, pluralism, especially in law, is a rather unwelcome guest because our understanding of law is closely connected with some basic legal features and principles, such as order, certainty and foreseeability. Nevertheless, legal systems can benefit from pluralism, as other social systems do; we have learnt that from the operation of the European Convention of Human Rights and its interpretation by the European Court of Human Rights. Pluralism in human rights protection has led to a widespread tendency of constitutional courts to apply laws which provide for higher protection of fundamental rights.

To prevent the negative effects of pluralism, such as legal uncertainty and lack of legal foreseeability, the cooperation among the interpreters of law is indispensable. In the case of the plurality of legal orders – the European and the national ones – which is the state of things in the European Union, we should differentiate between two types of inter-judicial cooperation: formal cooperation arising from the requirement of Article 267 of the Treaty on the Functioning of the European Union (TFEU-Lis), and material cooperation resulting from a desire to fill the gap created by the absence of a final arbiter.

Formal Inter-Judicial Cooperation: Article 267 TFEU-Lis-type Cooperation The first type of cooperation that makes a system of plurality of legal orders functional is the type of cooperation foreseen by the Treaties. These provided for an ideal delimitation of jurisdictions between the national judiciaries and the European judiciary. This cooperation is based on Article 267 TFEU-Lis. Here, we can speak about a true dialogue. The relationship between a national court and the European Court of Justice under the preliminary question procedure is not simply one of different jurisdictions. As was realized in the very early stage of the integration process, a national court and the European Court of Justice dispose of inevitably overlapping jurisdictions and a strict separation of matters of national law and of European law is not possible.[6] Therefore, the relationship of courts within this

6 However, the ECJ has repeatedly emphasized the clear separation of powers. The most recent assertion of this view was expressed in *Chacón Navas*:

> … it must be recalled that, in proceedings under Article 234 TEU (267 TFEU-Lis), which are based on a clear separation of functions between the national

procedure is not based on a strict separation of powers (jurisdictions), where a national court decides on the validity, interpretation and application of national law and the ECJ on the validity, interpretation and the way of application of European law. Instead, the national court and the ECJ are in constant dialogue, whereby the national court explains its problem with the application of European law due to its conflict with national law and suggests explicitly or implicitly possible ways how to solve the concrete legal issue. The ECJ, on the other hand, in order to give an effective answer on the interpretation of European law, needs to know and understand the facts and the specific application problems that arose in that concrete situation. This means that the ECJ has to interpret European law in the light of a competing national law, and thus, at least partially, to interpret the national law itself. Such a relationship implies real cooperation based on a direct inter-judicial dialogue. The legal basis for such a dialogue is found in Article 267 TFEU-Lis interpreted in the light of Article 4(3) TFEU-Lis, which provides for a sincere framework of cooperation between the Community (its organs) and the Member States (their organs). The obligation for cooperation binds not only all institutions of the Member States that exercise state power (including the judicial organs), but given ECJ's own case law, it obliges the Community institutions as well (including the ECJ). The dialogue-mode cooperation is in this sense a requirement of Community law.

Material Inter-Judicial Cooperation: The Question of the Ultimate Supervisor The second type of inter-judicial cooperation, on the other hand, is in deviation from Community law. As such, it is not and cannot be accepted by one of the parties – the European Court of Justice. Indeed, the ECJ has never softened its doctrine on the absolute supremacy of European law as formed by its decisions in *Costa*, *Internationale Handelgesellschaft* and *Simmenthal*.[7] However, the doctrines of many Member States' highest courts have yet to accept the doctrine of absolute supremacy of EU law. The group of "heretics" considerably broadened after the

courts and the Court of Justice, any assessment of the facts in the case is a matter for the national court. Similarly, it is solely for the national court before which the dispute has been brought, and which must assume responsibility for the subsequent judicial decision, to determine in the light of the particular circumstances of the case both the need for a preliminary ruling in order to enable it to deliver judgment and the relevance of the questions which it submits to the Court. Consequently, where the questions submitted concern the interpretation of Community law, the Court is in principle bound to give a ruling … (Case C-13/05, *Chacón Navas*, OJ C 224 of 16 September 2006, p. 9 paragraph 32; cf. also the exemptions from the "clear separation of functions" stated in paragraph 33 of the judgement)

7 Case 6/64, *Flaminio Costa v ENEL* [1964] ECR 585; case 11/70, *Internationale Handelgesellschaft v Einfuhr-und Vorratstelle für Getreide und Futtermittel* [1970] ECR 1125; and case 106/77, *Amministrazione delle Finanze dello Stato v Simmenthal S.p.A.* [1978] ECR 629.

two rounds of Eastern enlargement, and included the Czech Constitutional Court. Given that the ECJ has never reconsidered its doctrine on absolute supremacy despite the growing number of courts conditioning that doctrine, we may hardly speak about a dialogue here. The ECJ obviously does not reflect the Member States' highest courts' interpretation of its absolute supremacy doctrine.

In order to further conceptualize the cooperation between or among courts in the European constitutional space, we have to identify situations where the absolute supremacy of EU law is objected to by national judiciaries. There are two types of objections. The first arises when the Community exercises more powers than it possesses (than were conferred to it). Here, in order to intervene, the national constitutional courts differ as to the degree of perceived seriousness of breach on the principle of conferred powers. The prevailing approach has been one of restraint from exercising control when the Community acts within its conferred powers unless excess occurs so flagrant and serious as to cause breaches of inviolable provisions of the national constitutions.[8] The consequence of such serious excess is the non-application of the Community act in hand.

The second objection takes place when, somewhat paradoxically, the Community exercises less power than would be in compliance with the national constitutional order. That is the case when the standard of human rights protection on the Community/Union level is lower than the protection assured by the national constitution.[9]

Modes of Cooperation: Dialogue vs Bargaining

The current constitutional pluralism scholarship focuses on the question of material cooperation. Its dialogue idea is explained by the notion of a single channel of cooperation which works both ways: on one end of the channel, there are the Member States' (MS) constitutional courts and on the other, the ECJ. As has been emphasized above, two-way cooperation through dialogue is a feature of formal cooperation arising from the requirement of 267 TFEU-Lis. Conversely, material cooperation driven by *ultra vires* and *human rights protection tests* is far from being based on dialogue.

---

8 BVerfG, *Brunner et al. (Maastricht Decision)*, Case Nos 2 BvR 2134 and 2159/92 [1993], English translation in Oppenheimer 1994: 527–575; Polish Constitutional Tribunal, *Poland's Membership in the European Union (Accession Treaty)*, K 18/04 [2005], English translation available at http://www.trybunal.gov.pl/eng/summaries/wstep_gb.htm, accessed 20 January 2008); Czech Constitutional Court, *Sugar Quotas Regulation II*, Pl. ÚS 50/04 [2006] No. 154/2006 Coll., English translation available at http://angl.concourt.cz/angl_verze/ cases.php, accessed 5 August 2009.

9 BverG, *Wunsche Handelsgesselschaft*, Case No 2 BvR 197/83 [1986], English translation in Oppenheimer 1994: 462–497; *Sugar Quotas Regulation II* case; Czech Constitutional Court, *Lisbon Treaty*, Pl. ÚS 19/08 [2008] No. 446/2008 Coll., English translation available at http://angl.concourt.cz/angl_verze/cases.php, accessed 5 August 2009.

In this chapter it is claimed that there may be more channels of cooperation and hereafter it is analysed between which courts they work and in what ways; most importantly, this chapter looks into the modes of interaction in each case. Except for cooperation between the ECJ and the MS' constitutional courts (as in the current understanding), the MS' constitutional courts themselves might cooperate or form alliances (e.g., between Central and Eastern Europe (CEE) courts or between "old core" MS courts – the German, Italian and French).[10] The interaction within these channels presupposes cooperation, the existence of which is a precondition for pluralism to be beneficial. Further, there can be two modes of cooperative interaction: *dialogue* and *bargaining*. The basic difference between these two is that while *bargaining* is a process where each of the actors tries to gain maximum advantages and their strategy cannot be basically affected by the persuasiveness of the other actor's arguments, *dialogue* is a process where actors learn from each other and eventually one of the sides either accepts the argumentation of the other, thus realizing that their own arguments were refuted, or the actors manage to reach a common view.

To better understand the difference between these two areas of cooperation, this chapter inquires into the emerging cooperation between two new MS' constitutional courts, the Czech and the Slovak, and the European Court of Justice.

Formal and Material Inter-Judicial Cooperation in the European Doctrines of the Czech and Slovak Constitutional Courts

Formal Cooperation: The Preliminary Question

Both Constitutional Courts, the Czech and the Slovak, are rather reluctant to accept their role of referring courts under Article 267 TFEU-Lis. A common feature in both courts' approach to this question is avoiding direct clashes with the ECJ by postponing their final decisions. Confronted with an obligation arising under Article 234 TEC (267 TFEU-Lis), the Czech Constitutional Court (the CCC) in the *Sugar Quotas Regulation II*[11] judgement postponed its decision on whether it constituted a court, which ought to refer a case concerning the validity or interpretation of European law to the European Court of Justice for preliminary ruling. In order to moderate its indecision, the CCC asserted that the given questions were already answered by the ECJ, and therefore the doctrine *act clair* shall be, *in eventum*, applied. To be sure, the Court meant rather the doctrine *acte éclairé*. However, it is obvious that when the Court states that if it might be a court bound by 267 TFEU-

10 There is a theoretical possibility of some constitutional courts siding fully with the ECJ and thus creating yet a third channel between the ECJ and these "loyal" courts on the one hand and the other constitutional courts on the other.

11 Czech Constitutional Court, Pl.US 50/04, decided on 8 March 2008 (*Sugar Quote Regulation II*).

Lis, then the doctrine *acte éclairé* applies to its case, and the Court thus accepts the rule (and the obligation to refer a case to the ECJ for preliminary ruling) in order to apply one of the exemptions formulated in the *CILFIT* case.[12]

In the proceeding concerning the constitutionality of the Antidiscrimination Act (Law No. 365/2004 Coll.), the Slovak Constitutional Court (the SCC) was directly asked by the Slovak National Assembly as *amicus curiae* to refer a preliminary question.[13] The National Assembly wanted the Court to refer to the ECJ a question on the interpretation of Article 8, paragraph 8, of the Antidiscrimination Act. Although, formally, the question was not correctly formulated as it asked about the interpretation of a national law, the reason was, according to the National Assembly, that the contested provision of the Antidiscrimination Act transposed almost literally the provision of Article 5 of Council Directive 2000/43/EC,[14] and therefore needed to be interpreted accordingly. The Court refused to refer the preliminary question to the ECJ with the following argumentation: the questioned provision of Article 5 of the Directive rendered broad discretion to the Member States. The object of the proceedings before the SCC was the compliance of provisions of national law with the Slovak Constitution. In order to evaluate the constitutionality of the contested provision, interpretation of the Community legal norm was not needed. The Court was obliged to review the contested provision of the national law from the point of view of its constitutionality only. Therefore, there was no need to refer any question to the ECJ for a preliminary ruling (Mazák 2005a: 12).[15]

On the one hand, the reasoning of the SCC is not very persuasive thus far. Given that the provision of the national law is almost a literal transposition of Article 5 of the Directive, its interpretation should have been the same as in the case of the Directive's provision, and for defining that only the ECJ is competent. On the other hand, a strong argument in favour of the Court's decision is the fact that the Directive indeed leaves full discretion to the Member State as to whether or not it should adopt a provision concerning affirmative action.[16] The National Assembly would then be obliged to adopt a solution, which is in compliance with the national constitution, given the fact that neither of the two solutions (to allow affirmative action or not) would breach European law. This also means

12 Case 283/81, *Srl CILFIT and Lanificio di Gavardo SpA v Ministry of Health* [1982] ECR 3415.

13 Slovak Constitutional Court, *Antidiscrimination Act*, PL. ÚS 8/04 [2005]; Slovak original available at http://www.concourt.sk/rozhod.do?urlpage=dokument&id_spisu=31723, accessed 19 July 2010.

14 Council Directive 2000/43/EC [2000] OJ L180, of 19 July 2000.

15 The decision of the Slovak Constitutional Court was made in a separate resolution, and was not mentioned in the final judgement, which was the only one published.

16 Cf. the wording of the directive: "With a view to ensuring full equality in practice, the principle of equal treatment shall not prevent any Member State from maintaining or adopting specific measures to prevent or compensate for disadvantages linked to racial or ethnic origin."

that an interpretation of the Directive's provision (under the preliminary question procedure) is not needed.

Nonetheless, the Slovak Constitutional Court postponed once again its decision on whether it was a court under the meaning of Article 234 TEC (267 TFEU-Lis) in a decision of the Third Senate of 29 May 2007.[17] Referring to the ECJ's judgement in the *Ynos v Varga* case,[18] the SCC argued that because the relevant facts of the case took place before Slovak accession, the ECJ would have to deny its jurisdiction and therefore a reference for a question of preliminary ruling was inadmissible. Finally, the Slovak Constitutional Court examined in depth the preliminary question procedure in a judgement of the Fourth Senate of July 2008[19] concerning the extent of an entitlement of a commercial agent to an indemnity (*Commercial Agent* case). The petitioner, a commercial agent, claimed that the Regional Court in Bratislava deprived him of his constitutional right to be heard by a lawful judge when the Regional Court did not refer a preliminary question to the ECJ on the interpretation of certain provisions of Directive 86/653/EEC, transposed into the Slovak legal order by amendments of paragraphs 652–672a of the Commercial Code, applicable in his case. The question whether a non-reference to the European Court of Justice was a deprivation of the claimant's right to a fair trial had already appeared in proceedings before the Second Senate and was decided on 30 March 2005,[20] when the petitioner argued that the fact that the Regional Court in Bratislava and the Slovak Supreme Court as an appellate court did not refer the preliminary question to the ECJ deprived him of his right to a fair trial as assured by Article 46, paragraph 1, of the Slovak Constitution[21] and Article 6, paragraph 1, of the European Convention on Human Rights. The SCC did not examine the arguments of the petitioner and refused the petition as inadmissible for lack of jurisdiction due to the fact that the petitioner did not exhaust all available remedies, particularly the one of extraordinary appeal to the Supreme Court.

In the *Commercial Agent* case, the SCC reached a similar conclusion. It refused the petition for inadmissibility because the claimant could have filed an extraordinary appeal to the Supreme Court. Having said that, the SCC nevertheless clearly stated that the reason for extraordinary appeal lay in the fact that the Regional Court in Bratislava was incorrectly composed, meaning that the case of the petitioner was not decided by a lawful judge, and the lawful judge under these circumstances could have only been the European Court of Justice. Since Article 267 TFEU is directly applicable and forms part of national procedural law, national courts are obliged to refer a preliminary question to the ECJ when conditions

17 Slovak Constitutional Court, III. ÚS 151/07-14 [2007].

18 Case C-302/04, *Ynos kft v János Varga* [2006] ECR I-371.

19 Slovak Constitutional Court, (*Commercial Agent*), IV. ÚS 206/08-50 [2008].

20 Slovak Constitutional Court, II. ÚS 90/05-26 [2005].

21 Article 46, paragraph 1, of the Slovak Constitution reads: "Everyone may claim his or her right by procedures laid down by a law at an independent and impartial court or, in cases provided by a law, at other public authority of the Slovak Republic."

stipulated in Article 267 SFEU, as interpreted by the ECJ, are fulfilled. Given that a preliminary reference to the ECJ forms part of the national proceeding and only the ECJ is competent to answer questions concerning interpretation of European law, absence of the reference, when required, means that the national court answers that question instead of the ECJ. In other words, the question is answered (decided) by a judge who is not competent (an unlawful judge). The SCC thus adopted a rationale previously developed by the German Federal Constitutional Court.[22] The Slovak court shifted from the fair trial rationale (based on Article 46, paragraph 1, of the Slovak Constitution), which arose in the aforementioned case, to an examination of whether the claimant's right to a lawful judge (as assured by Article 48, paragraph 1, of the Slovak Constitution[23]) was breached. The SCC declared that the question of when a court was obliged to refer a preliminary question to the ECJ had to be answered and conditions laid down by ordinary courts. The SCC could not answer the question on when a preliminary question is obligatory (i.e., under what conditions). This is the task of the ECJ as "supervisor" of the preliminary question mechanism. In any case, the Slovak Court had to examine whether the communitarian judge was to be considered a lawful judge in the sense of Article 48, paragraph 1, of the Slovak Constitution and, therefore, whether a non-reference of a preliminary question to the ECJ breached one's constitutional right. The Court decided this question in the affirmative, however stating that the conditions under which a court was obliged to refer had to be developed by the ordinary courts, namely by the Supreme Court of Slovakia within its role as a harmonizer of ordinary courts' case law.

Soon after the Slovak Constitutional Court decided to supervise and enforce obligations arising from 267 TFEU-Lis within its jurisdiction by opting for a solution developed by the German Federal Constitutional Court (the lawful judge rationale), its Czech counterpart was confronted with the same question and had no way to escape it. In the *Pfizer* case,[24] the petitioner blamed the Czech Supreme Administrative Court (CSAC) for not submitting a preliminary question to the ECJ. The claimant's objection was based on their right to a fair process under Article 36, paragraph 1, of the Czech Charter of Fundamental Rights. The violation consisted of the fact that the court declined to join Pfizer as a party to the administrative proceeding on the registration of a medicinal product of its competitor. Pfizer considered the product in hand to copy its own product, which resulted in a breach of property rights. The CSAC confirmed the previous decisions of the administrative organ and the lower court, which declined to join Pfizer as a party in the administrative proceeding. The Court based its argumentation on a rather clear provision of national law. However, Pfizer argued that the CSAC should have

22 BVerfG, Order of 9 January 2001, *Europäische Zeitschrift für Wirtschaftsrecht*, 2001: 225.

23 Article 48, paragraph 1, of the Slovak Constitution reads: "No one shall be deprived of a judge. The jurisdiction of courts shall be laid down by law."

24 Czech Constitutional Court, *Pfizer*, II. ÚS 1009/08 [2009].

applied Community law[25] instead of national Czech law. The Constitutional Court, in line with its Slovak counterpart, skipped the "fair trial" rationale in favour of a more specific "lawful judge" reasoning.[26] The CCC asserted that the function of a constitutional court was to observe constitutionality. Thereby, Community law did not form a referential framework for the Court; it did not supervise whether national law was in conflict with European law. This was left to the ordinary courts, which were bound by the cogent provisions of European law that formed for them part of the applicable law. It was up to these courts to detect possible conflict and apply conflict-solving mechanisms (in general, by giving primacy to European law and, in case of the need for interpretation of an applicable European law, by turning to the European Court of Justice to get an authoritative interpretation as required by Article 234 TEC (267 TFEU-Lis)).[27] However, the CCC ought to intervene when the breach of Community law was flagrant, and especially when the ordinary courts disregarded a cogent provision of European law in such a way that the rule of law was endangered.

> Although the referral of a preliminary question is a Community law matter, the failure, in conflict with Community law, to make a reference may, in certain circumstances, also entrain a violation of the constitutionally guaranteed right to one's statutory judge. … A violation of the right to one's statutory judge comes about in the case where a Czech court (against whose decision there is no longer any further remedy afforded by sub-constitutional law) applies Community law but fails, in an arbitrary manner, that is, in conflict with the principle of the law-based state (Article 1 para. 1 of the Constitution of the Czech Republic), to refer a preliminary question to the ECJ. (*Pfizer* case, para. 21)

The CCC thus implicitly adopted the approach of the Slovak Constitutional Court that at first had declined to take over the obligations of ordinary courts to submit a preliminary question to the ECJ when required by European law in light of the ECJ's case law on Article 267 TFEU-Lis, and then, to rule on the conditions which oblige ordinary courts to submit a preliminary question. The CCC used the same reasoning as the SCC in postulating that in laying down conditions of

25 Directive 2001/83/EC [2001] OJ L311, of 28 November 2001, 67.

26 Article 36, para. 1, (on fair trial) reads: "Everyone may assert, through the legally prescribed procedure, his rights before an independent and impartial court or, in specified cases, before another body"; Article 38, para. 1, (on lawful judge) reads: "No one may be removed from the jurisdiction of her lawful judge. The jurisdiction of courts and the competence of judges shall be provided for by law." Cf. also the brief dissenting opinion of Judge Dagmar Lastovecká in the *Pfizer* case. Lastovecká insisted on a solution within the fair trial rationale rather than based on the lawful-judge one.

27 Czech Constitutional Court, *Application Primacy to European Community Law*, Pl. ÚS 12/08 [2008], English translation available at http://angl.concourt.cz/angl_verze/cases.php, accessed 5 August 2009.

referral for the ordinary courts, the CCC would have replaced the ECJ, which was the only court with jurisdiction over this matter. However, and again in accord with its Slovak counterpart, the CCC felt obliged to intervene when disregard for European law was perceived to be of such scale as to effectively breach Czech constitutionality as well.

> The Constitutional Court asserts that it deems as arbitrary action such conduct by a court of last instance applying a norm of Community law where that court has entirely omitted to deal with the issue whether it should refer a preliminary question to the ECJ and has not duly substantiated its failure to refer, including the assessment of the exceptions which the ECJ has elaborated in its jurisprudence. (*Pfizer* case, para. 22)

Both the Czech and the Slovak constitutional courts adopt a position that defers to the European Court of Justice established case law on Article 267 TFEU-Lis (ex 234 TEC). They agree that the ordinary courts of both countries are bound by requirements of Article 267 TFEU-Lis which forms part of the law and that a denial to follow such requirements results in a breach of these courts' duties. At the same time, both courts tacitly deny being subject to the very same requirement arising from the Treaty. Reason for the denial is found in the different role that constitutional courts reserve for themselves in the system – that is, to supervise constitutionality within their jurisdictions. In general, questions of European law cannot arise in front of them. European law will play a role in their reasoning only insofar as the matter touches upon constitutionality itself. Therefore, when ordinary courts disregard European law, the constitutional courts intervene only when the problem is of such importance as to affect the very constitutionality of their systems.

It is worth directing the attention of the reader also to the peculiar, although rather speculative, observation that the Czech Constitutional Court had avoided giving clear answers on the question of obligations of national courts under Article 267 TFEU-Lis and on its own role in that matter. Only after its Slovak counterparts worked out their position, the Czech Constitutional Court adopted the same approach (it has to be borne in mind that the wording of both countries' constitutional provisions on fair trial and lawful judge were quite similar) without mentioning the Slovak Constitutional Court's *Commercial Agent* case at all and instead referring to the German Federal Constitutional Court's case law (*Pfizer* case, para. 23).[28] Behaviour such as that of the CCC corroborates the idea about an increasing differentiation in the existing network of channels in the

28 To be sure, the SCC explicitly referred to the German Federal Constitutional Court as its source for drawing the lawful-judge rationale. From this point of view, it makes sense that the Czech court pointed to the same original source. However, the long struggle of both courts with the matter, and the timing of the CCC decision suggest that their decisions were not merely coincident.

European constitutional space. It seems that in this very concrete case, the Czech Constitutional Court wanted to "speak" both from the East to the West, and from the new Member States to the old. This claim will be further substantiated soon after the second sphere of inter-judicial cooperation in the European constitutional space is examined.

Material Cooperation: The Ultimate Supervisor

The space of material cooperation has been significantly determined by the wording of "the European clause" in the Czech and Slovak constitutions. The differences between "the European clause" in each of these constitutional orders partly explain the different delimitation of the scope of material cooperation with the ECJ.

In the Czech Republic, the government submitted a constitutional bill concerning the European Clause to the Parliament in March 2001. The governmental draft bill[29] of the constitutional amendment contained rather explicit reference to the effects of European law in the Czech Republic. However, it was altered by the Parliament. The respective Articles, which the deputies deleted, read:

> The Constitutional order, international treaties, which form part of the legal order and shall have precedence over laws, as well as laws and other legal regulations shall not be interpreted and applied to against obligations arising from the membership of the Czech Republic in an international institution ...[30]
> ... If the judge decides that the law applicable to the decided matter is contrary to an international treaty, which forms part of the legal order and shall have precedence over laws, he or she shall apply the provisions of this international treaty.[31]

Such a general interpretive clause,[32] consisting of an explicit command to the judge on how to solve conflicts, if enacted, would have meant giving European law effect fully controlled by the European Court of Justice.[33] Instead, a more moderate Euro-amendment was enacted, its core being formed by Article 1 paragraph 2, Article 10, and Article 10a of the Constitution. At first sight, Article

29 Chamber of Deputies, III. electoral term, press no. 884/0.

30 Article 10b of the Governmental draft bill.

31 Article 95, paragraph 2, of the Governmental draft bill.

32 See the special part of the Explanatory Report on Article 10b of the Governmental draft bill.

33 It is hard to speculate on how such provision would alter the CCC's approach taken in the *Sugar Quotas Regulation II* and subsequent cases. Although it is possible that the CCC would be able to reach its current doctrine despite such a general interpretation clause (i.e., foremost by establishing limited conferral of competences), its reasoning would be far more contestable.

10a creates way of conferring competences to the EU. Article 10 alongside Article 1, paragraph 2, provide for international treaties (including the European Treaties) to take effect within the Czech legal order (through precedence in application based on the monist approach). However, a sharp scholarly debate about which of the two constitutional provisions forms the basis for the effect EU law in the Czech Republic took over the national legal journals (Kühn and Kysela 2004; Kühn 2004a; Malenovský 2004, 2005).

On one hand, Article 10 and Article 1, paragraph 2, state that certain "treaties ... form part of the legal order; if a treaty provides for something different from what a statute provides, then the treaty shall apply" and the "Czech Republic shall observe its obligations resulting from international law"; on the other hand, Article 10a, paragraph 1, provides that "[c]ertain powers of the Czech authorities may be transferred by a treaty to an international organization or institution". From a classic, international law point of view, Articles 10 and 1 are clearly input provisions, while Article 10a is an output provision. Nevertheless, the majority of the Czech scholarship argued that Article 10a has a two-way effect regarding EU law.[34] This Article is, at the same time, the constitutional basis for conferral of competences to the Union organs and the constitutional basis for the validity and effects of EU law in the Czech Republic. It is the view of this author that this is the correct interpretation, as it distinguishes the European legal order from international law. It was the European Court of Justice that came up with the innovative and far-reaching account on the autonomous nature of the Treaties. However, the ECJ has not been fully consistent in whether the distinct nature of the Treaties also implies a separation of the European legal order from the national legal orders. This author's vies is that one of the most important reasons for which the ECJ differentiated the European legal order from international law was to prevent making the application of European law in the Member States' legal orders dependent on their internal rules on international law transposition. In other words, with the differentiation of the European legal order from international law the European Court of Justice asserted that the European legal order is autonomous from the national ones.

However, according to the Czech Constitutional Court:

> There is no doubt that, as a result of the Czech Republic's accession to the EC, or EU, a fundamental change occurred within the Czech legal order, as at that moment the Czech Republic took over into its national law the entire mass of European law. (*Sugar Quotas Regulation II* case, Section A-3, paragraph 4)

As far as the provisions of Article 10 and Article 1, paragraph 2, do not support the autonomous character of European law, the CCC opted correctly for Article 10a as legal basis of European law validity and applicability in the Czech Republic. Nevertheless, the quoted rationale on the "entire mass of European law being taken over into the Czech legal order" shows misunderstanding of the

34 For an opposite account see Malenovský 2008: 32–33.

autonomous nature of European law as separated not only from international law, but also from the national legal orders. This misconception can be explained by the already mentioned inconsistency of the ECJ's earlier decisions, where in the *Van Gend* case the Court claimed that the "Community constitutes a new legal order of international law for the benefit of which the States have limited their sovereign rights…",[35] while in the *Costa* case, the ECJ ruled that "[b]y contrast with ordinary international treaties, the EEC Treaty has created its own legal system which … became an integral part of the legal systems of the Member States …".[36]

If the Czech Constitutional Court deems European law as part of its legal order (as it obviously does) then, inevitably, it has to decide on its position/rank in the hierarchy of norms within the Czech legal order. The consequences for pluralism in the European Union are significant. If the entire mass of EU law is taken over into (that is, becomes part of) the Czech legal order, then constitutional plurality does not exist. However, the CCC does not, to a certain extent, object to the separation of powers within the system; that is, the CCC accepts that it is the European Court of Justice that exclusively interprets European law, that is, that the ECJ exclusively interprets part of the Czech legal order. Constitutional plurality is thus being replaced by institutional or interpretive pluralism. Institutional or interpretive pluralism is Daniel Halberstam's description of the US constitutional system (Halberstam 2009a: 328, 2009b). This kind of pluralism emerges as a consequence of the unsettled question of who is the final interpreter of the US Constitution. Halberstam employs this description in order to compare the US constitutional system with the European one. Applied to the developments in our case, where due to a misunderstanding on the nature of the European legal order by some MS' constitutional courts, such as the Czech one, constitutional pluralism changes into institutional or interpretive constitutionalism as far as these Member States' constitutional courts claim to be the ultimate arbiter on the part of the European constitutional space delimited by their claimed jurisdiction. For instance, the CCC adamantly rejects constitutional pluralism by including the "entire mass of European law" into its own legal order. As long as the CCC leaves the exclusive interpretive authority of European law to the ECJ, there is, indeed, no pluralism at all. However, the CCC denies the competence of the ECJ to interpret European law when it comes to the material core of the Czech Constitution. Here, an interpretative or institutional pluralism takes place because at this stage we have two institutions that hold a legitimate claim on being the final arbiter of a constitutional conflict.

The Slovak Euro-Amendment of the Constitution is rather closer to the original version of the Czech Governmental Bill than to its finally adopted version,

35 Case 26/62, *N.V. Algemene Transport – en Expeditie Onderneming van Gend & Loos v Nederlandse administratie der belastingen* [1963] ECR 1, 12 (emphasis added).

36 Case 6/64, *Flaminio Costa v ENEL* [1964] ECR 585, 593; Case 6/64, *Flaminio Costa v ENEL* [1964] ECR 585 (emphasis added).

as it explicitly tackles the question of primacy. The respective part of Article 7, paragraph 2, of the Slovak Constitution reads:

> The Slovak Republic may, by an international treaty, which was ratified and promulgated in the way laid down by a law, or on the basis of such a treaty, transfer the exercise of a part of its powers to the European Communities and the European Union. Legally binding acts of the European Communities and of the European Union shall have precedence over laws of the Slovak Republic.

The Slovak Constitutional Court has not so far contested the absolute supremacy of European law. The Slovak Constitution, unlike the Czech Constitution, does not contain an explicit eternity clause. The Slovak Constitution contains several provisions in favour of the effects of international law in the Slovak Republic; this fact, alongside the precedence clause mentioned above and in the absence of an eternity clause, makes the Slovak constitutional order more open towards the effects of the autonomous European legal order.[37] However, the SCC seems not to accept that it is a court under Article 267 TFEU-Lis (ex 234 TEC), as its jurisdiction and the ECJ's one do not overlap and thus a question of European law can hardly arise in a proceeding before the SCC.[38] This approach leads to a situation where the SCC transforms any question concerning European law into a question of national constitutional law (cf. *Antidiscrimination Act* case and *Commercial Agent* case). The Court avoids a clash with the ECJ due to its ability to transform a European obligation into a national constitutional obligation with the same effect. However, sooner or later the Court would have to deal with the scope of its precedence clause of Article 7, paragraph 2, that goes on to say: "Legally binding acts of the European Communities and of the European Union shall have precedence over laws of the Slovak Republic." The precedence clause may be interpreted as positioning secondary European law in-between the national Constitution and Slovak ordinary laws. Moreover, it does not solve the question of a possible conflict between European secondary law and an international treaty on human rights within the Slovak legal order (Azud 2003: 598 et seq., 2006: 344 et seq.).

Unlike its Slovak counterpart, the Czech Constitutional Court decided to assume the role of ultimate supervisor of the effect of European law in the Czech Republic. The Court developed its *ultra vires* test in the *Sugar Quotas Regulation II* judgement:

> [The] conferral of a part of its powers is naturally a conditional conferral, as the original bearer of sovereignty, as well as the powers flowing therefrom,

37 For the debate on further refining the Slovak Constitution (especially on how to enhance national parliamentary control over legislative decisions of the Slovak government in the Council of EU), see Somorová 2004 and Balog 2004.

38 For an analysis on this question cf. Mazák 2005a, 2005b.

> still remains the Czech Republic ... the conditional nature of the delegation of these powers is manifested on two planes: formal and substantive one. The first of these planes concerns the power attributes of state sovereignty itself, the second plane concerns the substantive component of the exercise of state power. In other words, the delegation of a part of the powers of national organs may persist only insofar as these powers are exercised in a manner compatible with the preservation of the foundations of state sovereignty of the Czech Republic, and in a manner which does not threaten the very essence of the substantive law-based state. ... According to Art. 9, para. 2, of the Constitution of the Czech Republic,[39] the essential attributes of a democratic state governed by the rule of law, remain beyond the reach of the Constituent Assembly itself. [reference added]

In the *Lisbon Treaty* case,[40] the Court broadened its referential framework. It applied, as a point of reference, the constitutional order of the Czech Republic taken as a whole, and not only its material core. The arguments of the Court were:

a. The subject of the review is primary law, not secondary law as in the previous proceedings.
b. The Lisbon Treaty is not a valid law yet and the Court is therefore not bound by an obligation of Euro-conforming interpretation.
c. Given that an international treaty under the meaning of Article 10a requires the same majority as is required for a constitutional amendment, to limit the review only to the "fundamental core" of the Constitution would to a large extent deprive the CCC of preliminary constitutional review of treaties, that is, of its core function.
d. The Constitution does not distinguish between "ordinary" international treaties under Article 49 and treaties under Article 10a.
e. The text of Article 87(2) of the Constitution explicitly envisages the whole constitutional order as a point of reference for this review, not only its fundamental core.
f. The Parliament's role is limited as it can only approve or disapprove an international treaty.

However, first, the CCC limited such an approach to solely an *ex ante* review on the constitutionality of an international treaty and, second, the Court throughout the *Lisbon Treaty* judgement repeatedly emphasized that the ultimate limits rested in the material core of the constitution, so that in fact its referential framework remained the material core. The Court also touched upon the question of the content of the constitutional core, although it tended to avoid giving a clear

---

39 Article 9, paragraph 2, reads: "Any changes in the essential requirements for a democratic state governed by the rule of law are impermissible."

40 Czech Constitutional Court, *Lisbon Treaty*, Pl. ÚS 19/08 [2008].

definition. According to the Court, it follows from Article 10a, paragraph 1, that only *certain* powers may be transferred by a treaty to an international organization. This Article must be interpreted in connection with Article 1, paragraph 1, and Article 9, paragraph 2, of the Constitution. It follows that the transfer of powers cannot go so far as to violate the very essence of the Republic as a sovereign and democratic rule-of-law-based state, founded on the respect for the rights and freedoms of human beings and of citizens, or to establish a change of the essential requirements for democratic rule in a law-based state. The Court admitted that the notion of a "sovereign state" is not uncontested and is hard to define at an abstract level (Bříza 2009: 149–150). Thus, the transfer of sovereign powers under the Constitution has certain limits.[41] In the words of the Court (in the *Czech Lisbon Treaty* judgement, paragraph 109):

> [t]hese limits should be left primarily to the legislature to specify, because this is *a priori* a political question which provides the legislature with wide discretion; interference by the Constitutional Court should come into consideration as *ultima ratio*, i.e., in a situation where the scope of discretion was clearly exceeded, and Art. 1 para. 1 of the Constitution was affected, because there was a transfer of powers beyond the scope of Art. 10a of the Constitution.

While the first exception from the absolute supremacy of European law lies in a serious and flagrant *ultra vires* action of the Community/Union (otherwise the CCC relies on the EU institutional framework that constitutes the control exercised by the ECJ which oversees that the Community/Union acts within its conferred powers); the second exemption follows the well-known *Solange I* argument of the German Federal Constitutional Court that it is for the national constitutional court to ultimately supervise the level of human rights protection in its jurisdiction. In the words of the Czech Constitutional Court in the *Lisbon Treaty* judgement (paragraph 196, summarizing the *Sugar Quotas Regulation II* doctrine):

> As regards possible conflict between the standard of protection of human rights and fundamental freedoms ensured by the constitutional order of the Czech Republic and the standard ensured in the European Union, it is appropriate to point out that protection of fundamental rights and freedoms falls in the area of the "material core" of the Constitution, which is beyond the reach of the constitutional framers (cf. Pl. ÚS 50/04). If, from this point of view, the standard of protection ensured in the European Union were unsuitable, the bodies of the

41 The German Federal Constitutional Court in its recent *Lisbon Treaty* judgement showed that delimitation of a rather concrete situation (based on the evaluation of transferred competences), after which sovereignty would be lost, was possible (BVerfG, (*Lisbon Treaty*), 2 BvE 2/08 [2009]; English translation available at http://www.bverfg.de/entscheidungen/es20090630_2bve000208en.html, accessed 5 July 2009.

> Czech Republic would have to again take over the transferred powers, in order to ensure that this standard was observed ...

The scope of material cooperation in the European constitutional space broadened with the accession of CEE countries, at the expense of formal cooperation. While formal cooperation works on a dialogue-mode, material cooperation tends to be bargain-focused instead. The Eastern enlargement has thus limited the inter-judicial dialogue and replaced it with bargaining to an extent that endangers judicial cooperation itself. What are the reasons for the non-cooperative behaviour of the new MS judiciaries?

Explanation for the Increasing Divergence in the European Constitutional Space: The Specific Features of CEE Judiciary's Transformation

Constitutional Culture

According to Ruti Teitel (1994: 170 et seq.), the prominent position of the constitutional courts in the constitutional design of post-communist states was a combination of the revolutionary reaction on the former regime and the transitional substance of the period in which they were established. The first reason consists of the fact that the communist regimes disposed of constitutional charters that ought to formally resemble democratic constitutions. However, the rights these charters granted were mostly just on paper. Due to the fact that the communist regimes left new governments with constitutions more or less adaptable to the new circumstances, the post-revolutionary effort was more concerned with the immediate need of economic reforms. Therefore the effort was directed to the transition towards the market economy and the creation of new basic charters was left for later time. The old constitutions were only quickly wiped of the most obvious totalitarian features. After all, the rights of individuals, the separation of powers and other principles resembling democratic liberal states could be found in these constitutions. What was needed was an independent and impartial institution separated from the legislature and the executive, which would give new meaning to the constitutional provisions and enforce them (Teitel 1994: 173). Constitutional courts filled, unlike ordinary courts, with new people not compromised by the former regime were the ideal candidates for the job. Their task was nothing less than to change the constitutional (legal) culture. The second reason for the prominence of new MS constitutional courts lies in the transitional substance of the new democracies which pressed the courts to assure the constitutionality of the flux of new laws and regulatory regimes without any delay. The constitutional courts were armed with centralized abstract review opened to a broad spectrum of petitioners, especially to political actors. According to Teitel, a new paradigm of active judicial review was established (Teitel 1994: 184–185) and the constitutional courts were embroiled in the essential political controversies of the day.

The absence of the rule of law, democracy and human rights protection in totalitarian regimes has signified, for the states of Central and Eastern Europe after the fall of the regimes, that the highest courts in these new democracies should obtain a symbolically prominent position in their systems of governance (Holländer 2003: 73).[42] During communism, in the absence of separation of powers, the judiciary, confronted with a question of vital state interests, followed the orders of the "Party and Government" (Kühn 2004b: 539).[43] The new constitutional courts enjoyed wide public support and disposed of enviable legitimacy in comparison with most of the other political actors in the system.

Over-separation of Powers

The way to transform "paper rights" into real ones was seen as the strict separation of the judiciary from the other branches. The constitutional courts established themselves as very active and influential actors that dictate the rules of the game to the other actors in the political system (Sadurski 2008: 3). They were prepared to protect this misbalanced separation of the judiciary from the other branches. The newly created constitutional courts of the post-communist countries therefore gained the respect of the public as the courts were independent guardians of social values (Zemánek 2006: 258). It turns out, at least for systemic reasons, that the position of constitutional courts in the new MS became relatively stronger compared to that in the old MS (Sadurski 2008: 3).

The "Juge-automate" Thesis

Considerable public support for constitutional courts in the countries of CEE stems from the doctrinal view of the role of the judiciary as the "judge as a mechanical interpreter of the law". In this perception, the function of the court itself in the system of governance cannot be attacked because the court only reads and applies the law made by the political organs. Bluntly put, the parliament enacts legislation, which the courts simply apply. It follows that an unjust judicial decision can be attributed only to the legislator and not to the judiciary that, from the nature of its function, cannot redress faulty legislation.[44] Errors in judicial decisions are seen

42 Holländer notices a "paradox of acceptance and denial" of constitutional courts in post-communist countries: while the public accepts the high authority of the constitutional court, the judiciary of the general courts maintain a critical attitude towards the constitutional court. Höllander sees the reason – in the words of Boštjan Župančič– in the "insufficient understanding of the relation between law and democracy" (Župančič 1998: 487).

43 For a picture of everyday reality of communist judiciary see Ulč 1972.

44 In 2002, Václav Havel, defending his nomination of Eliška Wagnerová as a Judge of the Constitutional Court at the Senate of the Czech Parliament, criticized this formalist approach to law (in Kühn's translation (2004b: 563)): "It is mechanical, I would like to say senseless, application of law, which almost becomes an object of some cult … It is

as due to personal faults of the judge because of lack of professional expertise or blemished reputation (e.g., if a judge who served during the totalitarian regime remains in office).[45] Put in other words, in post-communist political systems, the constitutional courts are not infallible because they are final, but they are the final arbiters because they are considered *ipso facto* to be infallible.[46] Paradoxically, this strictly positivist doctrine, which was developed in the late-nineteenth century under the influence of the Enlightenment in opposition to the "legal chaos of feudalism", was strongly condemned by Marxism-Leninism as "bourgeois", but in practice it lead to ultra-formalism of judicial interpretation (Kühn 2004b: 533 and 539; David and Brierley 1985: 242).[47] Yet another paradox is that the *juge-automate* concept, attributed to Montesquieu, who in *De L'Esprit des Lois* defines judges as *la bouche de la loi* (book XI, 6 (49)), is a misinterpretation put forward by Maillia-Garat, spokesman of the Napoleonic legislative assembly know as *Tribunat*, an organ filled by positivists. In fact, Montesquieu spoke about the opposite concept – the one of judge-made law ("judge is the speaking law" or *judex est lex loquens*) (Schönfeld 2008: 275). However, French bourgeois positivists attributed an opposite meaning to Montesquieu's thesis and Marxists-Leninists made it even more rigorous in order to overcome the bourgeois system.

Individual Rights above All

Wojciech Sadurski (2008: 4) notices that the states of the former communist bloc expected and believed that prospective EU membership would guarantee them a high standard of human rights protection, rule of law and democracy and prevent possible negative intrastate developments. After accession, paradoxically, the

---

an approach toward the application of law which does not permit any consideration of the law's sense, meaning or circumstances, any consideration of the probable legislative intent or even the core of law's value in a hard case. Although the law is a human product, it attains almost metaphysical authority." (stenographic record in Czech, the Senate of the Parliament of the Czech Republic, 14 March 2002, available at http://www.senat.cz/xqw/webdav/pssenat/original/ 11921/11921, 43, accessed 20 January 2008.

45 The judiciary in the systems of "real-existing socialism" lost almost all its prestige. This can be perceived as a consequence of combination of a bourgeois formalism, the communist doctrine of democratic centralism and socialist planned economy, which limited the courts' workload on deciding financially marginal family and civil cases (Kühn 2004b: 550).

46 A paraphrase of the words of the US Supreme Court Justice Robert Jackson in his concurrent opinion in *Brown v. Allen*, 344 U.S. 443 (1953) – "We are not final because we are infallible, but we are infallible only because we are final" – which signifies the difference in perception of the role of the judiciary in modern liberal democracies contrasted to the one in post-communist states.

47 "In bourgeois laws, the judge has become the pivot of the legal system. Socialist evolution has not made this error." (Szabó 1960, English translation in David and Brierley 1985: 242).

new MS felt that these standards could actually be threatened by the effect that European law would have on their lands.[48]

The explanation lies, according to Sadurski (2004: 7–75; 2008: 3), in the "sovereignty conundrum". The fall of the Soviet regime in CEE countries led to the restoration of full sovereignty which, contrary to the doctrine of limited sovereignty preached by the Warsaw Pact, was the basic constructive element of the new democracies. CEE countries have acceded to international organizations, one after the other; and constitutional scholars have been faced with the hard task of finding an adequate solution as to how to address the notion of a "weakened" state-sovereignty as a result of membership in these international organizations while chasing the shadow of the "limited sovereignty" connotation of the past.[49] Anneli Albi (2008: 79), on the other hand, sees the explanation in the negative reaction to the pre-1989 preference for the common interest over individual rights, which led to preference for individual rights over the interests of the society in the post-totalitarian period.

Eric Voeten offers empirical evidence on the dilemma of the post-communist states of CEE in his analysis on the politics behind the appointment process to the European Court of Human Rights (ECHR). Voeten shows that states aspiring to EU accession, in an attempt to increase their negotiating leverage before the European Commission, appoint activist judges in the ECHR,[50] thus signalling to the Union that they are prepared to ensure high standards of human rights protection (Voeten 2007: 693). Moravcsik (2000: 245–246) adds that states in transition want to secure the level of human rights protection that they have achieved against possible negative intrastate developments (the so-called "locking in domestic democracy").[51] Conversely, other states with high standards of protection are inclined to appoint non-activist judges to the ECHR because they classify their

48 Before EU accession, the majority of the CEE constitutional courts proclaimed that a "return to Europe" would ensure further democratic development of their countries. Conversely, after accession, they pleaded for democratic foundations against the absolute supremacy of EU law. An exception to the use of references to EU democratic standards was the Hungarian Constitutional Court in its ruling on free speech (judgement 18/2004 (V.25.) AB); cf. Sadurski 2008: 26–30.

49 A serene example of this ambivalence was shown by the Polish Constitutional Tribunal in its *Accession Treaty* case. The court, among others, dealt with the alleged conflict between the Polish Constitution and the right to vote and be elected in local elections ensured by the EU Treaty to citizens of other MS. The Court concluded that the limitation of Art. 62(1) of the Polish Constitution was not related to EU accession, but was assumed much earlier and constituted an obligation within the framework of the UN and the (European) Convention on Human Rights.

50 Contrary to the procedure in the ECJ, a judge nominated by the country of which the defendant is a citizen always sits on the bench.

51 Membership in the Council of Europe as a safety lock against undemocratic development is mentioned also by Sadurski (2008: 4); however, Voeten's empirical model is not able to prove such a hypothesis.

national level of human rights protection as sufficiently high and try to avoid external intrusion.[52]

All in All: Complicated Net of Channels and Modes of Inter-Judicial Cooperation in an Enlarged Union

The constitutional courts of the new MS find themselves caught in a dilemma. On the one hand, these new courts need to prove to the old MS that they have enough expertise to handle the effects of EU law in their jurisdictions,[53] while on the other hand they want to assert their authority and gain respect.[54] The constitutional courts of the old MS concluded in "Solange, chapter II" (Sadurski 2008: 1–2) that the protection of human rights provided by the Union is comparable to the one ensured at their national level. In contrast, the new constitutional courts, by confronting the ECJ's jurisprudence, try to make a different point: they want to assert that democratic standards reached by the new MS are comparable to that of the old MS. The new constitutional courts are prepared to show that they are, in fact, as competent as the constitutional courts of old MS to supervise the level of democracy and the rule of law in the EU and protect citizens against potential EU excesses. They wish to join the old Member States' constitutional courts in their supervisory function, and in cooperation with the ECJ, to ensure the democratic functioning of the Union.

52 Voeten (2007: 691–692) mentions the examples of the United Kingdom, Iceland and Austria; nevertheless, he suggests (2007: 676–677) yet another explanation: states with mature human rights protection would rather nominate activist judges who can help them let other states comply with liberal objectives, while their own protection of human rights would rarely be subjected to the ECHR review.

53 E.g., the Czech Constitutional Court in the pre-accession period took into account not only European law, but also the ECJ case-law – cf. cases *Škoda auto*, III. ÚS 31/97 and *Milk Quotas*, Pl. 5/01, the latter is available in English translation at http://angl.concourt.cz/angl_verze/cases.php, accessed 20 March 2008; cf. also the Polish Supreme Administrative Court's judgement of 13 March 2000 in *Senagpo*; see also Kühn (2005a: 566–567) and Zemánek (2006: 258–259), who quotes other examples ofEuro-friendly pre-accession decisions of the Polish Constitutional Tribunal.

54 Cf., on the one hand, the Euro-critical tone in the decisions of the Polish Constitutional Tribunal (*Accession Treaty* case), of the Hungarian Constitutional Court (*Agricultural Surplus* case), and partly also in the Czech Constitutional Court (*Sugar quotas II* case) that contrasted with the Euro-friendly results of the decisions. The Polish Constitutional Tribunal's decision in the *European Arrest Warrant* case is similar, although the result does not seem to be Euro-friendly at first sight (Sadurski 2008: 24–25).

Conclusion

This chapter aimed to rethink the current understanding of the European constitutional space in light of the Eastern enlargement, which brought the new constitutional thinking and language of the CEE constitutional courts (and scholars) into this shared space. The current scholarship's view of European constitutionalism is based on the coexistence of the MS constitutions and the EU constitutional charter. This peaceful coexistence is assured by a dialogue between multiple constitutional interpreters (the national constitutional courts and the European Court of Justice). This newly developed constitutional construct tries to replace the Kelsenian system, which might have worked well in centralized sovereign states of the Westphalian type, but is an obstacle for the development of the poly-centred European Union. The fundamental aspect of the Kelsenian system is the hierarchy of norms whereby the validity of a norm derives from compliance with a higher norm. After the fall of communist regimes, the CEE countries were faced with a process of reconstitutionalization. They looked back into their democratic interwar past and tried to revive these old concepts, albeit sometimes enriched with Western constitutional solutions and human rights achievements. However, this approach mostly neglected the 50-year development of Euro-Atlantic constitutionalism. After 15 years of reconstitutionalization, the old concepts were back. The doctrinal vision of the legal order that the constitutional courts in the new Member States in former communist countries have makes it intellectually difficult for them to grasp the idea of constitutional pluralism, which they try to avoid altogether by dragging the European legal order into their national orders. This foreign element in the European constitutional space limits its benefits and its further development. It creates new dense and complicated net of channels and modes of cooperation. Especially in the area of material inter-judicial cooperation, the constructive dialogue mode is vastly compromised by unilateral action with a bargaining taste. However, the declared openness of the vast area of the new Member States' constitutional law towards the effects of European constitutional principles and, though unwelcome, reformulation of European law requirements into national constitutional obligations have eventually lead to a significant transformation of national constitutional law, its interpretation and main principles.

References

Albi, A. (2008), CEE Constitutional Courts and Application of EU Law: Constitutional Rights versus Supremacy, in M. Hofmann (ed.) *Europarecht und die Gerichte der Transformationsstaaten*, Baden-Baden, Nomos, 77–96.

Azud, J. (2003), K otázke vplyvu vstupu SR do EÚ na suverenitu SR v kontexte článku 7 Ústavy Slovenskej republiky, *Právny obzor*, 86(6), 591–609.

Azud, J. (2006), Suverenita štátu a niektoré otázky jej obmedzení, *Právny obzor*, 89(4), 341–357.

Baquero Cruz, J. (2008), The Legacy of the Maastricht-Urteil and the Pluralist Movement, *European Law Journal*, 14(4), 389–422.

Balog, B. (2004), Úvahy o neschválenom návrhu novely Ústavy Slovenskej republiky, *Právny obzor*, 87(3), 202–228.

Bříza, P. (2009), Case Note: The Czech Republic, the Constitutional Court on the Lisbon Treaty Decision of 26 November 2008, *European Constitutional Law Review*, 5(1), 143–164.

David, R. and Brierley, J.E.C. (1985), *Major Legal Systems in the World Today. An Introduction to the Comparative Study of Law*, 3rd edn, London, Stevens and Sons.

Halberstam, D. (2009a), Constitutional Heterarchy: The Centrality of Conflict in the European Union and the United States, in J. Dunoff and J. Trachtman (eds) *Ruling the World? Constitutional, International Law and Global Government*, Cambridge, Cambridge University Press, 326–355.

Halberstam, D. (2009b), Pluralism in Marbury and Van Gend, in M.P. Maduro and L. Azoulai (eds) *The Past and the Future of EU Law: Revisiting the Classics on the 50th Anniversary of the Rome Treaty*, Oxford, Hart Publishing.

Holländer, P. (2003), *Ústavněprávní argumentace. Ohlédnutí po deseti letech Ústavního soudu*, Prague, Linde.

Hopmann, P.T. (1995), Two Paradigms of Negotiation: Bargaining and Problem Solving, *Annals of the American Academy of Political and Social Science*, 542(1): 24–47.

Kühn, Z. and Kysela, J. (2004), Na základě čeho bude působit komunitární právo v českém právním řádu? *Právní rozhledy*, 12(1), 23–27.

Kühn, Z. (2004a), Ještě jednou k ústavnímu základu působení komunitárního práva v českém právním řádu. *Právní rozhledy*, 12(10), 395–397.

Kühn, Z. (2004b), World apart: Western and Central European Judicial Culture, *The American Journal of Comparative Law*, 52(3), 531–567.

Kühn, Z. (2005a), The Application of European Law in the new Member States: Several (early) Predictions, *German Law Journal*, 6(3), 563–582.

Kühn, Z. (2005b), European Law in the Empires of Mechanical Jurisprudence: The Judicial Application of European Law in Central European Candidate Countries, *Croatian Yearbook of European Law and Policy*, 1, 55–73.

Kumm, M. (1998), Who is the Final Arbiter of Constitutionality in Europe? *Jean Monnet Working Papers*, 10/98, available at http://www.jeanmonnetprogram.org/ papers/98/98-10-.html, accessed 18 November 2008.

MacCormick, N. (1999), *Questioning Sovereignty. Law State, and Nation in the European Commonwealth*, Oxford, Oxford University Press.

Maduro, M. (2008), Interpreting European Law – Judicial Adjudication in a Context of Constitutional Pluralism, *Working Papers IE Law School*, WPLS08-02, available at http://papers.ssrn.com/sol3/papers.cfm?abstract_id=1134503, accessed 18 November 2008.

Malenovský, J. (2004), Ve věci ústavního základu působení komunitárního práva uvnitř ČR nebylo řečeno poslední slovo, *Právní rozhledy*, 12(6), 227–229.

Malenovský, J. (2005), Vítězství "dogmatiků" nad "pragmatiky" se odkládá, *Právní rozhledy*, 13(11), 408–412.

Malenovský, J. (2008), The Relations between Constitutional Law, Community Law and International Law according to the Czech Constitution: Still Ambiguities to be Resolved, in M. Hofmann (ed.) *Europarecht und die Gerichte der Transformationsstaaten*, Baden-Baden, Nomos, 31–39.

Marks, G., Hooghe, L. and Blank, K. (1996), European Integration from the 1980s: State-centric vs. Multi-level Governance, *Journal of Common Market Studies*, 34(3), 341–78.

Mayer, F. (2003), The European Constitution and the Courts. Adjudicating European Constitutional Law in a Multilevel System, *Jean Monnet Working Papers*, 9/03, available at http://centers.law.nyu.edu/jeanmonnet/papers/03/030901-03.pdf, accessed 20 March 2008.

Mazák, J. (2005a), Príspevok Ústavného súdu Slovenskej republiky při uplatňovaní práv a plnení povinností na komunitárnej úrovni, *Jurisprudence*, 14(6), 11–14.

Mazák, J. (2005b), National Judiciary after the Accession of the Slovak Republic to the European Union, *Zeitschrift für öffentliches Recht*, 60(4), 541–547.

Moravcsik, A. (2000), The Origins of Human Rights Regimes: Democratic Delegation in Postwar Europe, *International Organization*, 54(2), 217–252.

Oppenheimer A. (ed.) (1994), *The Relationship Between European Community Law and National Law: The Cases*, vol. 1, Cambridge, Cambridge University Press.

Pernice, I. (2002), Multilevel Constitutionalism in the European Union, *European Law Review*, 27(5), 511–529.

Pernice, I. (2006), The Global Dimension of Multilevel Constitutionalism. A Legal Response to the Challenges of Globalisation, in P.-M. Dupuy (eds) *Völkerrecht als Wertordnung: Festschrift für Christian Tomuschat/Common Values in International Law: Essays in Honour of Christian Tomuschat*, Kehl, Engel, 973–1006.

Pernice, I. (2009), The Treaty of Lisbon. Multilevel Constitutionalism in Action, *Columbia Journal of European Law*, 15(3), 349–407.

Sadurski, W. (2004), The Role of the EU Charter of Rights in the Process of Enlargement, in by G.A. Bermann and K. Pistor, *Law and Governance in an Enlarged European Union*, Oxford, Hart Publishing, 61–96.

Sadurski, W. (2008), "Solange, Chapter 3": Constitutional Courts in Central Europe – Democracy – European Union, *European Law Journal*, 14(1), 1–35.

Schönfeld, K.M. (2008), Rex, Lex et Judex: Montesquieu and *la bouche de la loi* Revisited, *European Constitutional Law Review*, 4(2), 274–301.

Somorová, Ľ. (2004), Vstup Slovenskej republiky do Európskej únie a ústavné zmeny, *Právny obzor*, 87(2), 140–149.

Stone Sweet, A. and Brunell, T.L. (1998), Constructing a Supranational Constitution: Dispute Resolution and Governance in the European Community, *American Political Science Review*, 92(1), 63–81.

Szabó, I. (1960), *A jogszabályok értelmezése*, Budapest: KJK.

Teitel, R. (1994), Post-communist Constitutionalism: A Transitional Perspective, *Columbia Human Rights Law Review*, 26(1), 167–190.

Ulč, O. (1972), *The Judge in a Communist State. A View From Within*, Columbus, Ohio University Press.

Voeten, E. (2007), The Politics of International Judicial Appointments: Evidence from the European Court of Human Rights, *International Organization*, 61(4), 669–701.

Walker, N. (2002), The Idea of Constitutional Pluralism, *Modern Law Review*, 65(3), 317–359.

Walker, N. (2003), Late Sovereignty in the European Union, in N. Walker (ed.) *Sovereignty in Transition*, Oxford, Hart Publishing, 3–32.

Zemánek, J. (2006), The Constitutional Courts in the New Member States and the Uniform Application of European Law, in I. Pernice, J. Kokott and C. Saunders (eds) *The Future Of The European Judicial System in a Comparative Perspective*, Baden-Baden, Nomos, 257–265.

Zemánek, J. (2009), Přezkum ústavnosti Lisabonské smlouvy: obsahové otázky, *Jurisprudence*, 18(1), 32–41.

Župančič, B. (1998), Od souboje ke smlouvě, aneb co vlastně ustavuje ústava, *Právník* 137(6), 476–498.

Chapter 6
The Constitutional versus the European Role of the Judiciary in Poland

Piotr Mikuli

Introduction

The purpose of this contribution is to discuss the role of the Polish judiciary in the context of applying the Polish Constitution, statutes and Community law. In a concrete case an ordinary court must be ready to solve potential conflicts between legal norms originating from different legal sources. This problem will be examined from the traditional point of view that an ordinary judge should always be subordinate to statute. This principle is entrenched in the Constitution of 1997, which states that judges, within the exercise of their office, shall be independent and subject only to the Constitution and to statutes (Article 178(1)).[1] Taking the above-mentioned doctrine into account, a number of constitutional lawyers (the author included) have expressed the conviction that control over the constitutionality of statutes should, in principle, be reserved exclusively for the Constitutional Tribunal. As we will see, however, this doctrine is not universally accepted in Poland.

It should also be noted that, under the doctrine of the subordination to statute, a judge does not have the right to refuse to apply a statute. This does not mean, however, that the application of law comes down to a simple subsumption of a factual state to a statutory norm.[2] Undoubtedly this process has, at least to a certain extent, a creative character. A judge should take into account not only established jurisprudence, but also varying views present in scholarship.

1 This construction seems to be even more restrictive than its German counterpart, which envisages the judiciary as bound by statute and the law (*an Gesetz und Recht gebunden*).

2 Zoll, A. (1996), Związanie sędziego ustawą [Subordination of a Judge to Statute], in J. Trzcinski and A. Jankiewicz (eds) *Konstytucja i gwarancje jej przestrzegania. Księga pamiątkowa ku czci prof. Janininy Zakrzewskiej* [*The Constitution and the Guarantees of Obedience to It. The Festschrift to professor Janina Zakrzewska*], Warszawa, Wydawnictwa Trybunalu Konstytucyjnego, 251.

Direct Applicability of the Constitution and its Consequences

Article 8, paragraph 2, of the Polish Constitution states that its provisions shall apply directly, unless the Constitution provides otherwise. According to Garlicki, in general, the direct judicial application of the Constitution may take three forms.[3] The first of these is the so-called "autonomous application" in which a constitutional norm forms the sole basis for a judicial decision. The second is "co-application" in which a judge uses a legislative norm as well as a constitutional norm because something is regulated by both.[4] The third and last form concerns the resolution of conflicts between the constitution and statutes.

As mentioned above, in both Polish doctrine and practice, the ability of ordinary courts to rule on the non-conformity of a statutory provision to the constitution is under dispute. It should be noted that similar discussions are taking place or have taken place in other Central and Eastern European (CEE) states including Russia. In the Czech Republic the conflict between the Constitutional Court and the Supreme Court was very evident and centred on the perception that the latter was a shelter for hardliners from the former regime. All of these "battles" in CEE states ended in victory for the constitutional courts, which, as W. Sadurski writes, have built a "monopoly over the constitutional adjudication".[5]

Returning to Polish scholarship, two different approaches can be discerned. The authority of the courts to decide on the nonconformity of a statutory provision to the constitution derives directly from Article 8, paragraphs 1 and 2, and Article 178, paragraph 1, of the Constitution. The former states that the Constitution shall be the supreme law of the Republic of Poland, and the latter stipulates that judges, within the exercise of their office, shall be independent and subject only to the Constitution and to statutes. Article 193 of the Constitution provides additional support for this approach. According to this provision any "court may refer to the Constitutional Tribunal a question of law concerning the conformity of a normative act to the Constitution, ratified international agreements or statute, if the answer to such a question of law will determine an issue currently before that court". This is very often interpreted to mean that the court should refer an issue to

3 Garlicki, L. (1999), Bezpośrednie stosowanie konstytucji. Wprowadzenie do dyskusji [Direct Applicability of the Constitution. An Introduction to the Discussion], in *Konstytucja w praktyce* [*The Constitution in Practice*], Warszawa, Biuro Rzecznika Praw Obywatelskich, 23 et seq.

4 L. Garlicki, within "co-application", distinguishes: a) "ornamental" co-application in which a judge stating the reasons for a judgement quotes a constitutional provision despite there being clear statutory provisions sufficient for resolving a case; b) "interpretative" co-application in which a judge determines a norm of the law on the grounds of a statutory norm and a constitutional norm; and c) "modified" co-application consisting of the interpretation of a statutory norm in such a way that its sense is grasped with reference to norms or principles of the constitution (see Garlicki, ibid.).

5 Sadurski, W. (2005), *Rights Before the Court. A Study of Constitutional Courts in Postcommunist States of Central and Eastern Europe*, Dordrecht, Springer,19ff.

the Constitutional Tribunal only when it is not convinced of the legitimacy of its own standpoint. Under this interpretation a court may refer a question of law to the Tribunal only if it does not itself know the answer. This is supposed to mean that, if a court is convinced about the conformity or nonconformity to the constitution of a given norm it should either apply this norm or omit it. The Supreme Court has taken this position in several of its decisions. For instance, in its reasons for the decision of 7 April 1998,[6] the Supreme Court decided that there was no obligation to refer a question of law to the Constitutional Tribunal. The Court further claimed that:

> ... referring questions of law, and in particular questions related to the conformity of a legal provision to the constitution, used by a court for the purpose of determining a given case, makes sense only if the court has doubts related to the conformity of that legal provision to the constitution and expresses this doubt in the substantiation of the question of law. If, however, the court does not conceive a doubt *ex officio* as to the conformity of that provision to the constitution applied by the court or if it decides that the party's motion for referring a question of law to the Tribunal is unfounded, because in the court's opinion the provision is in conformity to the constitution, then there is no obligation to refer such question to the Constitutional Tribunal.

Sadurski expresses a similar opinion, asking how one can reconcile the monopoly of a constitutional court with the duty of the courts to apply the constitution directly. He argues that direct application implies the right, indeed the duty, of an institution to refuse to apply a law that it finds to be unconstitutional.[7] However, opponents of this interpretation of the provisions of the Polish Constitution (the author amongst them) claim that the direct application of the Constitution by courts may, in fact, only take either of the first two forms characterized by Garlicki. From this point of view, the provisions of Article 178, paragraph 1, should be understood as a conjunction, that is to say that judges are subject both to the Constitution and to statute.[8] For ordinary courts a constitutional provision, or a constitutional provision together with a statutory provision, should be sufficient to enable the court to recognize its normative effect (which is only possible if such provisions are sufficiently clear and precise) or should determine the manner in which the

6 I PKN 90/98 OSNAPiUS no.1 item 6.

7 Sadurski, op. cit., 21.

8 See Mikuli, P. (2002), W sprawie ewentualnej możliwości kontroli konstytucyjności ustaw przez sądy (uwagi w związku z art. 8 ust. 2, 178 ust 1 oraz 193 Konstytucji RP na tle porównawczym [On a Possible Option for the Constitutional Review of Statutes by Courts – Comparative Comments Related to Article 8 para. 2, Article 178 para. 1 and Article 193 of the Constitution of the Republic of Poland], in J. Czajowski and M. Grzybowski (eds) *Szkice o zasadach i instytucjach ustrojowych II i III Rzeczypospolitej* [*Essays on the Constitutional Rules and Institutions of the 2nd and 3rd Republic*], Kraków, 189ff.

legal meaning of a statutory provision is defined (which adopts a form of the interpretation of the law in accordance with the constitution and may also be based on general constitutional principles). According to Garlicki:

> … every court will first have to address the question as to whether constitutional doubt really exists and whether the challenged provision is consistent with the constitution. If the court comes to the conclusion that doubt does not exist the problem will disappear immediately, because the court will simply state that it does not find any nonconformity with the constitution.[9]

In a sense this process is concerned with the interpretation of both statute and Constitution, which would suggest that it is indeed a direct application. Under such an interpretation, however, based on Article 193 of the Constitution, the court must refer a question of law if it wants to describe a statutory provision as inconsistent with the Constitution. The court cannot make such a decision unilaterally. Only the Constitutional Tribunal has the power to remove a given statutory provision from the legal system. According to Garlicki, the difference in wording between Article 178, paragraph 1, and Article 195, paragraph 1 (judges in the Constitutional Tribunal are subject only to the constitution), is noteworthy and means that the scope of discretion available to judges in the Constitutional Tribunal is different from the scope of discretion available to other judges when ruling on the application of statutes and on their conformity with the Constitution. It should be noted that the authority of the courts to verify conformity with the Constitution is not substantiated sufficiently clearly enough in the Constitution and that norms of competence cannot be implied. Trzciński indicates that:

> … norms of competence for constitutional state bodies must be clearly defined in the constitution. This is a requirement not only of the principle of the democratic state of law (Article 2 of the Constitution) but also the legality principle (Article 7 of the Constitution), especially that among the constitutional organs of the state there is an organ (the Constitutional Tribunal) the basic task of which is to verify the conformity of the law to the constitution.[10]

The Constitutional Tribunal on a number of occasions entered into debate with the Supreme Court and took the position that only the Constitutional Tribunal had the authority to verify whether statutes conform to the Constitution. In its decision of 4 October 2000,[11] the Constitutional Tribunal stated that:

9 Garlicki, op. cit., 28.

10 Trzciński, J. (2001), Normy kompetencyjnej nie można domniemywać [The Norm of Competence Can Not be Implied], a comment on the judgement of the Supreme Court of 4 July 2001, *Rzeczpospolita*, 5 December 2001.

11 Case P. 8/00.

> In a legally binding constitutional situation the position under which a ruling court may refuse to apply a statutory norm because of its nonconformity to a constitutional norm ... and to give a decision directly on the basis of constitutional regulation is unfounded. Such a position is not justified either by any principle expressed in the constitution of the direct applicability of constitutional provisions (Article 8, para.2) nor by any provision providing for the subordination of judges, within the exercise of their office, to the constitution and to statute (Article 178, para.1 of the Constitution). The general recommendations of the constitution in this case addressed to the legislator, do not allow [the legislator] to make, on their basis, individual decisions, and besides, the judge, being subject to the constitution, is not released from being subject to ordinary statute. Therefore it should be assumed that the right way to resolve doubts as to the conformity to a general constitutional norm of a particular statutory regulation used in a case is to refer a question of law.

In its reasons for its decision of 28 November 2001,[12] the Constitutional Tribunal stated that such arguments do not release courts (or any other organ of public authority) from the obligation to apply the provisions of the Constitution directly.

On the basis of the latest research, the current jurisprudence of the Supreme Court on the issue of the direct application of the Constitution cannot be said to be coherent, though it accepts that specific provisions may be recognized as inconsistent or consistent with the Constitution.[13] Different chambers of the Supreme Court have expressed various points of view concerning the results of Constitutional Tribunal decisions. There is no unanimous agreement between these chambers as to the applicability of provisions that lose their binding force to facts arising before the publication of the Tribunal's decision. This lack of agreement also applies to situations in which the Constitutional Tribunal decides to defer the date on which a statutory norm loses its binding force.

In turn, in the jurisprudence of the Administrative Supreme Court, as J. Trzciński and R. Hauser argue, one may observe a compromise between the two extreme approaches presented by the scholarship.[14] The court is not obliged to refer a question of law to the Constitutional Tribunal in three situations:[15]

---

12 Case K 36/ 01.

13 See Działocha, K. (ed.) (2006), *Basic Problems in Applying the Constitution of the Republic of Poland. Final Research Report*, Warsaw, Kancelaria Sejmu. The studies in this volume were prepared as part of a three-year research project financed by the State Committee for Scientific Research and carried out by 85 constitutionalists.

14 Hauser, R. and Trzciński, J. (2008), Prawotwórcze znaczenie orzeczeń Trybunału Konstytucyjnego w orzecznictwie Naczelnego Sądu Administracyjnego [Law-making Significance of Rulings of the Constitutional Tribunal in the Jurisprudence of the Supreme Administrative Court], Warszawa, Lexis Nexis, 26ff.

15 Ibid., and the judgements quoted there.

a. When statutory provisions were passed before the Constitution came into force and are not in conformity with the Constitution in terms of content.[16] In this situation a judge should apply the collision rule *lex posterior derogate legi priori*. Hence, he or she will limit themselves to pronouncing the fact that the most recent (i.e., constitutional) provision supersedes the older provision (a statutory one). This approach, in general, was also accepted by the Constitutional Tribunal.[17]
b. When statutory provisions are obviously not in conformity with the Constitution.[18] This happens if a constitutional provision and a statutory one concerning the same subject contradict each other. In such a case a judge should apply the rule *lex superior derogat legi imperiori*. Nevertheless he or she is only entitled to do so under the condition that constitutional provisions are self-enforceable, i.e., that they may constitute, as such, the basis for construing a legal norm.
c. When a judge is supposed to apply acts of secondary legislation (which in the hierarchy of the sources of law occupy a lower position than statutes).[19] It must be emphasized that, in fact, this approach has never been contested in the scholarship.

Judicial Applicability of EU Law

Assuming that the ordinary courts (in principle) are not entitled not to apply valid statutes when they seem to be contrary to the Constitution, one may ask why an ordinary judge has the right to disregard a statute when, in his or her opinion, it is in conflict with Community norms.

The Polish Constitution indirectly regulates the status of Community law.[20] Article 91(2) states that an international agreement ratified upon prior consent granted by statute shall have precedence over statutes if such an agreement cannot be reconciled with the provisions of such statutes. Primary Community law possesses this status among the hierarchy of legal acts. At the same time, Article 91(3) of the Constitution states that if an agreement, ratified by the Republic of

16 The judgements of the Supreme Administrative Court of 16 January 2006 and of 19 October 2006.

17 The judgements: 6 October 1998 (K 36/97), 8 December 1999 (SK 19/99), 8 March 2000 (Pp 1/99), but in the judgement of 28 November 2001 (K 36/01) the Tribunal turned out not to be consistent.

18 The judgement of the Supreme Administrative Court of 2 June 2000, as well two judgements of 24 October 2000.

19 Inter alia the following judgements of the Supreme Administrative Court: 20 December 2001, 14 February 2002, and 19 April 2006.

20 See Albi, A. (2005), *EU Enlargement and the Constitutions of Central and Eastern Europe*, Cambridge, Cambridge University Press, 78–82.

Poland, establishing an international organization so provides, the law established by it shall be applied directly and shall have precedence in the event of a conflict of statutes. Thus, this phrase refers to secondary Community law. Without any doubt, these provisions were directed to all courts.

Primary Community law, in the form of treaties, is also subject to verification of their conformity to the Constitution and here also the only organ that seems to be authorized to do this is the Constitutional Tribunal.[21] In this connection, ordinary courts are obliged to refer questions of law to the Constitutional Tribunal for an investigation of the conformity of an international agreement when issuing a decision depends on the answer to this question and the court is unable to resolve the conflict by interpretation in accordance with the Constitution. Certainly, because of the Constitutional Tribunal's authority to establish the conformity of international agreements to the Constitution both in the process of abstract *a posteriori* verification and incidental review, a conflict arises between the principle of superiority of the Constitution and the constitutional principle of respecting international law (Article 9 of the Constitution).[22] For this reason it must be assumed that the decision of the Constitutional Tribunal concerning the nonconformity of international agreements, referred to in Article 89, paragraph 1, of the Constitution, and the original Community law would have only internal results and would constitute an obligation on the relevant organs of the state to renegotiate, to breach the international agreement or to change the constitution.[23]

What is the authority of ordinary courts in relation to secondary Community legislation? The author is of the opinion that the Constitutional Tribunal has neither authority to decide on the conformity of the norms of secondary Community legislation to the constitution nor to express its opinion on the conformity of statutes to secondary legislation in an abstract review. It is difficult to regard secondary Community law as a "legal provision issued by a central State organ" (Article 188 Point 3).[24] The problem arises when we come to incidental control. There is some doubt in the scholarship as to whether a constitutional complaint can be lodged against a provision of a secondary Community law and whether the court can refer

21 See Błachut, P. and Mikuli, P. (2005), Uwagi o stosowaniu ustaw przez sądy w przypadku ich kolizji z prawem wspólnotowym [Remarks on the Applicability of Statutes in Cases Where They Conflict with Community Law], in J. Wawrzyniak and M. Kruk (eds), *Polska w Unii Europejskiej* [*Poland in the European Union*], Kraków, Zakamycze, 270.

22 Ibid., and the Polish literature quoted there.

23 Ibid.

24 Article 188 of the Polish Constitution exhaustively determines the competences of the Constitutional Tribunal. According to this provision, the Constitutional Tribunal shall adjudicate regarding the following matters: 1) the conformity of statutes and international agreements to the Constitution; 2) the conformity of a statute to ratified international agreements whose ratification required prior consent granted by statute; 3) the conformity of legal provisions issued by central state organs to the Constitution, ratified international agreements and statutes; 4) the conformity to the Constitution of the purposes or activities of political parties; and 5) complaints concerning constitutional infringements.

a question of law regarding the conformity of such a law to the Constitution or the conformity of a statute to secondary Community law.[25] A positive answer to this question could only flow from a statement that an item of secondary legislation is considered a "normative act", as referred to in Article 193 (on questions of law) and in Article 79, paragraph 1, of the Constitution (concerning the constitutional complaint).[26] It should be emphasized that, from the perspective of the general principles of Community law, the authority to verify the conformity of secondary Community law to the Constitution (similarly with primary law) would not be possible since Article 267 of Treaty on the Functioning of the European Union (formerly Article 234 of EC Treaty) provides, *inter alia*, that the Court of Justice shall have jurisdiction to give preliminary rulings concerning the interpretation of the Treaties as well as the validity and interpretation of acts of the institutions of the Community.

It should be noted that the opinion has recently been expressed that in assessing the constitutionality of a secondary Community law, the Constitutional Tribunal should remember that the Polish Constitution does not constitute an adequate reference norm for the control of such laws.[27] The only exception exists for those constitutional rules which may be perceived as potential obstacles in the process of delegating to the EU "the competence of organs of state authority in relation to certain matters" according to Article 90, paragraph 1, of the Constitution. Wojtyczek contends that there are several constitutional principles that make up "the identity of the state", therefore their infringement would make it impossible to transfer sovereign powers to an international organization or international institution. Amongst these principles he includes a requirement for the protection

25 The Constitutional Tribunal suggested such a possibility in its judgement of 11th May 2005.

26 Article 79, paragraph 1, of the Constitution: "In accordance with principles specified by statute everyone whose constitutional freedoms or rights have been infringed shall have the right to appeal to the Constitutional Tribunal for its judgment on the conformity to the Constitution of a statute or another normative act upon which basis a court or organ of public administration has made a final decision on his freedoms or rights or on his obligations specified in the Constitution."

27 Wojtyczek, K. (2007), *Przekazywanie kompetencji państwa organizacjom międzynarodowym* [*The Delegation of the Competence of Organs of State Authority to International Organizations*], Kraków, Jagiellonian University, 327. Wojtyczek nevertheless argues that the Constitutional Court is entitled to execute control over the constitutionality of secondary community law only in the context of the constitutional complaint. He excludes this possibility in cases of questions of law concerning a so-called normative act, as used in Article 193 of the Constitution, which should be interpreted in the light of enumerations included in Article 188 (see the previous note). In turn, Article 188 determines the subject of the constitutional complaint separately through direct reference to Article 79. See ibid., 236.

of human dignity and constitutional rights, the principle of statehood, the principle of democracy, the principle of social justice and the principle of subsidiarity.[28]

Another interesting issue that arises is the admissibility of any attempt to verify the conformity of national legislation created as a result of the implementation of Community law (i.e., its directives) with the Constitution. German jurisprudence may serve as a desirable example.[29] Taking into account the approach taken by the German Federal Constitutional Court in the *Facharztweiterbildung* case of 9 January 2001,[30] one may claim (a) that the requirements of the constitution bind a Polish legislator who transposes secondary Community legislation to the extent of freedom of regulation provided for a national legislator by the Community legislator, and (b) that within this area, the Polish legislator is subject to national verification of conformity with the Constitution. If, on the other hand, the Polish legislator is unconditionally bound by the Community legislator's directions, any domestic norms are not subject to verification of conformity with the Constitution by the Constitutional Tribunal. However, this approach was seemingly rejected by the Constitutional Tribunal in its decision of 27 April 2005 mentioned below (though this decision, as we will see later, concerned a European framework decision, not a directive) and has not found larger support in scholarship.[31]

The "Closed System" of the Sources of Law and the Doctrine of Subordination to Statute

The specific form of worship-of-statute often seems to shape current legal thinking in Poland. A good example in this context is the theory of the so-called closed system of sources of law envisaged in the Polish Constitution of 1997. While open to European integration, one may perceive this system as a new paradigm that is an obstacle to the creation of the law in the contemporary Polish state. This paradigm requires the preparation of a vast number of technical and complicated legal norms – a task for which parliament is often not prepared. In the meantime, in Poland, almost all legal issues must be anchored in statute. This is connected with Article 92 of the Polish Constitution, which states that regulations shall be issued on the basis of specific authorization contained in, and for the purpose of implementing, statutes. This authorization "shall always specify the organ appropriate to issuing a regulation, the scope of matters to be regulated and guidelines concerning the provisions of such an act". In this context, it should be emphasized that the Polish system concerning sources of law does not allow the executive to implement

28 Ibid., 284–299.

29 Błachut and Mikuli, op. cit., 273.

30 1 BvR 1036/99.

31 Kustra, A. (2009), *Przepisy i normy integracyjne w konstytucjach wybranych państw członkowskich UE* [*Provisions and International Norms in Constitutions in Selected Members States of the EU*], Toruń, TNOIK Torun, 317.

Community directives; this activity must always be carried out through a statute passed by the Polish Sejm and Senate.

The doctrine of subordination to statute should, then, be reformulated. However, the new paradigm of submission-to-statute does not automatically undermine the monopoly of the Constitutional Tribunal in adjudicating constitutional matters. The author is convinced that there are a number of arguments against the rights of ordinary judges to disregard statute on the grounds that they are not in conformity with the Constitution. If a judge decides not to apply a particular legal norm because it is unconstitutional, he must determine the content of a constitutional norm. This in turn, as scholarship emphasizes, often requires balancing constitutional values, and may result in a decision that differs from that determined by the Constitutional Tribunal. In turn, in the process of applying Community law, the ECJ is responsible for the construction of this law through the system of preliminary rulings that is obligatory at the level of national courts against whose decisions there is no judicial remedy (in Poland these are at the level of the Supreme Court). Consequently, the diffused system of the judicial review of legislation in the civil law system should always be complemented by some form of corrective mechanism in which a constitutional court or a supreme court plays an important role (*vide* Estonian, Portuguese, Maltese, Greek and Cypriot cases). In general, this factor consists of entrusting the highest courts or constitutional courts with the competence to consider the judgements of other courts on the unconstitutionality of normative acts.[32] In Greece, for example, the Special Highest Court settles controversies over whether the content of a statute is contrary to the Constitution when conflicting judgements are pronounced by supreme civil, criminal or administrative courts.

One may argue that a more flexible approach to the issue of the subordination of Polish judges to statute might be used in situations in which the Constitutional Court postpones the date on which a statute loses its binding force. The Tribunal has the right to do so according to Article 190, paragraph 3, phrase 1 of the Constitution which states that:

> A judgment of the Constitutional Tribunal shall take effect from the day of its publication, however, the Constitutional Tribunal may specify another date for the end of the binding force of a normative act. Such time period may not exceed 18 months in relation to a statute or 12 months in relation to any other normative act.

If the Tribunal makes use of this provision, an ordinary court deciding on a concrete case would have to decide whether or not to apply the statutory provision in question, which, even though it has been determined to be unconstitutional, has

32 Mikuli, P. (2002), *Zdekoncentrowana kontrola konstytucyjności prawa: Stany Zjednoczone i państwa europejskie* [*A Diffused Judicial Review of the Constitutionality of Law: United States of America and European Countries*], Kraków, Wydawnictwo Uniwersytetu Jagiellońskiego, *passim*.

not yet been deprived of its legal effect. In its jurisprudence the Tribunal itself has suggested that all subjects applying the law should take into account the fact that the Tribunal's rulings rebut the "presumption of constitutionality" of laws. One may argue that the rebuttal of the presumption of constitutionality potentially has an impact in the sphere of rights and freedoms of the person and the practice and functioning of the common and administrative courts.[33] However, judicial freedom in this matter would undermine to some extent the sense of the practice of postponement as well as possibly be perceived as inconsistent with Article 190, paragraph 1, which states that Constitutional Tribunal judgements shall be universally binding and final.

The dualistic attitude of ordinary judges to statutes, depending on the context (either constitutional or European), is not a uniquely Polish dilemma. It appears that everywhere a diffuse model of constitutional review has been absolutely rejected, i.e., it cannot coexist with the Kelsenian model. Moreover, an ambivalent approach to the judicial application of statutes can also be observed in the United Kingdom where judicial review of legislation does not take place, at least not in a strict sense. The issue in the UK may be linked to the application of the Human Rights Act (which implemented the European Convention on Human Rights) on the one hand, and the application of Community law on the other. The paradox here lies in the fact that whereas, in the first case, courts cannot strike down legislation violating conventional rights (they can only make a so-called declaration of incompatibility), in the second case they may disregard statutes. This was confirmed in *R v Secretary of State for Transport, ex parte Factorame (No. 2)*:[34]

> … it has been clear that it was the duty of a United Kingdom court, when delivering final judgement, to override any rule of national law found to be in conflict with any directly enforceable rule of Community law.[35]

Theories of Legal Pluralism and Their Weakness

Having two different approaches to the domestic legal system, in addition to the European one, may be perceived as very confusing, but can be justified, at least to some extent, by the theories of legal pluralism, i.e., the theory of constitutional

33 This issue has been widely discussed by Radziewicz, P. (2008), Wzruszenie domniemania konstytucjności aktu normatywnego przez Trybunał Konstytucyjny [Rebuttal of Presumption of Constitutionality of a Normative Act by the Constitutional Tribunal], *Przegląd Sejmowy*, 5, *passim*.

34 [1991] 1 AC 603.

35 Ibid., 658.

pluralism,[36] the theory of multilevel constitutionalism[37] or the theory of a multi-centric system of law.[38] These theories assume that in a modern state there are many coexisting bodies applying laws on the principle of the division of powers between domestic and external (European) authorities. According to these theories "a hierarchical position within one centre does not give a guaranty of influence on competences executed within the other".[39] Consequently the so-called looped hierarchy of legal norms should be substituted for the traditional hierarchy. This is described as interaction between various levels of norms. As Maduro observes:

> … constitutional pluralism identifies the phenomenon of a plurality of constitutional sources of authority that create a context for potential constitutional conflicts between different constitutional orders to be solved in a non-hierarchical manner.[40]

Theories of legal pluralism describe the actual state of facts, i.e., the relationships between domestic and European legal orders in practice. They prove that the problem of determining who has the last word when it comes to a conflict between norms issuing from these sources is unsolvable in a normative sense. Maduro illustrates this phenomenon with reference to the notion of counterpunctualism in the theory of music, which refers to the combination of different melodic lines in such a way that they harmonize with one another.[41] Maduro's concept of "counterpunctual law" explains that constitutional and Community orders may coexist with each other in a harmonic and peaceful way in spite of the fact that there is no hierarchical subordination between these sources and, therefore, no cohesive rules follow in the case of a conflict.

The theories of legal pluralism mentioned above are undoubtedly quite useful, especially with regard to the question of the formal validity of legal regulations. But, a question arises as to whether diversifying the validity and applicability of

---

36 See: MacCormick, N. (1993), Beyond the Sovereign State, *Modern Law Review*, 56(1). Walker, N. (2002), The Idea of Constitutional Pluralism, *EUI Working Paper LAW* No. 2002/1.

37 See Pernice, I. (1999), Multilevel Constitutionalism and the Treaty of Amsterdam: European Constitution-Making Revisited, *Common Market Law Review*, 4.

38 Łetowska, E. (2005), Multicentryczność polskiego systemu prawa i jej konsekwencje [The Multi-centrism of the Polish Legal System and Its Consequences], *Państwo i Prawo*, 4, *passim*.

39 Ibid., p. 3.

40 See Maduro, M. (2009), Courts and Pluralism: Essay on a Theory of Judicial Adjudication in the Context of Legal and Constitutional Pluralism, the paper circulated at the Constitutional Pluralism in the European Union and Beyond conference, Oxford, 20–21 March 2009.

41 Maduro, M. (2003), Counterpunctual Law: Europe's Constitutional Pluralism in Action, in N. Walker (ed.) *Sovereignty in Transition*, Oxford, Hart Publishing, *passim*. In the Polish literature his concept has been outlined by Kustra, op. cit., 351–353.

the law has such an important meaning. Constitutional pluralism eliminates, to some extent, the need to consider which system of law is superior, i.e., in general and in isolation from a particular case.

The author's opinion is that this approach may result in the future rejection of current methods of adjudication in conflicts between two legal orders within the abstract procedures of judicial review. However, it is not difficult to notice the smaller significance of legal pluralism in the process of the application of law. It results from the fact that national courts in every EU Member State must execute national as well as Community law: norms coming from two different centres are being applied by the same organs. Thus a classic hierarchy of legal acts/norms can be reconstructed, at least, for use in a particular case. The principle of a European-friendly interpretation of normative acts, though very useful, does not circumvent the dilemma of how to behave in a concrete case where a conflict between the constitution and Community law cannot be resolved through normal methods. After all, a judge is bound by the constitution.

Within legal pluralism *de lege ferenda*, the role of the Polish Constitutional Tribunal could be limited to resolving conflicts between primary Community law and the Constitution within the procedure of lower courts presenting questions of law. The Tribunal's rulings in this concrete procedure would have significance only as far as a particular case (not *erga omnes*) and would not deprive a Community of its internal effect (as has been explained above).[42] Nevertheless this would have to be linked to the amendment of the Constitution, especially the reformulation of the abovementioned Article 190, paragraph 1. This approach could constitute a method of assessing Community law from the point of view of constitutional values and could be treated as part of a constitutional dialogue between European and national judiciaries.[43]

The constitutional courts of CEE states have accepted approaches to European issues that are quite similar to those of many of their Western counterparts.[44] While they have, in general, expressed positive attitudes to the process of European integration, they have simultaneously "been very careful in elaborating their views on the absolute supremacy of Community law over constitutional

42 However, it should be emphasized again that this kind of decision would only have internal significance.

43 See in this volume T. Dumbrovský.

44 See, for instance, Decision of the French Constitutional Council of 9 April 1992 92-308 DC [*Maastrich I*] and the judgement of the Italian Constitutional Court of 18 December 1973 [*Frontini*, 183/1975] and of 8 April 1991 [*Giampaoli*, 168/1991]; the judgement of the Danish Supreme Court of 1998 (UfR 1998, 800) and the judgement of the Supreme Court of Cyprus of 11 November 2005 (case 294/2005).

norms".[45] Germany's *Solange cases* of 1974 and 1986[46] are sometimes perceived as an indirect precedent for Poland's Constitutional Tribunal, as well as for the constitutional courts of other CEE states. In their judgement of 11 May 2005,[47] the justices of the Polish Tribunal, referring to the concept of a multi-level system of sources of law, emphasized that:

> The existence of the relative autonomy of both national and Community legal orders in no way signifies an absence of interaction between them. Furthermore, it does not exclude the possibility of a collision between regulations of Community law and the constitution.[48]

The Tribunal simultaneously took the position that:

> Such a collision would occur in the event that an irreconcilable inconsistency appeared between a constitutional norm and a Community norm, such as could not be eliminated by means of applying an interpretation which respects the mutual autonomy of European law and national law. Such a collision may in no event be resolved by assuming the supremacy of a Community norm over a constitutional norm. Furthermore, it may not lead to the situation whereby a constitutional norm loses its binding force and is substituted by a Community norm, nor may it lead to an application of the constitutional norm restricted to areas beyond the scope of Community law regulation.[49]

In this ruling the Tribunal, *inter alia*, was also supposed to asses whether Article 249 of the EC Treaty is in conformity with Article 31, paragraph 3, of the Polish Constitution, specifically the conditions permitting the introduction of limitations to the enjoyment of constitutional rights and freedoms within the domestic legal system. The justices expressed the conviction that, although it is unjustified to transfer the requirements stemming from this constitutional provision directly to the field of issuing norms of secondary Community law, this does not preclude the possibility of reviewing legal provisions, including Community regulations, insofar as they are in force within the territory of Poland, from the

---

45 See: Piqani, D. (2007), Constitutional Courts in Central and Eastern Europe and their Attitude towards European Integration, *European Journal of Legal Studies*, v1(2), 20. In the article, D. Piqani also quotes the judgement of Estonia's Constitutional Review Chamber of the Supreme Court regarding the omission of Estonian currency as an example of "a clear acceptance of the ultimate supremacy of Community law".

46 See *Solange I* [1974] 2 CMLR 540; *Solange II* [1987] 3 CMLR 225.

47 See the case K 18/04 which concerned the constitutionality of the Accession Treaty.

48 English quotation taken from the translation published at the official website of the Tribunal' available at www.trybunal.gov.pl, accessed 19 July 2010.

49 Ibid.

perspective of observing the requirements laid down in Article 31, paragraph 3, of the Constitution. Some scholars argue that in this way the Polish Constitutional Tribunal, at least indirectly, recognized its competence to adjudicate on the compatibility of secondary Community norms with the Constitution.[50]

A second important decision, frequently criticized by many European lawyers, was a judgement passed just two weeks earlier (i.e., 27 April 2005) concerning the European Arrest Warrant.[51] The Tribunal held that the Criminal Procedural Code, which implemented the European Framework Decision, did not conform to Article 55 of the Polish Constitution.[52] While the Tribunal's decision was not, the author would say, "European-law- (EU law)-friendly", the justification for the ruling was just the opposite, though the Tribunal noticed that:

> The obligation to interpret domestic law in a manner sympathetic to EU law (so as to comply with EU law) has its limits. In particular, it stems from the jurisprudence of the Court of Justice of the European Communities (ECJ) that EU secondary legislation may not independently (in the absence of appropriate amendments in domestic legislation) worsen an individual's situation, especially with regard to the sphere of criminal liability.[53]

In its decision the Tribunal postponed the date on which this provision of the Code lost its binding force, thus enabling Polish authorities to fulfil European obligations without disruption. In 2006, Article 55 of the Constitution was amended so that the general ban on extradition could be reconciled with exceptions "if such a possibility stems from an international treaty ratified by Poland or a statute implementing a legal instrument enacted by an international organization of which the Republic of Poland is a member, provided that the act is covered by a request for extradition".

Conclusion

It must be noted that the constitutional courts of CEE states were not able to arrive at a new and freshly critical look at the relationship between domestic and Community law. This is not surprising, however, since the peoples of these states have only relatively recently "regained the possibility of the sovereign and democratic determination of their fate".[54] In this respect the citizens of these states, as well as their institutions, seem not to be ready for greater openness to supranational tendencies. A second explanation can be found in the fact that

---

50 See Kustra, op cit., 315 and the literature quoted there.

51 See case P 1/05.

52 Article 55 provided that "[t]he extradition of a Polish citizen shall be prohibited".

53 See note 21.

54 Phrase taken from the Preamble to the Polish Constitution.

a clear vision of the future of the European Union has not yet crystallized. On the contrary, it is quite blurred. This does not create favourable conditions for determining complex interactions between two branches of law: the domestic branch and the Community branch. Evident proof for the lack of bravery among the "fathers" of the Lisbon Treaty is the omission of a provision for the priority of Community law. A mention is found in the 17th Declaration to the Treaties, which, as all declarations, is not legally binding. Therefore, it is not bizarre that the national constitutions of the Member State, as well as the jurisprudence of constitutional courts, are prudent and nation-centred.

Perhaps in the future, together with the strengthening of integration, the multi-centric system of law might reshape itself into a new, mono-centric one that is European in character. Nevertheless, so far there has been no consent for such a strengthening from the Member States and their citizens. In these circumstances, to make the process of the application of law more elastic, it would be very helpful if the "European" role of judges was better entrenched in national constitutions. In this context Estonian regulations, at least at the theoretical level, seem to be a good example. Whereas Article 123 of the Constitution stipulates that Estonia must not conclude treaties that conflict with its Constitution, paragraph 2 of the Constitution of the Republic of Estonia Amendment Act (passed on 14 September 2003) allows the application of the Constitution to take into account rights and obligations arising from the Accession Treaty. The author is aware of the fact that these kinds of constitutional provisions, even though they may encourage judges to be more European-conscious, do not have to encourage judges to depart from traditional thinking on the constitution.[55]

On the other hand, a set of provisions in primary Community law addressing the role of national constitutions would also be desirable. The author is of the opinion that a possible constitutionalization of the superiority of Community law at the level of the European Treaties could be associated with a simultaneous recognition of national constitutional courts or other institutions of such type. The recognition of the role of national parliaments in a special protocol to the Lisbon Treaty could serve as an example in that respect.[56] Although conflicts between the constitutions of Member States and EC law are rare, one can imagine a special procedure which could be introduced in a situation when the constitutional court of a Member State contests the conformity of a provision of EC law with its national constitution. This kind of procedure could, for instance, include reaching a multilateral agreement on amending the provision of EU law. When such compromise becomes impossible,

55 See in this volume Kerikmäe.

56 See Protocol on the Role on National Parliaments in the European Union and Protocol on the Application of the Principles of Subsidiarity and Proportionality. This comes from the Preamble of the 1997 Constitution of the Republic of Poland. An English translation of the text is available at www.sejm.gov.pl/prawo/konst/angielski/kon1.htm, accessed 19 July 2010.

a Member State would have to change the constitutional provision in question or in an extreme case, leave the EU.

References

Albi, A. (2005), *EU Enlargement and the Constitutions of Central and Eastern Europe*, Cambridge, Cambridge University Press.

Błachut, P. and Mikuli, P. (2005), Uwagi o stosowaniu ustaw przez sądy w przypadku ich kolizji z prawem wspólnotowym [Remarks on the Applicability of Statutes in Cases Where They Conflict with Community Law], in J. Wawrzyniak and M. Kruk (eds), *Polska w Unii Europejskiej* [Poland in the European Union], Kraków, Zakamycze.

Działocha, K. (ed.) (2006), *Basic Problems in Applying the Constitution of the Republic of Poland. Final Research Report*, Warsaw, Kancelaria Sejmu.

Garlicki, L. (1999), Bezpośrednie stosowanie konstytucji. Wprowadzenie do dyskusji [Direct Applicability of the Constitution. An Introduction to the Discussion], Konferencja naukowa: *Konstytucja RP w praktyce*, [The Constitution in Practice], Warszawa, Biuro Rzecznika Praw Obywatelskich.

Hauser, R. and Trzciński, J. (2008), *Prawotwórcze znaczenie orzeczeń Trybunału Konstytucyjnego w orzecznictwie Naczelnego Sądu Administracyjnego* [*Law-making Significance of Rulings of the Constitutional Tribunal in the Jurisprudence of the Supreme Administrative Court*], Warszawa, Lexis Nexis.

Kustra, A. (2009), *Przepisy i normy integracyjne w konstytucjach wybranych państw członkowskich UE* [*Provisions and International Norms in Constitutions in Selected Members States of the EU], Toruń*, TNOIK Torun.

Łetowska, E. (2005), Multicentryczność polskiego systemu prawa i jej konsekwencje [The Multi-centrism of the Polish Legal System and Its Consequences], *Państwo i Prawo*, 4.

MacCormick, N. (1993), Beyond the Sovereign State, *Modern Law Review*, 56(1).

Maduro, M. (2003), Counterpunctual Law: Europe's Constitutional Pluralism in Action, in N. Walker (ed.) *Sovereignty in Transition*, Oxford, Hart Publishing.

Maduro, M. (2009), Courts and Pluralism: Essay on a Theory of Judicial Adjudication in the Context of Legal and Constitutional Pluralism, paper circulated at the Constitutional Pluralism in the European Union and Beyond conference, Oxford, 20–21 March 2009.

Mikuli, P. (2002), W sprawie ewentualnej możliwości kontroli konstytucyjności ustaw przez sądy (uwagi w związku z art. 8 ust. 2, 178 ust 1 oraz 193 Konstytucji RP na tle porównawczym [On a Possible Option for the Constitutional Review of Statutes by Courts – Comparative Comments Related to Article 8 para. 2, Article 178 para. 1 and Article 193 of the Constitution of the Republic of Poland], in J. Czajowski and M. Grzybowski (eds) *Szkice o zasadach i instytucjach ustrojowych II i III Rzeczypospolitej* [*Essays on the Constitutional Rules and Institutions of the 2nd and 3rd Republic*], Kraków.

Mikuli, P. (2002), *Zdekoncentrowana kontrola konstytucyjności prawa: Stany Zjednoczone i państwa europejskie* [*A Diffused Judicial Review of the Constitutionality of Law: United States of America and European Countries*], Kraków, Wydawnictwo Uniwersytetu Jagiellońskiego.

Pernice, I. (1999), Multilevel Constitutionalism and the Treaty of Amsterdam: European Constitution-Making Revisited, *Common Market Law Review*, 4.

Piqani, D. (2007), Constitutional Courts in Central and Eastern Europe and their Attitude towards European Integration, *European Journal of Legal Studies*, 1(2), 20.

Radziewicz, P. (2008), Wzruszenie domniemania konstytucjności aktu normatywnego przez Trybunał Konstytucyjny [Rebuttal of Presumption of Constitutionality of a Normative Act by the Constitutional Tribunal], *Przegląd Sejmowy*, 5.

Sadurski, W. (2005), *Rights Before Courts. A Study of Constitutional Courts in Postcommunist States of Central and Eastern Europe*, Dordrecht, Springer.

Trzciński, J. (2001), Normy kompetencyjnej nie można domniemywać [The Norm of Competence Can Not Be Implied], a comment on the judgement of the Supreme Court of 4 July 2001, *Rzeczpospolita*, 5 December 2001.

Walker, N. (2002), The Idea of Constitutional Pluralism, EUI Working Paper LAW No. 2002/1.

Wojtyczek, K. (2007), *Przekazywanie kompetencji państwa organizacjom międzynarodowym* [*The Delegation of the Competence of Organs of State Authority to International Organizations*], Kraków, Jagiellonian University.

Zoll, A. (1996), Związanie sędziego ustawą [Subordination of a Judge to Statute], in J. Trzcinski and A. Jankiewicz (eds) *Konstytucja i gwarancje jej przestrzegania. Księga pamiątkowa ku czci prof. Janininy Zakrzewskiej* [*The Constitution and the Guarantees of Obedience to It. The Festschrift to professor Janina Zakrzewska*], Warszawa, Wydawnictwa Trybunalu Konstytucyjnego.

Chapter 7
Structural Inconveniencies of the Treaty of Lisbon in the Czech Republic

Jiri Zemanek

Some political actors in Member States ("old" as well as "new" ones) are aware that a breach of "identity values" by an EU action could happen. The ratification process of the Treaty of Lisbon tested to what extent this awareness is a sincere one and may be taken seriously. A comparison of approaches by the German and the Czech constitutional courts exposes – mostly diverging – assessments in this respect.

In Search for Compensation for the Redefined Balance of Power at National Level

The ratification of the Treaty of Lisbon in the Czech Republic was a test of:

> capacity to reflect the developments within the EU and become active and responsible participants in the European debate ... with a Czech contribution democracy in the EU will be strengthened by the reinforced role of national Parliaments ... in contrast to other countries we did not pass a real discussion about the Constitutional Treaty ... Therefore, the ratification of the Treaty of Lisbon must be used as an opportunity to reflect European topics in the Czech debate and build up an informed view as a pre-condition for a self-confident and proactive membership.[1]

These prophetic words of a senior government representative became entirely true. The Treaty of Lisbon deals with the principles of execution of the Union powers, the decision-making process at the Union level and future changes of primary law in a way which interferes with the European agenda at the domestic level. The Czech Constitutional Court did not find the contested Treaty provisions to be in contradiction with the constitutional order, but invited a correction of

1 Alexandr Vondra, Deputy Prime Minister for European Affairs, in his preface to the consolidated Czech version of the Treaty on European Union and the Treaty on Functioning of the European Union, as amended by the Treaty of Lisbon, published by the Office of the Czech Government in 2008.

rules governing the formation of positions of the government in the Council of Ministers – to strengthen their democratic legitimacy and enforce the Parliament's power of political control over the government.

These shifts of concern required implemetation by legislative changes, which were passed in other Member States too, and in the Czech Republic resulted in the positive outcome of the process of ratification. At the moment there is continuing uncertainty about it (and not only because of President Vaclav Klaus, who indicated his hesitation about this step, but also due to fears about Ireland's second referendum on the Lisbon Treaty and – to some extent – also about the final steps of the ratification process to be taken in Germany and the Poland), but the Czech Parliament has amended the respective legislation – its rules of procedure,[2] e.g., in order to show the best possible face of Czech politics during the Czech Presidency of the EU Council.

This amendment, reinforcing the Parliament's control of powers relating to important European positions of the Government, balanced the internal effects of institutional change challenged by the Treaty of Lisbon. This was proclaimed by the Czech and German constitutional courts in their Lisbon judgements.

The recent preliminary review of the Treaty of Lisbon by the Czech Constitutional Court ("the Court")[3] and the German Bundesverfassungsgericht ("BVerfG")[4] has given the opportunity to (re)consider their perceptions of European integration. The BVerfG reaffirmed its earlier case law on *ultra vires* review of European legal acts, extended the control standard for autonomous, German-specific competences of substantial political importance ("constitutional identity"), both moderated by a recourse to the multi-level judicial dialogue, and – astonishingly – rejected the direct democratic legitimacy of the European Union (not being analogous to a state), the deficit of which – if not effectively counterbalanced by national parliaments – establishes constitutional limits for further integration. The Czech Court, in its earlier "European" case law inspired largely by the German doctrine,[5] was more self-restrained when identifying substantive grounds for constitutional review and less sceptical of European democracy in its concerns for the sovereign statehood.

---

2 Act no. 162/2009 Coll., amending Rules of Procedure of the House of Deputies (Act no. 90/1995 Coll.) and the Senate (Act no. 107/1999 Coll.).

3 Case Pl. US 19/08 *Lisbon I* of 26 November 2008; for the commentary see case note: Briza, P. (2009), The Czech Republic: The Constitutional Court on the Lisbon Treaty. Decision of 26 November 2008, *EuConst* 2009/1, 143–164; case Pl. US 29/09 *Lisbon II* of 3 November 2009 (English translation available at www.usoud.cz/view/726, accessed 21 August 2010).

4 BVerfG, 2BvE 2/08 of 30 June 2009.

5 See the first path-breaking cases Pl. US 50/04 *Sugar quotas* of 3 March 2006 and Pl. US 66/04 *European Arrest Warrant* of 3 May 2006.

An Evolving Constitutionalization of the EU under the Treaty of Lisbon

For some observers, the Treaty of Lisbon became the last step in the process of the institutional reform of the European Union which started 20 years ago. They assume that the capacity for political accord across the Member States about any innovative proposal has been exhausted, as the recent failed referenda and some troubled ratifications have evidenced. But, can the process of constitutionalization of European law really stop if it has been a means of advancing the European integration, even as a precondition for the process's survival in the increasingly globalized world? The correct understanding of the clause on "an ever closer union among the peoples of Europe"[6] does not limit the direction of Union's development to a federal European statehood, but includes adapting the Union's system to the changing environment of knowledge, economy, social and political matters and of law. If the Union becomes unadaptable to the course of affairs and their impact on the Member States, its decline could start. So far as the finality of the European project has not been defined, the Union's *habitus* remains transitory.

The process of the Union's adaptation was always only a reactive one, mostly reflecting the already established practice of its institutions by *ex post factum* treaty amendments and supplements. What is styled as "adaptation strategies" brings about lasting periods of Union incapability to act flexibly and effectively, which can be only partially relieved by the case law of the Court of Justice. The continual adaptation resembles crisis management. A model of continual Treaty adjustments and streamlining of terminology, avoiding its *sui generis* alibistic denominations, has been attempted already by the European Constitution with its bridging-*passerelle* clauses and other options of reinforced policies. Political elites in some Member States – authentic, traditionally Euro-restrained or populistic ones – became, as a result, worried about the risk of a self-evolution of European law to the detriment of the states' positions as "Masters of the Treaty".

The petitions for review of compliance of the Treaty of Lisbon with the Member States' constitutional orders, invoked by its ratification, challenged the national doctrines of European law on the basis of a comprehensive evaluation of *status quo ante*. Even though the new Treaty – the most extensive revision of the Union's foundations since Maastricht – is intended to consolidate rather than to further an advancement of European primary law, some judicial considerations indicated the intention to have a lasting impact on the debate about the future of the Union and to guide the next course of the process of European integration.[7] With this background, fears of a spontaneous extension of the Union's competences and their exercise outside a proper democratic control provoked recently unprecedented

---

6 Preamble of the former EC Treaty, Article 1 of the former EU Treaty, as well as Preamble of the new EU Treaty-Lis.

7 Thym, D. (2009), In the Name of Sovereign Statehood: A Critical Introduction to the Lisbon Judgment of the German Constitutional Court, *CMLRev* 1795, 1821.

statements by the BVerfG. Its findings received a rather critical response in the German academic community.[8]

As a Reason for a Constitutional Conflict?

It has already become the practice of national courts to seek the application of constitutional law in a manner compliant with European law obligations. The established fact is that some of them do so only with certain reservations.

The profile and the mode in which the national legal systems became open to influences of European law have reflected constitutional provisions, traditions and culture, as well as the local judicial ideology of the respective Member State. The Irish way requests a new reform Treaty to be adopted by an express amendment of the Constitution approved in a referendum, which then makes the position of European law in the domestic legal order quite stable. The French way necessitates the constitutional amendment on a case-by-case basis following the advice given in a preliminary review of the reform Treaty by the Constitutional Court. The German and Spanish way mostly avoids the direct amendment of the constitution, relying on its adaptation through a Euro-conforming interpretation and application, provided that the material core is not affected.[9]

There seems to be a potential conflict between European and national constitutional law. The problem arises when such a reservation is, first, vague and,

8 Besides Thym (ibid.), see also the contributions of the following authors published in 10 *German Law Journal* No. 8 – Special Edition (available at www.germanlawjournal.com/article.php?id=1155-1163, accessed 21 August 2010): Schönberger, Ch. (2009), Lisbon in Karlsruhe: Maastricht's Epigones At Sea; Schorkopf, F. (2009), The European Union as an Association of Sovereign States: Karlsruhe's Ruling on the Treaty of Lisbon; Halberstam, D. and Möllers, Ch. (2009), 'The German Constitutional Court says "Ja zu Deutschland!"; Tomuschat, Ch. (2009), The Ruling of the German Constitutional Court on the Treaty of Lisbon; Grosser, A. (2009), The Federal Constitutional Court's Lisbon Case: Germany's "Sonderweg": An Outsider's Perspective; Niedobitek, M. (2009), The Lisbon Case of 30 June 2009 – A Comment from the European Law Perspective; Wohlfahrt, Ch. (2009), The Lisbon Case: A Critical Summary; Kiiver, P. (2009), German Participation in EU Decision-Making After the Lisbon Case: A Comparative View on Domestic Parliamentary Clearance Procedures; Leibfried, S. and van Elderen, K. (2009), "And they shall Beat their Swords into Plowshares" – The Dutch Genesis of a European Icon and the German Fate of the Treaty of Lisbon; see also: Mayer, F.C. (2009), Rashomon in Karlsruhe, WHI-Paper 07/09, available at www.whi-berlin.de, accessed 21 August 2010, Gärditz, K.F. and Hillgruber, Ch. (2009), Volkssuveränität und Demokratie ernst genommen – Zum Lissabon-Urteil des BVerfG, and Classen, C.D. (2009), Legitime Stärkung des Bundestages oder verfassunngsrechtliches Prokrustbett?, both in *Juristenzeitung* 18, 872–889.

9 Cf. the case law of the German Constitutional Court on Art. 79, para 3GG, and plenty of commentaries on its role of *Ewigkeitsklausel*.

second, cannot be authorized – expressly or implicitly – or at least tacitly tolerated by the Treaty. In this case, the cohesion of European law could be endangered.

Up to now, this conflict has been manifested through judicial monologues rather than with an eye to the possibility for its resolution. The protection of the fundamental constitutional values amounts to national resistance of a different calibre than the earlier easy acceptance by Member States' courts of their mandate to enforce Community law by its direct application at the national level. The acceptance of the duty to revoke incompatible provisions of national (constitutional) law was slow and difficult, influenced by traditional doctrines on the effects of international law obligations within national legal orders[10] and ultimately, unchangeable principles which must always take precedence over any concurring legal provision of "extramural" origin.[11]

Criteria for Constitutional Review: Fundamental Values and *Ultra Vires* Clause

The Czech Constitutional Court in *Lisbon I* case[12] reasoned, first, that the Accession to the Union did completely render meaningless either the normatively supreme status of the constitutional order within the Czech legal system, nor the court's own position of an *ultima ratio*. It conditioned access to two requirements:

- First, to apply consistently the method of Euro-conforming interpretation of national law. This requirement, however, cannot have the character of an implicit amendment of the Constitution, since in the event of a clear conflict between the Constitution and the European law that cannot be settled by any reasonable interpretation, the Constitution, in particular its "material core", must take precedence.
- Second, to recognize, in general, the functionality of the European institutional framework (in particular the European Court of Justice) for ensuring review of the exercise of competences conferred on the Union. The Constitutional Court's position, however, may change in the future and the respective Union act would remain unapplied, if it appeared that this framework were dysfunctional. The Court assumes nevertheless that this can occur only in quite exceptional cases, for instance when abandoning the values the conferral of powers from the national to the Union level has

10 de Witte, B. (1999), Direct Effect, Supremacy and the Nature of the Legal Order, in P. Craig and G. de Búrca (eds) *The Evolution of EU Law*, Oxford, Oxford University Press, 177–213.

11 van Ooyen, R.Ch. (2006), *Die Staatstheorie des Bundesverfassungsgerichts und Europa*, 1st edn, Baden-Baden, Nomos).

12 The case *Lisbon I* was initiated by the Senate of the Parliament.

been based on, or when exceeding the scope of Union competences by adoption of an *ultra vires* act.

Concerning the "material core" of the constitutional order – the inviolable "essential requirements of a democratic state governed by the rule of law",[13] the Czech Constitutional Court refrained from defining its components as well as from making an enumerative list of its parts, in an abstract context and in advance, as it could prejudice a future self-serving definition based on cases decided at the time. It is possible to specify the content of this "material core" only on a case-by-case basis. The Court nevertheless mentioned at least some of them: fundamental rights, democracy, people's sovereignty, division of powers – not as a manifestation of its arbitrariness or (criticized) judicial activism, but to the contrary, as an evidence of its judicial restraint, which is perceived as a means of limiting the judicial power in favour of political processes and prevails over the requirement of absolute legal certainty.

The Court did not limit the preservation of the sovereignty of the Czech state/republic to the retention of national competences of essential, vital importance, constituting its "value identity" (as the BVerfG did in relation to Germany). It rejected setting in an authoritative way substantive limits to the conferral of competences to the Union. A catalogue of non-transferable competences could in the future become resistant to immediate political pressure and *ad hoc* interpretations and influenced by cases at issue at a particular time, as the petitioners requested. The petitioners were obviously encouraged by the German court's Lisbon judgement definition of *domaine réservé*, where an extensive conferral, encroaching upon several "sensitive" areas, was not found admissible.[14] In view of the role which the Constitutional Court plays in the Czech constitutional system, responsibility for such a decision is primarily political and cannot be adopted by the judicial branch of power. The Court can review it only from the point when the legislature, enjoying broad discretion, "manifestly exceeds" the content-related limits of conferral.[15] In both the German and Czech cases the Court did not want to practise a residual jurisdiction and was aware of its duty to refer the question to the ECJ for a preliminary ruling, but did not seem to be too eager to do so.[16]

13 "Eternity clause" of Article 9(2) of the Constitution, which must be read in conjunction to Article 1(1) of the Constitution: "The Czech Republic is a sovereign, unitary and democratic state governed by the rule of law, founded on respect for the rights and freedoms of man and of citizens."

14 Criminal law, monopoly on the use of force, fundamental fiscal decisions, guarantee of a just social order, culturally important decisions.

15 Under Article 10a, paragraph 1, of the Constitution only "certain" competences may be transferred.

16 An insertion of this duty in the Act on the Constitutional Court does not seem meaningful (a different opinion after *Lisbon* judgement of the BVerfG was expressed by a group of academics and judges – see www.whi-berlin.de – Material 01/09, accessed 21 August 2010).

Democratic Legitimacy of Union Decision-making

In the Czech Constitutional Court's opinion, the provision of the Treaty of Lisbon that "the functioning of the Union shall be founded on representative democracy"[17] governs processes at the European as well as at national level. The European Parliament is not an exclusive, but a complementary source of democratic legitimacy of European decisions since it stems from a delicate balance of both levels, without one necessarily outweighing the other. This *obiter dictum* contrasted with the opinion of the BVerfG, largely sceptical about the capacity of the European Parliament to play this role. Over time, the division of powers entrusted to European institutions has evolved into various normative procedures and now reflects the balance between both levels, authorizing the exercise of conferred competence by Union action. The Court rejected the unjustified assertion that representative democracy can only exist inside the sovereign states. The existence of elements of representative democracy at the Union level does not exclude the realization of the same elements at the national constitutional level. The conditions of conformity of the conferral of competences were not violated. For similar reasons the requirement of absolute equality among the voters of particular Member States is, therefore, not necessary; in other words, not all voters in each State get the same level of representation as each Member State is entitled to a pre-set number of elected members, and that number is not strictly related to the number of potential voters in each Member State.

The marked tendency to strengthen the role of national parliaments in the Union's decision-making by reinforced parliamentary scrutiny serves as a counterweight to the unbalanced division of powers within the European agenda at national level and not to the elimination of the Union's "democratic deficit".

The BVerfG was of a quite different opinion. It rejected the direct democratic legitimacy of the Union through the European Parliament, as it may perpetuate the Union's democratic deficit, if national parliaments cannot effectively scrutinize European affairs.[18] Its Maastricht-implicit appeal, which encourages a progressive empowering of the Union's democratic legitimacy, has not been now continued:

> As long as the European order of competences according to the principle of conferral in cooperatively shaped decision-making procedures exists … and as long as a well-balanced equilibrium of the competences of the Union and the states is retained, the democracy of the European Union cannot, and need not, be shaped in analogy to that of a state.[19]

More autonomous decision-making by a powerful European Parliament would be closer to the perspective of a European statehood – unauthorized, yet with a

17 Article 10 TEU.

18 Thym, op. cit., 1820.

19 Para. 272 German *Lisbon* judgement.

homogenous European *demos* as a new constituent power. The BVerfG attention to sovereign statehood (see below) influenced its position on the constitutional conditions for the scope of competences transferred to the Union and on the limits of European integration.

For the time being, the national parliaments of Member States as "Masters of the Treaties" fulfil the task of narrowing the democratic deficit. In the BVerfG assessment of European democracy, undoubtedly the major role was played by the "degressive proportionality" in the distribution of the nation quotas for European Parliament elections which resulted in electoral inequality (especially for German citizens) and fell short of regular statal democratic standards.

The difference between the constitutional assessments of European democracy under the Treaty of Lisbon can hardly be explained by the differences in the historical experience of both the German and Czech nations, which had totalitarian regimes, emphasizing the human dignity dimension of the right to free and equal participation of individuals in public authorities (including European ones).

State Sovereignty Reconsidered: Diverging Assessments

The BVerfG "innovated" in its "Lisbon" judgement by arguing that the preservation of sovereign German statehood requires the retention of national competencies "... of substantial political importance ... The principle of democracy therefore sets content-related limits to the transfer of sovereign powers, limits which do not result already from the inalienability of the constituent power and of state sovereignty".[20] The BVerfG then identified five areas of "untransferrable" competences,[21] each without clear qualitative criteria, essential for the necessary preservation of any meaningful democratic discourse at national level.[22] It seems that the only reference for this definition was the compilation and protection of the remaining national competences.

The BVerfG also annulled the accompanying law on parliamentary scrutiny of European legislation, requiring more specified guarantees for the Parliament's and the government's "responsibility for integration" through their greater involvement in the flexibility procedures for the future adjustments of the treaties.[23] Such a self-imposed assumption of policing borderline of Union competences gives the Parliament a margin of appreciation for infringments of its powers and facilitates the BVerfG's role as an ultimate guardian of the Constitution.[24] These procedures result in Treaty revisions and require national parliamentary approval before their

20 Paras 246 and 247 German *Lisbon* judgement.

21 See n 14.

22 Paras 249–252 German *Lisbon* judgement.

23 Para 236 German *Lisbon* judgement.

24 Thym, op. cit., 1803.

enactment by European institutions.[25] However, the BVerfG did not demand an *ex ante* enhanced parliamentary control of current Union's legislation in general, except for the new flexibility clause,[26] requiring ratification of the European decision before its implementation – as a protection of domestic *Kompetenz-Kompetenz*.[27] This is a suprising requirement since the flexibility clause serves the European secondary law-making, not an adjustment of European primary law.

Although the BVerfG has never had recourse to its warnings in earlier case law about control powers concerning European law acts as *ausbrechende Rechtsakte* – obviously because it found their activation unnecessary – it has now repeated its earlier justification of *ultra vires* review (without again mentioning expressly German fundamental rights guarantees) and, moreover, extended its review standards in respect of the principle of conferral to "... the inviolable core content of the constitutional identity" of the Basic Law[28] which is to be observed.[29] The "constitutional identity" includes the autonomous, country-specific democratic reserved powers in sensitive policy fields mentioned above. This may be understood as a warning against an evolution of European law through extensive interpretation by the Court of Justice.[30]

On the other hand, this *ex post* hostility of the BVerfG's reservations about European law, which could put the BVerfG into "a troublemaker" position as the guardian of the German national interest and diminish its influence on the future development of European law, was balanced by a hint of its constructive participation in the meaningful European judicial dialogue, enabling it to preserve its acquired judicial authority. The BVerfG relativized its sharp *obiter dicta* on national reserve powers by a statement that the standards for constitutional identity reviewable on national as well as on the European level, resulting from Article 4(2) TEU-Lis are parallel, complementary and inclusive: "In this respect, the guarantee of national constitutional identity under constitutional and Union law go hand in hand in the European legal area."[31] The complementarity means that the BVerfG should not have to disapply European legal acts as the consequence of identity review without due consideration of the Court of Justice's opinion on the national

25 Halberstam and Möllers, op. cit., 1243.

26 Article 325 TEU-Lis.

27 Paras 325–328 and 417 German *Lisbon* judgement.

28 Article 23(1) in conjunction with Article 79(3) of the Basic Law ("eternity clause").

29 Para. 340 German *Lisbon* judgement.

30 The BVerfG was aware of the ECJ's *Mangold* anti-discrimination judgement, controversial from the perspective of German law (case C-144/04 [2005] ECR II-9981), which became – as *ausbrechender Rechtsakt* – the first test case of the review standards extended by the *Lisbon* judgement of the BVerfG (see case 2 BvR 2661/06 *Honeywell*, pending).

31 Para 240 German *Lisbon* judgement.

constitutional identity obtained in the preliminary reference procedure.[32] However, this constructive relativization of the internal constitutional limits of European integration was destroyed by the BVerfG's rejection of European democracy in the name of sovereign statehood.

As already mentioned, the Czech Court, in its first "European" cases after the EU-accession, shared the BVerfG's doctrine[33] that the transfer of competences by the Treaty of Accession also implied acceptance of the effects of European law at the level of the national legal order. But, that transfer was conditional: the exercise of competences by the Union must not threaten "the material core" of the Constitution.[34] If such an autonomous, unilateral assessment puts a limit on the conferral of competence, is this limit of an absolute or a relative nature?

The Czech Constitutional Court was, in its *Lisbon I* judgement, aware of the European self-perception of "an ever closer union among the peoples of Europe",[35] but not to the extent that it would amount to a loss of statehood as a consequence of the change of identity of the Czech Republic as it became a constituent part of a European federal state. The Court did not share the juxtaposition between national and European constituencies which brought the BVerfG to a definition of constitutional limits for further integration and might only be overcome, once the constituent power (the citizens) decides to abandon national sovereignty and establish a European federation. For the time being, the Union must respect the national reservations, otherwise it would contradict the Constitution.

In a modern state, sovereignty is not an aim in and of itself, in isolation, but is a means of fulfilling the fundamental values on which the construction of a democratic state governed by the rule of law stands. The conferral of competences based on the free decision of a sovereign and the continuation of their exercise with the sovereign's participation in a pre-agreed, controlled manner, is not a sign of conceptual weakening, but – on the contrary – can lead to the strengthening of sovereignty. Therefore, the key manifestation of state sovereignty is not an

---

32 Thym, op. cit., 1812, who admits, that "the complementarity approach" may be read as an implicit reference to the concept of multi-level constitutionalism, denominated by the notion of *Verfassungsverbund*, the concept of which has been developed by Pernice, I. (2009), Multilevel Constitutionalism and the Treaty of Amsterdam, *CMLRev*, 703–729.

33 Cf. n. 5 above. The Court did not understand "the special relationship of protection of own nationals" as an obstacle to the Union efforts to ensure a high level of security of Union citizens by measures combating the crime phenomena, including coordination and cooperation between the police and judicial authorities, and by mutual recognition of the judgements in criminal matters. The Court waived the too broad understanding of this clause. Instead, the Court interpreted it as a mere reminder of the past repressive practices of the former communist police, i.e., in a way harmonious with the Framework Decision. At the end of the day the Court declared the respective implementation legislation compatible with the Czech constitutional order.

34 Zemanek, J. (2007), The Emerging Czech Constitutional Doctrine of European Law, *EuConst* 3, 418–435.

35 TEU, Preamble.

exclusive right, deriving its source from the monopoly of power, but a mere possibility of a disposition to transfer some competences (on a temporary or on a permanent basis).

The Czech Constitutional Court did not consent to the intention, expressed by the petitioners, to preserve through the catalogue of irreversible, eternal national competences state sovereignty as a *per se* attribute of statehood and an exclusive source of democratic legitimacy of the supranational power. Such a defensive approach, putting the constitutional limits with primarily a symbolic significance on European integration, attempts, in the main, to address the fears of the Parliament about its marginalization as the legislative branch of power and to calm the feelings of the general public who are worried about an alleged and proclaimed loss of national sovereignty. The understanding of state sovereignty as an end in itself[36] disclaims its perception as a mere means for realizing constitutional values at the most appropriate level instead of focusing on the availability of adequate democratic and rule of law-based guarantees of the execution of the scope of powers necessarily conferred on the Union by the Member States.

The Court was also aware, that the concept of "shared" (pooled) sovereignty of the Union as a *sui generis* entity can hardly be subsumed under classic categories of constitutional theory, as President Vaclav Klaus argued in his pleading before the Court. This concept was already used in the political Memorandum accompanying the Czech application for EU membership as early as January 1996.[37]

In the Czech constitutional context, the "material core", as a limit on the opening up of the domestic legal system, assumes exploration of the question, either as a provision recalling the past and precluding a restoration of the rule of totalitarian governance, which had played havoc with the former Czechoslovakia, or as a last-resort criterion of reference for scrutinizing Union action. The Constitution-drafters in autumn 1992, i.e., long before starting the negotiations on EU accession, were still worried about any future comeback of totalitarian practices. On the other hand, they obviously could not have intended to prejudice future developments of the process of integration in Europe and the participation of the Czech Republic in it. Citizens acted, when adopting, through their representatives selected in the elections in June 1992, the new Constitution, "[as] a part of the family of democracies in Europe and around the world".[38] Later case law outlined an assumption that the constitutional anti-totalitarian provision does not form part of the "material core".[39]

36 The letter of President V. Klaus to the Court in relation to its *Lisbon I* judgement.

37 Speaking about "the exchange of a part of national sovereignty for a shared supranational sovereignty and co-responsibility" as "an inevitable step to be taken for the benefit of its own country and the whole of Europe".

38 Preamble of the Constitution (Act no 1/1993 Coll).

39 The case *European Arrest Warrant*, op. cit.

Other Contested Points of the Complaint

The strategy used by the petitioners[40] in the Czech *Lisbon II* case was the following: they produced a self-made definition of the "sovereign democratic rule of law-State", allegedly missing in the constitutional jurisprudence, and tried to support their definition by references to the Court's previous case law. On this basis they questioned the Treaty of Lisbon – as a whole, as well as selected provisions – by references to, for example:

- its complexity that undermines legal certainty,
- the incapacity of the European Parliament to compensate for the "deficit of democracy" of the Union, which is possible to eliminate only in a state-like European federation (unauthorized by the Czech Constitution),
- the absence of "an imperative mandate" of the government by the Czech Parliament for all Union decisions concerning the Czech legislation,
- the non-neutral formulation of the Union´s objectives ("social market economy", "full employment", etc.),
- the lack of a clear exclusion of any future federative finality of the Union,
- the unclear conditions surrounding the suspension of membership rights,[41]
- the special relationship with neighbouring countries,[42]
- limiting Member States' foreign policies,
- the principle of representative democracy[43] found to be incompatible with the status of an international organization, founded on sovereign equality of its Member States,
- the promotion of "the general interest of the Union" by the Commission[44] as not being concrete enough, and the level of "European commitment" of the Commissioners, posing a discriminatory requirement for nominees not sharing the "European ideology",
- enhanced cooperation[45] making the cooperation between Member States impossible without a prior approval by the Union,
- the aim for governance at the global level[46] as unclear and not politically neutral,
- the common defence as an objective[47] contradicting the right of self-determination of peoples (with a reference to the BVerfG judgement in the Lisbon case),

40 The case *Lisbon II* was initiated by a group of 17 senators.
41 Article 7 TEU-Lis.
42 Article 8 TEU-Lis.
43 Article 10 TEU-Lis.
44 Article 17 TEU-Lis.
45 Article 20 TEU-Lis.
46 Article 21 TEU-Lis.
47 Article 42 TEU-Lis.

- the withdrawal from the Union[48] being not free of any political pressure,
- the exclusive competence of the Union[49] as inadmissible, since its non-execution by the Union could – as they claimed – deprive citizens of any means of enforcement of their right of self-determination,
- the Union's competence in criminal matters[50] and implied external powers as an encroachment on the vital functions of State,
- Union citizenship[51] and legal personality of the Union[52] as symptoms of a state-like federation,
- the method for distribution of seats in the European Parliament[53] as contrary to equality of the Member States (Germany – 12.6 per cent – versus Luxembourg – 0.8 per cent) as well as of the citizens,
- the competence of the Court of Justice[54] prejudicing an independent preliminary review of compliance of international treaties with the Czech Constitution by the Court.

The Court refused these objections as "apparently unjustified" and already existing under the Union *acquis* in force, as well as inadmissible, being *res iudicata* after *Lisbon I* case. Moreover, the Court reaffirmed its position on inviolable constitutional values, commenting that: "However, this principle [of interpretation of domestic law in conformity with EU law] cannot have the character of a kind of 'implicit Euro-amendment' of the Constitution. In the event of a clear conflict between the domestic Constitution and European law that cannot be cured by any reasonable interpretation, the constitutional order of the Czech Republic, in particular its material core, must take precedence."[55] The Court justified this limitation by the subject matter of the review – primary European law *de constitutione ferenda* – in the case of a not-yet-ratified treaty, the Euro-conforming interpretation cannot be applied.

In view of the role that the Court plays in the Czech constitutional system, responsibility for the decision on the scope of the conferral of competences is primarily political and cannot be appropriated by the judicial branch of power. The Court can review it only when the legislature, which enjoys wide discretion, "manifestly exceeds" the content-related limits of conferral under Article 10a, paragraph 1, of the Constitution, according to which only "certain" competences can be transferred.[56] Any consideration of the limits of conferral should have to reflect

48 Article 50 TEU-Lis.
49 Article 2, para, 1, and Article 3 TFEU.
50 Article 83 TFEU.
51 Article 20 TFEU.
52 Article 47 TEU.
53 Article 14, para. 2, TEU.
54 Article 218, para. 11, TFEU.
55 Para. 85 *Lisbon I* judgement.
56 Paras 110–111 *Lisbon II* judgement.

the overall protective measures taken at subnational, national and supranational level, which compensate for deficits occurring at other levels. "The material core" of the Constitution does not form an absolute constraint on European integration, a reference to which is not sufficient to push aside the operation of a Union legal act at the national level.

Reinforced Parliamentary Control over the "Lisbon" Structural Innovations

The Czech Court in its *Lisbon I* judgement[57] reminded the Czech legislature to strengthen the role that the Czech Parliament has to play when a "simplified revision procedure" of the treaties or so-called bridging (*passerelle*) clauses introduced by the Treaty of Lisbon are implemented.[58]

The amendments to the parliamentary scrutiny of governmental positions to the respective European proposals were adopted on 6 May, 2009,[59] and imposed the duty of direct notification of dissenting opinions of the Parliament in subsidiarity issues to the Union institutions, the minimum threshold and procedure for submission of the respective action by the Chambers of the Parliament to the Court of Justice, the parliamentary deliberations on Czech personal nominations to the Union institutions, the *ex ante* and explicit approval by each of the parliamentary Chambers to the listed cases of application of bridging clauses (general as well as special) binding on the representatives of the government in the European Council or the Council of Ministers (imperative mandate)[60] and the requirement for approval concerning the flexibility clause[61] only in the scope limited on application of this clause outside of the internal market.

The amendment act had been petitioned at the Court on 1 September 2009 by a group of Senators,[62] appealing to the Court[63] to *declare expressly* that:

- a total transfer of the state sovereignty to the Union in the future would be impossible,

57 Op. cit.

58 Paras 153, 165–167 and 174 of *Lisbon I* judgement.

59 Op. cit.

60 The only exception was the simplified amendment procedure under Article 48, para. 7, TEU-Lis where *in absentio* of any contradicting decision of a Chamber a tacit consent will be presumed. Otherwise the approval should be given by a simple majority, *per analogiam* (self-executing) international treaties (Article 10 of the Constitution) and might be subjected to a review of compliance of the respective Union draft act with the Czech constitutional order by the Court.

61 Article 352 SFEU.

62 Pl. US 26/09.

63 The petitioners used an unusual terminology: instead of Treaty of Lisbon, they speak about Treaty of Maastricht (TEU-Lis) and Treaty of Rome (TFEU).

- a minimum scope of national competence must be preserved "in all circumstances" and no *Kompetenz-Kompetenz* may be transfered (i.e., a ban on blanket empowerments) given that the Member States must "in all circumstances" remain "Masters of Treaties",
- the approval to the application of all bridging clauses must be given by a three-fifths majority in both parliamentary Chambers, (i.e., by the same vote as required for the Treaty of Accession),[64]
- the extension of the imperative mandate should compensate all cases of so-called democratic deficit of EU institutions,[65]
- the compliance of the treaties with the Czech Constitution can be saved only subject to a restrictive interpretation of their provisions,[66]
- the amendment of the Act by the Constitutional Court should introduce a new special procedure contesting Union acts against the criteria of reference of the Czech Constitution,
- the minimum threshold[67] necessary for submission of an action to the Court of Justice in subsidiarity issues as contrary to the principle of democracy (discriminating small political parties) should be abolished, and
- the Treaty of Lisbon must not be ratified by the President of the Republic until the above-mentioned legislation has been enacted.

The petition, largely inspired by the "Lisbon" judgement of the German BVerfG, disregarded the autonomy of the Union legal order, based on the principle of conferral of (certain) national competences. Therefore, on 6 October 2009, the Court rejected the claim for annulment of the "Lisbon"-reinforced parliamentary scrutiny as "apparently unjustified" on the following grounds:

- There was no reason to replace simple majority by a qualified (three-fifths) majority[68] in parliamentary preliminary scrutiny of governmental positions on the application of the general bridging clauses because the parliamentary approval is required only for a refusal, not for an approval of the draft clause. The applicable voting procedure (i.e., simple majority) makes the declared interest of the Parliament easier to protect than the one proposed by the petitioners (i.e., qualified majority). In addition, the

64 And that a non-passing of a Parliament's decision on the application of Article 48, para. 7, TEU-Lis should equal a disaproval of its application.

65 Including Czech personal nominations, which should also reflect the candidate's loyalty to the Czech Constitution.

66 Therefore, the Court must remain the final arbiter, able to dissaply the Union act, interpreted in contradiction of the Constitution.

67 Seventeen senators or 41 deputies.

68 Article 39, para. 4, of the Constitution for the approval of international treaties under Article 10a of the Constitution on the transfer of competence.

respective voting procedure when prescribed by the Constitution cannot be changed by a simple statute on parliamentary procedure.

- The constitutional principle of democracy does not require cutting the minimum number of MPs necessary for initiating an action on grounds of infringement of the principle of subsidiarity by a Union legislative act. Access to the right for the protection of minority rights by groups of MPs is thus not excluded and the limitation does not deprive the minorities of the essence of their right to protection.

The same conclusion was drawn on "an express declaration" on:

- the limits of transfer of competences,
- the minimum scope of powers of a sovereign state,
- the position of the Czech Republic as a "Master of the Treaties" forever,
- the necessity to extend the "imperative mandate" for all legislative decisions and personal nominations by the Union,
- the restrictive interpretation of Union law and the role of the Court as an ultimate guardian of the Constitution,
- the need to adequately amend the Act on the Constitutional Court, and
- the ban on the ratification of the Treaty of Lisbon until the above-mentioned points are enacted.

The Court had no jurisdiction to pronounce mere interpretative declarations, having no immediate concern with the merit. Instead, the real intention of the petitioners was to support the chances of another petition submitted later against the Treaty.[69] This was considered an inadmissible concern for the proceedings in question.

President Klaus's Objection to the EU Charter of Fundamental Rights

Following his phone call with the Swedish Prime Minister Fredrik Reinfeldt on 8 October 2009, and meeting with the President of the European Parliament Jerzy Buzek on 9 October, President Vaclav Klaus announced that: "Before the ratification, the Czech Republic must at any rate and in addition negotiate a similar exemption [from the application of the Charter of Fundamental Rights, as Poland and the United Kingdom did]. In this way a guarantee will be given to us that the Treaty of Lisbon cannot lead to a breakthrough of the so-called Benes' decrees [from 1940–46 on property confiscations, mostly of *Sudetendeutschen*]."

He justified this requirement by fear that "… the Court of Justice will review the compliance of legislation, practices and procedures of Member States with this Charter. It will make possible circumventing Czech courts and asserting immediately before the Court of Justice property claims of persons expelled after

69 The petition for the case *Lisbon II* was delivered on 29 September 2009.

WWII. The Charter enables even the review of valid decisions of Czech courts." He did not specify the form in which his requirement should have to be fulfilled.

Mr Ladislav Jakl, the secretary of the President's Office, said on Czech TV on 11 October 2009 that "the Irish way" – a political declaration made within the Presidency Conclusions of the European Council on 29–30 October 2009, protecting specific Irish proclaimed values and incorporated in the next treaty on accession – would not satisfy the President's requirement. He could rely only on a *hard opt-out* solution, legally binding from the very date of entry into force of the Treaty of Lisbon.

Mr Ales Pejchal, a member of the President's team of legal advisors, in an interview for the daily *Pravo* on 12 October 2009 said that the requirement attempts to resist an inventive interpretation of European law. Non-retroactivity of European law is generally accepted; but, Union citizens might claim at any national court their rights granted by the Charter[70] in so far as their legal status under the Treaty had been violated by a Member State. He referred to the early-1990 Czech legislation on restitution of property, confiscated during the communist regime, conditioning individual claims by the Czech nationality. The European Court of Human Rights in Strasbourg found this legislation not contradictory to the ECHR (European Convention on Human Rights), for which the condition of nationality is irrelevant[71] – in contrast to the findings of the UN Committee on Human Rights. Czech courts have the duty to recognize and enforce decisions of national courts of other Member States in civil law matters.[72] Mr Pejchal also admitted the existence of petitions from other Member States to the European Commission concerning Czech restitution affairs. Claimants often used the tactic of questioning the legality of the application of the Benes' decrees as the legal foundation for confiscations by *actio negatoria* and then suing for *vindicatio* under the legislation on restitution of property or simply under the civil law in force, with the aim of having the continuity of their property rights declared.

Mr Jan Brezina MEP of the European People's Party (EPP), in an article published by the daily *Pravo* on 12 October 2009, paid attention to the fact that the Charter did not extend the EU competences as well as to Article 345 Treaty on the Functioning of the European Union (TFEU) excluding any prejudice of the Treaty against the national rules governing the system of ownership and, therefore, did not share the fears of President Klaus. But, he was aware of the possible impact of the system of mutual recognition of civil law judgements on the topic (speaking about "a timed bomb") and proposed to channel these fears at the level of secondary EU legislation.[73]

---

70 He mentioned expressly Article 17 of the Charter – rights to property with reference to Article 2 TEU principle of non-discrimination.

71 Cases *Des Fours Walderode, Harrach, Gratzinger, Polacek, Pinc*, for example.

72 He referred to the Council Regulation 44/2001.

73 By limiting the field of application of Regulation 44/2001.

President Klaus had expressed no reservation against the Charter when he delegated to the government his constitutional power[74] to negotiate and sign the draft Treaty of Lisbon on the basis of the mandate given by the European Council in June 2007 to the Intergovernmental Conference. He did not mention the Benes' decrees, neither in his brief to the Constitutional Court nor in the oral hearing in *Lisbon I* and *II*. On the occasion of the delation of his constitutional powers to his government he disclosed only his doubts about the state-like status of the Union under the Charter and about the coexistence of three standards of protection of human rights (European, international, national).

The Court had already, in its *Lisbon* judgement, thoroughly analysed the compliance of the entire Charter with the reference criteria of the Czech constitutional order[75] and came to the conclusion, binding on all Czech public bodies, that there are no contradictions between them; Klaus's objection would have to be considered as *res iudicata*. Therefore, the second petition against the Treaty of Lisbon could no longer challenge the Charter.

The awareness of the Benes' decrees became topical during the parliamentary debates on the Treaty of Lisbon in February 2009. The consent by the Assembly of Deputies to the ratification of the Treaty was accompanied by a resolution (passed by more than 90 per cent of MPs), confirming the opinion that: "The legal status of the EU Charter of Fundamental Rights guarantees, without any doubts, that the Charter cannot be effective in a retroactive way and questions the legal and property relationships arising from the Czechoslovak legislation, in particular, that adopted within the period 1940–1946, as well as the existing case law of European and national courts on these legal and property issues."[76]

A couple of advisory opinions invited respectively by the European institutions (Ulf Bernitz, Jochen A. Frowein) and the Czech authorities (Lord Kingsland, Christian Tomuschat) such as the President of the Assembly of Deputies, the Czech Ministry of Foreign Affairs, the government, the Committee on European Affairs of the Senate and other bodies,[77] confirmed the non-retroactivity of European law when compared to that of the Benes' decrees.

The Czech Constitutional Perspective

The role of Czech President – elected by the Parliament (in 2008 with a weak democratic legitimacy of only a one vote majority) and not responsible to it (i.e.,

74 Article 63, para. 1(d) of the Constitution.

75 Paras 187–204 of the judgement.

76 For the reference to this reminder see para 35 of the European Council of 19–20 March 2009 Presidency Conclusions.

77 See the contributions, for example, of Christian Tomuschat and Jiri Zemanek in *Ist das tschechische Rechtssystem bereits EU-konform?*, from the colloquium, held by Friedrich-Ebert-Stiftung e.V. in Prague on 3 May 2001.

politically uncontrollable) – is drawn up complementarily: he/she has to moderate the constitutional system as a guardian of certain principles and political culture rather than implementing his/her independent, distinctive political programme. Therefore, he/she cannot force the other constitutional bodies to consider his/her political preferences.

President Havel has already achieved a substantial autonomy in the field of foreign policy, which falls in the list of *shared* presidential powers,[78] the exercise of which does require a countersignature by the Prime Minister. Conclusion and ratification of international treaties fall by no means within the President's full discretion.[79] But Havel's views did not differ significantly from those of the government. This flexible interpretation of the exercise of the shared powers became a real problem when President Klaus started to aspire to very different views from the government, especially in the area of European integration. The countersignature requirement is very difficult to implement fully in practice,[80] as the President *de facto* transformed his power to ratify international treaties into a personal veto prerogative.

President Klaus, through the non-ratification of the Treaty of Lisbon, apparently ignored the will of the democratically elected Parliament, the binding decision of the Constitutional Court, as well as denied his own act on the delegation of power to negotiate and sign this Treaty (see above). If he had refrained – after the Court's (expected) positive answer on compliance of the Treaty with the Czech Constitutional – from his duty to ratify, there were several (unprecedented) options as to how the current deadlock could be settled: the government could initiate a jurisdictional dispute before the Court (Article 87, paragraph 1k of the Constitution); the President's inability to perform his constitutional duty might have been a reason for adoption of a resolution by the Parliament, devolving performance of this duty *ad hoc* upon the Prime Minister (Article 66 of the Constitution); the President might have been asked to resign from his office (Article 61 of the Constitution); the President might have been prosecuted for high treason before the Constitutional Court on the basis of a charge brought by the Senate (Article 65 of the Constitition, impeachment) if he had been found to have violated the democratic order of the Republic (Act on the CC, Sec. 96) or Article 63, paragraph 1, of the Constitution on the President's power of ratification of international treaties, based on an essential presumption of observance of the Constitution by top state authorities, could have been amended by a supplement "... without any delay, otherwise this power will devolve upon the Prime Minister".

78 Article 63, para. 1, of the Constitution.

79 Kysela, J. and Kühn, Z. (2007), Presidential Elements in Government: The Czech Republic (continued), *EuConst* I, 91–113, 105.

80 President Klaus ratified The Rome Statute of the International Criminal Court, which was approved by the three-fifths majority in the Parliament in October 2008, as late as in May 2009; he delayed the ratification of the European Social Charter since couple of years, etc.

The implementation of any of these options was suspended during the time that the case *Lisbon II* was pending before the Court.[81]

The European Law Perspective

The position of President Klaus concealed non-retroactivity as it results from the rule of law as one of the principles common to EU Member States, as well as the horizontal provisions of the Charter, delimitating its field of application, its rules of interpretation and the level of protection for the rights it recognized.[82] His position also contested the operation of the principle of non-discrimination on grounds of nationality within the EC Treaty as a part of *acquis* in force.

The Benes' decrees presumed "state untrustworthiness" as a criterion for confiscations of property of Germans, Hungarians and other persons, who allegedly acted during the time of "lack of freedom" (occupation by the repressive regime of Nazi Germany during WWII) against the national interest (territorial integrity) of Czechoslovakia. Persons affected by the Benes' decrees during times of the postwar disorder and deprived of their rights or treated illegally should have – under specific circumstances, but on equal footing, regardless of their nationality – a right of access to Czech justice, which should review and – as the case may be – revoke their status under the decrees. The principle of non-discrimination on grounds of nationality codified by the EU Charter of Fundamental Rights changes nothing in *locus standi* of former *Sudetendeutsche* – Union citizens at present – before Czech courts and administration.

Everyone's equality before the law has not an absolute, but a relative nature: a different treatment may be only justified by an objective reason. "State untrustworthiness", used as a criterion by the Benes' decrees and approved by the Allies at the conference in Potsdam 1945,[83] cannot be considered at present as an objective reason justifying different treatment. Only the "objectively justified" past application of this criterion can be made – in an exceptional individual case – subject to the judicial review by a Czech court against the Czech legal standard, preceding ECHR- and EU-accession. A valid judgement can be reviewed by the European Court of Human Rights (ECtHR) only in relation to the rules on fair

81 The acceptance of these options by the general public was debatable, since other state bodies "tolerated" Klaus's arbitrary wilful behaviour and some media even glorified him for a long time; although 58 per cent of population feel his non-ratifying of the Treaty of Lisbon is detrimental to the position of the Czech Republic in Europe; and at the same time, for 62 per cent, he is the most popular Czech politician.

82 Articles 51–53 Charter.

83 The confiscation of Greek property by the Turkish administration after the occupation of the northern part of Cyprus (not recognized by international community) cannot – on the other hand – be considered as based on an objective reason (simple nationality).

trial. It cannot be reviewed by the Court of Justice in relation to the principle of equality, insofar as a link with European law (or its implementation at national level) is missing: the Treaty[84] does not prejudice the rules within Member States governing the system of property ownership (including property restitution, etc.).

Union fundamental rights *status quo* was already available on the basis of general principles of law and the case law of the Court of Justice.[85] The Charter respects the limits of powers conferred on the Union and does not extend any property claims to the prejudice of the Benes' decrees. There was no legal reason to require an additional opt-out from the Treaty of Lisbon.[86] At the end of the day, none of these scenarios was used: the European Council in December 2009 approved the attachment of Protocol No. 30 to the application of the EU Charter of Fundamental Rights in Poland and the United Kingdom.

Conclusion

The applicability of Member State law cannot be abandoned within a European state-like federation, but its applicability might be affected by modifications, reflecting subsequent changes of the Union's legal apparatus, insofar as the implementation of elements of statehood are concerned. Member State law must remain open to an inward reappraisal, if insistence on attributes of statehood could preclude the state's functions from being implemented through its participation in the project of European integration.

The original task of constitutional courts is to protect national constitutions against incompatible internal and external encroachments. The courts are used to recourse to considerable means of interpretation, neutralizing the encounter of conflicting norms and bringing them into a peaceful coexistence. The limit of such a restrained approach and the criterion of reference for *ultima ratio* judicial review are rules, the lowering of which is inadmissible, defined as "the constitutional core".

The constitutional courts in the Member States accepted an implicit change of their task when recognizing the Union's institutional framework as a guarantor of the execution of conferred powers in compliance with the common standard of values, subject to the Union not abandoning this standard.

84 Article 345 TFEU.

85 See "Explanations" to Article 51, para. 1, of the Charter, referred to by Article 6, para. 1, TEU-Lis.

86 President Klaus suggested, in the daily *Lidove noviny* on 16 October 2009, that an adequate guarantee "in the Irish way" of inviolability of the Benes' decrees could satisfy him, not necessarily an immediate hard opt-out, requiring the new ratification of the Treaty. On 18 October 2009, the Slovak Prime-Minister Robert Fico said on Czech TV that if there were to be ab opt-out clause Slovakia might join the Czech Republic.

This reservation witnesses ambiguity in the assessment of the relationship between European and national law as separate, but mutually bound systems: the task of controlling the limits for the execution of competences conferred on the Union is shared by European and national judicial authorities. Nevertheless, this does not entail a disclaimer by a constitutional court from its position of final guardian of the constitution. This approach demonstrates the understanding of the Union as a mere community of states, disregarding the civic dimension of the integration and the specific nature of legal systems based on non-hierarchical merits.

Invocation of an unlimited autonomy (*de facto*: of a conserving role) of the national "constitutional core" can undermine stabilization and modernization of the national legal system on the basis of the common – European and national – identity of values. In an extreme case, the Member State could fall into a precarious situation, forcing it to leave the Union.

One of the prominent objectives of the institutional reform of the Union was the reduction of its structural deficit, reflecting its specific (non-state) *habitus*. The existing deficiencies of democratic legitimacy of the European decision-making (viewed from the national perspective) may be "compensated" internally by reinforcing the national parliamentary scrutiny of European policies by the respective government. The respect of national constitutional identity without unilateral reservations should be able to avoid any obstruction to the development of Union law.

What is remarkable about the recent *Lisbon* cases is that the Czech Constitutional Court has emancipated itself in the assessment of European law from its former position of a *Lehrlinge* (apprentice) of the BVerfG. Even with its "European doctrine" not yet completed, the Court seems to be fairly "fit" for the post-Lisbon European judicial discourse.

References

Briza, P. (2009), The Czech Republic: The Constitutional Court on the Lisbon Treaty. Decision of 26 November 2008, *EuConst* 1, 143–164.

Classen, C.D. (2009), Legitime Stärkung des Bundestages oder verfassunngsrechtliches Prokrustbett?, *Juristenzeitung* 18.

Gärditz, K.F. and Hillgruber, Ch. (2009), Volkssuveränität und Demokratie ernst genommen – Zum Lissabon-Urteil des BverfG, *Juristenzeitung* 18.

Grosser, A. (2009), The Federal Constitutional Court's Lisbon Case: Germany's "Sonderweg": An Outsider´s Perspective, 10 *German Law Journal* No. 8 – Special Edition.

Halberstam, D. and Möllers, Ch. (2009), The German Constitutional Court says "Ja zu Deutschland!", 10 *German Law Journal* No. 8 – Special Edition.

Kiiver, P., (2009), German Participation in EU Decision-Making after the *Lisbon* Case: A Comparative View on Domestic Parliamentary Clearance Procedures, 10 *German Law Journal* No. 8 – Special Edition.

Kysela, J. and Kühn, Z. (2007), Presidential Elements in Government: The Czech Republic (continued), *EuConst* 1.

Leibfried, S. and van Elderen, K. (2009), "And they shall Beat their Swords into Plowshares" – the Dutch Genesis of a European Icon and the German Fate of the Treaty of Lisbon, 10 *German Law Journal* No. 8 – Special Edition.

Mayer, F.C. (2009), Rashomon in Karlsruhe, WHI-Paper 07/09, available at www.whi-berlin.de, accessed 21 August 2010.

Niedobitek, M. (2009), The *Lisbon* Case of 30 June 2009 – A Comment from the European Law Perspective, 10 *German Law Journal* No. 8 – Special Edition.

van Ooyen, R.Ch. (2006), *Die Staatstheorie des Bundesverfassungsgerichts und Europa*, 1st edn, Baden-Baden, Nomos.

Pernice, I. (1999), Multilevel Constitutionalism and the Treaty of Amsterdam, *CMLRev*, 703.

Schönberger, Ch. (2009), Lisbon in Karlsruhe: Maastricht's Epigones At Sea,10 *German Law Journal* No. 8 – Special Edition.

Schorkopf, F. (2009), The European Union as an Association of Sovereign States: Karlsruhe's Ruling on the Treaty of Lisbon, 10 *German Law Journal* No. 8 – Special Edition.

Thym, D. (2009), In the Name of Sovereign Statehood: A Critical Introduction to the *Lisbon* Judgment of the German Constitutional Court, *CMLRev*, 1795.

Tomuschat, Ch. (2009), The Ruling of the German Constitutional Court on the Treaty of Lisbon, 10 *German Law Journal* No. 8 – Special Edition.

Tomuschat, Ch. (2001), Die Benes-Dekrete – ein Hindernis für die Aufnahme der Tschechischen Republik in die Europäische Unieon?, in Ist das tschechische Rechtssystem bereits EU-konform?, Prag: Friedrich-Ebert-Stiftung e.V.

de Witte, B. (1999), Direct Effect, Supremacy and the Nature of the Legal Order, in P. Craig and G. de Búrca (eds) *The Evolution of EU Law*, Oxford, Oxford University Press.

Wohlfahrt, Ch. (2009), The Lisbon Case: A Critical Summary, 10 *German Law Journal* No. 8 – Special Edition.

Zemanek, J. (2001), Die Dekreten des Präsidenten Benes aus der Sicht des EU-Rechts, in Ist das tschechische Rechtssystem bereits EU-konform?, Prag: Friedrich-Ebert-Stiftung e.V.

Zemanek, J. (2007), The Emerging Czech Constitutional Doctrine of European Law, *EuConst* 3.

Chapter 8

Kafka, Kelsen and Supremacy: How European Courts Could Interact with a View to Fostering Constitutionalism

Alexander H.E. Morawa

Introduction

> [A Constitution is t]he vehicle of a nation's progress. It has to reflect the best in the past traditions of a nation; it has also to provide a considered response to the needs of the present and to possess enough resilience to cope with the demands of the future. … [T]he great generalities of the Constitution have a content and significance that vary from age to age and have, at the same time, transcendental continuity about them.[1]

> It is difficult to find a constitutional development that is more distant from [the] normative romantic vision of constitution making than the one we have observed in Europe since 1958. The process is devoid of opportunities for traditional constitutional enthusiasm.[2]

> The European constitutional balance urges a plural constitutional dialogue: a strong and daring European Court … needs to be surrounded by similar[ly] strong and daring interlocutors at national level.[3]

> The competition between national and Community pretensions with regard to ultimate legal authority, which results in intermittent yet fundamental conflicts, … results from the EU's own architecture, a hybrid between an international

1 Khanna, H.R. (2008), *Making of India's Constitution*, 2nd edn, New Delhi, Eastern Book Company, 3–4.

2 Sajó, A. (2005), Constitution Without the Constitutional Moment: A View from the New Member States, 3 *Int'l J. Const. L.* 243, 252.

3 Cartabia, M. (2009), Europe and Rights: Taking Dialogue Seriously, 5 *Europ. Const. L. Rev.* 5.

organisation and a Federal State in which it remains an open question as to who possesses ultimate legal authority.[4]

Learned Hand, judge of the United States Court's Appeal for the Second Circuit from 1924–1961 and one of the most highly regarded jurists in and beyond the United States, said in his 1959 volume called *The Spirit of Liberty*:[5]

> I often wonder whether we do not rest our hopes too much upon constitutions, upon laws and upon courts. These are false hopes; believe me, these are false hopes. Liberty lies in the hearts of men and women; …

In 2010, the legitimate question may be to ask where European liberty lies? Or, to be more pointed, one might wonder: is the liberty that the proposed European "constitution" promises truly at the heart of the European citizen?

In her recent article entitled A Constitution Between Past and Future,[6] Kim Lane Scheppele discusses the mindset of constitution drafters, in particular those that operate in a period of transition. She suggests that "constitution drafters invariably look even more towards the past than they do toward a future". She contends that "[i]n fact, this is impossible to avoid". Let us examine this claim in the context of the current European Communities' or European Union's legal order.

We may argue that the origin of the European Community was intended as an attempt to secure long-lasting peace and facilitate conflict resolution within a traditionally belligerent community of states by securing a sufficient level of mutual economic interdependence. Unlike other systems, such as the United Nations – where the United Nations Charter enjoys *de jure* an explicit supremacy over states' other international obligations[7] and is perceived as a quasi-constitution and thereby a guardian of the integrity of the international legal order – the European Communities' founding treaties did not claim to be constitutional in character, nor would that claim under any circumstances have succeeded.

The current constitutional debate, however, seems to be led by protagonists who look both backwards and towards a future characterized by an "ever closer union".[8] Thus, while the original idea of conflict avoidance through economic

---

4 Giorgi, F. and Triart, N. (2008), National Judges, Community Judges: Invitation to a Journey through the Looking-Glass – On the Need for Jurisdictions to Rethink the Inter-systemic Relations beyond the Hierarchical Principle, 14 *European Law Journal* 693, 709.

5 Hand, L. (1959), *The Spirit of Liberty*, Irving Dilliard (ed.), New York, Knopf, 144.

6 Scheppele, K.L. (2008), A Constitution Between Past and Future, 49 *William and Mary Law Review* 1377.

7 Article 103 of the United Nations Charter reads as follows: "In the event of a conflict between the obligations of the members of the United Nations under the present Charter and their obligations under any other international agreement, the obligations under the present Charter shall prevail."

8 The growing closer of the Union is also manifested in an increasing degree of unity of the legal order, including a tendency of the ECJ to emphasize the connections of the three

integration is still alive and strong, the current constitutional idea is driven by two core intentions: first, a European Constitution is viewed as a vehicle through which the imperfect and partly failing organizational structures within the European Communities can be repaired and turned into something more agreeable and lasting; second, the Constitution is supposed to include visionary elements that aim at the above mentioned greater unity of not just the European economy, but of European identity and European citizenry.

The above brief analysis goes hand in hand with the conclusion by Scheppele, who asserts: "Constitutions in their moments of creation cannot be inspired solely by imagined futures. Perhaps even more crucially, they encode imagined pasts."[9] Scheppele continues by advocating for "reclaiming the pre-constitutional past as a matter of constitutional enquiry".[10] Let us, again briefly, explore the backward- and forward-looking attitude of constitution drafters and of those who apply and interpret the constitution, namely the European Court of Justice and the various constitutional-level courts of the Member States.

Two of the defining legal issues of a constitutional structure that have attracted both public and scholarly attention in the recent past are, first, the European Court of Justice's power of judicial review and the scope thereof or, in other words, *van Gend & Loos*[11] and *Costa v. E.N.E.L.*[12] as the European version of *Marbury vs Madison*[13] and, second, the interrelationship of the supranational judicial body with its counterparts at the level of Member States, namely the national supreme and constitutional courts. The question raised in that context has been and continues to be whether this interrelationship can be one of confrontation or should be one of coordination. Tying the relationship issue together with the question of the scope of judicial review leads to one, presumably crucial question: what is a viable

---

pillars and to constitutionalize the third one. See Wessel, R.A. (2007), The EU's Foreign, Security and Defence Policy Fifteen Years after Maastricht: A Constitutional Momentum?, in Hans-Georg Ehrhart, et al. (eds), *Die Europäische Union im 21. Jahrhundert: Theorie und Praxis europäischer Außen-, Sicherheits- und Friedenspolitik*, Wiesbaden, Vs verlag, 305–306.

9 Scheppele, A Constitution Between Past and Future, 1380.

10 Ibid.

11 European Court of Justice, Case 11/70, *NV Algemene Transport- en Expeditie Onderneming van Gend & Loos v. Netherlands Inland Revenue Administration*, judgement of 5 February 1963, [1963] ECR 1.

12 European Court of Justice, Case 11/70, *Flaminio Costa v. E.N.E.L.*, judgement of 15 July 1965, [1965] ECR 585.

13 United States of America, Supreme Court, *Marbury v. Madison*, decision of 24 February 1803, 5 U.S. (1 Cranch) 137. The judgements of the ECJ in *Costa* and the Supreme Court in *Marbury* have been viewed as being judicial pronouncement about "basic empowering repositories – the Constitution in the United States, treaty in Community Europe": Puder, M.G. (2004), Supremacy of the Law and Judicial Review in the European Union: Comparing *Marbury v. Madison* with *COSTA v. ENEL*, 36 *Geo. Wash. Int'l L. Rev.* 567, 576.

model for multi-level judicial review in EU-Europe, taking into account both the constitutional history and reality of the European Union on the one hand, and national constitutional orders on the other hand?

National Constitutions as "National Treasures" and Kafka's "He"

Scheppele continues her analysis of constitution drafting by comparing a national constitution to a "treasure" and the drafters of that constitution as the preservers of *national treasures*.[14] The responses of certain national constitutional courts to supranational supremacy claimed by the European Union and its main protagonist, the European Court of Justice, indeed reflect a bit of an attitude that one would associate with the guardians of the Holy Grail. But it also relates to the question of identification, namely the identification of the population of European states with either the Union or their national entity as the defining factor. It also beckons the question which one, the Union or the national constitutional system, is seen as more likely to safeguard and be more reliable in advancing causes that are of common interest. This question neatly ties in with the question of whether national constitutional or supranational law as interpreted by their respective judicial guardians is in fact viewed more as an advance towards a desirable future. Scheppele in her article quotes from Franz Kafka's novel *He*, published in 1946. "He" in Kafka's text is a character caught "in a struggle between past and future":[15]

> He has two antagonists: The first pushes him from behind, from his birth. The second blocks the road in front of him. He struggles with both. Actually the first supports him in his struggle with the second, for the first wants to push him forward; and in the same way the second supports him in his struggle with the first; for the second of course is trying to force him back.[16]

When we claim that both the European Court of Justice (ECJ) and a national constitutional court are indeed protagonists of both the past and the future, our "He" in that scenario would be the European constitutional identity, and then it is indeed being pushed forwards and pulled backwards at the same time. The ECJ is, or rather was, the giver of supranationality of the Communities' legal order and thus clearly a strong protagonist of a future tight-knit European Union. This character as a creator of a legal order *sui generis* – although it does not amount to what one would properly call a constitutional legal order – also prompts the

14 Scheppele, A Constitution Between Past and Future, 1389.

15 Ibid.

16 Kafka, F. (1946), He, in *The Great Wall of China: Stories and Reflections* Berlin: Schocken Books, 276–77), quoted from Scheppele, A Constitution Between Past and Future, 1389.

Court to contribute to the past, here as a guardian of the self-made supreme and supranational order. The national constitutional and supreme courts are backward looking in that they are the protectors and preservers of the national treasure, namely their constitutions and what they stand for. But these courts are also by their own right forward-looking and future-oriented in that they further develop national law by themselves and incorporate that growing and expanding legal concept into the overall tradition of European law in a broader sense.

The question that then becomes essential is whether and how one can coordinate these parallel and sometimes conflicting systems of legal thought to ensure that, overall, there is a development towards a rights-centred constitutional legal future while at the same time the individuality and the coherence and functioning of a multitude of national constitutional orders are preserved as well. A growing trend in legal scholarship has suggested that "legal integration has proceeded through persuasion, mutual empowerment, and inter-court dialogue".[17] We shall explore further whether this judicial dialogue fits into the overall concept of constitutional development through judicial interpretation and what methodology may be suitable to accomplish the needs of a functioning judiciary and factual authority through coordination.

Constitutional Law-Making by Judges, or the Proper Role of the Judicial Branch in (Supranational) Constitutional Dialogue

The common reading of Montesquieu's approach to separation of power is that the three branches of government are relatively strictly and in any event purposefully separated. Thus, the judicial branch is not to undo and interfere with what is at the core of the power of the executive branch, such as foreign policy – the entire doctrine of a political question that is beyond the reach of the judiciary is an outstanding example of that principle.[18] Also, the legislative and judicial branches are rather carefully separated in that a judge, including a constitutional judge, is not to create law, but solely to interpret within certain clearly defined parameters the meaning of a legislative or constitutional text. Let us look into these issues from a very European perspective, yet without failing to duly consider the experiences of other systems of governance that are properly described as democratic.

With the proliferation of constitutional courts, in particular in the aftermath of the break-up of the Soviet Union and the Eastern Bloc, both the European (Kelsen) and American (*Marbury v. Madison*) approaches to constitutional adjudication have reappeared and gained strength. The process was historically predetermined,

17 Sweet, A.S. (2007), The Juridical Coup d'État and the Problem of Authority, 8 *German L. J.* 915, 925.

18 The political question doctrine is commonly understood to be a rule that excludes court action from those areas that are reserved, by virtue of a structural allocation at the constitutional level, for the legislative or executive branches of government.

in that European nations would routinely tend to follow a Kelsenian approach to constitutional review with the creation of separate constitutional tribunals entrusted exclusively with judicial matters that raise questions of a constitutional kind. However – with the general predominance of American legal thought in the process of re-establishing societies based on the rule of law in Europe in the 1990's – the philosophical foundations and their realization in practice of judicial review of the *Marbury* type also became rather influential in Europe.

Alec Stone Sweet, in his 2000 book *Governing With Judges*, places the modern type of constitutional court in some respects within the law-making process.[19] Referring to the power of European constitutional courts to conduct an abstract review of legislative acts, he emphasizes that when such courts exercise abstract review powers they operate "as a separate, but specialized, legislative chamber".[20] He suggests that constitutional courts become bodies involved in the law-making process in that they issue binding interpretations of a legislative act. He adds:

> Such rulings are formal, legally binding declarations stating that a legislative provision is to be considered constitutional if and only if that provision is interpreted exactly as the constitutional court does. Put differently, the judges rule that only one interpretation of a given legislative text, the one announced by the court, saves that text from being judged unconstitutional.[21]

Aharon Barak, the former president of the Israeli Supreme Court and a much criticized proponent of judicial activism, paints a quite different picture of the role of a constitutional type of court in his 2006 book *The Judge in a Democracy*: unlike Alec Stone Sweet, he here talks about not a formal, legal question of how to interpret a particular statute, but a broader question of "bridging the gap between law and society".[22] Proposing that a constitutional court should exercise partial activism and partial restraint, Barack formulates:

> I emphasized the importance of change in accordance with the general framework of the system, normative coherence, organic growth, natural development, continuity, and consistency.[23]

19 See Sweet, A.S. (1992), *The Birth of Juridical Politics in France*, New York: Oxford University Press,, and Sweet, A.S. (1994), Judging Socialist Reform: The Politics of Coordinate Construction in France and Germany, 26 *Comparative Political Studies* 443.

20 Sweet, A.S. (2000), *Governing With Judges*, New York: Oxford University Press, 62.

21 Ibid.,72.

22 Barak, A. (2006), *The Judge in a Democracy*, Princeton, Princeton University Press, 280.

23 Ibid., 281.

Thus, a constitutional judge is not a lawmaker influenced by the daily changes of the political will of the population, even of a democracy, but the guardian of a fundamental core of the legal order, which we may properly call the rule of law.

Marbury v. Madison has, as we have seen, not only dominated how courts in the United States interpret their own role as part of the constitutional order, but it has also influenced how judges and lawyers around the world see the role of the constitutional type of court. Stephen Breyer, a sitting Justice of the United States Supreme Court, centred his 2005 book around one thesis, namely that the United States Constitution was "centrally focused upon active liberty, upon the right of individuals to participate in democratic self-government".[24] Thus, he contends, the principle of participatory self-government was at the core of the constitutional structure that the founders of the United States Constitution had in mind. Is that true for European Union Europe; and more importantly, can it be incorporated as a guiding constitutional principle into the debate on creating a constitutional framework for a unified continent? If one considers that in the recent debate about supremacy of European law as opposed to constitutional predominance, conflict arose almost exclusively when the debate centred around individual freedoms and liberties, one might argue that Breyer's assertion of judicial supremacy may at least apply in a qualified fashion. Breyer is also a proponent of moderate judicial activism, although to a lesser degree than former justice Aharon Barak. Both are outstanding proponents of an approach to judicial interpretation that incorporates foreign and comparative legal analysis as well as the consideration of public international law documents and practice into domestic constitutional adjudication. The suggestion that the judicial discourse should in some way be globalized has given rise to a lot of debates, particularly in US constitutional scholarship. Laurence Tribe, in *The Invisible Constitution*, discusses the sentiments raised by scholars as well as by judges opposed to the incorporation of global legal thought into the domestic constitutional discourse, and concludes:

> Especially when one considers that the judicious use of global sources of insight is not a new phenomenon in our constitutional discourse, one should find this recently formulated antiglobalism at least presumptively puzzling – particularly in an era when law and culture, as well as economic life and sources of environmental concern, so thoroughly cross and transcend national boundaries.[25]

The European Communities and European Union are predominantly concerned with economic integration, but increasingly also the environment, security and a continental approach to citizenship. Even critics of the globalization approach in the US–American context leave much room for an argument that in Europe

---

24 Breyer, S. (2006), *Active Liberty*, New York, First Vintage Books, 21.

25 Tribe, L.H. (2008), *The Invisible Constitution*, New York, Oxford University Press, 186.

a dialogue between constitutional-type courts at all levels should indeed take place. Richard Posner, in his book *How Judges Think*, while being critical of the increasing references in US judicial practice to foreign sources of the law, still concludes:

> The problem is not learning from abroad; it is treating foreign judicial decisions as authority in US cases, as if the world were a single legal community.[26]

Now, the European Communities are indeed a single legal community. That is exactly what the European Court of Justice has emphasized ever since establishing Community law's unique character as a legal system *sui generis*, *in tandem* with the supremacy of European law over national law in all its manifestations. If Europe is indeed a community of law, that community is a community of both supranational, European law and national constitutional legal principles that enshrine the above mentioned "national treasures" and national identities codified in the constitutions – and interpretations thereof – of the Member States of the Communities. Should there not be an exchange along the lines of comparative constitutional law in a system that is so intensively linking a supranational legal order and a national constitutional identity? One should bear in mind in this context that the European Court of Justice itself continuously refers to the law and practices of the Member States when identifying an (emerging) European principle.[27]

National Constitutional Courts and European Law

The current relationship – or "interdependence"[28] – between national constitutional courts and the European Court of Justice has been described by Loïc Azoulai and Felix Ronkes Agerbeek as a calculated "equilibrium".[29] Their discussion of the jurisprudence of the French Conseil Constitutionnel concludes that that Court "allows for the *concurrence* of constitutional developments in Europe"[30] instead of fusing the various constitutional levels in support of European legal superiority. That characterization, while specific for French legal practice, may be considered

26 Posner, R.A. (2008), *How Judges Think*, Harvard, Harvard University Press, 353.

27 Iglesias, G.C.R. (2004), The Court of Justice, Principles of EC Law, Court Reform and Constitutional Adjudication, *European Business Law Review* 1116, 1119. See also the similar practice of the European Court of Human Rights: "It is legitimate when deciding whether a certain measure is acceptable under one of its provisions to take account of the standards prevailing amongst the Member States of the Council of Europe." Appl. 24396/94, *T. v. the United Kingdom*, decision of 16 December 1999, amongst many others.

28 Bauer, L. (2008), *Der Europäische Gerichtshof als Verfassungsgericht?* Baden-Baden, Nomos, 163.

29 Azoulai, L. and Agerbeek, F.R. (2005), Case Note, 42 *Common Market Law Review* 871, 886.

30 Ibid.

an adequate description of the practice of various other high courts. What we find can well be described as a shift from the German *Solange*-approach[31] that insisted on a reserved domain of national review of constitutionality at the very least in the field of human rights and fundamental freedoms, towards a sometimes formal, sometimes somewhat more substantive attempt to carve out a scope of constitutional review even within European Union substance matter; an example of the latter is the Spanish Constitutional Tribunal's ruling on the treaty establishing a Constitution for Europe,[32] where that court introduced a novel and somewhat artificial sounding distinction between primacy and supremacy to distinguish the effects of national constitutional and European community law.[33]

Some other current pronouncements of national constitutional courts about the status of European law in the domestic legal order and how to proceed in case of conflicts and controversies are illustrative for our further discussion. An example for an attempt to separate European law and national constitutional law matters on the formal plane is the jurisprudence of the Hungarian Constitutional Court. That Court in its practice "evade[s] the direct constitutional scrutiny of EU measures, but it will consider the constitutionality of the implementing measure without addressing the legality of the directive or the appropriateness of implementation".[34] It is noteworthy, however, that the Hungarian Court does in

31 Germany, Federal Constitutional Court, *Solange I*, judgement of 29 May 1974, BVerfGE 37, 271, and *Solange II*, judgement of 22 October 1986, BVerfGE 73, 339: "Solange die Europäischen Gemeinschaften, insbesondere die Rechtsprechung des Gerichtshofs der Gemeinschaften einen wirksamen Schutz der Grundrechte gegenüber der Hoheitsgewalt der Gemeinschaften generell gewährleisten, der dem vom Grundgesetz als unabdingbar gebotenen Grundrechtsschutz im wesentlichen gleichzuachten ist, zumal den Wesensgehalt der Grundrechte generell verbürgt, wird das Bundesverfassungsgericht seine Gerichtsbarkeit über die Anwendbarkeit von abgeleitetem Gemeinschaftsrecht, das als Rechtsgrundlage für ein Verhalten deutscher Gerichte oder Behörden im Hoheitsbereich der Bundesrepublik Deutschland in Anspruch genommen wird, nicht mehr ausüben und dieses Recht mithin nicht mehr am Maßstab der Grundrechte des Grundgesetzes überprüfen …", and subsequently the *Banana Market Case*, judgement of 6 July 2000, BVerfGE 102, 147 and, most recently, the Lisbon Treaty decision on 30 June 2009, 2 BvE 2/08, which has been termed, much like before the *Maastricht* decision, BVerfGE 89, 155, "Solange III": see Ziller, J. (2009), Solange III, or the Bundesverfassungsgericht's Europe-friendlyness. On the decision of the German Federal Constitutional Court over the Ratification of the Treaty of Lisbon, 5 *Rivista Italiana di Diritto Pubblico Comunitario* 973–95, and Makowski, K.D. (1995–1996), Solange III: The German Federal Constitutional Court's Decision on Accession to the Maastricht Treaty on European Union,16 *U. Pa. J. Int'l Bus. L.* 155).

32 Spain, Constitutional Tribunal, Opinion 1/2004, dated 13 December 2004, on the Treaty establishing a Constitution for Europe, summarized by de la Torre, C. (2005), Case Note, 42 *Common Market Law Review* 1169.

33 See ibid.,1187.

34 Varju, M. (2009), On the Constitutional Issues of EU Membership and the Interplay between the ECHR and Domestic Constitutional Law Concerning the Right of Assembly and Freedom of Expression, 15 *European Public Law*, 295, 300 with further references.

fact engage in sometimes rather "robust"[35] constitutional scrutiny and that, in any event, a finding that implementing legislation is unconstitutional does in practice mean that community law is at least to a degree scrutinized in substance and cannot be implemented in domestic law.[36]

The contemporary practice of the Italian Constitutional Court is instructive with respect to a more substantive discourse on European legal supremacy: Its practice is characterized by an initial rejection of primacy and supremacy of community law,[37] followed by a gradual acceptance of a limited supremacy complemented by the reserved power of the Constitutional Court to protect fundamental rights and principles enshrined in the national constitution.[38] In its 1984 *Granital*[39] decision, the Italian Constitutional Court changed its attitude and adopted the European Court of Justice's approach of supremacy, while maintaining that "whenever a community rule infringes a fundamental principle or right of the Italian constitutional system, it will be for the constitutional court ... to decide the hierarchy of norms".[40] With this line of jurisprudence the Italian Constitutional Court preserved its own authority to give precedence to its fundamental constitutional principles, a strategy particularly relevant in the context of fundamental rights and freedoms. It comes as no surprise that subsequent practice was in line with the European Court of Justice's own jurisprudence, emphasizing the principles which are common to the European legal system as decisive and accepting the European Charter of Fundamental Rights as an auxiliary, but also authoritative means of interpretation.[41] It would seem that since 1984 European law was perceived by the Italian Constitutional Court as "not ... separate, but as coordinated with the national legal order. The two legal orders are now seen as integrated."[42] Della Cananea stresses in this context that "[o]nce it is accepted that there is not a single constitutional document, but a plurality of documents having constitutional nature, the dialogue between courts becomes increasingly important."[43] He also correctly emphasizes that constitutional plurality as established by the practice of the Italian Constitutional Court mandates not only dialogue, but also leads to inevitable conflict, particularly in the field of fundamental rights and freedoms.

The Italian Court's dealing with European Union law offers interesting parallels to its most recent decisions concerning the domestic status of the

---

35 Ibid.

36 See ibid.

37 See decision of the Constitutional Court No. 14/1974, para. 14.

38 Decision of the Constitutional Court No. 536/1995, *Frontini*. Cf. Rossi, L.S. (2009), Case Note, 46 *Common Market Law Review* 319.

39 Decision of the Constitutional Court No. 170/1984.

40 Rossi, Case Note, 320.

41 See decisions of the Constitutional Court Nos. 393/2006 and 394/2006; cf. Rossi, Case Note, 320.

42 della Cananea, G. (2008), The Italian Constitutional Court and the European Court of Justice: From Separation to Interaction?, 14 *European Public Law* 523, 529.

43 Ibid.

European Convention of Human Rights. In two decisions dated 24 October 2007,[44] the Constitutional Court applied a newly amended provision of the Italian Constitution, Article 117(1), and found that that provision guarantees "superior legal authority to the European Convention over and above ordinary domestic statute law".[45] On the other hand, both European Union law and Council of Europe human rights law are subject to the ultimate test by the Italian Constitutional Court as to their compatibility with fundamental principles of the Italian Constitution. It is remarkable that the above decisions were issued in the context of fundamental rights and freedoms where it seems apparent from general public international law that the national legal order is entirely free to establish guarantees that surpass those established by international treaties. Thus, public international law maintains its force only in so far as it guarantees not only minimum standards, but *de facto* maximum standards. However, Mirate shows convincingly that there is a crucial difference between the approach of the Italian Constitutional Court to European human rights law and European Union law: "The constitutional review could assess the conformity of the ECHR provisions, as interpreted by the European Court, with references to 'any constitutional clause', and not only, such as in the relationship with the EU law, having regard for the 'general fundamental principles' of the domestic constitutional order."[46] The Constitutional Court thus clearly gives preferential status to European Union law as opposed to ordinary treaty law, notwithstanding the fact that the European Convention of Human Rights has "a special character ... as a treaty for the collective enforcement of human rights and fundamental freedoms"[47] "compris[ing] more than mere reciprocal engagements between Contracting States".[48] European Union law thus is clearly superior and enjoys interpretative priority, which seems, at first glance, to be in compliance with the European Court of Justice's own demand under the *Costa v E.N.E.L.* line of jurisprudence.

The Polish Constitutional Tribunal in the *Arrest Warrant Case*[49] had to assess the constitutionality of the European arrest warrant, which provides for extradition of Polish nationals upon request by the prosecuting authorities of other Member States. The Tribunal declared the national implementation of the European arrest

44 Constitutional Court of Italy, decisions Nos. 348 and 349/2007.

45 Mirate, S. (2009), A New Status for the ECHR in Italy: The Italian Constitutional Court and the New "Conventional Review" on National Laws, 15 *European Public Law* 89, 89.

46 Ibid., 102.

47 European Court of Human Rights, *Loizidou v. Turkey*, judgement of 23 March 1995, Series A, No. 310, para. 70.

48 European Court of Human Rights, *Ireland v. the United Kingdom*, judgement of 18 January 1978, Series A, No. 25, para. 239.

49 Polish Constitutional Tribunal, *Case of the Constitutionality of the European Arrest Warrant National Implementation*, judgement of 27 April 2005, No. P 1/05, quoted by Leczykiewicz, D. (2006), National Courts, 43 *Common Market Law Review* 1181, 1191, and the criticism therein on p. 1188.

warrant to be unconstitutional and rightly referred to principles of fundamental rights protection and the sources therefore in European Union law in its decision. When it came to assessing whether there was a principle that states should not extradite their own nationals, however, the Tribunal failed to engage in an exercise of assessing and identifying the constitutional judicial traditions of the Member States. This has been criticized by commentators as an interpretive inconsistency, as the exercise of filling the abstract European norm with concrete contents by referencing national constitutional law provisions and interpretations would have added credibility and weight to the argument of the tribunal.[50]

A 2006 judgement of the Estonian Supreme Court reflects "judicial disquiet about this supremacy principle that is not dissimilar to cases in the (older) Member States in earlier years".[51] Here, the Estonian Supreme Court did indeed give unqualified support for the principle of supremacy of European Union law in the context of assessing the authority to establish and issue currency that arose in the context of Estonia's prospective membership in the single currency. The court here held that, in principle, constitutional provisions that were not compatible with EU law were not applicable and therefore suspended. This interpretation of the so-called defence clause of the Estonian Constitution lead to the dissent of certain justices of the Supreme Court who found it to be too far reaching and suggested that the case law of the European Court of Justice did not require unconditional application of all European Union legislation, but rather provided for certain exceptions to that.[52]

The Czech Constitutional Court's 2008 decision on the constitutionality of the Lisbon Treaty[53] is another example of a national court's attempt to undertake a balancing act between reserving a domain for itself in European decision-making while at the same time demonstrating pro-European attitudes. Holding that the not yet ratified Lisbon treaty enjoyed lesser status in domestic law than secondary Community law – an approach that is open to criticism – the Court found that it would have to be tested against the entire constitutional order, and not merely against the "fundamental core" as established in the earlier *Sugar Quotas* case.[54] In an apparent attempt to combine a perceived European legal principle of subsidiarity even in the context of fundamental rights – Article 53 of the Charter

50 Leczykiewicz, National Courts, 1188.

51 D'Sa, R. and Lafranque, J. (2008), Getting to Know You: The Developing Relationship between National Courts of the "Newer" Member States and the European Court of Justice, with Particular Reference to Estonia, *EBLR* 311, 319.

52 Ibid., at 318 et seq.

53 Czech Republic, Constitutional Court, Case Pl. ÚS 19/08, Collection No. 446/2008, decision of 26 November 2008, reported by Bříza, P. (2009), The Czech Republic: The Constitutional Court on the Lisbon Treaty, Decision of 26 November 2008, 5 *European Constitutional Law Review* 143–164.

54 Czech Republic, Constitutional Court, Case Pl. ÚS 50/04, Collection No. 156/2006, decision of 8 March 2006. The Court still "emphasized the prominent position the fundamental core enjoys". Bříza, The Czech Republic, 148.

of Fundamental Rights – with a *Solange II*-like conditional recognition of the "functionality of the EU institutional framework for ensuring the review of the scope of the exercise of conferred competencies",[55] the Court easily arrived at its conclusion that the Lisbon Treaty was in conformity with the constitution.

The practice of the constitutional courts of new Member States has undoubtedly added a new dimension to the discourse on supremacy and European–national coordination. Whether these judgements are to be explained as "an attempt to reinforce [domestic constitutional courts'] inter-institutional position"[56] at home or a certain docility[57] towards the, for them, new European legal order and its protagonist, the ECJ, we find a clear preference for both constitutional integrity and Euro-friendly interpretation, which does not always work out. Sadurski characterizes the relationship between the national and supranational legal orders in the East as "not a picture of audacious judicial defiance in the face of Europe. But nor is it a picture of timid deference towards the EJC's doctrine of supremacy."[58] There is, however, a degree of parallelism in – subdued and cautious – judicial defiance towards EU law in the West and the East, as the case law shows, and that points in the direction of shared concerns, irrespective of the duration or "tradition" of European integration in a given Member State. We may take the progressing expansion of the European legal area as a feasible starting point for a reflection on the more fundamental issues of constitutional–supranational interaction, with a view to at least gradually remedying the deficiencies that still prevail in that area.

The Parameters for Interaction: The Hierarchy of Norms and Normative Constitutional Coordination

Before turning to the application of a participatory constitution-making scheme under dual national/supranational judicial guardianship, we have to set the stage. The outer limits for our explorations are twofold: first, the formal hierarchical framework for constitutional adjudication within a multi-level system of governance and, second, the deliberately informal interactive give-and-take amongst the actors, that is, in particular the judicial bodies, national on the one hand, above-national on the other hand. This author believes that neither one can exist without the other, even though attempts have been made to state just that both by the ECJ

55 Bříza, The Czech Republic, 150 and 161.

56 Sadurski, W. (2008), "Solange Chapter 3": Constitutional Courts in Central Europe – Democracy – European Union, 14 *European Law Journal* 1, 34.

57 Bobek, M. (2008), The Fortress of Judicial Independence and the Mental Transitions of the Central European Judiciaries, 14 *European Public Law* 99, 109, suggests such a docile executor-attitude of the Central and Eastern Europe (CEE) judiciary with reference to Ćapeta, T. (2005), Courts, Legal Culture and EU Enlargement, 1 *Croatian Yearbook of European Law and Policy* 23.

58 Sadurski, "Solange Chapter 3", 29.

– unqualified supremacy of European law, including national procedural law,[59] and even over national constitutional law[60] including pre-existing treasured values[61] – and by national courts – absolute reserved domain of national constitutional law.[62] As Weiler contended as early as 1991, "no core activity of state function could be seen as still constitutionally immune from Community action …".[63] Thus, even the core constitutional pillars of national law (or, the crown jewels amongst the national treasures) are at the very least *interacting* with European law.

Miguel Poiares Maduro offers a sophisticated and frank analysis of the interpretation of European law by the judiciary within the parameters of pluralism.[64] He defends a teleological approach to interpretation in general and in European law specifically, but more interesting for the present purposes is his discussion of the proper use of comparative law: is it aimed at discovering the "best law" or "a tool for the construction of a common law"?[65] He asserts that European judicial decision-making has "to balance the respect of national legal traditions with the need to accommodate them to the specific needs of the EU legal order" and, consequently, to follow the "requirement of consistency".[66] Maduro reintroduces a concept that we have discussed before, namely that constitutions as well as the founding treaties must be "open to the future" and are thus many times based on abstract and broad principles rather than regulations at the micro-level, which leads to "development and reinterpretation".[67] Indeed, teleological interpretation and comparative (constitutional) law are instruments of development and change, and that fact has caused extensive controversies between their proponents and those who favor an originalist or textual approach to interpreting constitutions,

59 Commission Notice on the Enforcement of State Aid Law by National Courts, *OJ C 85, 9 April 2009, 1–22:* "Given the supremacy of Community law, national courts must leave national procedural rules unapplied if doing otherwise would violate the principles [of European law pertaining to state aid]."

60 European Court of Justice, Case 11/70, *Flaminio Costa v. E.N.E.L.*, judgement of 15 July 1965, [1965] ECR 585.

61 European Court of Justice, Case 106/77, *Amministrazione delle Finanze dello Stato v. Simmenthal SpA*, judgement of 9 March 1978, [1978] ECR 629, para. 21: "[E]very national court must, in a case within its jurisdiction, apply Community law in its entirety and protect rights which the latter confers on individuals and must accordingly set aside any provision of national law which may conflict with it, whether prior or subsequent to the Community rule."

62 Such as those expounded on by the Czech Constitutional Court in the *Sugar Quotas* case or underlying the objections of the German Federal Constitutional Court in *Solange – Banana Market*.

63 Weiler, J.H.H. (1991), The Transformation of Europe, 100 *Yale L. J.* 2403, 2416.

64 Maduro, M.P. (2007), Interpreting European Law: Judicial Adjudication in a Context of Constitutional Pluralism, 2 *European Journal of Legal Studies* 1, 1.

65 Ibid., 6.

66 Ibid., 7.

67 Ibid., 12.

for instance in the United States.[68] In Europe, on the other hand, the comparative method is highly esteemed in theory and practice.

Poiares Maduro continues by saying that "EU law does not challenge the constitutional identity of national constitutional orders because it is grounded on the same legal values".[69] This is true, currently, to a great extent, but not entirely. The fact that there were relatively few head-on constitutional collisions between the ECJ and national high courts is an indication of relative *de facto* harmony, but cases where legal values were not shared, or more pertinently where legal values are shared amongst national constitutional adjudicators against the (already expressed or assumed) will of the ECJ have happened. Most remarkable in this respect are not so much the underlying stories or rights concerned, but the fact that a plurality of European national courts find that *they* should be the ultimate guardians of their respective constitutions. That is a momentous piece of evidence for *less than perfect* harmony. The question of who should wield the ultimate power of judicial review is fundamental in constitutional design, and the absence of a clear and commonly accepted answer is proof of significant intra-systemic deficiencies.

One might wish to argue that the entry into force of the Treaty of Lisbon[70] and the now existing formal "primary law" quality of the Charter of Fundamental Rights of the European Union of 7 December 2000[71] together with the three pillars[72] approach to fundamental rights protection may change the realities of EU human rights law substantially, thus rendering inter-court dialogue less, or not at all important: the Charter, the ECHR and the fundamental rights "as they result from the constitutional traditions common to the Member States"[73] form a "union" of sorts of human rights standards, with the latter two elements constituting "general principles"[74] of EU law. While it is debatable whether the European Court of Human Rights' (ECtHR) casuistic case law itself has sufficiently crystallized what would amount to working "general principles",[75] the inclusion of

68 See, for a critical discussion of the grounds for rejecting the comparative approach, Markesinis, Sir B. (2006), Judicial Mentality: Mental Disposition or Outlook as a Factor Impeding Recourse to Foreign Law, 80 *Tul. L. Rev*. 1325.

69 Maduro, Interpreting European Law, 17.

70 Treaty of Lisbon amending the Treaty on European Union and the Treaty establishing the European Community, signed at Lisbon, 13 December 2007, OJ 2007/C 306/01.

71 OJ 2000/C 364/01.

72 Pernice, I. (2008), The Treaty of Lisbon and Fundamental Rights, in Stefan Griller and Jaques Ziller (eds) *The Lisbon Treaty. EU Constitutionalism without a Constitutional Treaty?*, Vienna, New York, Springer, 235–56, 240.

73 Article 6(3) (ex Article 6 TEU).

74 Ibid.

75 The February 2010 Interlaken Declaration on the Future of the European Court of Human Rights, available at http://www.eda.admin.ch/etc/medialib/downloads/edazen/topics/europa/euroc.Par.0133.File.tmp/final_en.pdf, accessed 27 July 2010, para. 4, for

"constitutional traditions" clearly means the explicit reiteration of the *status quo*, namely EU and national dualism in filling the rights with concrete contents and the consequential potential for intra-system controversies. The right of individuals to challenge regulatory actions of Union agencies directly before the ECJ[76] certainly strengthens the procedural position of individuals, and thus may serve as a tool for enhancing civil society participation in the development of a common European law of fundamental rights. Yet, it does not appear that this tool has much to do with the issue of Community versus national constitutional-type rights divergences *per se*. Thus, unfortunately, despite being a major step forward, Lisbon seems to not have resolved the problem.

If it were true that the shared legal values were indeed a solid basis for a European "common law", "promoting communication between" legal orders in order to "reduce or manage[...]"[77] their potential conflict would suffice. Then, a delegation of powers from the Community level to the national courts similar to the delegated power of national courts envisaged by the ECJ with respect to safeguarding the right to an effective remedy against Community law in *Jégo Quéré* [78] would suffice; national courts would need to establish within their constitutional order a mechanism to ensure that pronouncements in matters affecting EU law were coordinated with other high courts and the ECJ.

If our European legal harmony is, much like the European project in its entirety, fragmented and conditional, then we still – Lisbon notwithstanding – suffer not so much from communication deficits, but from the absence of core elements of a European law that would qualify as a constitutional system. The three pillars of fundamental rights in the new Article 6 TEU is evidence of that fragmentation: why would one need to prescribe that the Charter, as a rather comprehensive document, is in continued need of enlightenment by the ECHR – a treaty that, as is being discussed, will be subjected to a *broader* national margin of appreciation with the increasing subsidiarity of the Convention procedure, the narrower, cassation-style jurisdiction of the ECtHR, and the logical consequence of a *broader power of national courts* to interpret the ECHR authoritatively, albeit within certain European minimum standards – and by national constitutional traditions? The absence of a core constitution is not necessarily bad at all, but needs to be

instance, has "[s]tressed the importance of ensuring the clarity and consistency of the Court's case law", thus at least between the lines admitting a lack thereof; several proposals include the reinvigoration of the little used advisory procedure, in a new format, to permit the Court to render judgements of fundamental importance in a pre-emptive, rather than reactive fashion: see Council of Europe (ed.) (2009), Contribution of the Secretary General of the Council of Europe, in *The Future of the European Court of Human Rights, Preparatory Contributions*, 36–48, 41.

76 Article 2, clause 214(c) and (d) of the Treaty of Lisbon.

77 Maduro, Interpreting European Law, 17.

78 ECJ, Case C-263/02P, *Commission v. Jégo Quéré & Cie SA*, judgement of 1 April 2004, [2004] ECR I-3425, para. 31.

recognized first, then responded to. Should we opt for replacing real harmony with empty claims of coordination, future conflicts will have to be resolved without a reference framework, and we are constructing the European legal "building" on sand.

Let us add Kelsen to Maduro and we will likely get somewhere: Kelsen's thinking does not create a strictly positivist formal *Stufenbau* of the law. Rather, "the theory of legal hierarchy is ... committed to a substantive conception of legality".[79] Hierarchically higher norms thus must also have a valid claim to substantive legality in order to prevail. In a multilayered legal reality as Europe faces today, a test of substantive legality also must undergo a plurality of levels of tests. The validity of a norm must always be assessed by reference to the legal order(s), or *Rechtsordnung(en)*, it operates in and there is no "abstract validity" irrespective of a normative context.[80] If we assume that the European legal order is one composed of 27 national systems and one supranational (complemented by another international one, the European Convention on Human Rights, or more generally operating within the framework of public international law), then the "concrete validity" of any norm claiming superiority will have to be formally and substantially in accord with the entire *Rechtsordnung*. The establishment of pure formal hierarchical superiority of a norm – or let us call it supremacy – is insufficient since it does not answer the second part of the question, namely if the norm is substantively compliant with the constitutional *Grundnorm*, which is a multi-level one. The task is finding a basis for concluding what the constitutional consensus is: is it the common European standard, or is it the – possibly lone dissenting – national standard? Is it for the national or the super-national court to establish (a) what the law is, (b) what the common standard is and whether a particular national norm complies with it or not (including a possible interpretation that renders it at least *de facto* compliant), and (c) what happens if there is a conflict? A full answer to these questions is embedded in a multitude of layers of legal and political decision-making processes and cannot be given in the present context. What can be offered, though, is a sketch of possible ways and means for European and national judges to coexist and ultimately cooperate both within a sound formal framework and within a structure that encourages mutual coordination and exchange.

The Kelsenian triangle of normative hierarchy provides a simple yet sophisticated model for positively resolving constitutional dilemmas within the emerging constitutional order of Europe. We simply need to place alongside the European legal system, which certainly maintains its supreme rank in the overall structure, a national triangle of hierarchal norms. The European law triangle will

79 Vinx, L. (2007), *Hans Kelsen's Pure Theory of Law*, Oxford, Oxford University Press, 83.

80 See Jestaedt, M. (2008), Konkurrenz von Rechtsdeutungen statt Koexistenz von Rechtsordnungen, in Hauke Brunkhorst and Rüdiger Vogt (eds), *Rechts-Staat*, Baden-Baden, Nomos, 233, 235.

have at its top not a formal, but a substantive "constitution" which to define will remain the sole domain of the European institutions, with the European Court of Justice taking the lead. Provisions from this substantive constitution trump not only all other normative provisions within the European law triangle, but also in the nature of things, are untouchable by any domestic or legal provisions, irrespective of their rank and value as national treasures.

Clearly, the overall acceptance of this substantive constitution will greatly benefit from an increased democratic legitimization process after its creation, as well as from the strengthening of democratic representation and adherence to fundamental rights as a duty of Community institutions.[81] Both democratic participation in the creation of European legal norms and the emergence of a European citizenry that will take an active, if not proactive role in litigating its own rights and entitlements before both national/international tribunals, will enhance said legitimacy.

National constitutional provisions will occupy in the above scheme a qualified role and position that ranks just below European constitutional norms; where exactly it ranks, and what its effects are, depends on their substantive quality as well. Thus, both normative systems are subject to the same standard when it comes to asserting their superiority. While national law, including constitutional provisions, will always rank below the European constitutional structure, the top

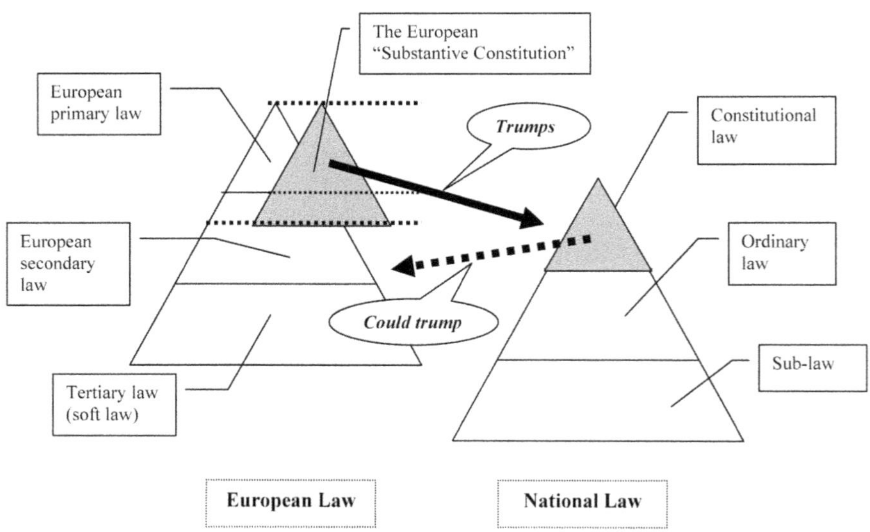

Figure 8.1 Proposed European constitutional triangle

81 See Sadurski, W. (2006), "Solange Chapter 3": Constitutional Courts in Central Europe – Democracy – European Union", EUI working paper LAW No. 2006/40, 32 (this is the same content as that published in 2008).

of the constitutional pyramid of the national legal system – those are the ones that form a core of the constitutional identity or the top of the national treasure as defined by national constitutional courts, or those that find a basis in a qualified common European legal principle (discussed *infra*) – will serve as a proper corrective element that reigns in, if necessary, European legislative acts that endanger the integrity of a constitutional system.

We thus have a non-homogenous concept of what is supreme and constitutional in character, as opposed to what is merely formally supreme, and that applies to European law as much as to national (constitutional) law. The benefits in contemporary Europe are apparent: first, the European Constitution can assert itself without the formal process of adoption or, in other words, a continued coordinated effort to build and sustain it will suffice. This not only reflects the crucial difference between national and supranational constitutions, but also the different role the various branches of supranational government play as opposed to their national counterparts. The interaction between judicial interpreters of the law cannot be a substitute for the lack of a "constitutional moment",[82] or an emotion that flows into a substantive constitution at such a moment; the absence of it means that the constitution that emerges "does not contribute to a sense of union, or the formation of identity, among the members of the society to which it applies".[83] But, provided that the other parameters are right, the heterogeneity and parallelism of constitutional processes can forge the communality that is lacking.

Second, this is also an exercise on constitutional realism, in that the processes by which a quasi-constitutional framework has been elaborated so far is legitimized by continued operation. The role of the European Court of Justice, in particular, can be sustained.

Third, a substantive constitution will remain flexible and will allow continuous interpretation in light of present-day circumstances. Within a system that lacks both founding fathers and a constituency that "willed" the constitution, such a non-static concept is particularly feasible, purposeful and legitimate, in particular if and as far as the future will see an increase in democratic participation in both law-making and law-setting, the latter through an active litigation practice in the common interest.

Fourth, the European lawmaker would be called upon to specify more clearly – with a view to influencing the contents of the substantive constitution – which of its texts shall be considered fundamental, and thus constitutional, thus asserting a rightful place of the legislature in the European political process and a partner of the ECJ, but also a means to employ "checks and balances". This should allow a more precise practice of legislating the "identity" of Europe, as opposed to administrative legislation, which overlooks, or deliberately excludes, the more fundamental questions.

---

82 See Ackerman, B. (1998), *We the People*, Harvard, Belknap Press/Harvard University Press.

83 Sajó, Constitution Without the Constitutional Moment, 243.

In a system that is characterized by a lack of homogeneity, similarly heterogeneous constitutional concepts are only natural, and in fact beneficial. With such a construction of supreme law, there is an organized exchange and dialogue possible, if not likely, that has tangible outcomes. We will need to explain the concept further, of course.

Substantive Constitutionalism and Substantive Supremacy

A Substantive Notion of a Constitution and Substantive Constitutionalism

There were debates as to whether the proposed European Constitution would qualify as a constitution or as a treaty. The overwhelming majority of national decision-makers regarded it as a treaty, while a few acknowledged it had elements of a factual constitution.[84] Let us depart from traditional notions even further than those who propose a multi-level constitutionalism of sorts: the present author suggests that we focus instead on a substantive definition of a constitution.[85] This is novel for the more positivistic systems of legal thought to which the majority of the Central and Eastern European systems undoubtedly belong. It is not that radical, however, if viewed (a) from a European perspective,[86] (b) from a public international law point of view. and (c) from other contexts, namely those of valid legal systems that lack a formal written constitution, or rather exist without one. One need not go so far as to rely on the Supreme Court of Israel which, in its famous

84 Albi, A. (2007), Introduction: The European Constitution and National Constitutions in the Context of 'Post-national Constitutionalism, in Anneli Albi and Jacques Ziller (eds), *The European Constitution and National Constitutions*, Alphen aan den Rijn (NL), Kluwer Law International, 1, 5 et seq.

85 Substantive characteristics of a constitution as core elements of constitutional constructivism are being discussed, for instance, in the US: see e.g., Fleming, J.E. (1993/4), Constructing the Substantive Constitution, 72 *Tex. L. Rev.* 211 and Fleming, J.E. (1995/6), Securing Deliberative Autonomy, 48 *Stan. L. Rev.* 1.

86 See Lenaerts, K. (2004–2005), The Constitution for Europe: Fiction or Reality, 11 *Colum. J. Eur. L.* 465, 467), who asserts that the – failed – constitutional convention "marked a switch of perspective, from a formal constitution enacted through substantive treaty-making, to a substantive constitution the adoption of which is operated in the end by formal treaty-making". Lenaerts here refers to "the insertion of the Charter of Fundamental Rights … as an expression of values common to the peoples of Europe … and the precise and transparent identification of the Union's exclusive and shared competences and thus their allocation between the Union and the Member States, as well as the distinction between the legislative and the executive power of the Union, each with its own set of decision-making procedures and legal instruments [as] represent[ing] major additional steps towards the building of an effective Constitution" and, accordingly, substantive constitutionality.

1992 *Mizrachi Bank* judgement,[87] created the constitutional status of so-called Basic Laws – statutes adopted by the Knesset in a form not different from ordinary laws and not intended by the legislative body to become a formal constitution – on the basis of their formal title,[88] but also, one may argue, their substance matter: amongst the first two such Basic Laws recognized to be constitutional in character was, after all, the Basic Law: Human Dignity and Liberty.[89] Rather, constitutional advancement many times involves the enhancement of a written constitution by accepting the parallel and complementary existence of a penumbra[90] of rights, processes and positions which can be "discovered"[91] and thus in a way created by courts. A failure to amend a constitution – or a treaty – does not mean that that document cannot be interpreted and indeed expanded by interpreting it as a "living instrument".[92] As Bardo Fassbender writes in 1998 when describing the constitutional quality of the UN Charter together with the Charter-based "world order treaties",[93] we should adopt "the notion of a substantive constitution (as

87 Israel, Supreme Court, C.A. 6821/93 *United Mizrachi Bank Ltd. v. Migdal Cooperative Settlement*, 49(4) Piskei Din [P.D.] 221, abridged in 31 *Israel Law Review* 764 (1997).

88 See Navot, S. (2007), *The Constitutional Law of Israel*, Alphen aan den Rijn (NL), Wolters Kluwer, 42 et seq.

89 See Rensmann, T. (2007), *Weltordnung und Verfasssung*, Tübingen, Mohr Siebeck, 273, who emphasizes the value-oriented method of interpretation in constitutional adjudication such as the *Mizrachi Bank* judgement.

90 See United States of America, Supreme Court, *Griswold v. Connecticut*, decision of 7 June 1965, 381 U.S. 479.

91 Fish, W.B. and Key, R.S. (1998), The Constitutionalization of Law in the United States, 46 *Am. J. Comp. L.* 437, 440.

92 As reflected in the constant jurisprudence of the European Court of Human Rights beginning with *Tyrer v. the United Kingdom* judgement of 25 April 1978, Series A, No. 26, para. 31. The Court's case law suggests that it is indeed possible to incorporate an essentially new right into the Convention by means of judicial interpretation, and that doing this is formally reserved for a special formation of the Court, the Grand Chamber. See Appl. 23459/03, *Bayatyan v. Armenia*, judgement of 27 October 2009, where the right to conscientious objection to military service – a right "not included among the rights and freedoms guaranteed by the Convention" (see Appl. 7565/76, *Conscientious Objectors v. Denmark*, decision of 7 March 1977, 9 DR 117, affirmed in the subsequent practice of the Commission and Court) – was at issue, and where two judges found that an enhanced interpretation of the Convention was called for: "My preliminary conclusion in the case at hand was to relinquish and allow the Grand Chamber to re-examine the issue/revisit the case law/and maybe to take a step further and to state that to sentence someone who refuses to do military service on grounds of conscience would be in violation of Article 9." Dissenting opinion of judge Fura, at para. 6.

93 Fassbender, B. (1998), The United Nations Charter as Constitution of the International Community, 36 *Colum. J. Transnat'l L.* 529, 588).

opposed to a formal or written one) to describe that larger segment of a community's legal order which encompasses its key rules".[94]

To avoid confusion, the term substantive constitution exceeds what it has been defined as in European scholarship and rather encompasses what Brentford calls "subjective constitution", or "a constitution which has social legitimacy and is embedded in the social-substrate of the State [here – Communities] by virtue of fundamental principles of law."[95] These rules include an effective and active exercise of citizenship.[96]

Subsidiarity and the Constitution

The principle of subsidiarity can here only be discussed very briefly. In an essay on levels of European sovereignty, Konrad Schiemann, a judge of the European Court of Justice, discusses the distributive decision-making process within a multi-level system of governance. He emphasizes that "[t]he doctrine of subsidiarity requires decision-making to be distributed to the lowest appropriate level".[97] He continues by concluding that "there is no *a priori* higher claim of validity for national constitutionalism vis-à-vis European constitutionalism".[98] From a more substantive viewpoint, other authors contend that there is a fundamental structural and historically grounded difference between constitutional level norms at the national and European level. Haltern, for instance, distinguishes between national law, which "possesses a rich texture of cultural resources, upon which it can be grounded"[99] and European Community law, which lacks a historical foundation as well as an identity and thus requires, for the establishment of purposeful stability, the "restless and continuous generation of law through political action".[100] Haltern continues by saying that the European Union realized that lack of original

94 Ibid.

95 Brentford, P. (1998), Constitutional Aspects of the Independence of the European Central Bank, 47 *Int'l & Comp. l. Q*. 75, 78.

96 Cf. Eleftheriadis, P. (1996), Aspects of European Constitutionalism, 21 *E. L. Rev*. 32, 38.

97 Schiemann, K. (2007), Europe and the Loss of Sovereignty, 56 *ICLQ* 475, 483.

98 Ibid., 484. The author finds that "in the context of present-day Europe, it is artificial to assume the national polity as the natural jurisdiction of a full representation and participation".

99 Haltern, U. (2007), Europa – Verfassung – Identität, in Christian Calliess (ed.), *Verfassungswandel im europäischen Staaten- und Verfassungsverbund*, Tübingen, Mohr Siebeck, 9, 25. "Nationales Recht besitzt eine reiche Textur kultureller Ressourcen, auf die es sich stützen kann."

100 Ibid., 30: "Die selbsterzeugte, hektische Handlung ist notwendig, um Europa Sinn angedeihen zu lassen. Es gibt keine Zeit und keinen Raum, den Sinn aus Texten abzulesen. Stabiler Sinn kann sich unter diesen Bedingungen nur einstellen, wenn er rastlos und unablässig neu durch politische Handlung generiert wird."

cultural resources, which every nation state possesses, and attempted to replace these foundations with a quantitative analysis of norms' acceptance amongst Europe's citizenry. This, he asserts, remained by and large without success.[101] The foundational difference in our two legal systems is also reflected in the problems of the "real life existence" of our parallel normative systems, to be discussed next.

Legal Parallelism

The parallelism of European and national norms, including those of a constitutional status, prompts a much repeated desire for a "political order on the basis of a pluralistic rather than a monolithic conception of the existence of political power and legal authority".[102] Walker speaks of a political reality that displays a "novel plural or compound configuration" where states and other post-state political entities coexist in a "generalized process of mutual infiltration ... rather than as the negotiation and maintenance of clear boundaries as in the case of traditional inter-state relations".[103] He adds an argument that relates to the existence of national treasures, namely that a "*via media* between a constitutional sensibility that is bound by existing statist understandings and one which is entirely dismissive of them".[104] Schiemann proposes that a new constitutional model should create a reality "where different authoritative orders and circles overlap, compete and collaborate".[105] Other authors logically conclude that, at the level of judicial parallelism, what is needed is a "plural constitutional dialogue"[106] between equally strong and equally adventurous judicial bodies at the national constitutional and at the European levels.

We shall discuss further whether coordination and dialogue are indeed the proper terms to describe that interaction. This author proposes instead to speak of *cohabitation* of the parallel systems, since the interaction between national and supranational courts in our context that will be established below resembles in many ways the process of give and take between roommates who share, on the one hand, the benefits of a place to live together, but also, on the other hand, the need to work together closely irrespective of many different backgrounds and attitudes to life. The common purpose is to keep the place inhabitable at the very least, or to beautify it further as the ultimate goal. Other than a married couple living together – the marriage contract here would be an explicit and detailed European constitution – our roommates do not necessarily have to give up their

101 Ibid.

102 Schiemann, Europe and the Loss of Sovereignty, 487.

103 Walker, N. (2006), EU Constitutionalism in the State Constitutional Tradition, European University Institute Working Paper Law No. 2006/21, 16.

104 Ibid.

105 Schiemann, Europe and the Loss of Sovereignty, 487.

106 Cartabia, Europe and Rights: Taking Dialogue Seriously, 7.

individualism – sovereignty – to subscribe to a common goal that is of paramount importance. Also, roommates may decide at a certain point in time to move on and leave the common place of residence.

Francis Jacobs assures us that "there is no formal solution to the problem of the relationship between EC Law and national law".[107] Let us assume that such a formal solution is neither likely to emerge nor necessary or even desirable for a pluralistic European legal area. In fact, much like roommates need to fight about more or less essential issues concerning their living arrangements occasionally, the constituent parts of any union based on the rule of law need an outlet for their intra-system discomfort. One school of thought seems to be that a national court taking a stand will, if nothing else, give it some leverage against the Union's and the other constituent parts' courts. Anderson refers to the emergence of an ECJ civil rights doctrine from the threats of disloyalty of the top judicial bodies of Germany and Italy.[108] Sauer considers loyalty an inherent element of multi-level systems of governance. He argues that loyalty and implied powers – another legal concept frequently invoked in the European context – read together mean that the national authorities, including the judicial branch, have "implied cooperational duties".[109] Sauer here borrows from the German concept of *Treu und Glauben* and suggests a prohibition of *widersprüchliche[s] Verhalten*,[110] or *venire contra factum proprium*. However, we would be gravely mistaken if we believed that multi-level systems attain the highest level of effectiveness at times of conflict-free coordination. Instead, constitutional dialogue benefits from occasional frictions which require the involved actors to reflect on their position and to adjust or reassert them in light of a fruitful discourse with their peers. Mere discourse without rules may be interesting, but is not likely to yield a result that advances the cause which is, indeed, European harmonization. Harmony presupposes common goals, but not at all willingness to be assimilated.

Substantive Supremacy

We have argued earlier in favour of a substantive notion of a constitution. This is the place to advance the idea of substantive supremacy, which corresponds to the

107 Jacobs, F.G. (2007), Supreme Courts and their Limits: the European Court of Justice, as Seen from the Viewpoint of an Advocate General, in Meinhard Hilf (ed.), *Höchste Gerichte an ihren Grenzen*, Berlin, Duncker & Humblot, 39, 45.

108 Cf. Anderson, D. (2000), Shifting the Grundnorm (and other Tales), in David O'Keeffe (ed.), *Judicial Review in European Union Law*, The Hague, Kluwer Law International, 343–360, 349.

109 Sauer, H. (2008), *Jurisdiktionskonflikte im Mehrebenensystem*, Berlin, Heidelberg, New York, Springer, 409, with reference to Peters, A. (2003), International Dispute Settlement: A Network of Cooperational Duties, 14 *EJIL* 1.

110 Ibid.

material definition of legal norms that have the attribute of being constitutional in character. Schiemann gives the example of marriages, which he says "can last a lifetime without there being a clear role about who takes a decision in the event of a disagreement".[111] While creative, this comparison is not quite accurate, since the relationship between European nations and the Communities resembles less a marriage, and more the daily interactions of a group of very diverse roommates. Schiemann's call for an "elaborated principle of subsidiarity",[112] however, deserves unconditional approval. Much like in the relationship between roommates, the "coherence of the legal order at the European level is not the only value that a European legal order should or does in fact embrace".[113] In the field of fundamental rights and freedoms, Cartabia finds merit in an approach where the 27 constitutional orders, the European Convention of Human Rights as a threshold document for human rights implementation in EU Europe and the unwritten constitutional principles established by courts and the ECJ should be placed alongside each other.[114] With this plurality of constitutional traditions even in human rights, and the mix of systems of thoughts that are either individualistic or dignity-based, the ensuing catalogue of rights is bound to remain somewhat inconsistent and not fully overlapping.[115] Another area where the coordination between the European and the national levels of law is of paramount importance is what Kumm calls the issue of "political self-determination".[116] Thus, in order to develop a workable concept of supranational–national interaction, one will have to take into account not only the area of rights and freedoms (where of course the majority of the discussion and the judicial discourse were located so far), but also the other areas of both national- and EU-constitutionalization.

We have spoken of a substantive constitution and consequently of substantive supremacy. We must take only one additional step in our thought process, and that is to see what the fundamental constitutional principles of both the European and the national legal systems are, of course in a necessarily abstract fashion. Schiemann sets the parameters: he finds that, apart from human rights, democracy and the rule of law constitute what he calls "fundamental constitutional principles"[117] of the Community. That, this authors believe, is a workable concept, in that next to fundamental rights or, in other words, individual self-determination we find democracy as the co-term describing European political or collective self-determination. Add to this rule of law, with all its implications of formal

111 Schiemann, Europe and the Loss of Sovereignty, 486.

112 Ibid.

113 Kumm, M. (1999), Who is the Final Arbiter of Constitutionality in Europe?: Three Conceptions of the Relationship between the German Federal Constitutional Court and the European Court of Justice, 36 *Common Market Law Review*, 351, 385.

114 See Cartabia, Europe and Rights: Taking Dialogue Seriously, 16.

115 See ibid., 18.

116 Kumm, Who is the Final Arbiter of Constitutionality in Europe?, 379.

117 Schiemann, Europe and the Loss of Sovereignty, 487.

Rechtsstaatlichkeit and substantive lawfulness in the sense of rightfulness, and you have probably the full area of fundamental constitutional matters covered. These are, by their very nature, also the areas where confrontation within the multi-level system of governance and judicial power will most likely occur.

Confrontation will occur if values at the national and at the European level are not shared.[118] True conflict only arises when tolerable substantive supremacy of European law cannot apply, or in other words, when an "evolutionary interpretation of national constitutions … consistently with the ECJ case law"[119] cannot be accomplished. Such conflicts would indeed be procedurally unsolvable and substantially deadlocked if we were operating within an inflexible and absolute system of supremacy in the former sense. Vassilios Skouris, referring to the ECJ's judgements in *Omega*[120] und *Schmidtberger*,[121] makes clear that in the field of fundamental rights and freedoms there is no need for "identical treatment of human rights in the entire European Union into every detail".[122] In *Omega*, Skouris emphasizes, the Court has made clear that a limitation of a freedom secured by Community law pursuant to a human right guaranteed by national constitution is not judged on the basis of whether there is a common approach of all Member States towards protecting that particular fundamental right.[123]

The answer to the question of what norm is supreme in constitutional dialogue lies not in the dialogue itself – which, after all, is *merely* a process – but in a balancing test that seeks to identify, to the extent possible, the objective basis for any claim to supremacy from either national or European law. That test is both a substantive one, and one that requires a procedural framework. The basis is the simple truth that in all law some provisions are more fundamental than others.

A dialogue that is purpose-driven and credible requires not just a firm framework within which it takes place, but also a structure that allows it to establish, or rather steers it towards establishing, a coherent practice of normative supremacy. Not

118 See Cartabia, Europe and Rights: Taking Dialogue Seriously, 20.

119 Jacobs, Supreme Courts and their Limits, 46.

120 ECJ, Case C-36/02, *Omega Spielhallen- und Automatenaufstellungs-GmbH v. Oberbürgermeisterin der Bundesstadt Bonn*, judgement of 14 October 2004, [2004] ECR I-9609.

121 ECJ, Case 112/00, *Eugen Schmidberger v. Republik Österreich*, judgement of 12 June 2003, [2003] ECR I-5696.

122 Skouris, V. (2007), Höchste Gerichte an ihren Grenzen – Bemerkungen aus der Perspektive des Gerichtshofes der Europäischen Gemeinschaften, in Meinhard Hilf et al. (eds*), Höchste Gerichte an hren Grenzen*, Berlin, Duncker & Humblot, 19, 36: "Denn die Entscheidung von Grundrechtsfällen erfordert häufig die Berücksichtigung nationaler oder regionaler Besonderheiten, sofern man nicht eine bis ins Detail einheitliche Grundrechtshandhabung in der gesamten Europäischen Union möchte."

123 Ibid., 37: "Das Urteil Omega ist besonders interessant im Hinblick darauf, dass es nicht verlangt, dass die auf ein Grundrecht gestützte Einschränkung einer Grundfreiheit einer allen Mitgliedsstaaten gemeinsamen Auffassung darüber entspricht, wie das betreffende Grundrecht am besten zu schützen ist."

a standard that is formally superior, but one that is substantively superior or, in simpler terms, "better", deserves recognition. Fortunately we do not operate in a vacuum when discussing what qualifies as "better" in this context, but can draw from international and comparative practice.

One manifestation of said practice is sufficiently comparable to European (EU) law and distinctly successful in establishing a regional, quasi-constitutional legal order within Europe: the European Convention of Human Rights. The ECHR system has for a long time recognized "national treasures" by adopting a clear-cut approach that the Convention-guaranteed rights are merely minimum standards that can be exceeded and surpassed by national legal provisions safeguarding fundamental rights and freedoms. This standard clearly requires a classification of national protection as "better" and the European Court of Human Rights as the Convention's supervisory tribunal to apply tests that qualify, and in certain circumstances quantify a national law and its implementation in practice as substantively superior to the minimum guarantees under the Convention.[124] Whenever the conflict within European law occurs in the realm of fundamental rights, that standard clearly is applicable by analogy. Thus, in assessing the superiority, or supremacy, of European EU law, it is not efficiency of the normative issue that counts; nor is it the usefulness of a norm in the interest of establishing a society governed by law and order, or the needs and requirements of a free-market economy, even if it is enshrined in fundamental freedoms such as within the European Communities. Instead, the primacy of a norm in direct conflict between international and national law derives from it being *better* in protecting and preserving individual freedoms, but also better in the sense that it is more adequate to build a society on the foundations of the rule of law.

The European human rights system does not stand alone with a substantive quality standard of rights collision: the Inter-American Court of Human Rights and its famous advisory opinion on the compulsory membership in an association of journalists[125] had to address a collision of a primary treaty (the Inter American Convention on Human Rights) and parallel treaties, which the government of Costa Rica invited the Court to utilize as a source for restrictive interpretation of the rights and freedoms enshrined in the American Convention. The Court's rejection of such an approach – the borrowing of more restrictive or, in the result, "worse" rules – was absolute and unequivocal. This is not to suggest that national

124 This author deliberately and cautiously leaves out a discussion of the possible ramifications of the "new" post-Protocol 14 ECtHR's limited cassation-style jurisdiction on the "better" standard. Truth be told, it may well be that the existing demand for a national approach to surpass in quality a minimum Convention standard, in order to be sustained, will yield to a "common good" standard, which may recognize too much of a national discretion in applying the Convention. Only the future can show.

125 Inter-American Court of Human Rights, *Compulsory Membership in an Association Prescribed by Law for the Practice of Journalism*, advisory opinion OC-5/85, November 13, 1985, Series A, No. 5.

constitutional law would rank on an equal footing with primary community law. Nor did the Inter-American Court find that other treaties, such as those adopted within the European Human Rights system or that of the United Nations, would stand on an equal footing with the primary treaty it had to apply. Yet parallel human rights protection systems have enough in common to allow at least a comparison by analogy with constitutional systems of, say, a traditional Western European country with a longstanding tradition of democratic values and a new accession country that has recently emerged from a dictatorial or quasi-dictatorial system of government. As much as European law seeks to achieve a common European standard in many areas, the global human rights regimes – and what is meant is both those that are truly global and those that contribute regional perspective to the emergence of global standards – have at least the harmonizing intent in common, which is accompanied by a healthy degree of competition and constructive conflict in the interest of furthering and advancing the standards.

Admittedly, the standard is not immediately transferable to the area of other issues of a constitutional character of the law including all those regulations of an economic or non-economic character in the three pillars of European law that have no explicit or implicit nexus to fundamental rights or freedoms. In those other areas, an assessment of whether a norm that is national is 'better' than a norm that is supranational cannot simply follow the result of an assessment whether it is more individual minded than a competing norm.

This first approach to identifying substantially superior norms is complemented by a methodology that borrows from comparative constitutional law, and thus from the system of legal thought most closely related to multi-level legal governance. Comparative constitutional law methodology is not alien to either the international or the supranational field of legal interpretation. Both the European Court of Human Rights and the European Court of Justice apply methods of comparatively assessing how certain areas of the law are handled at the domestic level with the intent to identify common – regional – standards. Comparative constitutionalism, while it indeed promotes "the learning and experimentalism … among different legal orders",[126] requires a depth of methodology and sophistication of procedure. Superficial, blank references to the mere outcome of other judicial pronouncements are a true obstacle and cause substantial damage to the credibility of the methodological approach of comparing. Assuming that we speak of comparative constitutional methodology that is viable, we can extract from it, at the very least, the principle of distinguishing. Comparatists do not blindly follow the guidance of foreign systems and the solutions that courts within those systems have proposed for particular legal questions, but apply adequate and properly explained standards to arrive at the conclusion of whether they should follow or distance themselves from foreign practice. The exercise of distinguishing also has a component of time and circumstances to it, in that distinguishing happens frequently when constitutional systems advance beyond what comparable systems (be they historically,

126 Maduro, Interpreting European Law, 7.

structurally, regionally or geographically comparable, or comparable on the basis of family membership) provide in a certain area of law. One may say that such systems are self-identified as objectively "better", but that self-identification must be without arrogance. A more advanced system must not succumb to a system of lesser status, and that is true not only in the field of fundamental rights, but also of other constitutional, including structural and organizational issues that can properly be the subject of comparative constitutional analysis. Both approaches are starting points, and no claim is made here that they will – or should – suffice as a constitution-making standard without further elaboration and practice. Indeed, further refining the approach will be required and will be most desirable. Also, the process and standard suggested is *per definitionem* time-sensitive in that it demands further development and adjustments as the overall constitutional structure matures.

The Constitutional Project, the ECJ and National Courts

There is disagreement in scholarship about the true role of the European Court of Justice in coordinating between and consolidating European and national law. While only some authors go as far as to describe the relationship between the European and national courts as being similar to that between "the federal judiciary and the state judiciary",[127] at least in the constitutional realm there is widespread consensus that the ECJ plays "a central role in constitution building",[128] or that "the constitutionalization of Europe was mainly a traditional project of the ECJ".[129] The ECJ is truly more constitutional in stature, as Tsagourias contends,[130] than the International Court of Justice, for instance. However, it was still created by treaty and even if that treaty has attained a status of a legal system *sui generis* by pronouncement of the very court that it created, and that court now sees itself, and is seen as different from treaty-based international tribunals,[131] the system still lacks

127 Biondi, A. (2009), How to Go Ahead as an EU Law National Judge, 15 *European Public Law* 225, 226.

128 Tsagourias, N. (2007), The Constitutional Role of General Principles of Law in International and European Jurisprudence, in Nicholas Tsagourias (ed.), *Transnational Constitutionalism*, Cambridge, Cambridge University Press, 87. See also Mancini, F. (1989), The Making of a Constitution for Europe, 26 *Common Market Law Review* 5933, who writes: "If one were asked to synthetise the direction in which the case law produced in Luxembourg has moved since 1957, one would have to say that it coincides with the making of a constitution for Europe."

129 Claes, M. (2007), The European Constitution and the Role of National Constitutional Courts, in Anneli Albi and Jacques Ziller (eds), *The European Constitution and National Constitutions*, Alphen aan den Rijn (NL), Kluwer, 235, 235.

130 Tsagourias, The Constitutional Role of General Principles of Law, 87 et seq.

131 European Court of Justice, Opinion 1/91, *Draft agreement between the European Community and the countries of the European Free Trade Association relating to the*

certain elements of a true constitution. The rejection of the European Constitution and its downsizing into a reform treaty – the Treaty of Lisbon – may indeed lead to a "renewed confidence"[132] of national courts to challenge the supremacy of EU law. In any event, at least in the field of constitution-building, the vision of a friction-free coexistence of national and supranational juridical bodies working together towards the achievement of a common goal is a bit fictitious.

Münch's theory of constructing a European society by judicial decision revisits topics that are commonplace in the discussion of distribution of power. Referring to the permanent conflict between progressive and conservative forces, national and international judicial bodies, Münch insists that "for the result of [that conflict] the distribution of power is crucial. However, not simply power is relevant, but also the kind of power resources available to the relevant actors."[133] The distribution of power in the field of judicial bodies is one of formal superiority or, in the sense of Kelsen, legal normative supremacy. Given the overall context of Münch's article, the question of availability of resources refers back to the type of citizenry that is affected by regulation and acts to secure its own rights. With that, we are firmly back in the field of public interest advocacy and grassroots constitutionalism. We also see that the struggle for supremacy is related to the attitude of the bearers of the rights the struggle relates to. Thus, national constitutional courts may be said to be the proponents of the rights and interests of the less transnational, less mobile and less market-driven European citizenry, while the supranational adjudicative body, the ECJ, tends to favour those who want to take the full advantage of market and mobility liberties. We have thus returned to society-building at its core. The dispute between centralized supranational and decentralized national constitutional adjudication is the discourse of the identity of European citizenship and of the European Union as a whole. As it is true with constitutional law in general, it is not merely a question of formal supremacy or of political goals, but a more fundamental issue of identity.

Modern citizenship is always linked to democracy, or the lack thereof. The citizen we mean is "both ruler and ruled".[134] "Civic citizenship"[135] – the one form that the European Union can sustain – has three essential elements or dimensions: belonging, equal rights based on that belonging, and the entitlement, and also the obligation, to participate, (that is, polity membership).[136] These merely

creation of the European Economic Area, [1991] E.C.R. I-6079.

132 Claes, The European Constitution, 246.

133 Münch, R. (2008), Constructing a European Society by Jurisdiction, 14 *European Law Journal* 519, 540.

134 Bellamy, R. (2008), Evaluating Union Citizenship: Belonging, Rights and Participation with in the EU, 12 *Citizenship Studies* 597, 600.

135 Delanty, G. (1997), Models of Citizenship: Defining European Identity and Citizenship, 1 *Citizenship Studies* 285, 288.

136 See Bellamy, Evaluating Union Citizenship, 599.

serve as "status" functions that lead to the fourth dimension, "identity".[137] The "communitarian model" of citizenship focuses on the issues of identification and asserts that community is the basis for something that the state – or, arguably, a supranational entity – is merely and expression of.[138]

The combination of entitlements – rights – and obligations – duties – has been identified as an element of the "conservative model"[139] of citizenship, or one that emphasizes obedience, such as the payment of taxes or military service. However, "obligations" may also be interpreted as a more rights-oriented exercise of a duty to participate in society-building, possibly also through civic participation. A failure to fulfil such obligations faces no formal sanction, but a diminished ability to benefit from the achievements of society. In the constitutional context, participatory duties may be seen as those that make a society civic, namely, non-abstinence, or at the very least the taking part in the defence of rights-based claims through legal processes.

In the European context, there "has been no transfer of allegiance to the EU".[140] Or rather, the transfer has not been deliberate or intentional in the sense of an identity-building exercise. The new possibility under the Lisbon Treaty for citizens to challenge EU agencies' regulatory actions directly before the ECJ is no indication of an actual increase of allegiance "by litigation", so to say. The sole linkage between civil societies, or communities, is that there exists a "multi-level network of civil societies where national civil societies are partially Europeanized and European civil society composed of organizations and actors at the European level as well as national and infra-national organizations and actors involved in European issues and policies"[141] participate. Citizenship is still fundamentally national, even if it has been elevated to a European matter by non-individual actors, including through a rights-based approach as expressed in the case law of the European Court of Justice. For constitutional interaction, there is a role of nation-states in building the European citizenry, namely that of "developing a sort of connection between Europe and citizens".[142] The key elements of that, it is submitted, should be citizen participation in a bottom-up sense[143] and a focus on principles of good governance, such as "openness, participation, accountability,

---

137 Enjolras, B. (2008), Two Hypotheses about the Emergence of a Post-national European Model of Citizenship, 12 *Citizenship Studies* 495, 495, and Kymlicka, W. and Norman, W. (1994), Return of the Citizen: A Survey of Recent Work on Citizenship Theory, 104 *Ethics* 352.

138 See Delanty, Models of Citizenship, 291.

139 Ibid., 290.

140 Bellamy, Evaluating Union Citizenship, 609.

141 Enjolras, Two Hypotheses, 498.

142 Bee, C. (2008), The "Institutionally Constructed" European Identity: Citizenship and Public Sphere Narrated by the Commission, 9 *Perspectives on European Politics and Society* 431, 444.

143 See Enjolras, Two Hypotheses, 503.

effectiveness and coherence",[144] which are also core principles of national constitutional legal orders.

Solange 2009: Core Elements of Constitutional Law in the European Context

Constitutional courts ever since the German Federal Constitutional Court with its *Solange* jurisprudence have withdrawn to the position that despite European integration and unification, including in the field of law, there remain core elements of national constitutional law or identity which are beyond the reach of European law-making or European Court of Justice interpretation. This is not to suggest that lone dissenters, or a marginal minority of Member States, may, through their judiciaries, "reject further steps in European integration based on their particular constitutional provisions".[145] The question remains, where and how we can identify and define *acceptable* core constitutional concepts. If we decide to leave them solely in the discretion of national judicial bodies we allow a rather unconvincing and relatively random system of possibly contradictory, but in any event incoherent, core constitutional concepts that seek to reign in the European Court of Justice as well as the European lawmaker without giving them or the other Member States clear guidance as to the reach of the core concepts, as it were. A theory needs to be developed that attempts to strategically define and refine the concept of core elements. It is suggested that national constitutional courts could advance two reasons for qualifying certain principles as being part of the core of that constitution.

On the one hand, constitutional principles *essential* to the particular national constitutional order could be emphasized; on the other hand, the core concepts could derive from a comparative legal analysis of identified essential constitutional norms that emanate from what we could call a "European consensus", or common European traditions. A reliance on national constitutional traditions alone may have the advantage of allowing those core elements that are unique to that particular constitutional order to prevail, at least in the jurisprudence of that national supreme constitutional court. The weakness of that approach lies in the absence of a transnational foundation, which the second approach clearly offers. What is regarded as essential here may be of marginal significance there. It will be difficult to advance the cause of such a national preference in the absence of corroborating evidence of European significance. With the second approach, an identified common European approach towards certain constitutional elements forms a more solid basis for a national court to object to the Europeanization of its constitutional principles.

144 Bee, The "Institutionally Constructed" European Identity, 444.

145 Albi, A. (2005), *EU Enlargement and the Constitutions of Central and Eastern Europe*, Cambridge, Cambridge University Press, 177.

What remains to be discussed is how to arrive at an identified European consensus in that sense. We may derive guidance from the jurisprudence of the European Court of Human Rights, which has established standards in the context of common European approaches, which form the basis, at least sometimes, for establishing superior European standards notwithstanding the longstanding traditions of certain Member States to the European Convention of Human Rights.[146] In our situation, national constitutional standards may be the not so longstanding, if compared to European Community law, but rather the subjectively perceived better standards. We need a tool to assess that qualitative superiority or, in other words, to turn subjective constitutional perceptions at the national level into judicially recognizable standards that can interact with and, if the test of superiority is fulfilled, trump Community law. If so, we can relatively safely say that the European legal order is ready for a process that a US commentator feared most as a possible – but rather unlikely, in the non-European context of constitutional comparisons – outcome of comparative constitutional law:

> If constitutional interpretations are based even in part on foreign law, then under some circumstances, *a single foreign country would have the power to change the meaning of the United States Constitution.*[147]

The dialogue advocated for by many needs to be a form of two-way "engagement".

The "Engagement Model"[148]

From the judicial practice discussed above one can relatively easily deduce a duty of the judiciary to engage in a top-down as well as a bottom-up discussion of what we can term "constitutional traditions". In other words, both the European Court of Justice and national constitutional courts face a clear and straightforward obligation to discuss the constitutional traditions of the Member States on the one hand, and the general principles of European law, on the other hand. The principle

---

146 See Morawa, A.H.E. (2002), The "Common European Approach", "International Trends", and the Evolution of Human Rights Law. A Comment on *Goodwin and I v. the United Kingdom*, 3 *German Law Journal* 8, available at http://www.germanlawjournal.com/print.php?id=172, accessed 27 July 2010.

147 House Judiciary Subcommittee on the Constitution Legislative Hearing: H. Res. 97 and the Appropriate Role of Foreign Judgments in the Interpretation of American Law, 19 July 2005, Prepared Statement of Nicholas Quinn Rosenkranz, Associate Professor of Law, Georgetown University, Washington, DC, available at http://judiciary.house.gov/media/pdfs/rosenkranz071905.pdf, accessed 31 March 2006. Emphasis added.

148 The term is borrowed from Jackson, V. (2005), Constitutional Comparisons: Convergence, Resistance, Engagement, 119 *Harv. L. Rev.* 109.

of engagement derives less from exclusive pronouncements by the courts, but more from justifiable criticism of judicial decisions that failed to do so. Paramount amongst those is the decision of the Polish Constitutional Tribunal in the *European Arrest Warrant Case*.[149] The focus on national treasures here appears sometimes as an obstacle in the thought process: what is meant is not so much a national treasure, but a treasure that is owned by a national constituency of citizens.

Then, two citizenries compete, and not a supranational and a national entity. The national citizenry is a part of the European one, and thus the two overlap and form one in some respects. Testing national standards against European ones on their validity from a citizen's perspective, and not on the basis of their suitability as a constitutional norm, elevates our test from a formal one (level of norms) to a substantive one: protection value for citizens. Superiority, in a qualitative sense, then emanates from a norm's suitability for the proliferation of citizen rights and European citizens' integration, not of state subjugation to supranational law. Also, all of a sudden, the question of how to assess qualitative superiority is not impossible to answer any more; a norm or standard that protects a national citizenry against its own government and/or demands government action may be equally valid as a source of entitlements of the European citizenry *vis-à-vis* the Community. One needs to examine whether other legal orders within Europe know a comparable – and not an identical – claim, irrespective of how that claim is validated and enforced. And, with the European Court of Human Rights, we can then assert a European consensus that, at the very least, a national constitutional norm is backed by a plurality of other corresponding national norms, or "peer norms".

Their existence would trigger a duty of the European Court of Justice to *engage* its national counterparts. All of a sudden, we have not a duty of the national adjudicator to interpret national law in conformity with Community law, but a duty of the supranational judicial body to view Community law in light of a European consensus of regulatory, or constitutional purpose. Of course that would not allow a persistent objector to European integration on the basis of obscure national "treasures" to emerge and stall the process of establishing a coherent European rule of law. If, however, the European law derives its authority merely from formal supremacy, but lacks the quality that can reasonably be expected from any norm that forms part of a rule of law, the European Court would be required to explain itself. This would trigger two beneficial effects for European constitutionalization: first, a democratic dialogue of legal orders would take place in lieu of the still underdeveloped direct dialogue of European citizens and their representatives; second, in doing so, the ECJ would be able to further develop the substantive constitution.

---

149 Polish Constitutional Tribunal, *Case of the Constitutionality of the European Arrest Warrant National Implementation*, judgement of 27 April 2005, No. P 1/05, quoted by Leczykiewicz, National Courts, 1191.

The European Court of Justice, much like a national court engaging in a comparative constitutional law exercise, may accept, distinguish and ultimately reject a claim to substantial superiority of a national "core" constitutional provision, but then has a high level of duty to explain. That explanation itself, and the process of cross-judicial dialogue that will necessarily ensue, will not necessarily resolve any and all conflicts between European and national constitutional law, but will at the very least allow a structured exchange and a true dialogue within a structured, hierarchical framework.

Münch makes a strong argument that European law "[d]oubtlessly ... strengthens the individual against his/her community of origin and, in the case of migration into another EU Member Country, also against the community of indigenous citizens of his or her country of residence".[150] He distinguishes between those citizens who benefit from Europeanization and the open market, on the one hand, and those whose safety and security is, at least in their mind, better protected by national norms and societal context.[151] If we accept that there are indeed two types of European citizens and that public advocacy aimed at the greater good is indeed designed for the development of a constitutional-rights-based order, we can also make a logical deduction as to whether European or national law is more favourable for individual rights protection: locally minded citizens will presumably find more protection by their national constitutional order, while the mobile citizenry that is Europeanized in their outlook on life will find advantages in a pro-mobility and pro-individualism-minded European rights regime. Inter-European constitutional dialogue is thus in any event a form of minority protection. The minority protected would be those European citizens who, while benefiting from the overall openness of the market, nevertheless are more static than the "ideal" European transnational citizens who make the markets-related liberties and freedoms their own. The open question is that of what the European Union truly is about. It is a question of identity and citizenship. This chapter will end with a brief look at these concepts, and what they can contribute to European constitutionalization.

150 Münch, Constructing a European Society by Jurisdiction, 538.

151 Münch gives the example of consumer protection laws, where European law clearly assumes that consumers are informed individuals capable of making a rational choice, while national law sometimes starts from the assumption that consumers are to be protected against unfair practices by corporations. Ibid., 537.

Citizenship, Rights and the European Citizenry

The original founding treaties were perceived by some authors as establishing "an incipient form of European Citizenship"[152] that was, however, "ill-defined".[153] As Evans notes in a 1984 essay, "there is no inherent reason why states should not be able to contract treaty obligations that define their nationals for the purpose of the treaty concerned".[154] In the absence of a workable definition in the treaties, it was the European Court of Justice that crystallized a more effective, if still somewhat vague concept of European citizenship. The Court did that in three identifiable areas: [155] first, in the fields of freedom of movement,[156] social security[157] and access to education,[158] the Court approached the issue of citizenship in a non-discrimination context. Jacobs[159] then identifies a second category of court judgements related to citizenship in the context of the enjoyment of the market freedoms: in *Collins v Secretary of State for Work and Pensions*, for instance, the Court established a non-discrimination right in the context of allowances and linked this to citizenship

---

152 Levi-Sandri, L. (1968), Free Movement of Workers in the European Community, Bull. E.C. 11-1968, 5–8, quoted in Evans, A.C. (1982), European Citizenship, 45 *Mod. L. Rev*. 497, 501, and Plender, R.O. (1976), An Incipient form of European Citizenship, in Francis G. Jacobs (ed.), *European Law and the Individual*, Amsterdam, North Holland.

153 Evans, European Citizenship.

154 Evans, A.C. (1984), European Citizenship: A Novel Concept in EEC Law, 32 *Am. J. Comp. L*. 697, 687.

155 Jacobs, F.G. (2007), Citizenship of the European Union – A Legal Analysis, 13 *European Law Journal* 591, 593.

156 ECJ, *Criminal Proceedings against Bickel and Franz*, judgement of 24 November 1998, [1998] ECR I-7637, concerning the right to use one's own language in criminal proceeding for foreigners in case that that language is admissible to be used by nationals, and *Rudy Grzelczyk v Centre public d'aide social d'Ottignies-Louvain-la-Neuve*, judgement of 20 September 2001 [2001] ECR I-6193, concerning the right to a minimum subsistence allowance for a French national resident in Belgium. The Court related these rights to European citizenship.

157 ECJ, *Maria Martinez Sala v. Freistaat Bayern*, judgement of 12 May 1998, [1998] ECR I-2691, concerning the right to receive child-raising allowance in Germany by a Spanish national resident there.

158 ECJ, *The Queen on the application of Dany Bidar v. London Borough of Ealing and Secretary of State for Education and Skills*, judgement of 15 March 2005, [2005] ECR I-2119, concerning the payment of assistance for students studying abroad in the form of subsidised loan, where the Court however qualified such a right as pertaining only to those foreign nationals who had "established a genuine link with the society of "the state in which they reside and study". See also ECJ, *Commission v. Austria*, judgement of 7 July 2005, [2005] ECR I-5969, where the Court held that Austria was required to "ensure that holders of secondary education diplomas awarded in other Member States can gain access to higher and university education organised by it under the same conditions as holders of secondary education diplomas awarded in Austria".

159 Jacobs, Citizenship of the European Union, 595.

in that conditions and limitations to the entitlement were "justified on the basis of objective considerations that are independent of the nationality of the persons concerned".[160]

A third and emerging concept of European citizenship is a free-standing, independent or "enhanced"[161] right with practical effects of its own and without linkage to Community freedoms and/or migration.[162] In an opinion in the case of *Wijsenbeek*, Advocate General Cosmas advanced an approach to citizenship in the context of the right to movement that "stemm[ed] from the status as a citizen of the Union, which is not subsidiary in relation to European unification, whether economic or not".[163] While this free-standing concept has been questioned by others,[164] subsequent judicial practice has indeed provided some basis to the claim that citizenship rights are indeed emerging as an independent category of entitlements that are (a) not connected to the Communities' four freedoms, and (b) *lex specialis* compared to general human rights norms. Amongst such decisions are, for instance, judgements concerning the acquisition of the right to residence status in Member States, such as *Zhu and Chen*,[165] and those taking sides in the dispute over the direct effect of Article 18(1) EC – the right to move freely and reside freely within the territory of Member States of citizens of the Union – such as *Baumbust*,[166] the scope of which has been questioned since. Another example of an independently existing citizenship-related right are the cases related to personal names, of which that of *Garcia Avello* stands out.[167] It may well be argued that such citizenship-based entitlements with no apparent economic relevance are indeed a tentative move towards an independent right to citizenship,[168] whereas the earlier cases were connected to fundamental freedoms, in particular the freedom

---

160 ECJ, *Collins v Secretary of State for Work and Pensions*, judgement of 31 March 2004, [2004] ECR I-2703.

161 Spaventa, E. (2008), Seeing the Wood Despite the Trees? On the Scope of Union Citizenship and its Constitutional Effects, 45 *C.M.L.Rev.* 13, 23.

162 See ibid.

163 ECJ, Case C-378/1997, *Criminal proceedings against Florus Ariël Wijsenbeek*, opinion delivered on 16 March 1999, [1999] ECR I-6207, para. 85.

164 See Mather, J.D. (2005), The Court of Justice and the Union Citizen, 11 *European Law Journal* 722, 726.

165 ECJ, Case C-202, *Zhu and Chen v Secretary of State for the Home Department*, judgement of 19 October 2004, [2004] ECR I-9925, concerning the right to freedom of movement on the basis of community citizenship irrespective of under what circumstances the citizenship of another Member State had been acquired.

166 ECJ, Case C-413/99, *Baumbust & R. v Secretary of State for the Home Department*, judgement of 17 September 2002, [2002] ECR I-7091.

167 ECJ, Case C-148/02, *Carlos Garcia Avello v Belgium*, judgement of 2 October 2003, [2003] ECR I-11613.

168 Jacobs, Citizenship of the European Union, 598.

of movement, and thus remain subordinate to these economic freedoms, as Mather contents.[169]

Apart from the yet to be clarified question of a possible (limited) direct effect of Article 18 EC – meaning that the right at issue, such as that to residence, is directly enforceable by individual citizens in national courts and thus trumps a traditional area of national law that was always within the domain of the sovereign states, namely the right to say "who belongs" – one more aspect limits the reach and scope of community citizenship: that is the question of the legal regime that regulates the acquisition of citizenship. In its jurisprudence, including the case of *Zhu and Chen*, "the Court of Justice has done very little, if anything at all, since 1992 to reduce the monopole powers of the [M]ember [S]tates, thereby perpetuating the inequities which exist across the entire EU in respect of requiring citizenship".[170]

Exploring visions of the future of a European citizenship, Kostakopoulou contends that "Europe could thus become the setting for the more ambitious transition to a post-national tableau and the prototype for a cosmopolitan experimentation".[171] The vision appears to be that multiple levels of communities are created by the citizens as members or, in other words, constructive citizenship.[172] If multiple citizenship thus creates community, the result "can only be conceived of as a genuinely heterogeneous European public".[173] We shall explore whether a heterogeneous public can be governed by a heterogeneous legal system which – much like citizens can be Europeans and nationals at the same time – can consist of European norms and constitutional principles at the same time.

The Citizenry and Mobilization as Preconditions for Constitutional Advancement

Much has been written in recent years about the increasing value and importance, also from a legal point of view, of the right to, and practical meaning of, European citizenship. Historically, Europeans as individuals were neither instrumental to European economic integration nor considered the bearers of rights and entitlements under the law of the European Communities. Neither general rights

---

169 See Mather, The Court of Justice and the Union Citizen, 732 et seq.

170 Ibid., 724; see also Kostakopoulou, D. (2007), European Union Citizenship: Writing the Future, 13 *European Law Journal* 623, 626, who emphasizes that with said jurisprudence the "international law maxim that determination of nationality falls within the exclusive jurisdiction of the Member States" is being upheld.

171 Kostakopoulou, European Union Citizenship, 626.

172 Ibid., 643; Kostakopoulou developed this theory earlier on in her 1996 essay Towards a Theory of Constructive Citizenship in Europe, 4 *Journal of Political Philosophy* 337.

173 Ibid.

and freedoms – apart from those associated with the basic freedoms of economic exchange – nor the political participation in the processes of creating European law were apparently considered essential. The executive-branch focus of the institutional organization of the European Communities and the weakness of parliamentarianism and participatory democracy serve as evidence. After all, the Communities were created by treaty and not by constitution, even if one would use a particularly pragmatic definition of constitution[174] or one that gives credit to the stature of a text within an overall legal system, which would then include the European Convention on Human Rights.[175]

However, comparative scholarship has clearly identified individual citizen mobilization as a crucial factor for the advancement of constitutionalization, in particular in the field of rights and freedoms. Charles Epp, in his book *The Rights Revolution*, has brought this to the point:

> [R]ights are conditioned on the extent of a support structure for legal mobilization. Under conditions in which a support structure is deep and vibrant, judicial attention to rights may be sustained and vigorous; under conditions in which a support structure is shallow and weak, judicial attention to rights is likely to be intermittent and ineffective.[176]

Epp expands his concept that constitutional rights are constituted in cooperation with an active and involved civil society beyond the initial phases of rights creation: "The continuation of nascent rights revolutions beyond their initial phases has also depended on broad support outside the judiciary."[177] Rachel Cichowski, in her study on *The European Court and Civil Society* (in which she focuses on gender equality and environmental protection issues), reviews the parameters under which public interest litigation can flourish.[178] The author notes that public interest litigation in Europe has had a considerably shorter history and was, even at the beginning of

---

174 The constitutional character of the founding treaties is being emphasized, for instance, in German scholarship, but one must bear in mind that the term *verfassungsrechtlich* there is clearly not used in a strict technical sense. See, e.g., Oppermann, T., Classen, C.D. and Nettesheim, M. (2009), *Europarecht*, 4th edn, Munich, C.H. Beck, 202, MN 6 and 7, who characterize the treaties as "verfassungsrechtliche 'Gründungsakte' der Union" and the process of their adoption as "definitiv gemeinte konsentierte 'Verfassungsgebung' ...".

175 European Court of Human Rights, *Loizidou v. Turkey*, judgement of 23 March 1995, Series A, No. 310, defining the "Convention as a constitutional instrument of European public order (*ordre public*)."

176 Epp, C.E. (1998), *The Rights Revolution*, Chicago, The University of Chicago Press, 198–199.

177 Ibid., 199.

178 Cichowski, R.A. (2007), *The European Court and Civil Society*, New York, Cambridge University Press.

the twenty-first century, "minimal, yet present".[179] Gormley writes, in 2000, of chances for an enhanced public interest activism in EU Europe, but concludes that such participation would require Community action to get started and would, in any event, take place at the legislative level.[180] Other authors' assessment is even more pessimistic: Wernicke, for instance, finds that public interest litigation is "virtually impossible"[181] and concludes that European Union law has reduced citizens and their representative organization to the role of mere informers, who can suggest but by no means have a right to action by the European Commission.[182] Much in line with Epp's argument, Cichowski finds civil society participation in the early stages and the continuation of social change through litigation crucial and discovers a "shift from individual discrete action to more formalized group action".[183] She then argues that "movement activism can be instrumental in altering political and legal processes in a way that influences the construction of new rules and procedures that serve as subsequent political opportunities for action. In this way, social movement activism becomes an integral force in the construction of governance",[184] but also in maintaining the momentum of the process of ongoing constitutionalization.

Citizen activism in the field of implementing claims through the judiciary – as opposed to the various forms of involvement in law-making and executive policymaking – commonly manifests itself in the form of public interest litigation. We shall use the term broadly here, meaning any form of use of the courts of law with the benefit of society as a whole or an identifiable segment of society in particular in mind, even if it takes the form of individual, and indeed even "commercial" litigation,[185] and will only later narrow the term down to such action that aims at or has the intended side-effect of advancing European constitutionalization.

179 Ibid., 8.

180 See Gormley, L.W. (2000), Public Interest Litigation, in David O'Keeffe (ed.), *Judicial Review in European Union Law*, The Hague: Kluwer Law International, 190–201.

181 Wernicke, S. (2007), Au nom de qui? The European Court of Justice between Member States, Civil Society and Union Citizens, 13 *European Law Journal*, 380, 390.

182 Ibid., 391.

183 Cichowski, 16.

184 Ibid., 17.

185 This will allow us to examine litigation in the public interest in the material sense without being confined by the *locus standi* rules of the European Court of Justice, or the national supreme and constitutional courts, which have been viewed as a "judicial straight jacket": Gormley, L.W. (2001), Public Interest Litigation in Community Law, 7 *European Public Law* 51, 53. See ECJ, Case C-321/95P, *Stichting Greenpeace Council (Greenpeace International) and Others v. Commission*, judgement of 2 April 1998, [1998] ECR I-1651, para. 28: "[W]here, as in the present case, the specific situation of the applicant was not taken into consideration in the adoption of the act, which concerns him in a general and abstract fashion and, in fact, like any other person in the same situation, the applicant is not individually concerned by the act."

There is an intrinsic link between public interest litigation and judicial activism, the very act and/or mindset of judicial officers that has been vilified by many as a breach of both constitutional orderliness and judicial decorum, which they believe must manifest itself in judicial self-restraint, if not deference to the other branches of government. This is not the place to elaborate further on the ongoing debate, but the author should disclose that he finds merit in P.N. Bhagwati's observation:

> If we analyze the true nature of the judicial function, it will immediately become apparent that judicial activism ... is an essential part of the judicial process.[186]

Feldman has convincingly articulated a common sense fact, namely that whether and to what extent litigation in the public interest is permitted in any given constitutional structure defines civic participation: "in a civic republican tradition in which citizens are expected or permitted to achieve self-fulfilment by participating in political decision-making, ... there is good reason to ... develop constitutional theories which allow citizens to act to secure public interests ... "[187] If we accept that in Europe we encounter a dual civic citizenship – the national one, articulating both a sub-Union political affiliation and a rights-bearing status under domestic constitutional law, and a European one, crafted primarily by judges and, as we have seen, still fragile and somewhat undefined – the wider implications are clear: citizen-driven constitutionalization is mandated both by the democracy paradigm enunciated by a common European "rule of law"-framework and guarded by constitutional courts as well as the European Court of Justice as the body that finds these common standards, and by the multi-level governance concept, which places the dual citizen as a subject of both national and supranational law in the midst of all these various processes. We have a seminal question to answer: shall the citizen be the proverbial lab rat, or shall he or she be an integral part of shaping the new constitutional order. To this author, the answer is clear.

Conclusions

If the European Union wants allegiance, it needs a true citizenry. The citizen is also a natural corrective *vis-à-vis* the professional judiciary, as the Anglo-American concept of a jury of one's peers demonstrates.[188] Thus, if the ECJ so

186 Bhagwati, P.N. (1984/5), Judicial Activism and Public Interest Litigation, 23 *Colum. J. Transnat'l L.* 561, 562. Mr Bhagwati was then a justice of the Supreme Court of India, a tribunal well known for its activism.

187 Feldman, D. (1992), Public Interest Litigation and Constitutional Theory in Comparative Perspective, 55 *The Modern Law Review* 44, 70.

188 In a jury system, the "peers" dispense justice alongside the professional judges, and are subject to the ultimate review of and correction by professional judges, at least with respect to their interpretation of the law, if not the facts.

far has been the driving force behind Union constitutionalization, it may well be high time to hand that task over, in part and in concert with the judicial branch, to the citizens. The realm of fundamental rights is the natural playground for citizen activism. And it is the logical arena where the validity, or quality, of standards can be assessed in the discourse and competition of Community and national human rights standards.

With citizen involvement, one of the most compelling criticisms of the EU's constitutionality claims will become less prevalent: that of the lack of democratic participation. If the political process continues to fail to constitutionalize – Treaty of Lisbon to wit – let a citizen-driven judicial process continue to be the driving force. After all, that is not a novel idea, but the hard reality of EU law-making since the inception of the Communities.

National constitutional courts then are not a problem, but part of the solution. The substantive supremacy approach outlined above, while no miracle cure and quite possibly subject to vehement criticism, can be a starting point for a re-evaluation of intra-system interaction of judges.

References

Ackerman, B. (1998), *We the People*, Harvard, Belknap Press/Harvard University Press.

Albi, A. (2005), *EU Enlargement and the Constitutions of Central and Eastern Europe*, Cambridge, Cambridge University Press.

Albi, A. (2007), Introduction: The European Constitution and National Constitutions in the Context of 'Post-national Constitutionalism, in Anneli Albi and Jacques Ziller, *The European Constitution and National Constitutions*, Alphen aan den Rijn (NL), Kluwer Law International.

Anderson, D. (2000), Shifting the Grundnorm (and other Tales), in David O'Keeffe (ed.), *Judicial Review in European Union Law*, The Hague, Kluwer Law International.

Azoulai, L. and Agerbeek, F.R. (2005), Case Note, 42 *Common Market Law Review* 871.

Barak, A. (2006), *The Judge in a Democracy*, Princeton, Princeton University Press.

Bauer, L. (2008), *Der Europäische Gerichtshof als Verfassungsgericht?* Baden-Baden, Nomos.

Bee, C. (2008), The "Institutionally Constructed" European Identity: Citizenship and Public Sphere Narrated by the Commission, 9 *Perspectives on European Politics and Society* 431.

Bellamy, R. (2008), Evaluating Union Citizenship: Belonging, Rights and Participation with in the EU, 12 *Citizenship Studies* 597.

Bhagwati, P.N. (1984/5), Judicial Activism and Public Interest Litigation, 23 *Colum. J. Transnat'l L.* 561.

Bříza, P. (2009), The Czech Republic: The Constitutional Court on the Lisbon Treaty, Decision of 26 November 2008, 5 *European Constitutional Law Review* 143.

Biondi, A. (2009), How to Go Ahead as an EU Law National Judge, 15 *European Public Law* 225.

Bobek, M. (2008), The Fortress of Judicial Independence and the Mental Transitions of the Central European Judiciaries, 14 *European Public Law* 99.

Brentford, P. (1998), Constitutional Aspects of the Independence of the European Central Bank, 47 *Int'l & Comp. l. Q.* 75.

Breyer, S. (2006), *Active Liberty*, New York, First Vintage Books.

della Cananea, G. (2008), The Italian Constitutional Court and the European Court of Justice: From Separation to Interaction?, 14 *European Public Law* 523.

Ćapeta, T. (2005), Courts, Legal Culture and EU Enlargement, 1 *Croatian Yearbook of European Law and Policy* 23.

Cartabia, M. (2009), Europe and Rights: Taking Dialogue Seriously, 5 *Europ. Const. L. Rev.* 5.

Cichowski, R.A. (2007), *The European Court and Civil Society*, New York, Cambridge University Press.

Claes, M. (2007), The European Constitution and the Role of National Constitutional Courts, in Anneli Albi and Jacques Ziller (eds), *The European Constitution and National Constitutions*, Alphen aan den Rijn (NL), Kluwer.

Council of Europe (ed.) (2009), Contribution of the Secretary General of the Council of Europe, in *The Future of the European Court of Human Rights, Preparatory Contributions*.

Delanty, G. (1997), Models of Citizenship: Defining European Identity and Citizenship, 1 *Citizenship Studies* 285.

D'Sa, R. and Lafranque, J. (2008), Getting to Know You: The Developing Relationship between National Courts of the "Newer" Member States and the European Court of Justice, with Particular Reference to Estonia, *EBLR* 311.

Eleftheriadis, P. (1996), Aspects of European Constitutionalism, 21 *E. L. Rev.* 32.

Enjolras, B. (2008), Two Hypotheses about the Emergence of a Post-national European Model of Citizenship, 12 *Citizenship Studies* 495.

Epp, C.E. (1998), *The Rights Revolution*, Chicago, The University of Chicago Press.

Evans, A.C. (1982), European Citizenship, 45 *Mod. L. Rev.* 497.

Evans, A.C. (1984), European Citizenship: A Novel Concept in EEC Law, 32 *Am. J. Comp. L.* 697.

Fassbender, B. (1998), The United Nations Charter as Constitution of the International Community, 36 *Colum. J. Transnat'l L.* 529.

Feldman, D. (1992), Public Interest Litigation and Constitutional Theory in Comparative Perspective, 55 *The Modern Law Review* 44.

Fish, W.B. and Key, R.S. (1998), The Constitutionalization of Law in the United States, 46 *Am. J. Comp. L.* 437.

Fleming, J.E. (1993/4), Constructing the Substantive Constitution, 72 *Tex. L. Rev.* 211.

Fleming, J.E. (1995/6), Securing Deliberative Autonomy, 48 *Stan. L. Rev.* 1.

Giorgi, F. and Triart, N. (2008), National Judges, Community Judges: Invitation to a Journey through the Looking-Glass – On the Need for Jurisdictions to Rethink the Inter-systemic Relations beyond the Hierarchical Principle, 14 *European Law Journal* 693.

Gormley, L.W. (2000), Public Interest Litigation, in David O'Keeffe (ed.), *Judicial Review in European Union Law*, The Hague, Kluwer Law International.

Gormley, L.W. (2001), Public Interest Litigation in Community Law, 7 *European Public Law* 51.

Haltern, U. (2007), Europa – Verfassung – Identität, in Christian Calliess (ed.), *Verfassungswandel im europäischen Staaten- und Verfassungsverbund*, Tübingen, Mohr Siebeck.

Hand, L. (1959), *The Spirit of Liberty*. Irving Dilliard (ed.), New York, Knopf.

House Judiciary Subcommittee on the Constitution Legislative Hearing: H. Res. 97 and the Appropriate Role of Foreign Judgments in the Interpretation of American Law, 19 July 2005, Prepared Statement of Nicholas Quinn Rosenkranz, Associate Professor of Law, Georgetown University, Washington, DC, available at http://judiciary.house.gov/media/pdfs/rosenkranz071905.pdf, accessed 31 March 2007.

Iglesias, G.C.R. (2004), The Court of Justice, Principles of EC Law, Court Reform and Constitutional Adjudication, *European Business Law Review* 1116.

Jackson, V. (2005), Constitutional Comparisons: Convergence, Resistance, Engagement, 119 *Harv. L. Rev.* 109.

Jacobs, F.G. (2007), Citizenship of the European Union – A Legal Analysis, 13 *European Law Journal* 591.

Jacobs, F.G. (2007), Supreme Courts and their Limits: the European Court of Justice, as Seen from the Viewpoint of an Advocate General, in Meinhard Hilf (ed.), *Höchste Gerichte an ihren Grenzen*, Berlin, Duncker & Humblot.

Jestaedt, M. (2008), Konkurrenz von Rechtsdeutungen statt Koexistenz von Rechtsordnungen, in Hauke Brunkhorst and Rüdiger Vogt (eds), *Rechts-Staat*, Baden-Baden, Nomos.

Kafka, F. (1946), He, in *The Great Wall of China: Stories and Reflections*, Berlin, Schocken Books.

Khanna, H.R. (2008), *Making of India's Constitution*, 2nd edn, New Delhi, Eastern Book Company.

Kostakopoulou, D. (1996), Towards a Theory of Constructive Citizenship in Europe, 4 *Journal of Political Philosophy* 337.

Kostakopoulou, D. (2007), European Union Citizenship: Writing the Future, 13 *European Law Journal* 623.

Kumm, M. (1999), Who is the Final Arbiter of Constitutionality in Europe?: Three Conceptions of the Relationship between the German Federal Constitutional

Court and the European Court of Justice, 36 *Common Market Law Review*, 351.
Kymlicka, W. and Norman, W. (1994), Return of the Citizen: A Survey of Recent Work on Citizenship Theory, 104 *Ethics* 352.
Leczykiewicz, D. (2006), National Courts, 43 *Common Market Law Review* 1181
Lenaerts, K. (2004–2005), The Constitution for Europe: Fiction or Reality, 11 *Colum. J. Eur. L.* 465.
Levi-Sandri, L. (1968), Free Movement of Workers in the European Community, Bull. E.C. 11-1968.
Maduro, M.P. (2007), Interpreting European Law: Judicial Adjudication in a Context of Constitutional Pluralism, 2 *European Journal of Legal Studies* 1.
Makowski, K.D. (1995–1996), Solange III: The German Federal Constitutional Court's Decision on Accession to the Maastricht Treaty on European Union,16 *U. Pa. J. Int'l Bus. L.* 155.
Mancini, F. (1989), The Making of a Constitution for Europe, 26 *Common Market Law Review* 5933.
Markesinis, Sir B. (2006), Judicial Mentality: Mental Disposition or Outlook as a Factor Impeding Recourse to Foreign Law, 80 *Tul. L. Rev.* 1325.
Mather, J.D. (2005), The Court of Justice and the Union Citizen, 11 *European Law Journal* 722.
Mirate, S. (2009), A New Status for the ECHR in Italy: The Italian Constitutional Court and the New "Conventional Review" on National Laws, 15 *European Public Law* 89.
Morawa, A.H.E. (2002), The "Common European Approach", "International Trends", and the Evolution of Human Rights Law. A Comment on *Goodwin and I v. the United Kingdom*, 3 *German Law Journal* (No. 8).
Münch, R. (2008), Constructing a European Society by Jurisdiction, 14 *European Law Journal* 519.
Navot, S. (2007), *The Constitutional Law of Israel*, Alphen aan den Rijn (NL), Wolters Kluwer.
Oppermann, T., Classen, C.D. and Nettesheim, M. (2009), *Europarecht*, 4th edn, Munich, C.H. Beck.
Pernice, I. (2008), The Treaty of Lisbon and Fundamental Rights, in Stefan Griller and Jaques Ziller (eds), *The Lisbon Treaty. EU Constitutionalism without a Constitutional Treaty?*, Vienna, New York, Springer.
Peters, A. (2003), International Dispute Settlement: A Network of Cooperational Duties, 14 *EJIL* 1.
Plender, R.O. (1976), An Incipient form of European Citizenship, in Francis G. Jacobs (ed.), *European Law and the Individual*, Amsterdam, North Holland.
Posner, R.A. (2008), *How Judges Think*, Harvard, Harvard University Press.
Puder, M.G. (2004), Supremacy of the Law and Judicial Review in the European Union: Comparing *Marbury v. Madison* with *COSTA v. ENEL*, 36 *Geo. Wash. Int'l L. Rev.* 567.
Rossi, L.S. (2009), Case Note, 46 *Common Market Law Review* 319.

Rensmann, T. (2007), *Weltordnung und Verfasssung*, Tübingen, Mohr Siebeck.
Sadurski, W. (2008), "Solange Chapter 3": Constitutional Courts in Central Europe – Democracy – European Union, 14 *European Law Journal* 1.
Sajó, A. (2005), Constitution Without the Constitutional Moment: A View from the New Member States, 3 *Int'l J. Const. L.* 243.
Sauer, H. (2008), *Jurisdiktionskonflikte im Mehrebenensystem*, Berlin, Heidelberg, New York, Springer.
Scheppele, K.L. (2008), A Constitution Between Past and Future, 49 *William and Mary Law Review* 1377.
Schiemann, K. (2007), Europe and the Loss of Sovereignity, 56 *ICLQ* 475.
Skouris, V. (2007), Höchste Gerichte an ihren Grenzen – Bemerkungen aus der Perspektive des Gerichtshofes der Europäischen Gemeinschaften, in Meinhard Hilf et al. (eds), *Höchste Gerichte an ihren Grenzen*, Berlin, Duncker & Humblot.
Spaventa, E. (2008), Seeing the Wood Despite the Trees? On the Scope of Union Citizenship and its Constitutional Effects, 45 *C.M.L.Rev.* 13.
Sweet, A.S. (1992), *The Birth of Juridical Politics in France*, New York, Oxford University Press.
Sweet, A.S. (1994), Judging Socialist Reform: The Politics of Coordinate Construction in France and Germany, 26 *Comparative Political Studies* 443.
Sweet, A.S. (2000), *Governing With Judges*, New York, Oxford University Press.
Sweet, A.S. (2007), The Juridical Coup d'État and the Problem of Authority, 8 *German L. J.* 915.
de alTorre, C. (2005), Case Note, 42 *Common Market Law Review* 1169.
Tribe, L.H. (2008), *The Invisible Constitution*, (New York, Oxford University Press.
Tsagourias, N. (2007), The Constitutional Role of General Principles of Law in International and European Jurisprudence, in Nicholas Tsagourias (ed.), *Transnational Constitutionalism*, Cambridge, Cambridge.
Varju, M. (2009), On the Constitutional Issues of EU Membership and the Interplay between the ECHR and Domestic Constitutional Law Concerning the Right of Assembly and Freedom of Expression, 15 *European Public Law* 295.
Vinx, L. (2007), *Hans Kelsen's Pure Theory of Law*, Oxford, Oxford University Press.
Walker, N. (2006), EU Constitutionalism in the State Constitutional Tradition, European University Institute Working Paper Law No. 2006/21, 16.
Weiler, J.H.H. (1991), The Transformation of Europe, 100 *Yale L. J.* 2403.
Wernicke, S. (2007), Au nom de qui? The European Court of Justice between Member States, Civil Society and Union Citizens, 13 *European Law Journal* 380.
Wessel, R.A. (2007), The EU's Foreign, Security and Defence Policy Fifteen Years after Maastricht: A Constitutional Momentum?, in Hans-Georg Ehrhart et al. (eds), *Die Europäische Union im 21. Jahrhundert: Theorie und Praxis europäischer Außen-, Sicherheits- und Friedenspolitik*, Wiesbaden, Vs verlag.

Ziller, J. (2009), Solange III, or the Bundesverfassungsgericht's, Europe-friendlyness. On the Decision of the German Federal Constitutional Court over the Ratification of the Treaty of Lisbon, 5 *Rivista Italiana di Diritto Pubblico Comunitario* 973.

PART III
The Rule of Law and Policy-Making in ECC after Enlargement

Chapter 9
Raising the Standard? The Current Challenges in Human Rights Protection in Hungary

Bernadette Somody

Introduction

Human rights are a universal value. The currently valid international human rights standards were codified by the international community in the middle of the twentieth century. This is what Hungary looked to as a point of reference during the political transition of 1989 and these were the standards that came to constitute the contents of the catalogue of fundamental rights which was formulated in 1989 as part of the Hungarian Constitution. The Constitutional Court secured a high level of protection for civil and political rights and freedoms on the constitutional foundation which was created in view of the shared European standard of requirements.

Inevitably, however, there have been examples,[1] even in the recent past, when the European Court of Human Rights reprimanded Hungary because one of the Hungarian courts made a decision according to a statute which was in accordance with the Constitution but was not in harmony with the requirements of the European Convention on Human Rights. Clearly, in these cases the level of protection of human rights demanded by Strasbourg was higher than the standard of requirements in the Hungarian Constitution. Generally, however, the opposite is more characteristic. We may fairly say that usually the Hungarian Constitution and the interpretative practice of the Constitutional Court demand the same or often an even higher level of protection than the Strasbourg requirements, and are in many ways stricter when restricting fundamental rights than the Strasbourg criteria.

In the cases mentioned, the European Court of Human Rights made a decision about Hungary which led to improvement in the enforcement of a fundamental right.[2] At the same time it appears as though these days the international treaties on human rights, the European Convention on Human Rights and the practice of

---

1 *Bukta and others v. Hungary*, 25691/04, judgement of 17 July 2007; *Vajnai v. Hungary*, 33629/06, judgement of 8 July 2008.

2 E.g., as a consequence of the decision of the Strasbourg Court in the case of *Bukta and Others v. Hungary*, the Hungarian Constitutional Court acknowledged that pursuant to

the Strasbourg Court, as well as EU documents on fundamental rights are being perceived in academic and public debate in Hungary as powerful arguments, including a number of cases where they are used to justify ambitions to restrict fundamental rights. It is this latter tendency we are going to explore in this chapter. Clearly, Hungary can certainly not respond by shutting herself away from international influences and arguments. Thus the question arises – how should Hungarian human rights protection respond to arguments coming from international and EU law which weaken the Hungarian national standard for the protection of human rights.

In order to lay the foundations, the current system of the protection of human rights in Hungary will be briefly presented. The sources of fundamental rights and the criteria for restricting these rights will be described. When doing so, particular emphasis will be placed on the fundamental rights which appear in the later case studies (the right to the protection of personal data and the freedom of expression). The two case studies demonstrate the problem at hand through concrete instances. The case study related to data protection is set in the context of the implementation of the Directive 2006/24/EC on Data Retention[3] (Data Retention Directive) in Hungary. The other case study illustrates the issue of the criminalization of racist speech and Holocaust denial in Hungary with a particular focus on the Framework Decision of the Council of the EU[4] (Framework Decision). In the academic literature on the subject, problems similar to those explored in the case studies usually lead to the question of what kind of possibilities the national Constitutional Courts have in protecting their Constitution. In the present chapter, however, the problem is examined from a different perspective and different quarters are looked in for answers based on the national protection of fundamental rights.

The Current System of Human Rights Protection in Hungary

Sources of Fundamental Rights

The Constitution In Hungary the political transition of 1989 took place by peaceful means through negotiations between the communist and the opposition forces. The transition was subsequently codified by the 1989 act of amendment

---

the right of assembly, spontaneous demonstrations may be held, as well as rapid-response demonstrations. See Decision 75/2008. (V. 29.) AB.

3 Directive 2006/24/EC of the European Parliament and of the Council of 15 March 2006 on the retention of data generated or processed in connection with the provision of publicly available electronic communications services or of public communications networks and amending Directive 2002/58/EC.

4 Council Framework Decision 2008/913/JHA of 28 November 2008 on combating certain forms and expressions of racism and xenophobia by means of criminal law.

to the Constitution.[5] In the technical sense, the Hungarian Constitution, originally dating back to 1949, underwent a mere amendment in 1989,[6] but in terms of content a completely new Constitution was born which satisfies content criteria of constitutionality, including human rights standards.

Certain of the fundamental rights were already present in the text of the socialist Constitution before the transition. However, neither in content, nor in legal character did the provisions on fundamental rights satisfy the expectations of a constitutional state. Before 1989 the Constitution declared that in the Hungarian People's Republic citizens' rights are to be practised in harmony with the interests of the socialist society; the practice of such rights is inseparable from complying with citizens' duties.[7] Besides, before the political transition, the Constitution had no normative force; fundamental rights were not tied in with any guarantees to ensure their mandatory nature or render them enforceable. The 1989 revision of the Constitution brought a change in both respects. The current Constitution contains a separate and comprehensive chapter on human rights in line with European standards. The enforcement of these rights is secured by a complex system of guarantees (such as the Constitutional Court, the ordinary courts and the ombudsmen).

Fundamental rights are mostly laid down in Chapter XII of the Constitution, dedicated to Fundamental Rights and Duties, but several provisions regarding fundamental rights also occur in Chapter I on General Provisions. The fact that the catalogue of fundamental rights was placed at the end of the Constitution is due to historical reasons and this is also why certain fundamental rights appear in other chapters: the Constitution renewed in terms of content in 1989 was not altered in terms of structure; therefore it retained the structure of the socialist constitution.

Acts of Parliament If we review the Hungarian Constitution we find that it offers a comprehensive system of first-, second- and third-generation human rights. The contents, limitations and guarantees of the individual fundamental rights are discussed in detail and defined by the acts of Parliament. This follows from the general clause of the Constitution on the restriction of fundamental rights, whereby in the Republic of Hungary regulations pertaining to fundamental rights and duties are determined by acts of Parliament.[8] As we can see, the Constitution lays down a stricter requirement regarding the form of restricting fundamental rights than the European standard. It does not accept a statute of any level which is adequately

5 Act XXXI of 1989.

6 The number for the Constitution of the Republic of Hungary is still Act XX of 1949.

7 Text of the Constitution before 23 October 23 1989, Article 54(2).

8 Article 8(2).

accessible and formulated with sufficient precision to enable the citizen to regulate his conduct,[9] but will only accept acts of Parliament as a suitable source of law.

The stipulations of the Constitution regarding regulation by acts of Parliament are decisive for all fundamental rights. Besides, the Constitution also prescribes, as a further guarantee, that passing an act of Parliament on a particular fundamental right requires the votes of two-thirds of the Members of Parliament present. It is important to emphasize that prescribing a qualified majority is not an indicator of the value or significance of the fundamental rights in question. The fundamental rights thus regulated are not more important or more valuable than those regulated in acts passed by an unqualified majority. Demanding a two-thirds majority goes back to political considerations: the Constitution demands a two-thirds majority with regard to issues in which agreement between the government side and the opposition was deemed particularly important from a political point of view by the political powers which negotiated the amendment of the Constitution in light of the original circumstances of the political transition.[10]

One example of regulation passed by a two-thirds majority is the right to the protection of personal data. According to Article 59 of the Constitution, in the Republic of Hungary everyone has the right to the protection of personal data. This article also prescribes that a majority of two-thirds of the votes of the Members of Parliament present is required to pass the act on the protection of personal data. Act LXIII of 1992 on the Protection of Personal Data and the Disclosure of Information of Public Interest (Data Protection Act) was created in order to implement the stipulation of the Constitution just mentioned.

Article 61 of the Constitution lays down the freedom of expression. This regulation, however, does not lay down an obligation to create an act on the freedom of expression nor does it stipulate that the issue be regulated through a qualified majority, despite the fact that, when judged by the practice of the Constitutional Court, freedom of expression is ranked second on the list of fundamental rights (which has crystallized from Constitutional Court practice), preceded only by the right to life and human dignity.[11] Regulations on the freedom of expression are contained in a number of different acts, with the most important limitations being laid down by the Criminal Code.

Decisions of the Constitutional Court Decisions of the Constitutional Court represent vital sources for fundamental rights. The Constitutional Court interprets and applies regulations of the Constitution regarding fundamental rights both in its

9 See *The Sunday Times v. United Kingdom*, 6538/74, judgement of 26 April 1979, p. 31, para. 49; *Silver and Others v. United Kingdom*, 5947/72, 6205/73 etc., judgement of 25 March 1983, p. 33, paras. 87, 88; *Malone v. United Kingdom*, 8691/79, judgement of 2 August 1984, p. 27, paras. 66, 67.

10 See Decision 4/1993. (II. 12.) AB.

11 For a formulation of this by the Constitutional Court see the section headed Criteria for Restricting Fundamental Rights.

procedures of constitutional review and in abstract interpretation of provisions of the Constitution. The principles laid down in the holdings of the decisions of the Constitutional Court are mandatory for all; they have *erga omnes* effect. Besides, such pieces of interpretation of the Constitution, as they occur in the reasoning part of the Court's decisions, represent a further source regarding fundamental rights since these also reveal the way in which the legislator, the courts and authorities that apply the law define fundamental rights.

The practice of the Constitutional Court also served as the test for the restriction of fundamental rights ("test of necessity and proportionality"), which is an issue we shall come back to later.

The contents and main guarantees of the right to the protection of personal data were also outlined in a decision of the Constitutional Court in 1991.[12] The subject of the constitutional review was the regulation on the state population register. According to the decision, the application of general and uniform personal identification codes which can be used without restriction was unconstitutional.

In this decision the Constitutional Court did not interpret the right to the protection of personal data as a traditional protective right. By taking into consideration the active aspect of this right, the Constitutional Court interpreted it as a right to informational self-determination. Thus, the right to the protection of personal data meant that everyone has the right to decide about the disclosure and use of his/her personal data. Consequently, approval by the person concerned is generally required to record and use personal data, and the entire route of data processing and handling must be made accessible to everyone, i.e., everyone has the right to know who uses, and when, where and for what purpose, his/her data. In exceptional cases, a statute (an act of Parliament) may order obligatory personal data-processing and prescribe the manner in which these data may be used. Such a statute restricts the fundamental right to informational self-determination, and is constitutional only if it is in accordance with the general constitutional requirements for the restriction of fundamental rights (Article 8(2) of the Constitution, on the test of necessity and proportionality).

Data subjects have to be ensured the opportunity to monitor the route of their data during the processing and to enforce their rights. The Constitutional Court defined proportionality as an essential requirement of data-processing. According to the decision of the Constitutional Court, adherence to the purpose to be achieved is a condition of, and at the same time the most important guarantee for exercising, the right to informational self-determination. It follows from the principle of adherence to the purpose to be achieved that collecting and storing data without a specific goal, "for the purpose of storage", for an unspecified future use are unconstitutional. The other basic guarantee is the restriction on the transfer and publication of data. Personal data may be transferred to a third party and data-processing systems may be combined only if all the conditions for data-processing are met with regard to each personal datum. The content elements and guarantees

12 Decision 15/1991 (IV. 13.) AB.

of the right to the protection of personal data which were thus defined by the Constitutional Court were codified, in 1992, by the Data Protection Act mentioned earlier.[13]

The Constitutional Court also offered an interpretation of the contents of the freedom of expression. The decision which defined the later interpretation of the Constitution was created in 1992.[14] It was about the constitutionality of the regulation on "incitement against a community".

In this decision the Constitutional Court declared that the freedom of expression has a special place among constitutional fundamental rights – in effect it is the "mother right" of several freedoms, the so-called fundamental rights of communication. Several fundamental rights, which the Constitution mentions by name, come under the category of communication rights: freedom of the press, which also covers freedom of the electronic media; freedom of artistic and literary creation; freedom of the distribution of works of art; freedom of scientific research; and freedom of teaching scientific knowledge. To this category belong, furthermore, freedom of conscience and religion, freedom of assembly and freedom of association. Moreover, this category covers freedom of information, freedom of access to, and disclosure of, data of public interest. They are preconditions of the sound formation of opinions. The sum total of communication rights enables an individual to take part in the social and political processes in a well-informed and responsible manner.

Freedom of expression, as the mother right of communication rights, receives enhanced constitutional protection. As the Constitutional Court has put it, although the privileged place accorded to the right of freedom of expression does not mean that this right may not be restricted, it necessarily implies that the right to free expression must only give way to a few rights; that is to say, the acts of Parliament restricting this freedom must be strictly construed.

Content-neutral protection is highly important among the constitutional principles of freedom of expression laid down by the Constitutional Court. The Constitutional Court has stated that the right to free expression protects opinion irrespective of the value or veracity of its content. No speech may be restricted when assessed merely on the basis of its content; the prohibition of a speech only becomes compatible with the Constitution if its consequences are considered. According to the decision of the Constitutional Court, only this approach meets the requirement of ideological neutrality. The freedom of expression has only external boundaries: until and unless it clashes with such a constitutionally drawn external boundary, the opportunity and fact of the expression of opinion is protected, irrespective of its content. In other words, it is the expression of an individual opinion, the manifestation of public opinion formed by its own rules and, in correlation to the aforesaid, the opportunity of forming an individual opinion built upon as broad information as possible that is protected by the Constitution. The

13 Jóri 2005: 71.

14 Decision 30/1992 (V. 26.) AB.

Constitution guarantees free communication – as individual behaviour or as a public process – and the fundamental right to the freedom of expression does not refer to the content of the opinion. Every opinion, good or damaging, pleasant or offensive, has a place in this social process, especially because the classification of opinions is also the product of this process.

International Law and EU Law The Republic of Hungary is a signatory to a number of universal and regional agreements on human rights. The European Convention of Human Rights, as the most significant from the perspective of Hungarian thinking about fundamental rights, is focused on here, as is the construction which offers the most effective mechanism for rights protection. The Convention was promulgated in Hungary in Act XXXI of 1993.

According to Article 7(1) of the Constitution the legal system of the Republic of Hungary accepts the generally recognized principles of international law, and harmonizes the country's domestic law with the obligations assumed under international law. In Hungary, international human rights treaties become integrated in the domestic legal system at the time of their promulgation (a dualist transformation model). Domestic law has to be in harmony with the contents of the human rights treaties thus promulgated and in terms of the hierarchy of sources of law; acts of Parliament promulgating a human rights treaty enjoy priority as opposed to domestic acts. This follows from the power of the Constitutional Court to examine conflicts between international treaties and domestic law. Should the Constitutional Court establish that a statute at the same or lower level than the statute promulgating the international treaty conflicts with the international treaty, it annuls in whole or in part the statute in conflict with the international treaty.[15]

At the same time, the Constitution also enjoys priority compared to international treaties. Through its power of constitutional review the Constitutional Court examines whether the acts of Parliament promulgating international treaties and the international treaties that have been integrated into these acts are in accordance with the Constitution. If the Constitutional Court declares that the international treaty in question or one of its stipulations is unconstitutional, it declares the act promulgating that treaty unconstitutional. Such a decision of the Constitutional Court does not affect the international obligations of the Republic of Hungary, but the legislator must secure the harmony between the domestic law and the obligations assumed under international law, which may even take the form of an amendment to the Constitution.[16]

The enforcement of fundamental rights may also be affected by EU law. In this context, the typical question that occurs is to what extent the Constitutional Court is entitled to examine the harmony of EU law with the requirements of the Hungarian Constitution regarding fundamental rights. What we can conclude in this respect from the decisions of the Hungarian Constitutional Court is that the Court

15 Act XXXII of 1989 on the Constitutional Court, Article 45(1).

16 Decision 4/1997 (I. 22.) AB.

examines the constitutionality of the domestic statute implementing community law regardless of the fact that it is based on the Community law itself. However, it is an open question what sort of possibilities are open to the Constitutional Court should there be any collision between a directly applicable community law and one of the provisions of the Constitution.[17]

Criteria for Restricting Fundamental Rights

The Constitution establishes a system of independent institutions protecting fundamental rights. The main elements of the system are the Constitutional Court, the ordinary courts of law and ombudspersons with general and specialized competence. As has already been mentioned above, Hungary also transposed the European Convention on Human Rights into the domestic legal system in 1993, which secures the enforcement of the European human rights standards laid down by the Convention and the practice of the European Court of Human Rights.

The Constitutional Court serves as the main body for the protection of the Constitution, including the fundamental rights. The Constitutional Court has a broad competence when compared to corresponding institutions in other countries, especially in reviewing the constitutionality of statutes. It secures the protection of fundamental rights chiefly through the constitutional review of the laws regulating and restricting fundamental rights and by annulling them should they prove unconstitutional.

The basis for the protection of fundamental rights by the Constitutional Court is the general clause of the Constitution regarding the restriction of all fundamental rights. The clause declares that, in the Republic of Hungary, regulations pertaining to fundamental rights and duties are determined by acts of Parliament; such acts, however, may not restrict the basic meaning and contents of fundamental rights.[18] The regulation comprises two criteria: (1) The first step prescribes, as we have mentioned earlier, the level at which fundamental rights are to be regulated and, within that, restricted. It lays down that fundamental rights should be restricted by acts of Parliament, which thus constitutes a more strict formal criterion than the European standard. (2) The second step, following the model of the German Constitution, lays down the requirement that the essential content of fundamental rights is inviolable. Thus it marks the extent to which, in terms of content, a fundamental right may be affected by a regulation if it appears in a source of law which is formally satisfactory, i.e., in an act of Parliament.

In the typical case, the practice of the Constitutional Court does not consider the essential content of fundamental rights as something objective. The essential content cannot be determined once and for all. Whether or not a restriction affects the essential content can only be ascertained on a case-by-case basis regarding every single instance of restriction. The essential content of a fundamental right

17 Trócsányi and Csink 2007; Sonnevend 2007a: 967–968.

18 Article 8(2).

is affected by a restriction which fails what is called the test of necessity and proportionality.[19] According to the formula used by the Constitutional Court and formulated mostly on the basis of instances from Germany and Strasbourg, a regulation that restricts a fundamental right is only constitutional if the restriction is suitable to achieve a legitimate objective of the legislator and also if it meets the requirement of proportionality and necessity. The individual fundamental rights of people may be restricted on the basis of the legitimate objective of protecting the fundamental rights of others, the state's duty to institutionally (objectively) guarantee fundamental rights, and the achievement of certain constitutional public objectives. The state may only use the tool of restricting a fundamental right if it is the only way to secure the protection or the enforcement of another fundamental right or liberty or to protect another constitutional value; that is to say, it is the only way to protect the above legitimate objectives. The constitutionality of restricting a fundamental right also requires that the restriction comply with the criterion of proportionality; the importance of the desired objective must be proportionate to the restriction of the fundamental right concerned. In enacting a limitation, the legislator is bound to employ the most moderate means suitable for reaching the specified purpose. Restricting the content of a right arbitrarily, without a forcing cause, is unconstitutional, just like doing so by using a restriction of disproportionate weight compared to the purported objective.[20]

Within the practice of the Constitutional Court, a certain hierarchy has evolved among the different fundamental rights from the point of view of liability to restriction. Two of these rights deserve particular attention. At the head of the hierarchy we find the right to life and human dignity which has been declared absolute. As was mentioned above, the right to life and human dignity is followed by the freedom of expression which, as the Constitutional Court has declared, receives enhanced constitutional protection. The special importance of freedom of expression means that there are very few other rights that have precedence over it and the acts of Parliament restricting this freedom have to be interpreted narrowly.[21]

As we have seen, the Constitution, contrary to seminal international treaties on human rights, does not name the possible grounds for restricting fundamental rights in its general clause on the restriction of human rights, nor do we find such objectives in the provisions on individual fundamental rights. The grounds which are legitimate in constitutional terms for restricting human rights may be ascertained on the basis of the practice of the Constitutional Court. The chief ground for restricting human rights can be to protect the fundamental rights of others. Besides, the Constitutional Court accepts as legitimate justification the state's obligation to protect fundamental rights. In other cases, it has accepted, for

19 Halmai and Tóth 2003: 131–133.

20 See e.g. Decision 30/1992 (V. 26.) AB and Decision 39/2007 (VI. 20.) AB.

21 Decision 30/1992 (V. 26.) AB.

instance, reference to public peace as a justification.[22] Restriction of fundamental rights may be justified primarily by the protection of other people's fundamental rights; while other justifications in connection with public interest (such as public peace, morals, law and order, safety) are seen as very feeble arguments in favour of restricting fundamental rights. According to some approaches, these arguments are in themselves insufficient as a ground for restricting fundamental rights except if they entail or threaten infringement upon concrete existing rights.[23]

Case Studies

The case studies below concern the right to the protection of personal data and the freedom of expression. Hungarian law secures a high degree of protection on both of these rights. Both of these fundamental rights face serious challenges these days. As regards data protection, the challenges include the ever-newer possibilities offered by technological development, as well as the demands made by anti-terrorist efforts.[24] Freedom of expression is challenged by society's call for state intervention against exclusion (racism, anti-Semitism or homophobia).

Implementation of the Data Retention Directive

During the totalitarian regime, citizens' lives were totally transparent for the state, while the operation of the state remained totally secret. The 1989 declaration of so-called informational freedoms (data protection and public access to data of public interest) symbolizes the opposite of the totalitarian regime. László Majtényi, the first Hungarian Commissioner for Data Protection and Freedom of Information, said:

> Information rights are among the most significant achievements of the revolution of the constitutional state. This is the axis, or at least one of the axes, around which the world is turning round. The information philosophy of the party state needed to be turned right the way round: from a non-transparent state and a transparent citizen to a transparent state and a non-transparent citizen.[25]

The gesture of inserting the right to personal data protection into the constitutional catalogue of the fundamental rights had a unique significance: it provided one of the means to demolish the myth of the state's omnipotence and omnipresence by constitutionally guaranteeing transparency for its citizens. It was

---

22 For the latter see, e.g., Decision 30/1992 (V. 26.) AB.
23 Balogh 2000: 132: Sólyom 2001: 406–408.
24 Sonnevend 2009: 169–170.
25 Majtényi 2006: 17.

followed a very strict Data Protection Act in which the concept of the right to self-determination was adopted.[26]

According to the Hungarian regulation, personal data shall not be processed unless the data subject has given his/her consent. Data-processing can be ordered by an act of Parliament (which means the restriction of this right), but only if this is the only way to secure the protection or the enforcement of another fundamental right or liberty or to protect another constitutional value (test of necessity and proportionality). According to the proportionality principle, personal data shall be processed only for a specified purpose, in order to exercise a right or perform an obligation. This purpose shall be complied with in all phases of the data-processing. No personal data shall be processed unless indispensable and suitable for the achievement of the purpose of the data-processing, and only to the extent and for the duration necessary to achieve that purpose.[27] The Constitutional Court has also expressly declared in its already quoted Decision 15/1991 (IV. 13.) AB that the collection and processing of personal data in the absence of a definite purpose and for arbitrary future use are unconstitutional.

The vulnerability of this protection and the European influences affecting it may be illustrated by the regulation on data retention. The Data Retention Directive requires the Member States to ensure that communication providers must retain, for a period of between six months and two years, necessary data as specified in the Directive to identify the parties involved in a communication and its traffic data. The data are required to be available to competent national authorities in specific cases, "for the purpose of the investigation, detection and prosecution of serious crime, as defined by each Member State in its national law".

Even prior to this, however, the Hungarian Act on Electronic Communications stipulated that providers of electronic communications services, for compliance with the requirements of disclosure authorized national security bodies, investigating authorities and the competent court of justice for the protection of national security, national defence or public safety and for the prosecution of criminal acts and any unauthorized use of the electronic communications system, shall retain for three years the traffic data of the communication.[28] Such a regulation was clearly unconstitutional as it was diagonally opposed to the Constitutional Court's repeatedly quoted decision which prohibits data-processing for "the stock" (i.e., without previously defined purposes) without previously defined purposes, but nobody attacked the provisions before the Constitutional Court.

When Hungary implemented the Directive,[29] the period of data retention was reduced, but in other respects the European expectation was used as an argument for the restriction of the right to data protection to a greater degree than the EU

26 Szabó and Székely 2005: 252–253.

27 Data Protection Act, Article 5(1)(2).

28 Act C of 2003 on Electronic Communications, Article 157(8 b, text before 15 March 2008.

29 Act CLXXIV of 2007.

required. This is clearly illustrated by the fact that instead of the legislator defining those serious crimes, the investigation, detection and prosecution of which may justify the processing of the related data (which was required by the Directive), it further softened the purposes which may justify data retention, despite the fact that they had been rather loosely defined even beforehand. According to the new rules, electronic communications network operators and providers of electronic communications service are required – for the purpose of compliance with any request made by the investigating authority, the public prosecutor, the court or the national security service pursuant to the authorization conferred in specific other legislation, with a view to discharging their respective duties – to retain the traffic data.[30] As we can see, this regulation has also omitted enlisting national security and other similar purposes listed in the earlier regulations, even though the organizations entitled to request data have far more extensive tasks than defined in the Directive. Following a petition by the Hungarian Civil Liberties Union (HCLU), the regulation is before the Constitutional Court at the moment.[31]

The Data Retention Directive[32] allowed each Member State to postpone until 15 March 2009 the application of the Directive to the retention of communications data relating to Internet access, Internet telephony and Internet email. Sixteen of the Member States took this opportunity, but Hungary was not among them.

Criminalizing Racist Speech and Holocaust Denial

The Hungarian practice of protecting fundamental rights faced up to the problem of the possible sanctioning of hate speech as early as 1992. This is when the Constitutional Court issued its decision[33] about regulating "incitement against a community" in which it laid down the constitutional principles of freedom of expression. Among other things, the Constitutional Court declared that the right to free expression protects opinion irrespective of the value or veracity of its content. No speech can be restricted purely on grounds of its content – the prohibition on any kind of speech can only be rendered constitutional by its consequences. By emphasizing a content-neutral and formal concept of the freedom of expression the Constitutional Court surpassed European standards.[34] This was the background for the "test of incitement to hatred" which the Constitutional Court laid down at this time and has consistently enforced on a number of occasions since then. Pursuant to that test, the criminalization of incitement to hatred complies with the Constitution because incitement has the danger of causing violence and injury to the rights of individuals. By contrast, the Constitutional Court found it unconstitutional to criminalize abusive language that reviles or disparages the Hungarian nation or a

30 Act C of 2003 on Electronic Communications, Article 159/A(1).

31 HCLU 2008.

32 Article 15(3).

33 Decision 30/1992 (V. 26.) AB.

34 Sólyom 2001: 218.

nationality, a people, a denomination or a race, because that crime can also take place if that expression of opinion did not involve any injury to rights of individuals. Such an abstract disturbance of public peace was not found to be a constitutionally sufficient justification for restricting free expression by instruments of criminal law. The above-mentioned Criminal Code category of "abusive language" did not mount an external obstacle in the way of free expression; it qualified as punishable an opinion on the grounds of its content.

This standpoint of the Constitutional Court has put a halt to almost two decades of ambition for legislation in which Parliament repeatedly tried to penalize certain opinions purely on the basis of their content, such as racist, anti-Semitic or otherwise exclusive utterances.[35] The Constitutional Court has persisted in maintaining the following interpretation of the freedom of expression:

> Historical experience shows that on every occasion when the freedom of expression was restricted, social justice and human creativity suffered and humankind's innate ability to develop was stymied. The harmful consequences afflicted not only the lives of individuals but also that of society at large, inflicting much suffering while leading to a dead end for human development. Free expression of ideas and beliefs, free manifestation of even unpopular or unusual ideas is the fundamental requirement for the existence of a truly vibrant society capable of development. ... Only through self-cleansing can a political culture and a soundly reacting public opinion emerge. Thus one who uses abusive language stamps himself as such and in the eyes of the public he will become known as a "mudslinger." Such abusive language must be answered by criticism.[36]

There was only one hate-speech-related decision in which the Constitutional Court diverged from the basic principle of content-neutral protection. In this decision the Constitutional Court decided that criminally sanctioning the "use of symbols of despotism'[37] was constitutional. The decision was heavily criticized in the relevant literature, precisely for diverging from the principle of content-neutral

---

35 Decision 30/1992 (V. 26.) AB; Decision 12/1999 (V. 21.) AB; Decision 18/2004 (V. 25.) AB; Decision 95/2008 (VII. 3.) AB.

36 Decision 30/1992 (V. 26.) AB.

37 Section 269/B of Act IV of 1978 on the Criminal Code: (1) Anyone who a) distributes; b) uses in front of a large public gathering; c) exhibits in public, swastika, the SS sign, an arrow-cross, the hammer and sickle, a five-pointed red star or a symbol depicting the above commits a misdemeanour – unless a graver crime is realized – and shall be punishable with fine. (2) The person who commits an act defined in paragraph (1) for the purposes of disseminating knowledge, education, science, or art, or for the purpose of information about the events of history or the present time shall not be punishable. (3) The provisions of paragraphs (1) and (2) do not extend to the official symbols of states in force.

protection.[38] In turn, the Strasbourg Court reprimanded Hungary for applying the rules which the Constitutional Court found constitutional in the case of *Vajnai v. Hungary*.[39]

Today there are two clearly outlined professional stances existing side by side in Hungary. Representatives of the one opinion champion the attitude of the Constitutional Court described above – in other words the content-neutral protection of the freedom of expression. They believe that racism should not be approached with a criminal sanction, but instead exclusion ought to be handled by means of social policy.[40] Representatives of the other opinion propagate the revision of the earlier viewpoint of the Constitutional Court and the criminalization of exclusionist speech. This kind of argumentation relies heavily on references to international treaties and EU law.[41] Draft proposals aimed at criminalization, including a proposal aimed at amending the Constitution, also refer to international law and EU sources.[42]

Efforts to criminalize racist and exclusionist speech, as well as Holocaust denial, usually refer to three international and EU documents. The first is the European Convention on Human Rights and its interpretation by the Strasbourg Court. The Strasbourg Court has repeatedly declared that the justification of a pro-Nazi policy could not be allowed to enjoy the protection afforded under Article 10 and that there is a category of clearly established historical facts – such as the Holocaust – whose negation or revision would be removed from the protection of Article 10 by Article 17.[43] In this context the Hungarian argumentation does not take into account that the Convention prescribes a minimum level of protection for the freedom of expression, and thus the practice of the Strasbourg Court only creates the possibility of criminalization for the states that are parties to the Treaty but does not prescribe it as an obligation.

The second relevant document is the United Nations International Convention on the Elimination of All Forms of Racial Discrimination of 21 December 1965. According to Article 4(a) of the Convention, the States Parties shall declare an offence punishable by law all dissemination of ideas based on racial superiority or hatred. In Hungary the Convention was promulgated by Decree-law 8 of 1969, which means that this happened well before the post-communist transition. The Hungarian legal system indeed does not satisfy the above quoted obligation. One of the reasons for this, however, is that criminalizing the acts in question would offend the principle of the content-neutral protection of the freedom of expression and thus the Constitution itself. In the Hungarian legal system the

38 See e.g. Halmai 2000.

39 *Vajnai v. Hungary*, 33629/06, judgement of 8 July 2008.

40 *Tézisek a szólásszabadság védelmében* 2009; Sárosi 2009: Simon 2009: Halmai 2009.

41 Bárándy and Berta 2008; Halmai 2008: Uitz 2009.

42 Bill T/9584 (4 May 2009); Bill T/9861 (27 May 2009).

43 *Garaudy v. France*, 65831/01, decision of 24 June 2003.

Constitution enjoys priority as against the obligations assumed under international law and thus the decree-law promulgating this treaty could even be annulled by the Constitutional Court were there a petition proposing this.

Third, we have to mention the Framework Decision of the Council of the European Union. According to Article 1(1)c), each Member State shall take the measures necessary to ensure that the following intentional conduct is punishable:

> publicly condoning, denying or grossly trivialising crimes of genocide, crimes against humanity and war crimes as defined in Articles 6, 7 and 8 of the Statute of the International Criminal Court, directed against a group of persons or a member of such a group defined by reference to race, colour, religion, descent or national or ethnic origin when the conduct is carried out in a manner likely to incite to violence or hatred against such a group or a member of such a group.

In order to sustain the content-neutral protection of the freedom of expression, Hungary could make reference, with a fair chance of success, to another provision of the Framework Decision. According to Article 7(2), the Framework Decision:

> shall not have the effect of requiring Member States to take measures in contradiction to fundamental principles relating to freedom of association and freedom of expression, in particular freedom of the press and the freedom of expression in other media as they result from constitutional traditions or rules governing the rights and responsibilities of, and the procedural guarantees for, the press or other media where these rules relate to the determination or limitation of liability.

We can see that content-based criminalization of racist speech and Holocaust denial goes against the Hungarian Constitution and the interpretation it has been consistently given by the Constitutional Court for almost two decades. We can also see that the above-mentioned international and EU documents leave more freedom for the Hungarian legislator in terms of criminalization than the justifications of the proposals allow us to see. Despite this fact, the legislator would willingly accept lowering the protection level at the Constitutional Court, even by amending the Constitution.[44] This is clearly shown by a speech made by an MP, Dr Zoltán Szabó, in Parliament during the debate of the amendment of the Constitution:

> The Constitutional Court, whose task is not to create a Constitution but to offer authentic interpretations of it, has declared that the Constitution protects the

44 One may argue that lowering the protection level of freedom of expression means increasing that of the right to human dignity so the general level of human rights protection does not decrease. However, it has to be taken into consideration that not all forms of racist speech and Holocaust denial affect other individuals' fundamental right to human dignity.

> freedom of expression regardless of the value and veracity of the opinion voiced. This was declared by the Constitutional Court, therefore this is what the current Constitution does. The present Constitution will continue to do this until we change it. We, the two-third of us in this House, have the power to achieve that in the future the Constitution should not protect the freedom of expression regardless of value and veracity but should indeed present a firm boundary when the opinion is lacking in certain value contents or truth contents. This is what this draft proposal is about. Thus the fact that the Constitutional Court has declared this indicates to me precisely the need to modify the Constitution not the lack of such necessity.[45]

This proposal to amend the Constitution was not accepted by Parliament, but further such attempts are to be expected in the near future.[46]

Conclusion

Fundamental rights were integrated in the Hungarian Constitution in one single act of revision in 1989. The legislators in essence copied the international minimum standards into the Constitution and complied with the pressure to retain social rights (which had previously figured in the socialist Constitution). This was followed by the decisive role of interpretation by the Constitutional Court – on the basis of the above-mentioned Constitutional foundation it built up a body of human-rights-related legal material which can be seen as equally valuable as the Western European examples.[47] What is more, as its first Chair László Sólyom declared, the Constitutional Court considered it its mission to *raise* the minimum level of requirement represented by the text which had borrowed the international minimum standard.[48] This practice of the Constitutional Court includes defining the criteria for restricting fundamental rights, as well as the two decisions presented earlier which elaborate the constitutional contents of the right of informational self-determination and that of freedom of expression. Overall, we may conclude that both the practice of the Constitutional Court and the related legislation on fundamental rights have created a high level of protection to fundamental rights, even by European standards.

The incorporation of fundamental rights into the Constitution in 1989 and their interpretation by the Constitutional Court in the 1990s were not preceded

45 Szabó 2009.

46 Among recent events, the amendment of the Criminal Code has to be underlined. On 22 February 2010 the Parliament adopted a new act criminalizing the public Holocaust denial. It seems certain that the act will be the subject of *ex post* constitutional review before the Constitutional Court which could be initiated on the basis of *actio popularis*.

47 Sólyom 2003: 17.

48 Sólyom 2001: 118.

in Hungary by an organic process of development. It may be stated that Hungary is a relatively new Central Eastern European democracy where, on the one hand, the standard of human rights protection is high even compared to the general European standard, but on the other hand, lacking in a history of slow and organic development, it is not solid enough. Since the system of fundamental rights and freedoms was built up in a very rapid way, it is rather vulnerable and inescapably leads to the thought that it could be destroyed with almost the same rapidity. As László Sólyom aptly put it, "throughout the successive waves of democratisation the reception time of human rights gets exponentially shorter".[49] One wonders – would it take just as little time to demolish them?

To be sure, we must emphasize positive European influences: the Hungarian system of human rights was based on and determined by the common European values, especially the European Convention on Human Rights and the related case law. The latter was of significant importance for the practice of the Constitutional Court, although in the argumentation their role rarely went beyond an auxiliary, confirming function.[50] Besides the positive effects generally acknowledged, an attempt has been made in this chapter to shed light on some of the challenges that the Hungarian human rights system is facing, especially in connection with EU membership. Currently, we are experiencing that European tendencies in the field of human rights and the protection of the Constitution by the Constitutional Court may also come into conflict in such a way that the input from international and EU law and their argumentation weaken the Hungarian standard of the protection of fundamental rights. The question is what sort of answers the national protection of human rights should give to such impact of international law and the European Union.

As was already indicated at the beginning of this chapter, the answer to the problem is typically sought within the powers of the Constitutional Court. The Hungarian Constitutional Court examines domestic legislation which is based on EU law implementing the directives, and has the power to declare it unconstitutional and to annul it.[51] On this basis, the Constitutional Court would annul the legal regulations implementing the Data Retention Directive (as proposed by the Hungarian Civil Liberties Union), but in fact this would only postpone finding a solution to the constitutional problem. After all, if the directive itself is opposed to the Constitution it cannot be implemented in a way which is in harmony with Hungarian requirements regarding fundamental rights.

We have also seen that if any document is unconstitutional (and if on this basis the document in question is subject to review by the Constitutional Court), this still does not present a real obstacle. In order to make sure that the law that criminalizes racist speech does not fail the constitutional review of the Constitutional Court

49 Sólyom 2003: 15.

50 Sólyom 2001: 202–209.

51 Decision 17/2004 (V. 25.) AB; Decision 744/B/2004. AB. Other possibilities open to the Constitutional Court regarding EU law are at present an open question.

there have even been proposals that the Constitution be amended.[52] In the last case study it was also shown that an international treaty does not even need to be of such a nature as to force a change in the Constitution. The fact that the practice of the Strasbourg Court does not consider the criminalization of Holocaust denial as contrary to the Convention was used in Hungarian argumentations in order to further this otherwise unconstitutional criminal legislation and to justify the amendment to the Constitution that this would require. The author of a dissertation on the Hungarian Constitution, Gábor Attila Tóth, claimed in 2009, that: "[i]n 1989–1990 … for a moment it might have seemed as if [Hungary] would be the first to acknowledge any rights and the last to restrict them. Twenty years later the picture that emerges is the reverse: if the external environment calls for the protection of rights, the country will make this possible, if international law allows for restriction on rights, the country will demand it."[53] The approach to and method for constitutional legislation presented above practically render it unnecessary to look to the Constitutional Court as a possible source of protection for the Constitution.

The idea of amending the Constitution renders the constitutional regulation of fundamental rights relative – the same is true of that interpretation of the Constitution in which two different measures of the fundamental rights are simultaneously at work: the domestic law based on EU law has to comply with a far lower level of constitutionality than other domestic legal regulations. EU law need not meet the general constitutional requirements (test of necessity and proportionality), but it, as a system, has to provide a certain minimum protection for fundamental rights (the objective essential content, the core of the rights). This interpretation, which exists only in constitutional theory in Hungary, is similar to the approach of the German and Italian constitutional courts.[54] Accepting the difference between the two standards of the protection of human rights, in this current author's opinion, however, does not reflect the negative consequences of EU law weakening the national standard of the protection of human rights.

The first question is the following: should Hungary preserve the present standard of human rights protection in all details or does European cooperation necessitate some compromises? The author of this chapter is committed to a high level of protection with regard to both data protection and the freedom of expression. At the same time we must admit that the tools of constitutional law are not sufficient to enforce a higher level of protection than the common European standard. For sociological and diplomatic reasons, the existing legal guarantees cannot function sufficiently, either.[55] As for the conflict between the Constitution and the norms of international and EU law, decision-makers respond, ultimately, by modifying

52 According to Article 24(3) of the Constitution: "A majority of two-thirds of the votes of the Members of Parliament is required to amend the Constitution."

53 Tóth 2009: 282.

54 Sonnevend 2003: 33–34, 2007a: 965–966, 2007b: 503–504.

55 Sonnevend 2009: 174.

the Constitution. It seems certain that the Hungarian standard of the protection of fundamental rights will be the result of a compromise with the European standard. Many claim that this is an acceptable solution; in fact it is expressly the desirable reaction.[56]

The case studies, however, also illustrate that we do not need to make all allowances for every issue that comes into question by reducing the standard of protection of fundamental rights. The implementation of certain provisions of the Data Retention Directive might have been postponed by a declaration; the practice of the Strasbourg Court allows for, but does not oblige, countries to criminalize Holocaust denial; and the UN Convention (or the act promulgating it) could also be subjected to a constitutional review by the Constitutional Court. Furthermore, the Framework Decision also allows Member States to refer to their constitutional traditions. These possibilities, however, have not been and still are not being considered in Hungary.

In order to avoid making unnecessary allowances on the one hand, and to make inevitable compromises more easily acceptable on the other hand, the following steps appear viable for a Member State:

- In these cases, in order to preserve the national protection of fundamental rights one self-evident solution would be *to strengthen the role of the national Parliament* in EU law-making and the public control exercised by Parliament over the government. This would, at the same time, contribute to the transparency of the EU-related activities of the government.
- The national protection of fundamental rights rests on the national Constitution as a foundation, the stability of which is one of the crucial guarantees of fundamental rights. In Hungary there are no rules to stabilize the Constitution by rendering amendment an exceptional last resort. Technically speaking, the Constitution may be entirely freely amended by a vote of two-thirds of the Members of Parliament. Further procedural standards and requirements could be introduced in order to *secure the stability of the Constitution.* Short of these, however, it is up to the power which creates the Constitution (in Hungary the two-thirds of the Members of Parliament) to recognize the significance of the stability of the Constitution.
- Legal experts as well as NGOs are responsible for emphasizing that the text of the Constitution is a normative document based on certain clearly definable moral criteria and reflecting a relatively stable value system. This value system constitutes a coherent structure of mutually interdependent elements. The Constitution is not an unalterable legal norm, but it cannot be modified each time the legislators sense social outrage. In case of a change it is crucial to preserve the value principles and internal structure and cohesion of the Constitution.[57]

---

56 Ibid.: 176; Sajó 2004: 89, 92.

57 *Tézisek a szólásszabadság védelmében* 2009.

In the background of insisting on the national standard of the protection of fundamental rights, as András Sajó points out,[58] we might detect a general distrust regarding the European Union. The EU's mechanisms protecting fundamental rights are perceived as distant, and not much is known about their effectiveness, either. So long as we accept this, the compromises which will inevitably have to be made about the standard of protection of fundamental rights might be made more easily acceptable by *disseminating information about the EU and the protection of fundamental rights within the EU*.

The regulation on data retention is based on the criminological consideration whereby the retention of traffic data can lead to identifying a larger number of crimes. Sanctioning racist speech is explained with reference to changes in historical and social conditions and particularly to the increase in extremist phenomena. These explanations are based on preliminary considerations which are of a historical, sociological and social psychological nature, rather than a legal nature. In order to justify the above-mentioned argumentation it would be important to have access to these *results from the social sciences*.

Certain analysts believe that during the 20 years that have gone by since the political transition of 1989, a high national standard of protection for fundamental rights has become outdated. This standard of protection for fundamental rights was a reaction to the totalitarian regime of the past. Today, however, this is no longer seen as required in an EU Member State;[59] therefore there should be no concerns about making the required compromises.

The point of departure of this chapter was that the Hungarian standard of human rights protection is high, but not sufficiently stable. The European influences (including the effects of the EU) on this standard could be double-edged: they may strengthen as well as weaken it. As for the latter effect, in certain cases the level of protection accepted in the EU requires the decrease of the relatively high national standard. If we are not careful and we open the door to the possibility of lowering the national standard of fundamental rights protection to the common European minimum on the basis of the above argumentation, and without further considerations we might step onto a slippery slope. All of this might lead to a more substantial lowering of the standard of fundamental rights than is inevitable.

References

Balogh, Zs. (2000), Alapjogi tesztek az Alkotmánybíróság gyakorlatában, in G. Halmai (ed.) *A megtalált Alkotmány?* [*The Constitution Found?*], Budapest, Indok, 122–44.

58 Sajó 2004: 94.

59 Ibid.

Bárándy, G. and Berta, A. (2008), Gyalázkodás – elfogadott törvényjavaslat – elutasító alkotmánybírósági határozat (Országgyűlés: igen, Alkotmánybíróság: nem), *Magyar Jog*, 12, 808–818.

Halmai, G. (2000), Hátramenetben az alapjogvédelem?, *Fundamentum* 3, 69–83.

Halmai, G. (2008), Erőszaktilalom és "társadalmi stressz". *Élet és Irodalom*, 15 August 2008.

Halmai, G. (2009), Gyilkosok, uszítók, gyalázkodók. *Élet és Irodalom*, 13 March 2009.

Halmai, G. and Tóth, G.A. (2003), Az emberi jogok korlátozása, in G. Halmai and G.A. Tóth (eds), *Emberi jogok*, Budapest, Osiris, 108–135.

HCLU (2008), Constitutional Complaint Against Hungarian Telecom Data Retention Regulations, available at: http://tasz.hu/en/node/826, accessed 15 July 2009.

Jóri, A. (2005), *Adatvédelmi kézikönyv*, Budapest, Osiris.

Majtényi, L. (2006), *Az információs szabadságok. Adatvédelem és a közérdekű adatok nyilvánossága*, Budapest, CompLex.

Sajó, A. (2004), Miért nehéz tantárgy az együttműködő alkotmányosság? *Fundamentum* 3, 89–96.

Sárosi, P. (2009), A múlt kontrollja. Miért nem szabad büntetni a holokauszttagadást? *Magyar Narancs*, 7 May 2009, 49.

Simon, É. (2009), Védeni az ellenséget, *Népszabadság*, 21 May 2009.

Sólyom, L. (2001), *Az alkotmánybíráskodás kezdetei Magyarországon*, Budapest, Osiris.

Sólyom, L. (2003), Sólyom László előszava, in G. Halmai and G.A. Tóth (eds), *Emberi jogok*, Budapest, Osiris, 14–20.

Sonnevend, P. (2003), Alapvető jogaink a csatlakozás után, *Fundamentum* 2, 27–37.

Sonnevend, P. (2007a), Magyar Alkotmány és EU-csatlakozás, in A. Jakab and P. Takács (eds), *A magyar jogrendszer átalakulása. 1985/1990–2005*, Budapest, Gondolat – ELTE ÁJK, 964–9.

Sonnevend, P. (2007b), The Position of the Hungarian Constitution after the Accession to the European Union, in A. Jakab, P. Takács and A.F. Tatham (eds), *The Transformation of the Hungarian Legal Order 1985–2005*, The Netherlands, Kluwer Law International, 502–6.

Sonnevend, P. (2009), Alapjogvédelem és nemzetközi kihívások, in L. Majtényi and M.D. Szabó (eds), *Mi fenyegeti a köztársaságot?*, 169–76.

Szabó, M.D. and Székely, I. (2005), Privacy and Data Protection at the Workplace in Hungary, in S. Nouwt, B.R. de Vries and C. Prins (eds), *Reasonable Expectations of Privacy?*, The Hague, TMC Asser Press, 249–84.

Szabó, Z. (2009), Speech No. 220. Session No. 216, 9 June 2009. *Országgyűlési Napló*, available at http://www.parlament.hu/internet/plsql/ogy_naplo.naplo_fadat?p_ckl=38&p_uln=216&p_felsz=220&p_szoveg=&p_felszig=220, accessed 1 August 2009.

Tézisek a szólásszabadság védelmében (2009), Eötvös Károly Intézet, available at http://www.ekint.org/ekint/ekint.news.page?nodeid=275, accessed 1 July 2009.

Tóth, G.A. (2009), *Túl a szövegen. Értekezés a magyar alkotmányról*, Budapest, Osiris.

Trócsányi, L. and Csink, L. (2007), Alkotmány v. közösségi jog: az Alkotmánybíróság helye az Európai Unióban, *Jogtudományi Közlöny* 2, 63–69.

Uitz, R. (2009), Valami megbomlott, *Magyar Narancs*, 7 May 2009, 50.

Chapter 10

Constitutionalization and the Media in Post-enlargement Central and Eastern Europe

Katrin Nyman-Metcalf

Introduction

Constitutionalization in the narrowest sense of the word means that a country adopts a constitution which is the supreme law in that country and from which the competence to enact laws, as well as the hierarchy of laws, is derived. However, as a phenomenon constitutionalization includes more than just this basic aspect. To be a constitutional democracy, the country not only needs to ensure that laws and regulatory decisions are formally made in accordance with the system set up by the constitution, but also that the constitution and the rights it sets out are applied in practice, at all levels of society. The accession process to the European Union (EU) includes various criteria to ensure that proper constitutionalism – the outcome of the process of constitutionalization is achieved.

External pressure is not enough however. In a constitutional democracy, people have expectations that the rights in the constitution will be enforced. When they have such expectations they can exercise pressure through the political system and civil society to achieve or strengthen proper constitutional protection. People no longer accept corruption and abuse of power as something normal in society. To achieve this "real" constitutionalism there must be an understanding in society of what a constitutional state is: one with the rule of law, proper organs to enforce this and respect for the rights set out in the constitution. The media has an important role in fostering such understanding, provided media is in a position to act independently in favour of constitutionalism. Reforming media, and not least the legal landscape of the media, is an important ingredient in the reform process in countries in transition.

The EU is the most important source of influence on the process of constitutionalization that has been going on in East and Central Europe since the fall of Communism in the late 1990s, although the European Court of Human Rights, the Council of Europe and other international organizations also play a part. Although decision-makers will be in direct contact with EU organs and other international bodies and will use EU material directly, the public receives these influences in the version given to them by media. Media becomes the filter through which ideas are transmitted – the ideas as adopted and adapted by the society are reflected in media, which in turn again influence society's norms. The media is the spider in the web of developments in any society and its role is clearly seen, especially in societies in transition.

This chapter does not deal with the process of constitutionalization in a given country. Instead, it outlines the importance of media in shaping and supporting the process of regardless of the national setting. The chapter explains a process, which to a large extent is valid irrespective of the specific national laws and cultures. Although many issues are universal, the discussion has a special emphasis on Eastern and Central Europe and the developments in this region, especially since 1989, including the relevance of EU influence for this particular aspect of constitutionalism.

The chapter first gives a background to the role of media and its ability to play a role, namely by briefly discussing freedom of expression. This leads on to the matter of rule of law or rule by law, the importance of which is seen particularly in relation to the media. The third section concentrates on democracy, with the fourth section going into more detail in relation to the agenda-setting role of the media as an instrument in the process of constitutionalization. Finally, media law is examined in some more detail. After the general section on media legislation, the different approach for different types of media, the importance of mentality for media consumption and the use by authorities of the media are presented. All the different aspects of how media and the regulation of it contribute to the process of constitutionalization are briefly drawn together in the concluding remarks.

Freedom of Expression

People's expectations help shape the environment for successful constitutionalism, and the media undoubtedly plays a role in this. However, there is something of a "chicken and egg" issue: what comes first? Can media only act positively when the constitutional protection for the freedom of expression is already strong or can media push to strengthen this protection? Do laws have to guarantee media freedoms before media can play an active role or can media help to push the general positive developments even without such (functioning) legal protection? Not just media laws as are of interest, but also measures such as legal provisions on libel and slander, broadcasting licensing regimes and rules for media professionals (such as accreditation of journalists) that, although legitimate, can be misused by a regime that is not willing to allow proper media freedom even after the formal abandoning of censorship.

Underlying the discussion is the importance of freedom of expression. This freedom is recognized in most major human rights instruments, such as in Article 19 of the International Covenant on Civil and Political Rights[1] and Article 10 of

1 New York, 19 December 1966, 999 UNTS 171, in force 23 March 1976.

the European Convention on Human Rights (ECHR).[2] It is an important human right, as well as a prerequisite for the exercise of many other rights and freedoms. The European Court of Justice (ECJ) has recognized the importance of freedom of expression as stated in Article 10 ECHR.[3] This freedom needs to be accompanied by rules in order to be effective and in order for it not to conflict with other rights. This is especially true in relation to modern forms of communication that reach a large number of recipients and have a great impact. There is an important interrelationship between media and the rule of law in that media is important for the functioning of the rule of law, and rule of law must prevail for media to play a positive role.

Most media legal issues are within the competence of the Member States rather than the EU. At the EU level legal instruments mainly aim at reducing potential obstacles to free movement. The ECJ has established that broadcasting is to be seen as a service[4] and that it should be covered by the rules for free movement of services. To make free movement possible, certain common standards exist at the EU level. However, this division of competence with a smaller role for the EU is only possible as it is built on a background of respect for freedom of expression and free media that is a prerequisite for EU Membership. There may not be much in the way of concrete rules related to media in the accession process of the new EU Members or of the current candidate countries, but media features in the accession process and is important not just in its own right but also as an underlying feature of other issues.

Rule of Law or Rule by Law

Especially in societies in transition, the distinction between law as rhetoric and law as regulating rules may be quite great. Law as rhetoric in this context means the adoption of new laws, a demonstration of the ability of the government to act, at least as much as to allow adoption of laws. The difference compared with law as regulating rules is that in this latter case the laws enacted are also respected and implemented.[5] It is a sign of a constitutional state that the law as rhetoric is translated into law as regulating rules and that the law both as enacted and as implemented is in accordance with the constitution. Taube defines the notion of constitutionalism as the use and evolution of a normative constitution.[6] This is also what shows the difference between rule of law and rule by law. A society can be ruled by law without meeting the requirements for a proper constitutional society, if the authorities are not themselves constrained by laws – ultimately by

2 Rome, 4 November 1950, ETS 5-1950, in force 3 September 1953.

3 European Court of Justice Case C-260/89 ERT.

4 European Court of Justice Case 155/73 Saachi.

5 Jonsson 2003: 3.

6 Taube 2001: 63.

the constitution – but can pass laws and interpret them with impunity, as they like and as fits the political views of the day. Rule of law gives supremacy to the laws – again, ultimately the constitution – as the framework for activities by authorities, be they rule-making or decision-making activities.

Rule of law and democracy are not the same thing, but are closely connected. True democracy requires a constitution and legality, and that the laws of the process are followed.[7] Democracy without rule of law is difficult to imagine and in any case could only work for a very limited period in some extreme circumstance – otherwise it is not democracy, but just elections without real substance or meaning. In the same way, rule of law without democracy is inconceivable; such a situation would instead be rule by law when laws do exist but when they lack the legitimacy that democracy gives them.

One key element of a society ruled by the rule of law is that there is legal certainty. For media legislation this existence or absence of certainty is amplified, as an uncertain media will resort to self-censorship, and thus perhaps creating even more negative effects of the absence of certainty. Broadcasters or newspapers will not be established if there is uncertainty about whether or for how long they will be able to operate; thus plurality is prevented. Plurality takes a while to achieve and cannot be done through law, although law is essential as a foundation against which plurality can grow. Furthermore, plurality is not the same as diversity. Many media outlets do not automatically entail many different views. The lack of legal certainty will result in the inability of a proper, pluralistic and also diverse media market to flourish. By necessity, countries in the midst of a major reform period experience a lot of changes to their legislation, a lot of law-making in a short time and an absence of stability of institutions. This does not need to be so negative if the direction of the law-making is the same and if the authorities make efforts to avoid negative consequences of changes in the law – there can be legal certainty even in situations of legal change.

Authors have different views on whether constitutionalism includes elements of legal culture and legal history or whether it can be defined as a legal concept by itself.[8] In the view of the present author, the concept should be seen as a legal concept standing on its own and not interpreted in light of cultural and traditional issues. It is another matter that constitutionalization – the way to reach constitutionalism including what reforms it entails in a given structure – will be influenced by factors external to the legal system (practical issues), as well as by legal factors external to the constitution (various laws and other normative acts). However, to have a concept of constitutionalism that can be applied to different circumstances helps to keep the ideal for legal reforms "clean" and suitable as a universal aim. The process will differ in place and time, but the end result as a legal concept is universal.

7 Fogelklou 1998.

8 Jonsson 2003: 11; as well as Kis 2003 and Sajó 1999.

Peters and Schwenke put it well when they warn that culture-based moral relativism may pay a high price as it can easily be made a handmaiden of dictators.[9] Even if leaders of transition countries may be more wary than autocratic leaders in how they present the relativism of rights, when this goes to the essence of the rights and their protection rather than to details of their implementation, it must be recognized for what it is: limitation of the internationally recognized, and most often also nationally explicitly protected, human rights. Freedom of expression is something of a favourite right to limit due to cultural factors.[10] Rule of law means priority to law in its role as giving rights and protecting rights and freedoms also *vis-à-vis* the authorities.

The Media and Expectations of Democracy and Rule of Law

The media is an essential component in the transition to democracy and in respect for human rights as it disseminates reforms and thus creates expectations. The media is the reflector of what goes on in society and also has the potential to act as an amplifier.[11] The media will thus play a role in any process of change. In countries where the official media has been slow to reform, unofficial media has occurred early in the transition and promoted this. In most Eastern and Central European countries, in the transformation process the media was a mixture of underground and unofficial media, and foreign media targeted at the specific countries (like Radio Free Europe or Voice of America), as well as the official media, first cautiously and then more boldly, moving away from just towing the party line. In many cases the official media was quite slow to react and found its role diminished as people were well aware of the fact that the official media could not be relied upon to report the truth. For years, people had got used to reading between the lines and consumed official media in the (near) absence of anything else, but once change started, people expected the media to be part of the process. The 20 years that have passed since the changes in East and Central Europe, have seen a major change to the media landscape globally, and with today's many fast-moving, interactive media channels the pressure on the media to reflect reality

9 Peters and Schwenke 2000: 819.

10 An example of the autocratic view on cultural relativism of rights can be seen in a not very recent, but in any case illustrative, quote from the then Chinese Prime Minister Li Pang in an address to the UN Security Council in 1992 as quoted by Müllerson: "In essence, the issue of human rights falls within the sovereignty of each country. A country's human rights situation should not be judged in total disregard of history and national conditions." Müllerson 1994: 203–04, fn. 135.

11 The present author discusses these issues in the specific context of selected countries in transition (Latvia, Russia, Thailand, Turkey and to some extent Serbia) in the forthcoming (2010) book *Lighting the Spark. The Role of Transformational Institutions* (with P. Bergling and A. Fogelklou).

has also changed. The crisis in Iran in 2009 is but one example of this: authorities still try to control the media image and do it with much the same tools as before (expelling journalists, blocking foreign media, etc.), but with much less success as people can use Internet and mobile telephones to participate in the global media landscape in a manner which it is almost impossible to totally block.

If media is to be able to play the role of reflector and preferably also that of amplifier of reforms, a basic level of media independence and pluralism must exist. The extent of independence and freedom needed before media can have any instigating role can vary. In this context, various factors come into play, such as availability of different sources of media, ownership and management of the media (as even in authoritarian societies there may be more than just direct government-controlled media), cultural preferences and the civil society. What is clear is that neither media law itself nor even a broader base, including laws on related issues, is enough to create an environment for free and independent media. This is also a practical matter – a matter of the actual availability of media outlets.[12] At the same time, legislation is important and a proper regulatory framework is necessary to allow free media to flourish. This covers constitutional protection of freedom of expression, specific legal regulation of media for both broadcasting (that normally is regulated by the state) and print media (that in most democracies is only subject to self-regulation), as well as other legislation that indirectly affects media content (provisions on incitement to hatred and violence, libel and slander rules, as well as election-related legislation).

During the process of EU accession, Eastern and Central European states have dealt with media legal issues at different levels and in varying fashions. Independent regulatory systems have been set up although the exact design of these varies quite a lot (between independent regulatory bodies or independent functions within another body, such as a ministry, or between sector specific or general regulators, etc.). Advertising rules, including in relation to advertising in elections have been created, criminal codes updated related to libel and slander, and so on. Many countries have introduced laws on media ownership, the content of which varies quite a lot.

Media sets the agenda and shapes expectations on a country's move towards constitutionalism. If media is able to act as a watchdog, governments will be more accountable and developments more sustainable as the development of the country will be elevated to a position of interest for people. Free media creates a momentum and, as can be seen from authoritarian countries that have allowed certain media freedoms, this momentum may be difficult to stop. Strict repression may be needed if the momentum has reached a certain level – up to this level, countries that wish to maintain an illusion of freedom may attempt "softer" repression, such as practical restrictions on media or auxiliary legal restrictions.

In the early phase of change, the media will act either without any proper regulation or legal framework or by "stretching" the pre-transition framework;

12 Discussion in, e.g., Oertel 2003.

the real test for what the media landscape will be like comes a bit later in the reform process when authorities take charge of what in a transitional stage is often a chaotic picture and create the rules under which the media will have to act. After a period of more or less underground publications distributed privately and some pirate radio-stations, comes a time for media to be handled by proper business entities, broadcasters applying for frequencies and laws preventing media concentration and other potentially negative effects of a free media market. Challenges against an independent and pluralistic media market do not only come from direct authority involvement, but may also be based on domination of media by a few businesses or a few individuals promoting a certain agenda. In the Eastern and Central European Members States the problems for media tend to be related to a lack of real pluralism, the presence of high concentrations of outlets, as well as to some extent to the still exaggerated use of libel and slander legislation. In Hungary, for example, former Prime Minister Orban won a libel lawsuit in January 2010 against a newspaper that reported a publicly made statement (by a politician) that was deemed libellous. This was in contradiction with best European practice, where media should not be held liable for publishing attributed statements as such liability risks stifling free debate in media. The relevant law in Hungary is in the process of change, which has been welcomed by media professionals as well as international observers. In Slovenia there is a pending case brought by the prosecutor of criminal defamation, including a claim for large damages against a Finnish investigative journalist, as well as a related civil case brought by a former Prime Minister.[13] In both these cases the situations have arisen in countries with otherwise good records of freedom of the media, but the fact that such cases are brought by politicians indicates that there may still be a lack of understanding about the standards of freedom of expression – which also protect critical speech – that should form part of European standards.

In certain EU candidate countries there are still problems with more direct political interference with media or legal obstacles for free media. Croatia was criticized for limited independence of the regulatory system in initial screening reports by the European Commission, which led to changes to the relevant laws and systems, which in turn led to a positive evaluation.[14] In Macedonia it is the public service broadcaster that is subject to political pressure.[15]

---

13 OSCE Representative on Freedom of the Media, report 4 March 2010. The Slovenian case is criticized by journalists' organizations as well, e.g., Journalists without Borders, available at http://www.rsf.org/Former-PM-sues-Finnish-journalist.html, accessed 3 August 2010.

14 European Commission, Screening Report, Chapter 10, Information Society and Media (June/July 2006), latest evaluation on progress towards meeting the standards of the *acquis communitaire*, available at http://www.ec.europa.eu/enlargement/pdf/croatia/screening_reports/screening_report_10_hr_internet_en.pdf, accessed 3 August 2010.

15 EUROPA (2010), FYROM – Audiovisual and Culture – Summaries of EU Legislation, available at http://europa.eu/legislation_summaries/enlargement/ongoing_

Agenda-setting and Symbol-manipulation by the Media

In democratic states with a free media most commentators will agree that the media sets the political agenda as well as reports on it.[16] This so-called agenda-setting theory was first launched by Shaw and McCombs in 1972. The theory explains how the media does not just reflect newsworthy matters, but actually determines what it is that becomes newsworthy. Shaw and McCombs claimed that the main importance of mass media was its ability to organize the world, and even if it cannot tell people what to think, it will tell them what to think about.[17] The authors provided empirical examples from the United States to support the theory, which as an explicit theory was new in the 1970s, even if the idea that media could decide what people would think about had been launched even earlier. This possibility of media putting things on the political agenda has been increasingly recognized over the years and many studies, especially in the United States, have repeatedly shown a correlation between what the media reports and what people think is important.[18] The media does not necessarily report what is objectively important, but it decides what it thinks is important and then reports on it. The decision on what is important may be influenced by various factors, such as editorial decisions of the journalists and editors, preferences of the media owners, commercial considerations and so on.

Media as an agenda-setter is a phenomenon of democracies with a free media, as the state-imposed media in authoritarian states shows a different dynamism of the state organ – mass-media interplay. The agenda-setting theory cannot be applied unless it is the media itself that decides what the issues are that it should launch into the public mind. In countries undergoing reform, at some point in the process the media acts or at least attempts to act as a catalyst for reform. This is one instance when the media attempts to decide what to put on the political agenda. The role varies between countries, including between countries that otherwise show similarity in their reform processes. The differences normally depend on a combination of various factors, such as different regulations, different ways in which authorities use the media, the public's mentality or external factors pushing for reform. Populist media, tabloids, soaps and other such means may be used in a more subtle way to influence the population (*panem et circences*) as a way to reduce pressure for more freedoms and reforms, or potentially as a means to

---

enlargement/cu0003_en.htm, accessed 3 August 2010.

16 See for example McQuail 2000.

17 Shaw and McCombs 1972, 1977; and Shaw, McCombs and Weaver 1997. The authors studied the role of the media in US presidential elections. Their studies showed how the media was decisive in what things people were interested in. This kind of correlation that later became seen as almost obvious had not been clearly seen or understood before, which is what made the so-called agenda-setting theory so noticed.

18 Examples in Griffin 2006 and McQuail 2000.

promote popular desire for reform. This also becomes a factor influencing what the media landscape in a transition state will look like.

The transition from authoritarian to democratic governance does not follow any one model as is agreed by academics as well as practitioners.[19] Authors list different factors that determine how a state must react in response to a repressive past and what influence law can have in the process: the specific legacy of injustice, legal culture and political traditions. The process of constitutionalization and harmonization with the EU must take this into account. Law in countries in the process of democratization will be a means of demonstrating and setting down new understandings, but the background against which this will happen will depend on the mentioned factors, as elaborated by Teitel. Such factors – or, in other words, reality – and not an ideal theoretical point determine the success of transition.[20] Apart from its direct normative function, law also has a role as a symbol of power, as a means of communication between the government and those governed. Public mentality will always influence the effect of law and the perception of it, not least its symbolic value.[21] The way authorities use law and the way in which people see it are both shaped by the general mentality and relation to symbols within a given society. In an individualistic society with a more critical approach to authority, manipulation through symbols of power, such as law, must be different than in a society (or in the elements of society) where people have a more trusting approach to power. The difference between the Baltic States (especially Estonia) and Russia can be mentioned as an example, with Estonia as an example of an individualistic state and Russia as one where a strong central power is expected. Strong opposition and dissident movements, a legacy of freedom, the repressive system as an element of foreign occupation rather than as a national political current are all relevant for how people will read signals emitted by authorities, whether in the shape of laws or otherwise. Media – in many ways a contact point between those governing and those governed – provides the main means to create and manipulate symbols.[22] Podgorecki explains how the media, together with other tools, is used to change normative declarations into "real" ideology and create collective false consciousness.[23] The success of such transformation into a

19 In recent debate, many commentators have questioned the sometimes stressed relevance of the difference between "preconditionists" and "universalists". The debates are centred on the question as to whether a state must be ready for democracy or whether certain reforms can be supported or even imposed in any event. These notions can easily become too superficial. There are always so many aspects that determine the success of reforms that it is not easy to categorize these in the groups of preconditions or not. See, e.g., Berman 2007, especially at 28–31.

20 Teitel 2000.

21 Legrand 1996: 60–61. These here mentioned issues were discussed a lot in the late 1990s, in the heyday of transition studies in Europe.

22 La Spina 1996: 45–46 and Teitel 2000: 220.

23 Podgorecki 1996, especially at 11.

collective belief determines the possibility to change perceptions again when the system changes and the imposed collective belief is no longer imposed.

The EU accession of a country and its integration into the European cultural and legal sphere brings with it perceptions, consciousness and collective beliefs. These include freedom to choose and to think freely. The media should reflect freely what society is interested in and, through a combination of market forces and some targeted policies (such as public service broadcasting), the idea of media as an independent reflector of society rather than a tool of repression and propaganda is introduced. Such a transformation is not always easy, but a constitutional state without free media is inconceivable.

Media Legislation

Freedom of the media is a key element of freedom of expression, something which enjoys constitutional protection in most countries. Governments that want to portray themselves as being – or moving towards being – democratic tend to make great efforts to transmit signals of greater freedoms for media than those that they really allow. In societies moving backwards from the viewpoint of protection of rights (like Russia), limiting media freedoms (but preferably without admitting to it) becomes essential. The role of the mass media is a key element in the study of transition to democracy. Most researchers would agree on the importance of media in any democracy or democratization process.[24] However, the importance of media regulation is a less well-examined topic in academic, as well as practical democratization, discussions and democratization assistance. Any regulation of media is a balance of what sometimes appears as a thin line between censorship and legitimate regulation. A simplistic starting point may be that censorship is

24 Habermas regards the media as a crucial factor in the transition to liberal democracy, as the media creates the public sphere in which individuals can discuss things in a way that leads to accountability and democracy. For the media to have this role it must report on issues of government and similar: it must be able to do this and be interested in doing so (Habermas 1991). Modern academic debate on the role of the media in democracies often concentrates on the latter aspect and the "dumbing-down" of media. The media pays less attention to serious issues of real interest for society and more to mass entertainment, creating especially among less-educated people what can almost be seen as a situation of living in an unreal world of celebrities and reality shows while not being interested in political processes or basic issues of society. Another trend in media research is the study of interactive media, internet blogs and similar, where ordinary people have a role in media content and may to some extent take over from media professionals, thus eventually also influencing the agenda-setting role. Among many authors discussing these trends from various viewpoints are Chomsky and Herman 2002 and various chapters in Curran and Gurevitch 2000. See also McQuail 2000.

bad, regulation may be good – or is at least not necessarily bad – and the two are definitely not the same thing.[25]

It is important to understand the legal and regulatory background against which the media acts in order to fully understand the role of the media in the transition to constitutionalism. Laws alone will not create a free and pluralistic media, but its importance for allowing such a market to develop cannot be underestimated. The legal and regulatory background should consist of as few laws as possible concerning print media, that should act freely – provided it follows basic criminal or civil laws on such matters as incitement to violence, indecency and protection of minors, or defamation. Broadcast media, on the other hand, should be regulated by an independent regulatory agency that can provide an organized frequency spectrum management and minimum broadcasting standards, but that otherwise is as unrestrictive as possible. The frequency spectrum provides an objective reason for regulation of broadcast media. As a limited global resource that does not recognize national borders, frequencies must be handled in a global manner, something which is done through the International Telecommunications Union (ITU). The ITU rules require that states have a national system for frequency regulation, and implement the international regulation on state level.[26]

Especially in societies where outright censorship is abolished, but the society has not yet undergone full liberalization and democratization, various ways of using legislation or practical means of pressure to prevent media from being "too free" may gain in importance. State ownership of printing facilities and/or limited supplies of ink in Russia in order to limit the printing of newspapers are examples of such indirect pressure. Defamation law, accreditation of journalists, disproportional limitations on issuance of broadcast licenses and state ownership or other monopoly of transmission facilities and newspaper distribution systems are other such examples. Defamation and libel laws are popular tools to silence journalists, as this is often the avenue that is left when censorship and other restrictions are abolished. Defamation legislation is generally regarded as an acceptable limitation to freedom of expression, provided it is used in a reasonable and proportional manner that is not more restrictive than the right that it aims to protect (the right to privacy and dignity) requires. Almost all countries have defamation legislation and many have both criminal and civil defamation laws.[27] In most European democracies criminal defamation is used sparingly. However,

25 Many democratic rule of law states have an explicit ban on censorship in the constitution, which provides an important interpretative tool for any media regulation.

26 Article 10 ECHR expressly recognises that broadcast licensing is not a limitation of freedom of expression.

27 International organizations such as the Council of Europe and the Organization for Security and Co-operation ion Europe (OSCE) promote the abolition of criminal defamation and have pushed this through in some transition countries (such as, Bosnia Herzegovina and Georgia), but the campaign is made more difficult by the fact that it is not possible to claim that this is a European standard.

this is not necessarily a solution to the problem of using defamation legislation to silence uncomfortable media, as exorbitant demands for compensation in civil cases often pose even more of a problem.

The basic concepts and structure of media legislation are similar in most countries regardless of type of legal system, with the main – and indeed very crucial – difference being whether there is prior control and censorship of media or not. General prior control is regarded as totally incompatible with a democratic state. Even as early as in the Swedish law on press freedom in 1766 or in Blackstone's *Commentaries on the Laws of England* from 1765, the idea of prohibiting any form of censorship or prior restraint of the press was launched. For a democratic state, this remains a key concept. Electronic media regulation has progressed in a different manner, largely due to the fact that such media uses the frequency spectrum, which is a limited natural resource.[28] Broadcasting is furthermore seen to have a different impact than print media. This is due to its immediacy and the stronger effect on the audience that visual and audio messages are thought to have. Another reason for the different regulation is that broadcasting (especially television), ever since its inception, has been seen as a very important means to communicate messages, thus being something over which governments want to ensure a certain control. The same reason led to early television in many countries being run by the state or at least through public bodies. This has changed in more recent times, with liberalization of broadcasting and public service broadcasting remaining (if it exists) as just one actor on the broadcasting scene. Liberalization has also led to regulation of broadcasting being moved from direct government control to independent regulators that should be objective, non-political and transparent, and with the independent regulators providing the possibility of appeal. Even in countries with a liberalized broadcasting sector and an independent regulator, the principle however remains that decisions on issuing broadcast licences, as well as the oversight of licensees, contains demands on programming, not just as prohibitions of negative matters, but also as requirements for types of content. Protection of minority rights, through allowing access to broadcasting, is just one example.[29] Even if broadcasting is regulated in a different manner than the printed press, prior control of content in this sphere also is incompatible with freedom of expression.

Printed Press and Broadcast Media

In countries with freedom of expression, the printed media is normally totally free as there is no limitation on the number of outlets possible and ordinary criminal legislation is thought to be sufficient to deal with any negative occurrences in the printed press. Other than this, the press should ideally also have a system

28 Discussed in Rönning 2007.

29 Nyman-Metcalf 2008.

of self-regulation that ensures ethical and quality standards through intervention by the industry itself. Self-regulation is especially suitable for ethical questions and issues related to a fair and honest procurement of news and information, as authority intervention in matters such as these would risk restricting the freedom of the press.[30] Laws and formal regulation may still be needed for issues of libel and slander, copyright violations and access to information. Protection of privacy also needs some protection in law, but this is an area where it is important that not too many restrictions are put on the free debate, so self-regulation can be important to set the framework within which the press should operate, with official regulation only entering the scene when these limits are transgressed.[31]

Incitement to crime and to hatred and violence is prohibited in most countries regardless of how it is carried out, but the media is clearly the main means for doing any such incitement. Hence any prohibitions will restrict what the media can say. Both broadcasting regulation and self-regulatory systems for the press (or for all media, self-regulation can also encompass broadcast media) normally contain special rules about incitement and the application of such rules is often among the more controversial regulatory issues. Just as someone's freedom fighter is someone else's terrorist, what is a legitimate political message for someone is a call for violence and hatred to someone else. Leaving the media in a post-conflict society in the hands of those that started a war is dangerous, as many real examples show.[32] The media can also start the conflict in the first place.[33] The media is recognized to have played an important role in inciting violence, as well as maintaining the level of tension between ethnic groups after the conflict, during the wars in former Yugoslavia.[34] Even today it is in the countries of former

---

30 The International Federation of Journalists voices this widely accepted industry view on the difference between self-regulation and regulation through law, see http://www.ifj.org/en/pages/quality-in-journalism, accessed 3 August 2010.

31 Among many European Court of Human Rights cases on this issue are *Lingens v. Austria* (8 July 1986 Series A, No. 103), *Nilsen and Johansen v. Norway* (GC 23118/93, ECHR 1999-VIII) and *Karhuvaara and Iltalehti v. Finland* (53678/00, ECHR 2004 – X).

32 Kurspatric 2003: 210, stresses the importance of looking at the media in an internationally lead rebuilding process after a war, not leaving the media in the hands of those responsible for the war. See also Nyman-Metcalf 2008.

33 The famous case of Radio-TV *libre des milles collines* in Rwanda provides a frightening illustration of how the media can have a very real inciting effect. Broadcasts on this broadcaster, as well as Radio Rwanda and the journal *Kangura*, are regarded as having been instrumental in inciting the campaign of violence in Rwanda. See, e.g., International Federation of Journalists, www.ifj.org.

34 The Kosovo public service broadcaster provided almost a textbook example of incitement in its treatment of an event in 2004 of some Kosovo Albanian children drowning in unclear circumstances. The incident was blamed on Serbs, even if the purported evidence was scattered and contradictory, and furthermore the incident was used as an excuse to broadcast very nationalistic Albanian concerts instead of regular broadcasting content, thus possibly contributing to setting off the riots that erupted in March 2004 and lead to several

Yugoslavia where problems of incitement to hatred in the media are the most frequent in a European context.

In most countries where the media is not totally free, but also not totally controlled, the printed press is more independent and shows signs of more plurality than the broadcast media. There are many reasons for this: the longer tradition of press freedom compared to that of broadcasting, the practical fact that there tends to be more of printed press and it is easier to set up than broadcasters, the perceived greater influence of broadcasting. New media such as Internet also tends to be allowed more freedoms than traditional media as its impact is still not as noticeable as that of the traditional mass-consumed media. Most people in any country do not actively seek information, but consume that which is readily available, predominately the main television and radio channels (broadcast news is normally the primary source of news) with popular daily newspapers added to that. The newspaper circulation is often even greater than shown by the official figures, as several people read one copy, people read newspapers in cafés and libraries and so on. Such practices tend to be more common in poorer countries and sooner rather than later after transitions. Only a minority actively seeks news from other than the main channels, which is why a country may allow certain freedoms for specialist media without experiencing a real challenge to the monopoly of their manufactured media image.

Media ownership matters a great deal for media independence as it is difficult to image a pluralistic and independent media if it is all state owned. But the ownership versus influence question is far more complex than a difference between state and private ownership. A situation with many different owners does not by itself mean diversity. Furthermore, if owners do not guarantee editorial independence, media may not be the mouthpiece of authorities that it is in totalitarian states, but it may still be unable to play a role as an independent watchdog. Another phenomenon is that a government can exert a lot of influence over media through commercial owners. Apart from the very direct impact media owners have, there is an important indirect effect through advertising.

In order to fully understand the situation for the media in a certain country, a knowledge and understanding of all factors influencing the media is required, also including the media infrastructure and ownership. Furthermore, fear and self-censorship may play a role in the difference between media situations in different countries going through what otherwise may be somewhat similar periods of change. Among EU Members from Eastern and Central Europe, Bulgaria experiences problems with organized crime targeting investigative journalists and regrettably appearing able to do so with impunity, although recent developments

deaths. See the Kosovo broadcast regulator www.imc-ko.org, accessed 3 August 2010. The author worked as legal advisor to this regulator between 2003 and 2006, and was member of its Council in 2006–07. See also OSCE Representative on Freedom of the Media The role of the media in the March 2004 Events in Kosovo", available at http://www.osce.org/documents/rfm/2004/04/2695_en.pdf, accessed 3 August 2010.

seem to indicate a more active approach by authorities.[35] International support to media in reforming countries is a potentially important factor, but in no way a solution to problems of unreformed media systems.[36] Although it may often be beneficial for the transition to have foreign support, the danger that, e.g., a foreign media outlet will remain "too foreign" must not be forgotten. People's expectations and tastes may change with time, but to immediately project an entirely new way of presenting information is not likely to have an immediate impact on the broad population. Instead is more likely to lead to rejection of the particular media outlet. The media does set agendas, but not in a vacuum, but projected on expectations of people.

Public Perceptions and the Media

Although statements that some people are different and do not want democracy should not be used as an excuse to stop development, it is a fact that there is less popular pressure for reform in certain countries than in others and the objective reasons for this are not always clear. How and when the media starts shaping the pressure is a key factor. As for Russia, economic reform that has led to greater wealth and availability of consumer goods (and in the media context, availability of popular entertainment including foreign entertainment) has not entailed any important pressure for political reform. The bureaucracy resists reform; the will to reform is not there at the top and there is not much pressure from below.[37] Public opinion influences how people see the media, and the media influences public opinion. Media legislation is just one of the building blocks in the panoply of measures to influence the end product that the usual consumer will consume. Media legislation is on the one hand legislation for specialists rather than for the broad public, but on the other hand has a great impact on the public, setting the scene for the media landscape of a country. The regulation of the media and how it gets its opportunities to operate may not be known by the broad public, who may not know the road the media outlets have to travel to get to disseminate the final product. This also means that restrictions and censorship may not be known

35 Violence against journalists was singled out by the OSCE Representative on Freedom of the Media in his report of 4 March 2010.

36 International organizations often prefer to support media outlets directly rather than media regulatory systems, which may lead to situations when a broadcaster supported by the international community does not get a licence from a regulator implementing best international (and/or European) principles of regulation (often to some extent equally supported by the international community, normally even in the shape of the same countries or organizations), because it does not meet minimum requirements. On the whole, the international support tends, however, mainly to be for media outlets, which can create problems if there is no proper legal and regulatory background against which the media can act or at least which will suffer from lack of sustainability of the support.

37 See, e.g., Bomsdorf 2003.

by the public as their very nature ensures they do not get known. In a time of globalization, the public may find out about restrictions to the normal channels through alternative channels (as they do in democracies), but this takes time and may not reach more than the elite.

An active civil society may help to ensure that restrictions in media legislation, various means to close down media outlets, restrictions against journalists and other such acts become known to the public. Such an active civil society will spread the knowledge obtained by a few, through more active media consumption, to the broad public. In some countries, at the very moment of the transition – as in the various velvet, rose or orange revolutions in recent years – the spreading of such information is an important element in triggering the revolutions and the calls for change. With a certain maturity of the revolutions, unless the civil society manages to build a lasting platform for itself, this information dissemination will decrease and people will go back to getting their information from a few major channels.

The media cannot ignore the link between the media message and people's expectations. People expect to read and see something in the media and if the media provides something completely different, this may mean that people do not read or watch it or that they project their views on it and interpret it wrongly. Corruption can be taken as an example – if people expect corruption and take that as natural, it is that much more difficult to root it out. There will not be any shame involved in corruption that could be used to induce people to stop being corrupt. The media should help change such perceptions, but does not always do that; it may, instead, reinforce such perceptions because it builds on the expectations that already exist. One may be tempted to think that an outside push could help to create this change, but widespread, extremely negative comments some years ago, even in successful post-transition countries like Latvia and Lithuania, about Soros Foundation influence over the media and society show that it is difficult to have too much outside influence in changing perceptions. In 2006, a Latvian minister proposed legislation to limit activities such as those of the Soros Foundation – namely NGO activities funded by international donors – activities targeted at, e.g., combating corruption. The proposed legislation did not pass, but it highlighted that it was possible even in an open society like Latvia to create negative propaganda based on the fact that there was international support.[38] If external influence exists, it must be discreet and contribute to changing expectations of people and what they are given at the same pace – a pace suitable for each society. How to adapt this pace and still not fall into the trap of culture-based moral relativism is a challenge especially for external influence over reform processes and the media in such processes.

38 http://www.bertelsmann-transformation-index.de/181.0.html?L=1, accessed 3 August 2010.

Media Strategy of the Authorities

The possibility for the media to reflect certain issues and thus to contribute to constitutionalization is of little value if it does not use its opportunities, if it even has the possibility to do so. From a time when the authorities told the media exactly what to say there has to be a transition to a time when it decides itself what to say, but in order to have a maximum effect it must, when doing this, manage to pick the topics that are important for the transition of the country. It is not easy, even in the most mature democracies, to have a truly independent and pluralistic media that provides a quality product which appeals to the broad population. In a country in the process of reform, this is even more difficult. To add to the difficulty, in the process of Europeanization there are many complex factors that need clarification. The population is interested, but needs to get information in a fashion that is adapted and suitable, but the media may only to a limited extent be able to provide such information.

In a rapidly changing media environment, there is a danger of other negative occurrences in addition to state control – such as a monopolization by big businesses or certain parties or just a "dumbing-down" of the media. It may look tempting to use regulation to avoid this and to some extent it may be possible, although using regulation to create pluralism should never extend to getting involved in content – just in setting the scene in which pluralistic content can happen. This is done through broadcast licensing and through press support to maintain diversity, measures that require proper legal framework and careful implementation so as not to become a back-door way of government influence over media content.[39]

In an atmosphere of a lack of professional and investigative journalism it is possible for authorities or other interests to plant articles and to otherwise get certain stories into circulation, sometimes even without there being explicit payments for them. Corruption will be reported if it is about a business rival, but evidently not about the owner of the newspaper or broadcaster in question. But also, corruption may not be reflected at all if there is no business interest one way or another and authorities are not promoting investigative journalism.[40] Direct political media outlets are more easily categorized, whereas the real interests behind business ones are more difficult to understand. Increased transparency would remedy this, but such transparency rarely exists. The oligarchs in Russia were prime examples of how personal and business interest set the media agenda – this is now more or less history with a state-controlled media in Russia. Media freedom as created in legislation and supported by the state is a crucial element for media's role in society, but so are media ownership and other means of influencing media by various interests. Manipulation of the media is very important and it exists in most

39 In addition, support measures may come into conflict with competition law and state aid law.

40 Although provided the media has achieved a certain degree of freedom, corruption as a topic may be reflected simply because it is commercially attractive. Sájo 1998: 43.

countries, although often both the media and the manipulators would deny it. In a generally untransparent society it is almost impossible to know the extent of manipulation.

The media is the means through which the governing authorities can sell their views, on reform or on stagnation. Media strategies and the dialogue between the media and the authorities are new features in societies where the earlier method was that the media was fed what it should say and just simply had to say it. For real impact in a setting of choice for the media, authorities should have a media strategy to make sure that their message is spread. At the same time, it is important that the state does not get too involved in media issues through laws and binding rules, so it must be up to authorities first of all to create an attractive media message and, secondly, up to the media to report it or not. Creating a media strategy for an authority that may have been used to dictating what the media should say is not easy, neither is it easy for the media to know how to deal with issues when it is no longer told what is newsworthy or not.

In all societies, media reactions are to some extent politicized and the media is most interested in political events and personality issues rather than in the everyday work of authorities. When looking at the media role, authorities must recognize the fact that journalists often like packaging in order to report something. The authorities must make themselves interesting in an intelligent way. The media strategy of institutions is crucial to determine the role the courts themselves can transmit to the public. A lack of investigative journalism will mean that the media picture transmitted is largely the one the institution wants transmitted.

Conclusion

Media plays a key role in the process of constitutionalization. A free and pluralistic media is not just important in its own right as a key feature of democracy, but it helps to reflect and amplify reform processes going on in a country in transition. The media is part of the process of Europeanization, but to a large extent still depends on local, national factors. The media creates expectations, but also reflects expectations of its audience. Agenda-setting of the media is not an absolute, but a mutual process between audience and media – the more so, the freer the media. If people want to read or hear about something, this pushes the media to deal with it. If people are interested in corruption they will want the media to report on the struggle against it. If this is perceived as interesting, the media will report more and more about it and people will become all the more interested. However, the media cannot just wait for people to expect to hear about something, but it must sometimes create the expectation.

There are many forces other than just intervention by authorities that shape the media and lead to it being free or not, being a factor pushing for reform or not. Media legislation is very important and in this context it is necessary to keep in mind that different types of legislation are relevant, not just the media laws as such. Legal reforms that influence media to some extent form part of the EU accession process, even if most media issues remain in the national competence and it is mainly the general framework that is influenced by EU harmonization. But legislation is far from the only or even the main factor that affects media freedom. The media itself is also not the only factor that pushes for change, although it is the means to get wider dissemination of what goes on. A free and independent media would be unlikely to exist in a society that does not have other foundations for a successful society, such as a functioning civil society. Not only is this needed to help spread messages, but also to pick up the expectations raised through the media so that the expectations are not lost when something becomes less newsworthy.

Given the role of the media in authoritarian societies, it is perhaps not surprising that it does not easily come to play an independent role when the society changes. There is no tradition of investigative journalism, and it can be observed in places where through strong foreign presence (like Bosnia Herzegovina and Kosovo) there is an actual possibility for the media to act freely, and even assistance given to it to do so, that investigative journalism takes a long time to occur. Rather than the media being the independent force that puts pressure on politicians and pushes for reforms, it stays in its role of a supporter of state power and the mouthpiece of the authorities. Independent-minded journalists will often lack support, financial means and even skills to challenge the established media. Foreign assistance may help overcome this, but this may not always be sustainable and there is a danger of creating media that does not appeal to the broad masses, as it is seen to be too much of a foreign import.

Russia provides an interesting example of how the media must be controlled to control society. The reverse actions of Putin would be very hard, if not impossible, if he did not control media. If people's expectations were shaped by a media that did push for reforms, it would be very hard to reverse trends towards more freedom. The fact that people can get access to other information through some more-liberal media outlets, or even through travelling abroad, has limited impact as long as the main media outlets are controlled and their agenda is that of the government. The control over the media thus presents itself as perhaps the main obstacle to a proper reform: the positive influence of reforms striving for constitutionalization are not allowed to permeate into the structure of society and light sparks for further reform. Where there is a desire to halt or reverse constitutionalization, stopping the free media is a priority and success in doing so will determine the success in reversing the trend.

References

Berman, S. (2007), Lessons from Europe, *Journal of Democracy* 18(1), 28–41.

Bertelsmann Transformation Index BTI (2010), Latvia country report, available at http://www.bertelsmann-transformation-index.de/181.0.html?L=1, accessed 8 March 2010.

Bomsdorf, F. (2003), Die gesellschaftliche Dimension des russischen Wandels, *Europäische Rundschau* 31(2)2, 19–30.

Chomsky, N. and Herman, E. (2002), *Manufacturing Consent: The Political Economy of the Mass Media*, New York, Pantheon.

Curran, J. and Gurevitch, M. (eds) (2000), *Mass Media and Society*, 3rd edn, London, Arnold.

EUROPA (2010), FYROM – Audiovisual and Culture – Summaries of EU Legislation, available at http://europa.eu/legislation_summaries/enlargement/ongoing_enlargement/cu0003_en.htm, accessed 3 August 2010.

European Commission, Screening Report, Chapter 10, Information Society and Media (June/July 2006), latest evaluation on progress towards meeting the standards of the *acquis communitaire*, available at http://www.ec.europa.eu/enlargement/pdf/croatia/screening_reports/screening_report_10_hr_internet_en.pdf, accessed 3 August 2010.

Fogelklou, A. (1998), Principles of Rule of Law and Legal Development, in Sevastik, P. (ed.), *Legal Assistance to Developing Countries*, The Hague, Kluwer, 32–60.

Griffin, E. (2006), *A First Look at Communication Theory*, 6th edn, New York, McGraw-Hill. Jonsson, A. (2003), Constitutionalism and Changing Concepts of Rights in Post-Communist Societies. The case of Slovenia, Department of East European Studies, Uppsala University, Working Papers 79 (October 2003).

Habermas, J. (1991), The Structural Transformation of the Public Sphere. An Inquiry into a category of Bourgeois Society, Cambridge, Mass., The MIT Press.

Kis, J. (2003), *Constitutional Democracy*, Budapest, Central European University Press.

Kurspatric, K (2003), *Prime Time Crime – Balkan Media in War and Peace*, Washington, DC, United States Institute of War and Peace.

La Spina, A. (1996), Modes of Legal Intervention and Totalitarian Effectiveness, in Podgorecki, A. and Oligiati, V. (eds), *Totalitarian and Post-Totalitarian Law*, Dartmouth, Aldershot, 39–69.

Legrand, P. (1996), European Legal Systems are not Converging, *International and Comparative Law Quarterly* 45, 52–76.

McQuail, D. (2000), *MacQuail's Mass Communication Theory*, 4th edn, London, Sage Publications.

Müllerson, R. (1994), *International Law, Rights and Politics*, London and New York, Routledge.

Nyman-Metcalf, K. (2008), Media Policy through Regulation: Freedom of Expression in a Process of Change, in Frandberg, A., Hedlund, S. and Spaak, T. (eds), *Festskift till Anders Fogelklou*, Uppsala, Iustus, 203–18.

Nyman-Metcalf, K., Bergling, P. and Fogelklou, A. (forthcoming 2010), *Lighting the Spark. The Role of Transformational Institutions.*

Oertel, B. (2003), Viel Presse – wenig Freiheit, *Osteuropa* 53(1), 19–32.

OSCE (2010), The Representative on Freedom of the Media Miklos Haraszti, *Regular Report to the Permanent* Council, 4 March 2010 (FOM.GAL/1/10/ Rev.2), available at www.osce.org/documents/rfm/2010/03/42896 en.pdf, accessed 7 March 2010.

OSCE (2004), Representative on Freedom of the Media, The role of the Media in the March 2004 Events in Kosovo, available at www.osce.org/documents/ rfm.

Peters, A. and Schwenke, H. (2000), Comparative Law beyond Post-Modernism, *International and Comparative Law Quarterly* 49 (October), 800–34.

Podgorecki, A. (1996), Totalitarian Law: Basic Concepts and Issues, in Podgorecki, A. and Oligiati, V. (eds), *Totalitarian and Post-Totalitarian Law*, Dartmouth, Aldershot, 3–37.

Rönning, H. (2007), Broadcasting Regulation vs. Freedom of Expression and Editorial Independence, *Nordicom* 2 (2007), 9–19.

Sájo, A. (1998), Corruption, Clientelism, and the Future of the Constitutional State in Eastern Europe, *East European Constitutional Review* Spring, 37–46.

Sajó, A. (1999), *Limiting Government, An Introduction to Constitutionalism*, Budapest, Central European University Press.

Shaw, D.L. and McCombs, M. (1972), The Agenda-Setting Function of Mass Media, *Public Opinion Quarterly* 36 (Summer), 176–87.

Shaw, D.L. and McCombs, M. (eds.) (1977), *The Emergence of American Political Issues: The Agenda-Setting Function of the Press*, St. Paul, Minn., West.

Shaw, D.L., McCombs, M. and Weaver, D.L. (1997), *Communication and Democracy: Exploring the Intellectual Frontiers in Agenda-Setting Theory*, Mahwah, N.J., Lawrence Erlbaum.

Taube, C. (2001), *Constitutionalism in Estonia, Latvia and Lithuania*, Uppsala, Iustus.

Teitel, R.G. (2000), *Transitional Justice*, Oxford, Oxford University Press, 213–28.

Chapter 11
The Rule of Law and the Rise of Populism: A Case Study of Post-Accession Bulgaria

Daniel Smilov

Populism and the Rule of Law in East European Context

There is a serious difficulty with the concept of populism: it is often abused in political discourse.[1] By calling someone a "populist", people are often just expressing their negative evaluation of the actor or her political agenda. Nevertheless, if we discuss political players such as the Kaczynski brothers in Poland, Fico in Slovakia, Ataka and GERB (*Grazhdani za evropeysko razvitie na Balgariya* [Citizens for European Development of Bulgaria]) in Bulgaria – or the ones who are often referred to as "populists" – several common characteristics come to mind.[2]

First, populists in the region appeal to the people or nation as a whole, as opposed to corrupt and impotent political elites. In other words, they present themselves as an alternative not to a specific political party or platform, but as an alternative to the existing scheme of representation and the political system as a whole.

Secondly, populists are (although to a varying degree) against the key idea of liberal democracy: that the political majority is limited in important ways by constitutional constraints. The Central European family of populism is openly majoritarian: it is centred around the belief that the consent of the majority is the ultimate ground of legitimation in politics. Therefore, this type of populism is particularly opposed to the idea of minority rights.

Thirdly, and again to a varying degree, populists challenge at least some elements of what they see as the "liberal consensus" of the transition period: market-oriented reforms, integration in the Euro-Atlantic organizations, rejection of nationalistic language and behaviour, respect for minority rights, freedom of religion, sexual orientation, etc. Populists "challenge" all these "taboos", deplore

---

1 See Schmitter, P. (2006), *A Balance Sheet of the Vices and Virtues of 'Populisms'*, paper delivered at the conference the Challenge of New Populism, organized by the Centre for Liberal Strategies, Sofia, in May 2006.

2 For a discussion of populism in Eastern Europe see Mudde, C. (2002), In the Name of the Peasantry, the Proletariat, and the People: Populism in Eastern Europe, in Meny, Y. and Surel, Y. (2001), *Democracies and the Populist Challenge*, Basingstoke, Palgrave.

the "political correctness" of liberalism, and give an opportunity for the citizens to discuss problems which have been "bracketed out" by the mainstream parties.

Finally, at least in some countries, the advent of populism was accompanied by a turn to an understanding of politics as a clash of personalities, rather than as a clash of ideas. Issues of personal integrity became central in the political processes primarily through a succession of anti-corruption campaigns and activities. The example of Bulgaria well illustrates the original nexus between the rise of populism and the prioritizing of corruption as a social problem. The ex-tsar Simeon II – first among a succession of populist politicians in the country – won landslide elections in 2001 on an anti-corruption ticket.

Senses of Crisis of Liberal Democracy

Part of the problem with populism is that there is no general agreement as to the nature, depth and character of the danger that it presents to liberal democracy. Generally, there are two types of reactions to the political developments under discussion. First, there are those who believe that the described problems are nothing but temporary aberrations from the norm within young and inexperienced liberal democracies. These aberrations are due to "transition fatigue", post-accession relaxation of political standards, or disappointment with the speed with which market reforms create welfare. On this interpretation, these temporary problems will be gradually overcome with the continuous integration of the region in the EU and the consolidation of democracy. This optimistic interpretation relies on the strength of liberal democratic institutions and the rule of law in Central Europe. In some of its versions, however, it is recognized that the crisis might have some more lasting implications, as the revision of the structures of political representation, and especially the way political parties function.[3]

Secondly, there are others who would go as far as to compare the current crisis of liberal democracy with its demise in the interwar period, when right- and left-wing extremists subverted the democratic order by abusing its instruments of representation. These reactions to the phenomenon are typical of political analysts, journalists and others, especially when populism comes in a more radical form – as in the case of Ataka, in Bulgaria, or the anti-Semitic outbursts during the mass protests in Hungary. Admittedly, this is a slightly paranoid and alarmist interpretation, but there is *prima facie* evidence in its support as well. Open authoritarian leanings are most evident in Russia and Ukraine, but even in EU Member States from Central Europe there are signs of growing intolerance to vulnerable minorities, such as the Roma and homosexuals, resurgence of anti-Semitic feelings, calls for taking politics to the streets, and even occasional

3 See, in particular, Schmitter, P.C. and Trechsel, A.H. et al. (2004), *The Future of Democracy in Europe: Trends, Analyses and Reforms*, Strasbourg, Council of Europe Publishing.

outbursts of political violence.[4] It is true that the constitutional framework of liberal democracy is still mostly intact, but within this framework the dominant mode of making politics is becoming illiberal. In other words, the most popular tool to mobilize public support becomes the attack against liberal policies and principles in different areas of governance: from immigration and welfare to EU integration matters.

This chapter does not attempt to give an answer to the question which of the above-discussed senses of crisis is closer to reality. Rather, it explores the more lasting impacts of the new populist *Zeitgeist*[5] on the rule of law and the politics of the judiciary. The main idea is that political populism has often neglected repercussions in the activities of judges and courts – the supposed guardians of the rule of law. Formally, the institutional framework might still be in place, but its *modus operandi* might actually turn it into an instrument of anti-liberal and anti-democratic politics.

Courts, Populism and the Rule of Law

Courts have different functions in a modern liberal democracy, which could hardly be reduced to a straightforward application of the law as a set of rules. Explicitly or implicitly, courts are authorized to interpret the law, sometimes even to develop and change it, and, ultimately, to contribute to the elaboration of public policies.[6] Further, the law has a serious expressive potential, and courts could use this potential quite freely in many situations. They are also entrusted with the supervision of the fairness of political competition, and last, but not least, they are empowered to regulate their own affairs. The above-described rise of populist politics has potential implications for all of these areas of judicial activity.

---

4 For the link between mass demonstrations, populism and anti-liberal doctrines, such as Carl Schmitt's understanding of representation, see Smilov, D. (2008), The Power of Assembled People: The Right to Assembly and Political Representation, in Sajo, A. (ed.), *Free to Protest: Constituent Power and Street Demonstration (Issues in Constitutional Law)*, The Netherlands, Eleven International Publishing.

5 Mudde, C. (2004), The Populist Zeitgeist, *Government and Opposition* 39(4).

6 This is a view that has been defended most powerfully by authors such as Raz, J. (1979), *The Authority of Law. Essays on Law and Morality*, Oxford, Clarendon Press; (1986), *The Morality of Freedom*, Oxford, Clarendon Press; (1994), *Ethics in the Public Domain*, Oxford, Clarendon Press; Barak, A. (1989), *Judicial Discretion*, New Haven, Yale UP; (2005), *Purposive Interpretation in Law*, Princeton and Oxford, Princeton University Press. See also Sunstein, C., Schkade, D., Ellman, L. and Sawicki, A. (2006), *Are Judges Political? An Empirical Investigation of the Federal Judiciary*, Washington, DC, Brookings Institution Press.

Courts as Regulators of Political Competition

Courts are most exposed to political pressures when they act as supervisors of the fairness of the political process. *Bush v. Gore*[7] has demonstrated that even the courts of established democracies could not avoid partisan pressures in their decision-making. The rise of populism in Eastern Europe amplifies the impact of certain political pressures on the courts, pressures which could be grouped in several categories.

First, there is a tendency of mainstream parties to restrict competition by populist newcomers through legal, constitutional and quasi-constitutional mechanisms. Courts could become instrumental as blocks to such newcomers in this context. This is possible because senior judges, and especially constitutional judges, are often appointed through partly politicized procedures, which are dominated by the mainstream parties as represented in parliament, the government, or the presidency.

Further, cartelization of mainstream parties is a process which is familiar to students of contemporary democracy:[8] the main parties stick together in order to obtain state privileges and to deny new competitors entry into the political process. In the circumstances of rising populism, established elites feel increasingly insecure: people are alienated from them (low party membership, lack of large pools of small donors, lack of ideological commitment and loyalty). These conditions intensify the tendencies among established parties to form cartels with the aim of blocking political competition. Helped by the judiciary, mainstream parties may actually turn the constitution into an instrument for the perpetuation of their staying in power.

Secondly, if the mainstream parties feel threatened both by newcomers and by the judiciary, or other independent centres of power, they might launch a campaign against these centres of power by trying to change the constitutional rules that grant newcomers independence and autonomy. In this case as well, the rule of law may be the ultimate victim, especially if the end result is political domination over areas which might be better left free from partisan influence (public media, judiciary, etc.).

Examples of this type of politicization of the courts are not hard to find. President Putin, as a plebiscitarian populist leader, has managed to ensure political control over the judiciary, which resulted in a series of high-profile cases against recalcitrant oligarchs, such as the notorious case against Mikhail Khodorkovsky[9]

---

7 531 U.S. 98, 12 December 2000.

8 See Katz, R. and Mair, P. (1995), Changing Models of Party Organisation and Party Democracy, *Party Politics* 1(1).

9 For a concise description of Khodorkovsky's judicial ordeal see en.wikipedia.org/wiki/Mikhail_Khodorkovsky, accessed 17 August 2010. It is quite indicative that immediately after Khodorkovsky announced his political ambition to campaign in the 2008 presidential elections, prosecutors stated that they believed that there were grounds for

– at the time a serious potential competitor and political opponent of the Kremlin. The administrative and police pressure on Gary Kasparov – a current leader of the opposition in Russia – is also remarkable:[10] this pressure has not been reigned in by judicial bodies in any way, which just demonstrates the political subservience of the judiciary.

Courts as the Makers of Public Policy

In the circumstances of rising populism, there are suitable conditions for the courts to become fora for the making of some types of public policy. Mainstream liberal parties have willingly passed an increasing number of difficult political decisions to the judiciary in sensitive areas such as privatization, restitution, the legacy of the communist past, etc. Hidden behind the authority of international or constitutional rules, domestic elites are often willing to avoid taking responsibility for sensitive and unpopular decisions. Further, the judiciary itself has been active in taking the opportunity to block unpopular policies of governments on the basis of legal rules and principles. It is reasonable to expect that the reduction of the scope of democratic politics leads to the expansion of the scope of the decision-making activities of other bodies, and, especially, judicial bodies. This process could have a lasting impact on the rule of law.

Populist pressures are most apparent in the area of criminal policy and the fight against organized crime and corruption. Romania and Bulgaria are cases in point: in these two countries, the European Commission and other organizations have repeatedly stated that policies in these areas are wanting, and that visible results are difficult to detect.[11] This criticism has been accompanied by significant public pressure for decisive action, which is fuelled by populist politicians, who are eager to portray the whole mainstream establishment as criminal and corrupt. Apart from the rising popularity ratings of these populists, the combined result of these pressures have been the transfer of significant powers to judicial and prosecutorial bodies. In Romania, a special, well-funded prosecutorial unit targeting high-profile corruption has been set up. In Bulgaria, insistent calls for special organized crime courts have been made, and the prosecutor general (who is part of an independent

---

further indictments of the ex-oligarch for money-laundering. There was a possibility that he left jail on parole in the spring of 2007. In case of further indictments, this possibility would become irrelevant.

10 For instance, Kasparov was arrested for the organization of an allegedly illegal public demonstration (14 April 2007). At the time of the annual conference of the Russian opposition in the autumn of 2006, Kasparov's office was raided by special police units.

11 For an account of the pre-accession negotiations between EU and Bulgaria and Romania on the issue of judicial reform, see Smilov, D. (2006), EU Enlargement and the Constitutional Principle of Judicial Independence, in Sadurski, W. Czarnota, A. and Krygier, M. (eds) (2006), *Spreading Democracy and the Rule of Law? The Impact of EU Enlargement for the Rule of Law, Democracy and Constitutionalism in Post-Communist Legal Orders*, Dordrecht, Springer.

judiciary in the country) has been repeatedly asked to elaborate policies and strategies in relation to organized crime and corruption. The effect of this extension of policy-making powers of the independent judicial branch are difficult to assess at the moment, but there is one obvious effect which is to be attributed to populist pressures: the preservation of *incredibly high conviction rates*.[12]

A very interesting example of courts directly responding to populist pressures is presented by a decision of the Hungarian Constitutional Court. In the middle of the 1990s the liberal finance minister Bokros introduced much-needed austerity measures in order to ensure the financial stability of the country. The Court invalidated key elements of the package of legislation and, in practice, rendered it meaningless.[13] The judges did this by introducing a wide range of social and economic "acquired" rights of welfare. Although a year later the judges became more accommodating of neo-liberal measures, they set a specific political *bon-ton*: that there are acquired welfare rights from which political parties cannot deviate. This tone contributed to the entrenchment of a policy of ever-increasing public spending, the flourishing of populist rhetoric, which ultimately led to the 2006 crisis when it became clear that most of the "acquired" rights can no longer be supported by the state. In the ensuing events, the mainstream parties started accusing each other of being responsible for the severe financial problems (although public spending and statist politics had been a common ground between them for most of the transition period). Ultimately, spontaneous protests, and even street violence, broke out when it became clear that in the pre-election campaign the ruling Socialist PM Gyurchany had not necessarily been exhaustive as to the scope of austerity measures which needed to be adopted after the elections of 2005. The issue of whether this pre-electoral brevity constituted a political lie was set to be explored in massive public demonstrations in which football hooligans, conspiracy theorists, anti-Semites and opposition leaders (not always in this order) made their views known in the major Budapest squares. The thus-far stable parliamentary democracy was successfully bypassed and temporarily pushed in the corner by a populist and plebiscitarian political action.

Courts and Identity Politics

The law expresses the identity of a given political community as a whole, or at least this is what every populist would argue. Therefore, the rise of populism entails an increasing pressure on the courts to make sure that the law expresses the identity of the people, the nation, or even the dominant religious denomination. These

---

12 See the report of the Centre for Liberal Strategies (2006), The Judiciary: Independent and Accountable. Performance Indicators of the Bulgarian Judicial System, available at http://www.cls-sofia.org/uploads/files/Projects%20files/1162302106__final_report_english.pdf, accessed 17 August 2010.

13 For an account and analysis of these events see Sajo, A. (1996), How the Rule of Law Killed the Welfare Reform, *East European Constitutional Review*, Spring 1996.

pressures are not an invention of Eastern Europe – on the contrary, their origin should be traced to the Western part of the continent. After all, the failure of the EU Constitutional Treaty should be attributed to a degree to the widespread belief that the Treaty was expressive of a "European identity". This imagined identity was not recognized by various national populisms as their "own", which probably was the key reason for its failure. Be that as it may, there are other examples of European mainstream constitutional policies framed under populist pressures. The decision of the ECtHR in the *Refah Partisi*[14] case, in which the court approved the ban of an Islamist popular party in Turkey, was following the same identity-expressing logic. It is not that important for present purposes whether the court was right or wrong in its decision about the legality of the ban. More important is the reasoning of the judges, according to which the ECHR was held in principle incompatible with Islamic ideas of legal pluralism, with Islamic law (Sharia), and with the idea of *jihad*. This wholesale judgement of incompatibility between the ECHR and the key normative underpinnings of the Muslim world is hardly anything different from a bold declaration of a distinct (Western, European, civilized) identity by the Court. This element of the judgement made even many Turkish liberals angry. After all, the Strasbourg judges could have been much more careful in their language, attempting to distinguish between these elements in the Sharia, Islamic pluralism, *jihad*, etc., whose political pursuit would constitute a real and present danger in a liberal democracy. The wholesale incompatibility declarations could hardly be explained on grounds different from populist pressures on judges to enter into identity politics.

The repercussions of this and similar judgements on dress codes, veils, crucifixes in schools, etc., could be quite powerful in Eastern Europe. The region in general is very susceptible to overblown and paranoid interpretations of "militant democracy"[15] – the doctrine according to which democracy and the constitutional order should be guarded by "preventive" strikes against their opponents. In particular, these opponents are often seen among representatives of ethnic minorities nurturing secession or autonomy dreams. Greece, for instance, has put significant judicial pressure on members of the Macedonian Slav community by denying their right to association and assembly.[16] Across the border in Bulgaria, members of the same Macedonian community are regularly denied the right to form a political party, be that on constitutional[17] or on formal procedural grounds (this case will be considered in more detail below under the heading Courts and

14 *Refah Partisi (The Welfare Party) and others v. Turkey* (application nos. 41340/98, 41342/98, 41343/98, and 41344/98). The first judgement on the case by the ECtHR was in 2001, while the Grand Chamber ruled in 2003.

15 For a discussion of the concept see Sajo, A. (2004), What is Militant Democracy? Against What Should We Defend the State? in Sajo, A. (ed.), *Militant Democracy*, Utrecht, Eleven International Publishing.

16 *Sideropoulos and Others v Greece* (1998) 57/1997/841/1047.

17 Constitutional Court decision 1/2000, 29 February 2000.

Identity Politics. There are further instances of bans of communist parties for nothing more that their name and declared support for some form of communist ideology. The rise of identity politics, which populism spells, will hardly leave the courts and the judiciary unmoved – many of them will be tempted, and are already tempted, to join in.

Courts as Adjudicators in Politics of Personal Integrity

As mentioned above, there is a certain natal nexus between populism and personality politics. If political competition becomes more and more a competition of persons rather than ideas, it is reasonable to expect that the integrity of these persons will become more and more the subject of judicial proceedings. Recent events give support for such a thesis, starting with the sinister cases in Russia and Ukraine where political opponents have been physically threatened and attempts have been made to criminalize them: think of the attempt to poison Yuschenko before the Orange Revolution,[18] Khodorkhovsky's trials, Gari Kasparov's ordeals as the leader of the Russian opposition, and so on. In more benign regimes, the attacks against the personal integrity of the opponent took less sinister forms. In Romania, for example, 2007 – the first year of EU membership for the country – started with an attempt by top politicians to impeach each other. President Basescu was at the receiving end of these attacks. There are ongoing judicial proceedings against a former prime minister of the country – Adrian Nastase – as the accusations are about corruption.

One of the probably most threatening developments took place in Poland. There, the nationalist-populist political forces of the twin Kaczynski brothers originated a so-called second wave of "lustration". The idea was 20 years after the beginning of the transition to ultimately disclose all agents and collaborators of the communist secret services. More than 700,000 individuals were supposed to go through a screening procedure about their political past. The idea behind this operation was nothing less than total purification of the Polish political elite in the pursuit of moral and political integrity; the more cynical interpretation saw this operation as a tool for the conservative-populist forces to deal a death blow to the more liberal-minded political formations in Poland. The role of the courts in this procedure was crucial. First, the Constitutional Court had to assess the compatibility of the procedure with fundamental rights. Then, the judiciary had to enforce the rule that public figures failing to disclose information or to comply otherwise with the proceedings would be liable to serious sanctions: fines, dismissals, bans from pursuing a specific profession for a number of years. It was

18 For a brief description of this attempt see http://observer.guardian.co.uk/international/story/0,6903,1371999,00.html, accessed 17 August 2010.

not difficult to predict that the courts would be exposed to great politicization in this "integrity-guaranteeing" exercise.[19]

Populism and the Rule of Law in Bulgaria

Populism as a Reaction to Quasi-constitutionalism

Populism in Bulgaria, as in the rest of Eastern Europe, could be understood as a reaction to a process of excessive constraining of the space for the development of alternative visions of democratic politics. As a result of this constraining, the platforms of the major political parties came dangerously close to each other, which then opened space for more radical or simply extravagant newcomers to the political stage.

Constitutionalism did have a role to play in this process of the constraining of democratic politics. Constitutionalism usually means the commitment of political actors to the observation of constraining principles in the form of rights and separation of powers. In Eastern Europe, however, constraining went further than that traditionally accepted, due mainly to the EU pre-accession process. This process helped strengthen the constraining of the powers of political majorities mainly through the explicit reinforcement of a specific cross-party "transition consensus" embedded in the EU conditionality. The substance of this consensus was the political Copenhagen criteria together with the requirement for a "functioning market economy" "capable of withstanding competitive pressures". No serious political actor could deviate from these commitments, which gave them a *quasi-constitutional* status.

This process could be interpreted as "deep constitutionalization" of politics or 'quasi-constituonalization, since it reached much deeper into the political process than normal constitutions actually do. The more concrete expressions in Bulgaria of this deep constitutionalization were the following.

Economic Quasi-constitutional Constraint Economic policy was largely a discretionary area for the government until 1996 in Bulgaria. During these first transitional years, the Bulgarian Socialist Party was willing to engage in economic experimentation: it delayed the privatization process, loosened financial discipline for the financing of loss-making state owned enterprises, etc. As a result, the

---

19 Key articles of the 2007 Law were judged unconstitutional by Poland's Constitutional Court or Constitutional Tribunal of the Republic of Poland on 11 May 2007, making the role of the Institute of National Remembrance (IPN) unclear and putting the whole process into question. For a general overview of late lustrations see Cynthya, M. Horne (2007), *Late Lustration Programs in Poland and Romania: Better Late than Never?*, available at at http://www.allacademic.com//meta/p_mla_apa_research_citation/2/1/1/2/8/pages211286/p211286-1.php, accessed 17 August 2010.

financial situation in the country drastically deteriorated at the end of 1996, and the banking system virtually collapsed. In order to tackle hyperinflation, and to restore the trust in the banking system, the Bulgarian government established the so-called Currency Board, which fixed the rate of the Bulgarian Lev to the rate of the euro (the Deutsche Mark originally). This was the first significant constraint on political discretion in the area of the economy which deprived the government from the right to alter the exchange rate of the Bulgarian currency. The second major constraint was the conclusion of various agreements with the International Monetary Fund (IMF) and the World Bank, which provided loans in return for fast reforms in the area of privatization and the improvement of the functioning of the administrative apparatus. All of these limited significantly the room for the designing of radically different economic policies. Gradually, the two main parties – the UDF (Union of Democratic Forces), and more significantly the Socialists – recognized these constraints as fully legitimate. This recognition, however, brought their economic programmes very close together, and made them virtually indistinguishable after 1997. The beginning of the pre-accession negotiations for membership simply reinforced and further legitimated the already existing economic constraints. An additional consideration eventually also emerged – the potential membership in the euro zone, which would also require tight financial discipline in line with neo-liberal policies.

Political Quasi-constitutional Constraints The accession of Bulgaria to the EU and NATO imposed a virtual "political supervisory board" on the Bulgarian government. It had to report regularly to the EU Commission on progress in agreed upon reforms, as well as to coordinate its foreign policy with EU and NATO partners. The room for independent initiatives was decidedly decreasing, although of course it could not be fully eliminated. For instance, although the Bulgarian population was, on the whole, against the intervention of NATO against Milosevic's regime, the Kostov UDF government gave permission to NATO for the use of Bulgarian airspace for attacks against Yugoslavia; the only act of defiance was the refusal to accept Albanian refugees in Bulgaria.

In the area of substantive reforms of the administration and the judiciary, the influence of the EU Commission was very strong – a fact which has been well studied and documented. The overall result of the monitoring and the conditionalities was by and large positive from the point of view of the modernization of the country. But it needs to be said that political priorities were set up together by the Bulgarian government and the Commission. Due to this joint decision-making, some issues were raised as political priorities much higher in the public agenda that they would have been in other circumstances. Thus, the reform of the judiciary gained the status of a paramount concern in the period 2002–2007. It was the same with the fight against corruption and organized crime. In the same vein, areas in which the EU was not that interested – such as the reform of the public education system and healthcare – were systematically neglected by successive governments. The appropriation of public funds is a reliable indicator: while the budget of the judiciary was rising significantly from year to year (as were the salaries of the judiciary), the budget for the education system remained relatively stable (as were the salaries of teachers and university professors). This situation was the reason for a major strike in the school system in the autumn of 2007, which was the biggest strike seen in Bulgaria after the changes in 1989.

Judicial Constitutional and Quasi-constitutional Constraints The Bulgarian Constitutional Court and the Bulgarian judiciary have asserted themselves strongly during the transition period. During the 1990s, the Bulgarian Constitutional Court managed to "bracket out" from political competition at least four main areas: restitution of agricultural land, restitution of urban property, judicial independence and independence of the public electronic media. In all these four areas there was significant political disagreement. In the first two, the disagreement was between the left and the right: the BSP (Bulgarian Socialist Party) and the UDF. The Socialists opposed the restitution of property nationalized by the communist regime and, instead, introduced a scheme of compensation for the assets using state bonds. The UDF, with the decisive help of the Constitutional Court in this regard, prevailed: the principle of full restitution for nationalized assets was promoted to the rank of a constitutional principle.

Regarding the independence of the judiciary and the media, the political dividing line ran not so much between left and right, but between government and the opposition: throughout the 1990s, Bulgarian governments had tried to assert their influence in these areas. Here again the CC was quite instrumental in curbing these attempts.

Overall, the impact of the CC in this period could be assessed as positive, but again a side effect of this influence was the diminishing of the room for substantive political competition after the constitutionalization of particular questions.

Since the beginning of the new century, the CC has focused predominantly on the issue of judicial independence, interpreting this principle to prevent the possibility of any major reform of the judicial system. This has brought the Court as a whole in conflict with the political establishment: most of the parties at the present moment would adopt more radical reforms than the CC would be willing to permit. In any event, however, the constitutionalization of a very strict conception of non-interference with the judicial system has further decreased the possibilities for radically different ideas of judicial reform – a policy area which became central in the period 2001–2009.

International courts, and especially the ECtHR, have had a similar impact on the Bulgarian political process, although much more limited. One issue which comes to mind is the legitimacy of ethnic minority parties. The pressure of the Council of Europe and its bodies was key for the legitimization of the Movement of Rights and Freedoms, which is generally an ethnic minority party. Without the existence of such foreign standards, this legitimation would have been more difficult (all this does not mean that the ECHR standards of political freedom are fully applied in Bulgaria).

In terms of quasi-constitutional judicial constraints on political majorities one could point out the increasing assertiveness and the autonomy of the ordinary Bulgarian judiciary. The Supreme Administrative Court (SAC) is a case in point. This body attempted to play a significant role in some of the big privatization projects of the Simeon II government in the period 2001–2005. In coalition with some political actors, the SAC helped to block the privatization of the monopolistic tobacco company Bulgartabac. SAC also threatens to stall one of the major reforms in the education system by invalidating (again) the introduction of A-level exams. All these instances demonstrate that political majorities face increasing competition from independent judicial bodies in the policy-making process: constraints on the will of the majorities are increasing. The EU insistence on issues such as strengthening of judicial capacity, judicial independence, etc., have actually amplified these trends.

NGOs as Quasi-constitutional Constraints NGOs have not been a significant constraining factor in the Bulgarian political process, at least in comparison with the other abov- mentioned and listed factors. However, there have been examples where NGOs have been successful in the imposition of specific goals and priorities on political actors. The most prominent example of this was the anti-corruption programmes designed by the Coalition 2000 organization and the Centre for the Study of Democracy. With the help of significant foreign aid from the United States Agency for International Development (USAID), Coalition 2000 managed to raise public awareness of corruption and make anti-corruption one of the top priorities of government. While the results of these efforts are subject to intense debate, it is beyond doubt that the problem itself, as well as the strategies used to tackle it (measurements of corruption, design of action plans, creation of anti-corruption commissions and other bodies), were virtually imposed on political actors by NGOs and foreign donors. The EU granted further legitimacy to the NGO-initiated anti-corruption campaigns and compelled successive governments to take them seriously.

All these considerations suggest that the EU accession process has helped the entrenchment of a deep constitutionalism which imposes quite comprehensive and pervading constraints on the political process. This process provides us with a key for understanding the impact of populism on the rule of law in Bulgaria. We have to expect two types of pressures. On the one hand, there is the pressure on courts and the judiciary to stick with an expansive notion of quasi-constitutionalism typical of the transition period. This pressure would come from the traditional political forces, the parties of the liberal consensus. On the other hand, one could expect pressure on the courts from the new populist players, who would strive not only to unravel the liberal consensus of the transition period, which acquired a quasi-constitutional status, but also the constraints of "constitutionalism proper", such as constitutional rights and separation of powers. It is this dynamic that we set out to explore in the next part of the chapter.

Populism and the Bulgarian Judiciary

In this part of the paper offers an analysis of a series of short case studies which illustrate the different types of impact of populism on the rule of law in Bulgaria, following the analytical framework proposed in the first part of the chapter.

Courts as Regulators of Political Competition

Courts Used to Block Populist Newcomers The return of the former tsar Simeon II from long years of exile was an event which was greeted by welcoming demonstrations in Sofia and the other major cities of the country. The gathering of large masses of people sparked reminiscences of the first years of the transition, when the ex-communists were forced out of government by popular pressure. In the same revolutionary vein, in 1997 the Socialist government of Zhan Videnov resigned under the continuous pressure from street protests. Not surprisingly, in 2000–2001, the then-ruling government of Ivan Kostov (UDF) reacted rather nervously to the popular return of Simeon II to the country, and mobilized all of its resources with the intention of preventing him from participation in the political process. First, the Constitutional Court – in which the UDF had a clear dominance – banned Simeon II from participation in the presidential election because of residence requirements.[20] Secondly, and more controversially, a Sofia court denied registration to the National Movement Simeon II – the organization with which the ex-tsar was planning to take part in the parliamentary elections. The denial was grounded in procedural considerations – the lack of the required support as shown by the lack of signatures, etc; all of these were rather curious in the case of a political organization which was just about to win half of the seats in the Bulgarian parliament. All these efforts came to no avail, since Simeon II and NDSV (National Movement for Stability and Progress) managed to run in the elections even without being registered as a separate party: they used the registrations of two small and insignificant parties for that purpose.

The results of the June 2001 parliamentary elections were shocking: NDSV won more than 40 per cent of the vote and exactly half of the seats in the Bulgarian National Assembly. The result would have been an absolute majority in the parliament had it not been for several small parties which used Simeon II's name on their ballot without his authorization – some 3 per cent of the vote was lost on such parties through voter confusion. All established traditional parties – the right-

20 The 1991 Constitution requires that candidates for presidential office spend the five years in the country before the elections. This provision was introduced in 1991, specifically against Simeon II – ironically, it came to be applied 10 years later than originally planned. In this case, the Constitutional Court faithfully stuck to the plain text of the basic law, although on other occasions the CC has proved that it could rather creatively interpret constitutional provisions. For instance, several years before that the CC had returned all of the real estate property of Simeon II and his family, which amounted to millions of euros.

wing UDF, together with the left-wing Socialists – together won fewer votes than Simeon II's NDSV.

Courts Mobilized Against the Political Opponent: The Blue Coalition Case 2009
The fluid state of the Bulgarian party system, which had almost fallen apart due to the impact of the rising populists, intensified political competition dramatically. Established parties – even the once stable and powerful BSP – began to feel threatened and saw their resources for political mobilization weakened. Therefore, established parties with access to and influence over the high magistracy tried to capitalize on these relationships in order to block inconvenient political opponents. Thus, the ruling coalition of BSP and DPS (MRF – the Movement for Rights and Freedoms) attempted, in the Sofia city court, to block the registration of the successor to the UDF as a political party. The reasons for the denial of registration were very formalistic and ultimately the registration was granted. However, this happened only after the European parliamentary elections, and only after it was clear that the UDF would take part in the elections together with DSB in the Blue Coalition, regardless of the state of its registration. The case clearly illustrates the instrumentalization of the courts for the purposes of political competition.

Courts as Regulators of Public Policy: Penal Policy

Criminal Policy Area: The Fear of Acquittals According to original research carried out by the Centre for Liberal Strategies[21] in Sofia in 2006, in terms of duration of trial and pre-trial procedures as an indicator for the efficiency of the judicial system, Bulgaria does not differ dramatically from the practices in the EU member countries. (Civil cases – 350 days on average; criminal cases of common character – 835 days, the pre-trial phase included.) It should be stressed, nevertheless, that these practices are rather diverse, and that our judicial system is not a high scorer in either one of the categories – we are rather in the middle, and possibly more towards the end regarding criminal cases. What the study shows is that there is a considerable "in-between-institutions" time, which the cases spend

Table 11.1 Percentage of Convicted and Acquitted Persons from All Indicted Persons)

	% of convicted persons	% of aquittals
2002	64%	2%
2003	78%	1.5%
2004	78%	1%

21 http://www.cls-sofia.org/uploads/files/Projects%20files/1162302147__final_report_bg.pdf, accessed 17 August 2010.

between two courts, or between the court and the prosecutorial office. There is a serious potential for optimization in this regard.

Further, with respect to criminal cases, it is the duration of the pre-trial phase which draws attention. The accumulated duration here is 541 days, which is the overall time in the investigation and the prosecutorial offices (i.e., including the time during which cases are sent back for further investigation). This demonstrates that the pre-trial phase accounts for most of the duration of a common criminal case (835 days altogether). One should not immediately jump from here to the conclusion that the pre-trial phase is inefficient; other explanations are also possible. To begin with, the duration of the pre-judicial phase should be read together with the information about the "super-efficiency" of the prosecutorial office, demonstrated by the ratio between convictions and acquittals: around 80 per cent convictions as against only around 1 per cent acquittals of all indicted persons. When these two facts are combined, we get a difficult-to-interpret picture. It is quite possible, that in the Bulgarian criminal justice system as a whole there is a "fear" of acquittals. This increases considerably the relative weight of the pre-trial phase: either it has collected sufficient evidence for conviction, or the case is referred back to it for further investigation. The tendency to refer cases back increases the duration of the pre-trial phase.

Courts and Identity Politics

The Bulgarian Constitutional Court Decisions on OMO Ilinden and militant democracy Doctrines: Decision 1, 2000 Eight years after its first (rather liberal) decision on the closure of political parties, the judges faced a challenge against the constitutionality of a tiny Macedonian party. The challenge took place after the 1999 local elections, in which the party – OMO Ilinden-PIRIN – collected around 2,000 votes and managed to win only one mayoral place in a small village. Understanding the issue of the Macedonian national identity may require a long and complex discussion; yet, it is probably not too controversial to say that the modern Macedonian nation appeared only in the twentieth century, formed by the populations of Slavic origin living between Bulgaria, Serbia, Greece, and Albania. As the local elections in 1999 showed, a small part of the population in southern Bulgaria was willing to identify as Macedonians, both politically and nationally.

The challengers in this case argued that the establishment and operation of OMO Ilinden violated Article 11(4) and Article 44(2) of the Constitution, as well as the constitutional principles of the Preamble declaring the duty to protect the Bulgarian statehood and national unity. It was alleged that the party had a "separatist character", and that its goals ran against the unity of the Bulgarian nation. One argument invoked by the petitioners was that the party was the successor of an independent Macedonian association OMO Ilinden (formed in 1990) whose goal was the "founding of a Macedonian state through the secession of the Pirin region from Bulgaria".

First, the judges considered the issue of whether the registration of the party violated Article 11(4) of the Constitution. They held that:

> There is no separate Macedonian ethnos in the Republic of Bulgaria. Because of that, the Court does not find evidence that the registration of this organisation violates Article 11(4) of the Constitution and the prohibition to establish parties on ethnic ground.[22]

It seems that at this point the Court had reached the right conclusion for the wrong reason. The logic of this argument advanced an interpretation of Article 11(4) which is far less justifiable than the interpretation of this provision from the 1992 MRF decision. According to the new reading, Article 11(4) prohibited *minority ethnic groups* from establishing political parties; however, since there was no Macedonian ethnic group in the country (in the view of the judges), the Court did not find a violation of Article 11(4) in the OMO case.

In contrast, the old interpretation did not enter into the issue of what an ethnic minority party was, or the issue of whether there was a particular minority in the country. Rather, it simply permitted the registration of parties, as long as they were inclusive and did not threaten the constitutional order.[23]

Despite the dubious merit of the reasoning up to this point, the first three parts of the decision seemed to be more or less consistent with, or at least not directly contradicting, the doctrine of constitutionality of parties elaborated in the MRF judgement. The error in the fourth part of the decision, however, was far from insignificant. There, the judges developed another doctrine of unconstitutionality of parties based not on Article 11, but on Article 44(2) and which contained a prohibition of parties whose activity was "directed against the *sovereignty, the territorial integrity of the country*, and the unity of the nation" (emphasis added). The CC held that OMO violated this provision in the part of its judgement

---

22 Decision 1, 2000.

23 In the following paragraph, however, the judges resorted to a further argument, echoing the rationale of the previous doctrine:

> On the other hand, it could be asserted that a party is based on ethnic ground when its founding documents do not allow for membership of representatives of other ethnic groups. As evident from Art. 8 of the founding document of OMO Ilinden – PIRIN, all Bulgarian citizens can be its members.

The argument reinforced the requirement of "party openness" and "inclusiveness" from the 1992 decision, but this time, it seemed, the Court considered openness not as a decisive, but, at best, supporting consideration. The central point that the judges made was that in Bulgaria there was no Macedonian minority and therefore there could not be a party on "ethnic Macedonian ground". It was unclear from their reasoning whether, had there been a Macedonian minority in Bulgaria, it would have been sufficient for OMO to be open to other minorities in order to be recognized as constitutional. If openness is sufficient, the lack of a Macedonian minority argument would be irrelevant anyway – the judges' first argument would be redundant.

concerning the integrity of the country. The evidence revealing the violation, in the view of the judges, included the following:

a. A gathering of OMO supporters in 1991 and the adoption of a declaration calling, among other things, for the granting of political autonomy to Pirin Macedonia, the withdrawal of the Bulgarian "occupational" armed forces, and the disbanding of Bulgarian political parties.
b. The publication of two maps indicating the inclusion of Bulgarian lands in the territory of the Republic of Macedonia in 1993 and 1995.
c. Seven 1998 and 1999 interviews, memoranda and press conference statements of the leaders of OMO, in which they, among other things, "treat[ed] the Pirin region as part of Macedonia… and agre[ed] that the region should be cut off from Bulgaria, although they claim[ed] that the time for this ha[d] not come yet…"
d. Two campaign statements of the leaders of the party (during the 1999 local elections) in which they threatened to raise the issue of secession in case their requirements were not fulfilled by the government.
e. Finally, the Court accepted as evidence a 1999 letter on behalf of the party from a member of its governing body to the Open Society Institute, Budapest. In the letter, there were claims for political autonomy of the Pirin region and a statement that the rights of the Macedonians ranked higher than Bulgarian national sovereignty. (After the admission of the letter as evidence, OMO denounced it as an expression of its official policy.)

Not only did the Court hold that this evidence was sufficient to demonstrate that the activity of OMO Ilinden violated Article 44(2) of the Constitution in the part aimed at protecting the *territorial integrity* of Bulgaria, the judges further argued that every separate piece of evidence constituted a sufficient ground for the establishment of such a violation. The Court expressed the view that no "*effective* impact on the protected… [territorial integrity] is necessary" (emphasis added) for a declaration of the unconstitutionality of a certain political activity under Article 44(2). In other words, declarations, interviews, letters and statements – all of them forms of *speech* – could be interpreted as unconstitutional activity sufficient for the prohibition of a political party.

The restrictions on statements, containing calls inflaming hostility, is based on the enshrined in the Constitution values of toleration, mutual respect, as well as the prohibition on propounding hatred on racial, national, ethnic or religious grounds. These restrictions do not deny protection to the variety of contradictory beliefs, reflecting the competition of ideas and opposing view points.[24]

"The [hatred restrictions]… definitely target statements, which affect the interests of the social groups, formed on the basis of different characteristics – racial, ethnic, religious, political, national, social, sexual, etc. The exclusion

24 Decision 7, 1996, *Jurisprudence 1991–1996*, 140.

of such statements from the range of protected speech is consistent with the, proclaimed in the Preamble to the Constitution, universal value of tolerance, with the requirement of religious tolerance (Article 37(1)), and with the prohibition to create organizations, whose activity is directed toward the inflaming of racial, national, ethnic, or religious hatred (Article 44(2)).[25]

The political effects of the decision were purely negative. It contributed to the cooling of the relationship between Macedonia and Bulgaria. Also, the decision of the CC proved to be an embarrassment for Bulgaria because the country ultimately lost several cases brought by OMO in the ECtHR.

Still, despite the pressure from the Council of Europe, Bulgarian courts systematically deny (on formal and procedural grounds) to register OMO. OMO has become one of the sticking points, not only in Bulgarian relationships with Macedonia, but also *vis-a-vis* the Council of Europe. Most importantly for our purposes, the case indicates the rehabilitation of mild nationalism with its anti-minority bias in the jurisprudence of Bulgarian courts. This has become possible because of the change of the political climate.

Conclusion: The General Impact of Populism on the Rule of Law in Eastern Europe

The developments discussed in this chapter demonstrate that courts and the judiciary are by no means immune to the pressures of populism. Sometimes the judiciary is seen as the guardian of constitutional order against aggressive illiberal majorities. The truth is that often the guardian is also implicated in the political clashes between majorities and minorities, or are rendered ineffective by them. Very often, instead of being relatively impartial arbiters, courts become active participants in the political process or isolated, self-interested bystanders.

These facts *per se* do not render Ely's proceduralist ideal of reinforcement of political representation through judicial action irrelevant.[26] Indeed, in some cases courts have helped to improve democracy by curbing the power of aggressive majorities or by protecting vulnerable minorities. The whole question is about the dynamics of the process, however. Ely relied on the example of the Warren Supreme Court which responded positively to the rise of the civil rights movement and took on board many of its claims about equality and political participation of disadvantaged groups. This is a demonstration of the responsiveness of courts to rising political movements.

Are courts – as bodies bound by constitutional rights and principles – responsive only to liberal political pressure, however? The evidence for such a conclusion is unfortunately lacking. In the US, during the McCarthyism period in the 1950s, the Supreme Court did accommodate illiberal attitudes and positions. The already-

25 Ibid., 145.

26 Ely, J.H. (1980), *Democracy and Distrust*, Cambridge Mass., Harvard UP.

mentioned *Bush v. Gore* case is also indicative of the tendency of courts to go with rising political forces.

The Eastern European perspective, and the Bulgarian case studies more specifically, support such a conclusion. During the 1990s, there was a wave of liberalization in the region, which was marked by the rise of liberal political forces to power.[27] This was also the high point of constitutional courts which became instrumental in the entrenchment of the values of liberalism in the ex-communist societies. Success was different in the different countries, but, as a whole, constitutional review was established together with the belief that courts could curb the excesses of aggressive majorities or authoritarian leaders. The beginning of the new century spelled the rise of a new political fashion in Eastern Europe. Putin's plebiscitarian presidency extinguished not only liberalism, but democratic competition in Russia as well. Ukraine's never-consolidated democracy has slipped into instability with populist leaders pursuing altogether indeterminate goals. Even the new EU Member States of Central Europe are experiencing a rising tide of illiberal and populist parties and leaders which question many of the consensual goals and priorities of the transition period. Poland's flamboyant Kaczynski coalition, emitting anti-Semitic, anti-homosexual messages, and trying to criminalize its political opponents under the guise of lustration laws pursuing absolute "moral integrity", was probably the most striking example.

Courts, thus far, have been unable to put a stop to these developments. Although reactions to the rise of populism have not been unified, there has been no systematic and committed judicial resistance to populism in any of the countries in the region; accommodation of populist pressures, although to a different degree, has been much more common. In some of the countries, such as Russia, we have an almost total political subservience of the courts to the populist leader. In Ukraine, the Constitutional Court has become a player in the battle between different populists – the sense of judges being impartial arbiters has been ultimately lost. Elsewhere in the region, courts have succumbed to populist pressures in their policy-making on criminal justice issues, national identity questions, welfare policies and so on. Curiously, in some instances, courts have tried to prevent the entry of extremist, illiberal or simply populist actors by themselves adopting paranoid and illiberal strategies; the ultimate effect of such actions is also detrimental to the rule of law and constitutional democracy.

All in all, there is no evidence on the basis of which courts could be seen as staunch guardians of liberal constitutional values and principles in Eastern Europe – the record is too mixed for such an optimistic conclusion. Courts have proven sensitive and accommodating to rising political tides – the liberal one in the 1990s and the populist one of the present day. When the political infrastructure of a society is emptied of its liberal content, it is probably unwarranted to place hopes

27 For an account of the role of courts during the transition period, see Smilov, D. (2004), The Character and Legitimacy of Constitutional Review: Eastern European Perspectives, ICON (*Journal of International Constitutional Law*) 1.

in a single institutional mechanism – judicial review and independent judiciary – as the ultimate guardian of constitutional democracy. It could be argued whether courts have presented a "counter-majoritarian difficulty" in Eastern Europe, but thus far at least they have not presented a serious and committed counter-populist difficulty.

References

Barak, A. (1989), *Judicial Discretion*, New Haven, Yale University Press.

Barak, A. (2005), *Purposive Interpretation in Law*, Princeton and Oxford, Princeton University Press.

Centre for Liberal Strategies (2006), *The Judiciary: Independent and Accountable, Performance Indicators of the Bulgarian Judicial System*, available at http://www.cls-sofia.org/en/papers/the-judiciary-independent-and-accountable-performance-indicators-of-the-bulgarian-judicial-system-36.html, accessed 17 August 2010.

Ely, J.H. (1980), *Democracy and Distrust*, Cambridge Mass., Harvard University Press.

Horne, C.M. (2007), *Late Lustration Programs in Poland and Romania: Better Late than Never*?, available at http://www.allacademic.com//meta/p_mla_apa_research_citation/2/1/1/2/8/p211286_index.html, accessed 17 August 2010.

Katz, R. and Mair, P. (1995), Changing Models of Party Organisation and Party Democracy, *Party Politics* 1(1).

Mudde, C. (2002), In the Name of the Peasantry, the Proletariat, and the People: Populism in Eastern Europe, in Meny, Y. and Surel, Y. (2001), *Democracies and the Populist Challenge*, Basingstoke, Palgrave.

Mudde, C. (2004), The Populist Zeitgeist, *Government and Opposition* 4.

Raz, J. (1979), *The Authority of Law: Essays on Law and Morality*, Oxford, Clarendon Press.

Raz, J. (1986), *The Morality of Freedom*, Oxford, Clarendon Press.

Raz, J. (1994), *Ethics in the Public Domai*n, Oxford, Clarendon Press.

Sajo, A. (1996), How the Rule of Law Killed the Welfare Reform, *East European Constitutional Review*, Spring.

Sajo, A. (2004), What is Militant Democracy? Against What Should We Defend the State?, in Sajo, A. (ed.), *Militant Democracy*, The Netherlands, Eleven International Publishing.

Schmitter, P.C. (2006), *A Balance Sheet of the Vices and Cirtues of "Populisms"*, paper delivered at the conference The Challenge of New Populism, organized by the Centre for Liberal Strategies, Sofia, Bulgaria, in May 2006.

Schmitter, P.C. and Trechsel, A.H. et al. (2004), *The Future of Democracy in Europe: Trends, Analyses and Reforms*, Strasbourg, Council of Europe Publishing.

Smilov, D. (2004), The Character and Legitimacy of Constitutional Review: Eastern European Perspectives, *ICON* (*Journal of International Constitutional Law*) No. 1.
Smilov, D. (2006), EU Enlargement and the Constitutional Principle of Judicial Independence, in Sadurski, W., Czarnota, A. and Krygier, M. (eds), *Spreading Democracy and the Rule of Law? The Impact of EU Enlargement for the Rule of Law, Democracy and Consitutionalism in Post-Communist Legal Orders*, Dordrecht, Springer.
Smilov, D. (2008), The Power of Assembled People: The Right to Assembly and Political Representation, in Sajo, A. (ed.), *Free to Protest: Constituent Power and Street Demonstration (Issues in Constitutional Law)*, The Netherlands, Eleven International Publishing.
Sunstein, C., Schkade, D., Ellman, L. and Sawicki, A. (2006), *Are Judges Political? An Empirical Investigation of the Federal Judiciary*, Washington, DC, Brookings Institution Press.
Wikipedia, Mikhail Khodorovsky, http://en.wikipedia.org/wiki/Mikhail_Khodorkovsky, accessed 17 August 2010. http://www.cls-sofia.org/uploads/files/Projects%20files/1162302147__final_report_bg.pdf, accessed 17 August 2010.

Index

For Product Safety Concerns and Information please contact our EU
representative GPSR@taylorandfrancis.com
Taylor & Francis Verlag GmbH, Kaufingerstraße 24, 80331 München, Germany

www.ingramcontent.com/pod-product-compliance
Ingram Content Group UK Ltd.
Pitfield, Milton Keynes, MK11 3LW, UK
UKHW020014200926
475702UK00014B/1887

* 9 7 8 1 1 3 8 2 5 4 4 5 9 *